PRE-REFORMATION RELIGIOUS DISSENT IN THE NETHERLANDS, 1518–1530

J. Alton Templin

D1739175

University Press of America,® Inc.
Lanham · Boulder · New York · Toronto · Oxford

Copyright © 2006 by
University Press of America,® Inc.
4501 Forbes Boulevard
Suite 200
Lanham, Maryland 20706
UPA Acquisitions Department (301) 459-3366

PO Box 317
Oxford
OX2 9RU, UK

Library of Congress Control Number: 2006926154
ISBN-13: 978-0-7618-3526-4 (paperback : alk. paper)
ISBN-10: 0-7618-3526-1 (paperback : alk. paper)

⊖™ The paper used in this publication meets the minimum
requirements of American National Standard for Information
Sciences—Permanence of Paper for Printed Library Materials,
ANSI Z39.48—1984

Contents

Contents

Figures

Foreword

Texts on the sixteenth century Reformation usually identify The Netherlands with Anabaptists and Calvinists. Scarcely mentioned are the debates, conflicts, and persecutions that stirred the cities and countryside of the Low Countries in the decade following Luther's literary and pastoral critiques of the Roman church. From 1520 to 1530 The Netherlands teemed with calls for religious reform. By the end of the decade, Menno Simons was questioning the actual nature of the Eucharistic elements and the validity of infant baptism, but he was still a Roman Catholic priest. John Calvin was still a student of the Humanities and studying to be a lawyer in Orleans. The Synod of Dordrecht was another hundred years away. In fact, the word "Protestantism" itself was unknown until 1529. Yet, as Alton Templin points out in this study, change was already sweeping through The Netherlands. Texts inspired by later medieval thought, Humanistic writings, detailed analysis of scripture, and the ever-present treatises of Luther promoted pastoral change and theological re-evaluation. Evangelical monks and priests risked their vocations, freedom and lives. Printers put themselves and their livelihoods on the line. Uneducated laypeople, shoemakers, roofers, barbers, cloth makers, house painters, women, common folk with uncommon courage met in secret, studied the Bible and often paid the price for their dissent. Exiles, tongue borings, burnings, and drownings became commonplace as the Inquisition attempted to root out heresy. Templin, who recreates the fervor, danger and excitement of these people and their ideas, notes that the protests and sacrifices did not coalesce into a distinctive movement at this time. He demonstrates, however, that this cacophony of diverse, bold voices was able to incorporate some of the highest ideals of the sixteenth century Humanistic scholarship and integrity, the pursuit of religious and social freedom, and simplicity of faith and belief.

Templin suggests that he has a modest goal to "present a detailed summary of some of the most important, but not readily available, theological treatises of the period." This modest goal, however, is couched in a more exhaustive description of the political, social, intellectual, and spiritual world of the early sixteenth century Netherlands. Texts are placed in their contexts. The importance of Charles V's broad control of The Netherlands, the emperor's relationship with local authorities, the early appearance of the Inquisition in the Low Countries, edicts against heresies, trial records, correspondences, influential literary and theological discourses, scriptural translations, the pedagogies of the Humanist teachers, the daily rhythms of the monasteries, and even the musings of the spirituals who had become disenchanted with matter itself frame and inform the unfolding attempts at reform and the writings of the pivotal decade.

Templin follows other scholars in asserting the seminal impact of Erasmus and Luther on early dissent in The Netherlands. He also draws on more recent work to describe the influences of other late medieval writers such as Wyclif, Hus, John Pupper of Goch, and Wessel Gansfort. (He emphasizes the influence of the former two on Cornelis Hoen's justly famous treatise on the Eucharist.) Throughout his study, Templin consistently illustrates the wide spectrum of thought and issues that fomented in The Netherlands of the 1520s—that it was not simply a period of anti-sacramental revolt (as some scholars have implied) but a time of varied efforts to change the theological underpinnings and pastoral practices of the church.

In constructing his story of early dissent in The Netherlands, Templin introduces the reader to an array of unusual but seldom reticent characters, most of them unknown to all but a few Reformation scholars: Wouter (Gualterius), Hinne Rode, Barteld Laurens, Gerrit van Wormer, Willem Ottens, Dirk van Abcoude, Herman Gerrits, George Saganus, Johannes Sartorius, Cornelis Hoen, Johannes Pistorius (the first martyr for the Evangelical faith in the northern Netherlands), Gulielmus Gnapheus, Frederick Hondebeke, Nicholas van Broeckhoven, Gerard Geldenhauwer, Gerard Listrius, Cornelis Grapheus (secretary of Antwerp), and Augustinians such as Jacob Praepositus, Henry of Zutphen and Lambert de Thoren. Each one claims his place in history, a place rightfully established by his thoughts, words and deeds.

Templin also highlights some of the key texts of the period—most of which had the honor of making it into the *Index of Prohibited Books* by the middle of the sixteenth century. His summary of the texts and their salient points reveals the scholarship and passionate concerns of the period. The satirical *Lamentations of Peter* constructed imaginary dialogues between the apostles, early church writers like Ambrose, Jerome, Cyprian, Augustine, Hilary and Gregory, and Luther (who is visited by Jerome and Augustine) to criticize the mendicants and scholasticism, to encourage a return to the devotion and literature of the early church, and to support Luther's continuing efforts at reforming the church. Cornelis Hoen's *A Most Christian Letter* set the stage for a more radical interpretation of the Eucharist. The Dutch translation of the Gospel of Matthew with glosses and commentary readily embraced insights from the church fathers, the histories of Josephus; word studies in Latin, Greek and Hebrew; and the exegetical value of comparative scriptural texts. This "study" bible's evangelical conclusions: works righteousness is inadequate, God's grace is primary, humans are sinful, faith must be internalized, the sacrament of penance is questionable, and Christ is the only head of the church. The *Summa der godliker scrifturen*, a summary of the teachings of scripture, came to similar but often more radical conclusions: the sacraments as signs of inner faith (for example, there is no power in the baptismal water itself), pacifism, and the equality of men and women as equal inheritors of God's grace (says its anonymous author, "Eve was not taken from Adam's foot, but from his side"). As Templin so carefully and wonderfully implies, these were admirable treatises, written by thoughtful authors in extremely dangerous times.

This study is a significant contribution to the literature on the Reformation. Alton Templin has given the English reader access to previously obscure works and generally less-recognized early reformers and critics of the church. He has taken an immense amount of scholarship and archival materials and woven them into an expansive description of dissent in The Netherlands in the 1520s, richly rewarding in its lively vignettes, historical detail, and thorough analysis of the reformers' texts.

Timothy L. Bryan, Th. D.
Chairman of Humanities, Philosophy and Religious Studies
University of Phoenix, Colorado Campus
Westminster, Colorado

Preface

As I began my graduate studies at Harvard, I planned to specialize in major figures within the Continental Reformation. My study with George H. Williams, however, opened my eyes and directed my research projects toward wider fields. He guided me toward the Radical Reformation to broaden my understanding of the European scene. This also formed a more comprehensive historical and theological background for my chosen field of teaching Historical Theology and Church History. One seminar introduced me to Anabaptist developments, especially the life and work of Menno Simons. Further study concerning The Netherlands introduced the theological problems surrounding Jacobus Arminius and many discussions leading up to the Synod of Dordrecht (1618-1619). The theological emphases of Arminius were logical predecessors of my Methodist heritage. I knew the denomination was "Arminian" so I thought I should know the concepts to which this terminology made reference.

At about the same time I enrolled in seminars with another Harvard Church Historian, Heiko A. Oberman. His influence coupled with that of Williams convinced me that I should learn the Dutch language. Heiko Oberman led me through the growing pains in a new language and encouraged me to use as my main text for the Dutch study Maarten van Rhijn's *Wessel Gansfort* (1917). I later learned that van Rhijn had been a mentor and a major influence in Oberman's own theological development.

Some of Luther's first published writings were taken to the Netherlands in 1518 and were soon read widely. Other research in later seminars provided an acquaintance with some of the earliest reforming scholars in The Netherlands in the decade immediately following Luther's beginnings. These transition figures, although not solidly in what we might later call a "Protestant" category (because that designation did not yet exist), extended to the organization of the Anabaptists in The Netherlands. The organization of the Anabaptists in the Netherlands is usually attributed a visit by Melchior Hoffman in 1530. Consequently, I have concentrated on developments between the dates when Luther was first known in The Netherlands, and when the Anabaptist organizations began to develop (1518-1530). In the midst of this research I had a chance to spend a sabbatical year in Amsterdam reading both in the University of Amsterdam and the Free

University, also in Amsterdam. While there I was able to procure copies of the documents on which this study is based, many of which were not available elsewhere.

Three published articles, and three lectures given at professional societies, are the result of my continuing interest in this field. The published works are: 1) "Jan de Bakker: an early Martyr for the principle of Religious Freedom in The Netherlands," *The Iliff Review*, XXXI (Spring, 1974), pp. 17-29. This material is revised to form a portion of Chapter 10 in this study. 2) "Cornelis Grapheus (1482-1558): A Humanist Scholar of the Netherlands who recanted," *The Iliff Review*, XXXVI (Spring, 1979), pp. 3-18. The work of Grapheus forms a major portion of Chapter 6. 3) "*Oeconomica Christiana*: Biblical Humanism in The Netherlands, 1523," *The Mennonite Quarterly Review*, LVI (July, 1982), pp. 242-255. This published article, after revision, forms Chapter 9. All these materials are used in this study with the permission of the individual publishers. Some other lectures given at professional societies form parts of other chapters. This research has profited at many points, especially, from my contact with Dr. Johannes Trapman in The Hague. We have been acquainted many years, although we have met only occasionally. While I have worked most of the time far removed from The Netherlands, he has been kind enough to share his published writings concerning our mutual interests and he has also called my attention to writings of other scholars in the Netherlands who have published materials concerning the 1520s. He will recognize the places in this study which have benefited from his expertise.

This work attempts to bring to our attention some of the lesser-known scholars and many non-scholars involved in the earliest proto-Protestant dissent in The Netherlands. Although these writers and their documents from the 1520s were related to the larger movements for reform in Northern Europe, they have often been given less prominence and much of this material has not found its way into English-language Reformation studies. I hope these studies and theological analyses will illuminate the work of several of these key theological leaders, and that it will begin to fill in this gap concerning The Netherlands of the early 16th century.

Since I began my interest in Protestant developments within The Netherlands following the suggestions of Professors George H. Williams and Heiko A. Oberman, I consider this study one of the results of their influence extending over many years. Although both of these mentors died such a short time ago (2000, 2001 respectively), I am glad to acknowledge my thanks, although posthumously, for their original suggestions. Finally, I am glad to be able to bring this portion of the earliest proto-Protestant Reformation in The Netherlands to an English-speaking readership at this time. Some of these developments have been known in the scholarly community for more than a century, but usually have remained either in the Dutch or German language.

I should like to express my thanks and appreciation to three persons who have done extra work on my behalf to bring this publication to fruition. First, I am deeply indebted to Dr. Timothy L. Bryan, former student and long-time associate in Reformation studies. He read the entire manuscript and while serving as an editor located many places which needed clarification or more precise wording. For this I offer Dr. Bryan my sincere thanks. Additionally he graciously consented to write the Foreword which embodies his understanding and interpretation of this lesser-known phase of the earliest Protestant developments. Second, I have benefited from the assistance given to me by Adam Barnhart, recent graduate of The Iliff School of Theology, who shared his expertise in computer language. He offered excellent guidance and gave directions on principles of formatting these chapters according to the specifications of the publishers. After his analysis of the work he provided invaluable assistance in preparing the Index. Third, I wish to express my deep appreciation for the library staff of The Iliff School of Theology. I am especially indebted to Katie Fisher, circulation librarian, who has answered many requests for resources. Through their computer system she located documents, books and other materials I had not yet obtained on microfilm or on Xerox copies from The Netherlands or other European libraries.

J. Alton Templin
The Iliff School of Theology
Denver, Colorado
December, 2005

Acknowledgements

I should like to acknowledge, with thanks, the consideration given by editors of periodicals in which parts of this study have previously appeared in their publications. All appear here with their express and written permission.

An earlier version of Chapter 10 appeared as: "Jan de Bakker: an early Martyr for the principle of Religious Freedom in The Netherlands," *The Iliff Review*, XXXI, (Spring, 1974), pp. 17-29.

The substance of Chapter 6 first appeared as: "Cornelis Grapheus (1482-1558): A Humanist scholar in The Netherlands who recanted," *The Iliff Review*, XXXVI (Spring, 1979), pp. 3-18.

A lecture given at The Sixteenth Century Studies Conference in Kalamazoo, Michigan (1981), was subsequently published as *"Oeconomica Christiana:* Biblical Humanism in The Netherlands, 1523," *The Mennonite Quarterly Review*, LVI, (July, 1981), pp. 242-255. In a substantially revised form it is included as Chapter 9.

Introduction

I. Previous historical studies concerning this decade

Several studies in the past century or more have attempted to present a complete and connected story of the Protestant Reformation in The Netherlands. Some of the most well-known are: 1) Gerard Brandt, *The History of the Reformation and other Ecclesiastical Transactions in and about the Low-Countries* (4 vols.: London: T. Wood, 1720-1723); reprinted English translation in two volumes (New York: AMS Press, 1979; 2) J. G. de Hoop Scheffer, *Geschiedenis der Kerkhervormoing in Nederland van haar ontstaan tot 1531* (Amsterdam: G. L. Funke, 1873); 3) L. Knappert, *Geschiedenis der Nederlandsh Hervormde Kerk geduurende de 16e en 17e eeuw* (Amsterdam, 1911); 4) L. Knappert, *Het ontstaan en de vestiging van het Protestantisme in de Nederlanden* (Utrecht: 1924); 5) Johannes Lindeboom, *Het Biblisch Humanisme in Nederland* (Leiden: A.H. Adriani, 1913); and 6) J. Reitsma, *Geschiednis van de Hervorming en de Hervormde Kerk des Nederlanden* (The Hague: Martinus Nijhoff, 1949). All these works have been consulted for this study. This present analysis does not attempt to make any comprehensive overview such as these, but rather, will present a detailed summary of some of the most important, but not readily available, theological treatises of the period. Only one of these documents has appeared in English—Cornelis Hoen's writing on The Eucharist (See Chapter 5). There will not be any attempt to assume uniformity in doctrinal emphases or interconnectedness among the various writings. Rather, diversity will be the main emphasis which more accurately reflects the reality of this formative period.

Recent scholarship with respect to religious dissent in The Netherlands during the decade of the 1520s has resulted in one major survey and at least three doctoral theses. In 1991 a significant study appeared which summarized the influence of many individuals involved in the earliest "Reformation" in The Netherlands: *"Humanisme, Evangelisme en Reformatie in de Nederlands, 1520-1530,"* written by Bart J. Spruyt. He summarized the works of many of the scholars who are analyzed in several chapters in this study. His article is a good introduction to the earliest reform movements in The Netherlands. For the English-speaking student, however, it presents a problem because it was printed only in Dutch, and I have no indication that it will be translated. The collection in which this material appeared is entitled *Reformatie in Meervoud* [Reformation in its Plurality].[1]

Spruyt analyzed several factors to establish this plurality. **First**, there was no over-all organization, and no one issue which was addressed. **Second**, the lines of later distinctions between "Erasmian thought" and "Lutheran thought" were not clearly drawn. Many persons thought the movements emphasized the same types of reform, or at least were similar. **Third**, some reformers, especially those with a strongly humanist/educational emphasis [*humanitas*] sought to blend new humanist scholarship [concern for pure Latin or Greek and correct translations] with *libertas* [freedom from excessive restraint with respect to human ceremonies, laws and rituals] and *simplicitas* [a return to the simple gospel *philosophia christiana*] in place of a strong emphasis and dependence on scholasticism. Spruyt stated that sought "to free the church from the pressing burden of churchly requirements of commands and prohibitions, and from the tyrannical power of the Pope."[2] They sought to reform the church without a split—they sought a reform from within. **Fourth**, there were those who did not think they could reform the church from within and introduced new theological interpretations instead. Again, there were no uniform approaches or emphases.[3]

In addition to this summary, I have analyzed three recent theses to my own profit and have referred to them in appropriate places in this study. The first is Dr. C. Ch. G. Visser's, *Luther's Geschiften in de Nederland tot 1546* [Luther's writings in The Netherlands to 1546], (Assen, The Netherlands: Van Gorcum and Comp. N. V., 1969). Visser collected bibliographical information on two classes of publications. On the one hand, he analyzed Luther's works known to have been printed elsewhere but available in The Netherlands. On the other hand, and perhaps more significant for our study, he presented information on at least seventy-five different tracts of Luther actually published in The Netherlands, mostly before the end of 1530. One of these documents was an edition of the condemnations of Luther in 1519 by both the Universities of Cologne and Louvain/Leuven. The author also added information on printers and translators of the period. His thesis remains in Dutch, although the author concluded with a brief synopsis of each chapter in German.

The second is Dr. Johannes Trapman's, *Summa der Godliker Scriften (1523)* [The summary of the Holy Scripture (1523)]; (Leiden: New Rhine Publishers, 1978). This thesis, completed at Leiden, is an analysis of one of the earliest proto-protestant, or at least dissenting, writings. The *Summa* was a Dutch translation and modification of an earlier anonymous Latin tract, *Oeconomica Christiana* [*ca.*, 1520-1521]. This Dutch treatise was one of the two earliest writings banned specially by the Emperor in an order of 23 March, 1524. The Latin original, although probably written in 1520 or 1521, was not published until August, 1527, in Strasbourg or possibly Antwerp. The contents of this tract are analyzed in Chapter 9 of this study. This thesis remains in Dutch although Trapman included a chapter-by-chapter summary in French.

The third is Bart J. Spruyt's, *Cornelis Hoen (Honius) and his Epistle on the Eucharist* (1525). This thesis was completed in 1996, also at Leiden and published the same year (Houten, The Netherlands: 1996). He prefaced his study with a substantial chapter tracing the historiography of the early dissent in The Netherlands back to the beginning of the 16th century. Finally, he assessed the influence of Erasmus which he found to be a major theological source for Hoen's work. Spruyt also published a preliminary study of Hoen's work: *Ketter an het binnenhof* [Heretic at the inner court],[4] reflecting Hoen's service as a lawyer within the government in The Hague. This brief preliminary study remains in Dutch, while the finished thesis was published in English translation. Spruyt included a Latin edition of Hoen's letter on the Eucharist (and a German translation). For an English version one must go to Paul Nyhus's translation in H. A. Oberman, *Forerunners*, pp. 268-278.

In addition to these theses there are two other works which have proved helpful. The **first** is a study introducing the earliest reform movements in the Netherlands: Alastair Duke, *Reformation and Revolt in the Low Countries* (London: The Hambleden Press, 1990). Especially valuable as a parallel with this study are the first two chapters: "The Origin of Evangelical Dissent in the Low Countries," (pp. 1-28); and "The Face of popular dissent in the Low Countries, 1520-1530," (pp. 29-59). This British author briefly summarized the movement toward dissent and refered to many of the scholarly leaders whose works form the various chapters of this present study. While he provides the framework for the dissent, he does not provide any detailed analysis of the theology of any of these scholars. His concern is to give an overview extending another hundred years to the Synod of Dordrecht, 1618-1619.

The **second** significant work is a survey of the political background of The Netherlands during the first half of the Sixteenth Century. James D. Tracy, in his *Holland under Hapsburg Rule, 1506-1566: the Formation of a Body Politic* (Berkeley and Los Angeles: The University of California Press, 1990), covers a half century and provides political and economic background for the period of Emperor Charles V. He surveyed the tensions between the semi-independent provinces in The Netherlands as contrast to the centralizing tendencies of the Emperor. Tracy carried the story to 1556, the date of the Emperor Charles V's abdication.

One further source for an understanding of popular religion in the early 16thcentury, while not involving academic or theologically reasoned treatises, is the Chambers of Rhetoric [*rederijkerskamers*]. These were drama groups who entertained at various public festivities and were often free with their religious, or social, or political criticisms. Indeed, in his *Radical Reformation* (1992), George H. Williams briefly mentioned these groups with the comment that this movement "needs further investigation."[5] These tracts or dramas, however, are not considered in this study for two reasons. First, because of their complexity and widespread influence, an analysis of them would take us in a different direction from the humanist treatises and formal theological documents here analyzed. The second reason is even more compelling. Gary Waite has done extensive study of these groups and has published his findings in English.[6] I consider his articles and his extensive footnotes and bibliography a complementary study and a parallel analysis of this same period of time. In an interesting coincidence when George Williams called for "further investigation" concerning these groups, Waite's studies were in progress as Williams was submitting his final manuscript to the publishers, but because of the timing he evidently did not know of Waite's work. Also, coincidentally, I first became aware of Waite's research when he presented a paper on this subject at the Sixteenth Century Studies Conference at St. Louis, Missouri, in October, 1990. I had presented an earlier version of Chapter 4 of my study on the *Lamentations of Peter* at the same Conference.

II. An Overview of the Dissent in the 1520s

The focus of my study concerns one decade only—1520 to 1530—and provides some analysis of the theological works and ideas of many diverse scholars. To set the context of these dissenting ideas, Chapter 1 begins a generation earlier, in 1500 with the birth of the future Emperor Charles V. Because of his family connections and the various inheritances, he would become the dominant political influence in The Netherlands for the next half century. Chapter 2 analyzes the religious situation, especially the parallel contributions of Erasmus and Luther in The Netherlands. The interrelation between these two reformers, and the understanding and misunderstandings which Luther and Erasmus had of each other—as seen through their writings—continued even beyond the establishment of an Inquisition in The Netherlands in 1522. Each of the following chapters 3 through 11 lifts up certain documents and certain individuals who made their own unique contribution to the total complex of ideas and actions. Chapter 3 surveys many individuals active in the Humanist educational institutions, especially Latin schools in the major cities. Many of these individuals did not leave the Roman Catholic Church, but, nevertheless, contributed their efforts in education works and various Biblical studies. Sometimes they came under the scrutiny of the inquisitorial authorities. Chapter 4 analyzes a satirical lament in heaven by Biblical writers such as Peter, James, Luke and Paul, as well as Church Fathers including Ambrose, Jerome and Augustine. All these early writers complained that their works were not being read or taken seriously in the Church of the 16th century. Their writings, so they stated, were being superseded by Scholastic "sophists" such as Thomas Aquinas, Duns Scotus and others. Chapter 5 looks at a new interpretation of the Eucharist. Cornelis Hoen was a Humanist lawyer at the Court at The Hague. In 1521 he wrote—or perhaps compiled—a new interpretation of the Eucharist which denied transubstantiation and suggested that the elements were symbols or signs. His work, first published in Zürich by Zwingli in 1525, is compared with other texts of this period. Chapter 6 concerns Cornelis Grapheus, Humanist secretary of the city of Antwerp. As an editor, he was instrumental in having certain documents dating from the Late Middle Ages edited and published. Although these documents were almost a half-century old at the time, the ideas were confused with those of Martin Luther. Grapheus was imprisoned and forced to recant all his works. His emphasis, however, was probably more concerned with scholarly precision than agitation for church reforms like Luther. Several dissenting Augustinian monks form the basis of Chapter 7. On 1 July, 1523 the first two Augustinian martyrs in The Netherlands were burned in Brussels. They were conversant with many of Luther's doctrines. Others with similar ideas are included in this chapter as well.

Chapters 8 and 9 deal with two publications quickly condemned and suppressed in a special Edict of the Emperor in 1524. Chapter 8 concerns a secret Dutch translation of the Gospel of Matthew with several glosses or commentaries on the chapters frequently reflecting a non-Roman Catholic understanding. Chapter 9 presents a *Summa* or summary of the scriptures as understood by an anonymous author. One of the author's main emphases is baptism which should result in a "new person" with renewed human responsibility for one's own faith and actions within the community. This emphasis on baptism does not reflect a strict Lutheran interpretation but, instead, anticipates some of the main ideas of the Anabaptist movement of succeeding decades. (I used the Dutch edition published in 1882 by Professor Toorenenbergen in Amsterdam.) The first martyr for reforms within the church in the northern Netherlands is introduced in Chapter 10. One of his main actions had been to challenge the Roman Catholic sacrament of marriage, especially since it was not allowed for priests. Although a priest, he took a wife, whom he would neither renounce nor call his "concubine." Consequently, he was burned at the stake in The Hague. Chapter 11 introduces a Humanist editor who emphasized both the centrality of the Scriptures and a sincere pastoral concern for the sick and the suffering. His "*Troost ende Spiegel der Siecken*" [Trust and Mirror for the Sick] is a manual on pastoral care that challenged the callous practices of Roman Catholic priests. He fled to Germany. In Chapter 12 court records are used to document the government's attempts to control the dissenting tendencies and various popular reactions within the period, whether related strictly to Lutheran influences or dissent arising from other sources. These records show that some lay persons were often openly vocal and very confrontational in their religious dissent. Several examples are given, and the various punishments meted out to them are documented.

III. Geographical Factors

The geographical area referred to as The Netherlands in the 16th century was considerably larger than what we know today as the nation of The Netherlands. In the late Middle Ages and during the Reformation period the Burgundian Netherlands, much of which was later inherited by the future Emperor Charles V, included much of what we now know as The Netherlands and portions of Belgium as well. In addition, certain areas along the Rhine River in West Germany, such as the town of Goch, and the northwestern corner of France, including the cities of Lille and Dunkirk in the French province of Flanders, were all part of this inheritance. The Netherlands of the 15th and 16th centuries also included the present nation of Luxembourg. A map of 16th century Netherlands follows this introduction as Figure I.

A further complication in this period concerned the 17 separate provinces of The Netherlands, each of which had a different history and political tradition. Much of the area had been subjected to the Burgundian authorities for over a century. This included especially the provinces of Holland, Zeeland, Flanders and Brabant. Other territory came under the authority of Charles V during his own lifetime, through war, negotiation, or treaty. These were confined to the central and northeastern sections of the present nation of The Netherlands: Utrecht (1528), Overijssel (1528), Friesland (1524), Drenthe (1536), Gelderland (1543) and Groningen (1536). Consequently the authority which the Imperial forces could exercise concerning the religious inquisitions differed depending on the area.

In the intervening 450-year history many of the provincial names have been preserved. Some modifications came, however, for several reasons, including the wars of independence and the temporary truce of 1609, drawn at the approximate boundary between The Spanish Netherlands (now Belgium) and The United Netherlands (now often referred to popularly as Holland). Brabant, for example, was divided into three provinces: the province of Brabant (includes Brussels); the province of Antwerp (the province surrounds the city); and the province of North Brabant (in the southern portion of The Netherlands, including such major towns as Breda on the west and s'Hertogenbosch on the east). The old province of Holland, the economic center of the northern Netherlands, was divided between the provinces of North Holland (including both Amsterdam and Haarlem) and South Holland (including Rotterdam, Leiden and The Hague).

There are now eleven provinces in The Netherlands and nine in Belgium, and Luxembourg is a separate nation.

One further complication should be noted. The line of the Truce of 1609, dividing the United Netherlands on the north from the Spanish Netherlands on the south, did not divide according to language or ancient tradition. The language of the north provinces (with the possible exception of Friesland) was a form of Low German or *Plattdeutsch*, popularly referred to as "*Deitsch*," and still later "Dutch." This same language tradition, however, is preserved in the northern and western portions of Belgium where it was called "Flemish" in Flanders. A small area of northwestern France, including the city of Dunkirk, also preserves the Dutch/Flemish background. The southern portion of the sixteenth century Netherlands, on the other hand, used the language known as Walloon/French. Today much of Belgium uses both languages for such things as street signs. Some of the provincial or city names look quite different with both a Flemish/Dutch spelling and a French/Walloon version. Two examples are *Kortrijk/Courtrai* and *Luik/Liege*. We will use both names of many towns or cities in the southern Netherlands to avoid confusion when the different names might lead to uncertainty of location. The two major Belgian cities involved in this particular study are Antwerp and Brussels. Both of these also have two designations, but in this study we will use the commonly-accepted English spellings.

Despite the geographical, cultural, and language differences, however, the whole area was referred to as The Netherlands in the early 16th century. Because a large portion of the region came to the house of Hapsburg as a result of direct inheritance, the imperial authority could be more severe than it could in Germanic areas where there were Electors, Dukes, Counts and free cities to exert an intermediate authority. Almost as soon as Luther's works were known they were published in The Netherlands, especially in Antwerp, which was the commercial capital of the area (before this status was later assumed by Amsterdam). These writings were of interest for the scholars of the Northern Renaissance and the Biblical Humanists, and they were widely read. Likewise, many of the writings of Luther were circulated in the Augustinian monasteries of The Netherlands.

IV. Political Factors

For many reasons the Protestant movement in the Netherlands proceeded slowly for over a decade. *First*, there was no major leader to inspire followers and bring cohesion among the many individuals who were opposed to the Roman Catholic hierarchy and its sacramental system. *Second*, the Imperial political administration was much stronger in present-day Belgium and the Northern Netherlands (now The United Netherlands) than it was in the city-states of

Switzerland or the principalities of Saxony. There was neither a city council, nor a "Frederick the Wise" to provide a "buffer" between the Emperor and the people.

The area of The Netherlands, which Emperor Charles V theoretically controlled by hereditary right, was administered until 1530 directly by his aunt, the Regent Margaret of Austria. A genealogy of Emperor Charles V of Hapsburg follows this introduction as Figure II. It charts the complicated dynastic relations which brought his extensive inheritance into reality. These are further elaborated in Chapter 1.

Since centralized Imperial authority was felt to some extent in all parts of The Netherlands, ancient local rights and traditions were strained by the imposition of more rigid controls. Each region thought its rights were being challenged in a different way, so there were different levels of religious repression.[7] *Third*, because of this political situation an inquisition could be, and was, organized with an inquisitor general for The Netherlands. It was surprisingly effective in prohibiting widespread religious differences from organizing, although agitation from the citizens of the local legal authorities forced the first inquisitor out of power in 1523.

V. *Theological Factors and/or supposed abuses in The Netherlands*

In the early 16th century The Netherlands were brought together under the leadership of Emperor Charles V as a result of various opportune marriages in the few decades before. There was much individuality among the various areas, however, and local customs and local rights were steadfastly guarded against what seemed a larger and powerful influence from the outside. It is true that Charles V had been born in The Netherlands (in Gent/Gans, Flanders, now part of Belgium), but his attempts gradually to enforce common laws over all areas caused petitions, reactions, and quite different degrees of conformity to the new orders. As a result, there were many differences between various areas, not only in political and economic matters, but also with respect to religious practices. The Brethren of the Common Life, for example, had influence in certain areas; in other localities Erasmus and other Humanists were widely known .

Whereas Calvinism was organized in The Netherlands in the 1560s, and earlier the Anabaptists were prevalent from the 1530s, there were protesting movements, or at least protesting individuals, more than a decade before 1530. Nevertheless, it is probably not accurate to refer to them as "Protestant" at this time. There was much divergence within the proto-Protestant individuals and groups, as well as many variations within the Roman Catholic establishment itself. Before there was precision in the use of the term, all movements in this area that did not seem to be orthodox Roman Catholic were called "Lutheran," although many of them actually reflected little which would later be known as authentic Lutheranism.

There were, however, several tendencies in The Netherlands which can be loosely termed "dissenting" in the decade following 1520. Some of these were a reflection of Lutheran ideas spread in Augustinian monasteries at Antwerp and Dordrecht. There were other developments among the common people reflecting the continuing influence of the Brethren of the Common Life, a movement which emphasized education for other classes of society in addition to the clergy. Here also the Bible was translated and copied for wider reading. A third group reflected the new learning of "Biblical" or "Northern Humanism," as exemplified best by the Rotterdam-born scholar, Erasmus. The latter, suspected of heresy by some in his own church, was briefly in correspondence with Luther and, for several years lived until 1521 at Louvain/Leuven, the only university city in The Netherlands. Humanist criticism of Roman Catholic abuses was prevalent in the scholarly Latin schools.

There are many references to "Humanism," "Renaissance Humanism" and "Biblical Humanism" in these chapters, and these terms are used in this 16th century context. Some definition or clarification of these words may be in order, however, since the words "humanism" and "humanist" have taken on a much broader and less precise meaning in our own era. "Humanism" in all its forms in this period refers to the Latin concept of *studia humanitatis*, or studies of human concerns, and human culture in general. In contemporary education circles we still refer to the "Arts and Humanities," by which we mean literature and languages along with philosophical and/or religious issues. In contrast, we might characterize the earlier or medieval period as concerned with references to ideas beyond the human—heaven, angels, purgatory. Medieval art, as compared with Renaissance art, often exemplifies this striking contrast, since Renaissance art usually presents us with a realistic earthly landscape and seemingly real, everyday people or situations in place of Medieval creations populated by angels and Heavenly hosts.

The term "Renaissance" refers to a "re-birth" (*re-naissance* from the French), mainly a re-birth of interest in the Classical culture of ancient Greece and Rome, especially as exemplified in literature, languages, the human situation in the world, painting, sculpture, and architecture. This development quite naturally took on special characteristics depending on geographical location (for example, the Italian Renaissance as compared with the Northern Renaissance north of the Alps) and on specific interests of individuals or schools (for example, secular scholarship as compared with religious developments).

Renaissance Humanism was a philological method deeply involved in languages, translations, and editions of scholarly works, especially as these affected the whole intellectual culture. Paul Kristeller, a well-known scholar of Renaissance Humanism concluded,

I should like to understand Renaissance Humanism, at least in its origin and in its typical representatives, as a broad cultural and literary movement, which in its substance was not philosophical but had important philosophical implication and consequences. I have been unable to discover in the humanist literature any common philosophical doctrine, except a belief in the value of man [the human person] and the humanities and in the revival of ancient learning.[8]

William Bouwsma stated the objectives of "Humanism" slightly differently. Using Petrarch as his prime example, he thought that Humanism was concerned less with abstract thought, philosophy or metaphysics, and

was more concerned with individual human beings, with their changing thoughts, values, and feelings, and with human interaction in society. . . .Eloquence acquired by training in rhetoric was especially prized for its persuasive power. It was believed capable, as the humanists thought that the scholastic formulations were not, of penetrating the hearts of human beings, transforming the will, arousing the emotions, and accomplishing the world's work by inspiring action.[9]

For the Humanists, all types of literature were worthy of examination, whether Christian, non-Christian, or pre-Christian. Up-to-date translations were indispensable. No matter the text, human values and the practical aspects of ideas therein were emphasized. Biblical Humanism" especially in the Northern Renaissance, emerged from this atmosphere.

The term "Biblical Humanism" presupposes a methodology of careful linguistic study and accurate translations of the Bible. In addition, early Christian literature was also included. One of the best practitioners in this period was Erasmus, who edited and prepared for publication many Christian theological works from the first four centuries of the Christian era. In addition, Erasmus produced new editions of the Bible in Greek and Latin, and he wrote commentaries (or paraphrases) on all of the New Testament writings except for Revelation (as did Calvin a few decades later). The first concern of Biblical Humanists was always accuracy and well-stated prose. It was only secondary, and not a basic concern, that their work might result in new approaches to theology. Indeed, many Biblical Humanists remained in the Roman Catholic fold, although there were also many who realized that the implications of their thought led them in new directions. Over-all, the theological arguments of the Biblical Humanists were based more on careful linguistic analysis than on traditional interpretations which formed the basis of many of the theological arguments of the Medieval period. Thus it is not surprising that the Roman Catholic establishment was often suspicious, if not actually hostile, to these methodologies.[10]

In the decade of the 1520s the distinctions between Humanist theological conclusions and reforming doctrines were not clear. Although Humanism and the early Reformation developed at about the same time, they had different assumptions and different goals. Many Humanists did use their methodologies for the sake of the Reformation. (One of the best-known examples of this tendency was Philip Melanchthon, the close companion of Luther.) Others, however, used Humanist methods but remained within the Roman Catholic Church. (The best-known example of this tendency was Erasmus.)

The major objectives of Humanism were clarity of sources, correct translations, and the ability to analyze all sides of a given question. Their method was open-ended and the Humanists were concerned first of all with academic or intellectual conclusions. The Reformers were interested mainly in commitment to certain doctrines which by their nature eliminated certain other ideas which could not be comfortably incorporated into the new Reformed dogmas. Erika Rummel has written extensively about the Humanist attitude and methodology which was at times cooperative with and at other times, in tension with, developing Reformation ideas. She refers to this process as "confessionalizing."[11] Her bibliography includes extensive references to earlier usage of this same term. While her examples are largely from Germany, there were parallel developments in The Netherlands, which had significant cultural interchange with its neighbor to the east.

The gulf between Humanism and the Reformation became clear only after Erasmus and Luther's published debate over the "Free" or the "Bound" will (1524, 1525). In this exchange Luther reaffirmed his theological assumptions about the restrictions on the human will. Erasmus, on the other hand, evaluated various approaches to free will which the Roman Church had already affirmed. It was a non-commital exercise for Erasmus, a dogmatic assumption for Luther. The increasing "confessionalizing" of the Lutherans after the Diet of Worms and later after the Diet of Augsburg on the one side, and the development toward rigidity with respect to the Roman Catholic Church culminating in the Council of Trent on the other side made a Humanist, neutral, middle ground difficult. The gulf between the two confessions had become so deep by the time of Erasmus' death (1536) that the island in the middle where the Humanists might choose to stand was for the most part non-existent.

VI. The Late Medieval Church as compared with the Reformation: The Question of the "Forerunner."

The terminology of a "Forerunner of the Reformation," from a previous era, presupposed that there was a sharp break between the Reformation and all that went before. Consequently, so the assumption continues, since some individuals wrote about one or more of the ideas (or teachings) which would be analyzed again by one or more of the scholars in the Reformation period, they were called a "reformer" before there was a Reformation.[12] It seems more accurate now to think that the Late Middle Ages and the Reformation periods were part of a continuum. The 16th century can certainly be seen as an outgrowth or an elaboration of certain themes of the 15th century (or even of the 14th), but an analysis of the 15th century cannot be accurately understood and evaluated except in its own context, certainly not through 16th century hindsight.

Two specific examples of 15th century scholarship were closely related to the content of this study. In Chapter 6 we include some material on John Pupper of Goch (1420-1475), and in Chapter 5 a brief analysis of some concepts of Wessel Gansfort (1420-1489) seems germane to the discussion. While eschewing the older terminology "Reformers before the Reformation," however, Heiko Oberman analyzed this problem[13] and argued for continuity on many theological fronts. Often the earlier "forerunner" terminology arose in Protestant circles and was arbitrarily applied to earlier periods in an artificial or misleading comparison.. This superficial use of the "forerunner" fails to let concepts arise out of their own context. Instead, it presupposed an evaluation from a context several decades or centuries in the future.

VII. Changing understanding of the Sacraments, especially concerning the Eucharist

Earlier scholars referred to the early reformers in The Netherlands as "Sacramentarian," or "Sacramentists." They assumed that the reformers' main concerns involved the changing understanding of the Sacraments, most notably the Eucharist. Other scholarly studies in The Netherlands either lacked precision, or experimented with other terms. For example, a comprehensive, although old, study of the Reformation in The Netherlands referred only in passing to the term "Sacramentarians," where the author also used a synonymous term, "evangelical."[14] Several years later another historian from The Netherlands, J. Lindeboom, used the term, but he more often referred to the major reforming movement as "National Reformed" closely related to "Biblical Humanism."[15] L. Knappert returned to the term "Sacramentarians" in his historical survey.[16]

George H. Williams followed these earlier scholars, especially Knappert, and used the term "Sacramentist" as a designation of the earliest reforms within The Netherlands.[17] Williams noted that Luther used the term "Sacramentarian," or various versions thereof, for opponents such as Zwingli, Oecolampadius or Karlstadt, who refused to affirm the Roman Catholic understanding that the grace of God was both actually present and offered to the believer in the Eucharistic elements. At the same time, however, Williams recognized that in many different ways a spiritual "Real Presence" was a part of worship reform in The Netherlands. He recognized that Wessel Gansfort of The Netherlands, while continuing to affirm medieval understandings, also provided for a spiritual communion in addition to and outside the elements on the altar. Various reformers tended to sharpen the distinction between these two understandings (we might term them the Medieval— or literal—and the spiritual), and, in the case of Cornelius Hoen (See Chapter 5), even to place his whole emphasis on the spiritual aspect as a "sign" in place of any power within the transubstantiated elements on the altar. Hence the shift was from a realistic "Real Presence" to a typological "spiritual" presence "by, with and under" (Luther) or a symbolic presence within the individual believer himself (as variously understood by Zwingli, Oecolampadius, Karlstadt or Cornelis Hoen).

Williams's sense of the gradual change in interpreting the Eucharist is helpful for our understanding. There have been questions raised, however, about the term "Sacramentarian" or "Sacramentist;" and a growing realization that the shift in sacramental understanding was much broader than the Eucharist alone. Following Williams's lead, and perhaps employing some of the same sources, Cornelius Krahn used the term "Sacramentarians" in reference also to the early reform ideas in The Netherlands.[18] Indeed, he devoted one chapter to "The Evangelical Sacramental Reformation." An even more recent study by Arnold Snyder also uses the term,[19] and both Krahn and Snyder assert that the "Sacramentarian" understanding of the sacraments was one of the elements in the rise of Anabaptism, not only in The Netherlands, but also in Switzerland.

The problem of terminology has been specifically addressed by Johannes Trapman in The Hague.[20] He pointed to the lack of historical usage of the term (with the above understandings), and concluded that it is too nebulous, or affords too many shades of meaning to be of value in this discussion. Frequently the term "Sacramentarian," for example, has been used in the sense of *anti*-Sacramentarian; hence, it is at least imprecise if not utterly confusing. Furthermore, a modification or even rejection of the medieval understanding of the Eucharist was not consistent in The Netherlands. Indeed, while the various individuals surveyed in this study emphasized needed changes in the churches, many raised no question concerning the Eucharist.

If there is any emphasis which can be seen as a unifying theme in this decade of reform in The Netherlands, it might be some variation of the idea of freedom[21]— freedom from papal control; freedom from indulgences; freedom from various sacramental understandings; freedom from medieval church dogmas such as purgatory, or pilgrimages, or prayer through intermediaries such as saints and the Virgin Mary; and freedom from ceremonials or from clerical abuses. Likewise, many of the scholars from The Netherlands sought freedom to pursue their Humanist learning and have access to the best literature of their day. To be sure, no one person or one town embodied all of these emphases, but because of these diverse concerns, without expecting a unifying theological motif, we must analyze each person or group on its own merits.

Notes for the Introduction

1. W. de Greef, O. J. de Jong, J. van Oort, B. J. Spruyt, editors, *Reformatie Studies, Reformatie in Meervoud* (Kampen, The Netherlands: Uitgeverij de Groot Goudriaan, 1991). This article appears on pp. 26-54.

2. *Ibid.*, p. 27, *befrijding van de drukkende last van kerkelijke geboden en verbod-enen van de tirannieke macht van de Paus.*

3. These various pluralities are discussed on pp. 29-30.

4. B. J. Spruyt, *Ketter aan het Binnenhof: Cornelis Hoen en zijn tractaat tegen de transubstantiatieleer (1525)* (Heerenveen, The Netherlands: Uitgeverij J. J. Groen en Zoon, 1997.

5. George H. Williams, *The Radical Reformation*, (third edition.). Kirksville, Missouri: *Sixteenth Century Essays and Studies (*1992), pp. 98-99.

6. Gary K. Waite, "Popular Drama and Radical Religion: The Chambers of Rhetoric and Anabaptism, in The Netherlands," *Mennonite Quarterly Review*, 65 (1991), 227-255; *ibid.*, "Vernacular Drama and the early urban Reformation: The Chambers of rhetoric in Amsterdam, 1520-1550," *Journal of Medieval and Renaissance Studies*, 21 (1991), 187-206; *ibid.*, "Reformers on Stage: Rhetorical drama and Reformation Propaganda in The Netherlands of Charles V, 1519-1556," *Archiv für Reformationsgeschichte,* 83 (1992), 209-239.

7. For a thorough analysis of the political and economic aspects of The Netherlands of this period, see James D. Tracy, *Holland under Hapsburg Rule, 1506-1566: The formation of a Body Politic* (Berkeley, Los Angeles: University of California Press, 1990).

8. Paul Kristeller taught renaissance humanism and related topics at Columbia University for forty years, beginning in 1939. He summarized his understanding developed over a lifetime in an essay "The Humanist Movement" written as an introduction to a collection of his printed works in Paul Oskar Kristeller, *Renaissance Thought and its Sources,* (New York: Columbia University Press, 1979). This quotation is on pp. 31-32.

9. William Bouwsma, "The Spirituality of Renaissance Humanism," in vol. 17 of Jill Raitt, ed., *Christian Spirituality: High Middle Ages and Reformation* (New York: Crossroad, 1987), pp. 236-237.

10. See, for example, the excellent summary of this problem in Cornelis Augustijn, "Die Stellung der Humanismus zur Glaubensspaltung 1518-1530", pp. 141-153, in Cornelis Augustijn, *Erasmus der Humanist als Theologe und Kirchenreformer* (Leiden, New York: Brill, 1996).

11. Erika Rummel, *The Confessionalization of Humanism in Reformation Germany* (Oxford: Oxford University Press, 2000).

12. Karl C. Ullmann, *Reformers Before the Reformation: Principally in Germany and The Netherlands* (Trans. Robert Menzies, 2 vols., Edinburgh: T. And T. Clark, 1855).

13. Heiko A. Oberman, ed., *Forerunners of the Reformation: The Shape of Late Medieval Thought* (New York: Holt, Rinehart and Winston, 1966); especially "The Case of the Forerunner," pp. 3-49.

14. J. G. de Hoop Scheffer, *Geschiedenis der Kerkhervorming in Nederland van haar onstan tot 1531* (Amsterdam: G. L . Funke, 1873); p. 109.

15. J. Lindeboom, *De Confessioneele ontwikkeling der Reformatie in de Nederlanden.* (The Hague: Martinus Nijhoff, 1946); pp. 41-42. The same author analyzed his concept of the "National Reformed" much more completely in his earlier work: *Het Biblisch Humanisme in Nederland.* (Leiden: A. H. Adriani, 1913).

16. L. Knappert, *Het ontstaan en de vestiging van het Protestantisme in de Nederlande* (Utrecht: 1924).

17. George H. Williams, *The Radical Reformation* (Philadelphia: Westminster Press, 1962). This discussion is on pp. 27-37. Thirty years later he published a much-enlarged version: *The Radical Reformation.* (Kirksville, Missouri: Sixteenth Century Journal Publishers, 1992). In the later version he included substantially the same material on pp. 95-108.

18. Cornelius Krahn, *Dutch Anabaptism, Origin, Spread, Life and Thought (1450-1600)* (The Hague: Martinus Nijhoff, 1968). This was reprinted: (Scottdale, Pennsylvania: Herald Press, 1981).

19. C. Arnold Snyder, *Anabaptist History and Theology: An Introduction* (Kitchener, Ontario: Pandora Press, 1995). His reference to The Netherlands is on pp. 16-18 where he follows Williams; while his reference to Switzerland is on p. 53.

20. J. Trapman, "Le rôle des "Sacramentaires" des Origenes de la Réforme jusqu'en 1530 aux Pays Bas." *Nederlands Archief voor Kerkgeschiedenis*, 63 (1983), pp. 1-24.

21. B. J. Spruyt makes this a major emphasis in his study: "Reformatie en meervoud" [Reformation in its plurality], pp. 26-54 in *Reformatie Studies*, (Kampen, The Netherlands: de Groot Goudrian, 1991).

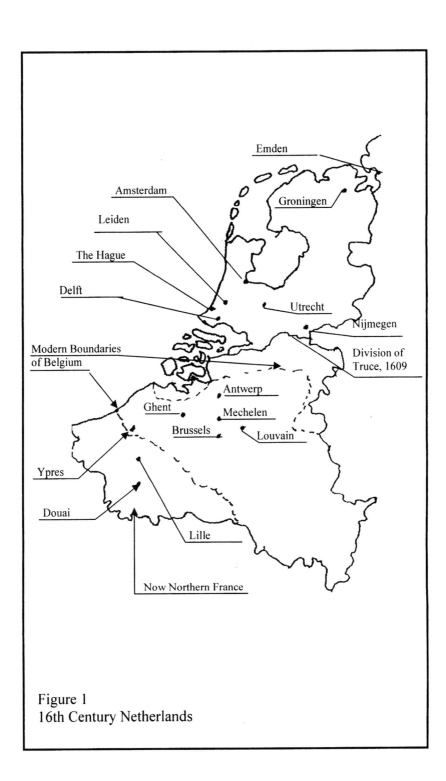

Figure 1
16th Century Netherlands

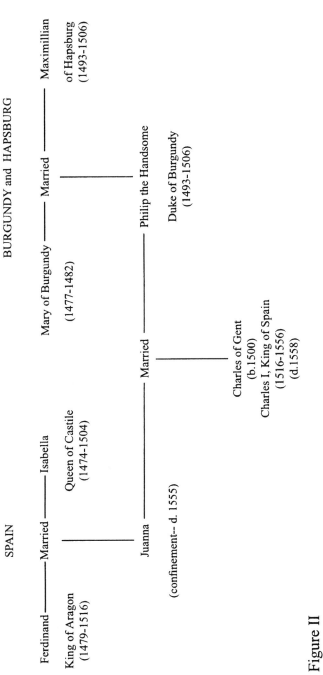

SPAIN   BURGUNDY and HAPSBURG

Ferdinand ———— Married ———— Isabella   Mary of Burgundy ——— Married ——— Maximillian
King of Aragon   Queen of Castile   (1477-1482)   of Hapsburg
(1479-1516)   (1474-1504)   (1493-1506)

        Juanna ———————————————— Married ———————————————— Philip the Handsome
                                                          Duke of Burgundy
  (confinement-- d. 1555)   (1493-1506)

                              Charles of Gent
                              (b.1500)
                              Charles I, King of Spain
                              (1516-1556)
                              (d.1558)

Figure II
genealogy of Charles V

Chronological Table

1500

24 February, in Gent/Gans [Flanders], Birth of Charles, of Hapsburg (later Emperor Charles V)

1503

PAPACY OF JULIUS II (Giuliano della Rovere, from Genoa), 31 October. 1503-21 February, 1513

1504

26 November, Death of Queen Isabella of Castile/Spain, maternal grandmother of Charles [later to be Emperor Charles V]

1506

25 September, death of Philip the Handsome, Duke of Burgundy. He was the father of Charles (later Emperor Charles V), who in turn became Duke of Burgundy on the death of his father

Margaret of Savoy (and of Austria) became regent for her six-year-old nephew Charles, and maintained that role most of the time to her death 1 December, 1530.

1513

PAPACY OF LEO X (Giovanni de' Medici, from Florence), 31 October, 1513, 1 December, 1521.

1516

23 January, death of Ferdinand of Aragon/Spain, the maternal grandfather of Charles [later Emperor Charles V]

14 March, Charles of Hapsburg (at age 16), became King of Spain

1517

31 October, Luther prepared 95 theses for classroom discussion on the abuse of indulgences

30 November, FIRST edict of Charles, King of Spain and Duke of Flanders, against blasphemy in The Netherlands

1518
1518 or 1519 Jacob Proopst (Praepositus) became prior of the Augustinian monastery in Antwerp

1519
5 January, SECOND edict of Charles against blasphemy in The Netherlands

12 January, Emperor Maximillian I died. He had been Holy Roman Emperor since 1493, and was the paternal grandfather of Charles of Hapsburg (soon to become Emperor Charles V).

28 June, election of Charles of Hapsburg as Emperor Charles V (at age 19)

30 August, (*penultima die mensis Augusti*) Condemnation of writings of Luther by the theological faculty of Cologne. They recommended they be burned.

7 November, Condemnation of writings of Luther by the theological faculty of Louvain/Leuven. They also recommended they be burned.

1520
25 March, Luther's *responsio* to the condemnations published

17 July, Papal Bull, *Exsurge Domine,* promulgated against 41 teachings of Luther. Luther received it on 10 October, and burned it on 10 December in Wittenberg.

8 October, Luther's books burned in Louvain/Leuven

12 October, Luther's books burned in Cologne

17 October, Luther's books burned in Liege/Luik

23 October, Charles crowned "King of the 'Romans', actually "King of the Germans" in Aix la Chapelle (Aachen). Charles was crowned by the Pope in Bologna, but not until 24 February, 1530. Abdicated, 1556.

10 December, Luther burned the papal document, *Exsurge Domine,* and other theological tracts

1521
3 January, Papal Bull, *Decet Romanum Pontificem* promulgated—excommunicating Luther and his followers. [See Appendix, # I].

17 February, THIRD edict of Charles, now Emperor and King of Spain as well as Duke of Flanders, against blasphemy

20 March, FIRST EDICT of Charles, Emperor, against Luther's teaching (*leerstelsels*) and books, especially in The Netherlands

17 and 18 April, Luther was questioned before the Diet of Worms

26 April, Luther was allowed to leave Worms to go back to Wittenberg, with the promise of a safe conduct. On 4 May, while he was in the Thuringian moun-

tains, he was taken prisoner by friendly forces, and hidden in the Wartburg castle (he was there from 4 May, 1521 to 1 March, 1522).

8 May, the Imperial Edict of Worms, condemning and banning Luther, was promulgated in Latin, signed by the Emperor 26 May

8 May, A similar edict written for The Netherlands, also condemning Luther was issued in Dutch/Flemish and in French/Walloon.

August, Praepositus, prior of Augustinian monastery in Antwerp, returned from study in Wittenberg, having received his degree *Baccalaureus Biblicus* and Licentiate in Theology.

28 October, Erasmus left Louvain/Leuven for Basel where he arrived 15 November

5 December, Praepositus, as prior of Augustinian monastery in Antwerp, questioned and imprisoned

6 December, The Bishop of Kamerijk/Cambrai authorized inquisitional powers for Jacob Masson (Latomus) and Nicholas Baechem of Egmond, to try Praepositus for heresy

1522

PAPACY OF ADRIAN VI (Adriaan Florensz, from Utrecht), 9 January, 1522-14 September, 1523.

After 13 January, Herman Gerrits (Gherardi) of Utrecht recanted his nine articles [See Appendix, # II].

5 February-23 April, Cornelius Grapheus in prison in Brussels

9 February, in Brussels, Praepositus's "recantation" with thirty "Lutheran" arguments which he denied under pressure [See Appendix, # III].

23 April, Frans van der Hulst appointed inquisitor in Charles's territory of The Netherlands.

23 April, Cornelius Grapheus was forced to renounce and condemn his theological articles [See Appendix, # IV].

6 May, Luther's books burned in Antwerp

July, second imprisonment of Praepositus. (He escaped, and by August was in Wittenberg with Luther)

October, Henry of Zutphen fled from Antwerp to Bremen

1523

February, Cornelis Hoen in prison for a short time until March. Then he was again imprisoned to be released in October.

5 February, Cornelis Grapheus imprisoned

1 June, Pope Adrian named Frans van der Hulst inquisitor in the Netherlands, adding authority of the church to that of the empire the previous year

1 July, two monks burned in Brussels (Augustinians—Johann van Esschen and Heinrich Vos, of Antwerp). [See Brother Henry's 62 articles which he was forced to deny, Appendix, # V].

PAPACY OF CLEMENT VII (Giulio de' Medici, from Florence), 19 November, 1523-25 September, 1534

There were complaints against inquisitors with authorities reasserting privileges of the States of The Netherlands

1524

23 March, Emperor Charles V promulgated an edict against printers. Singled out for his condemnation were two documents: *Summa der godliker skrifturen*, and a translation and commentary on the Gospel of Matthew published in Amsterdam. The author of the former remains anonymous, the latter was issued by a Franciscan, John van Pelt.

1 April, the Emperor's SECOND EDICT against Luther's works

Cornelis Hoen died at an advanced age

September, publication of Erasmus' *De Libero Arbitrio*.

10 December, Henry of Zutphen murdered by a mob in Dithmarschen (Germany)

1525

April, Cornelis Woutersz in prison. A longer imprisonment would be in 1527.

15 September, Pistorius (Jan de Bakker) in prison and executed in The Hague [See a summary of his beliefs in Appendix # VI].

24 September, the Emperor's THIRD EDICT against Luther's works.

August/September, Zwingli's publication of Hoen's letter concerning the Eucharist

December, publication of Luther's *De Servo Arbitrio*.

1526

17 July, the Emperor's FOURTH EDICT against Luther's works.

1527

14 March, the Emperor's FIFTH EDICT against Luther's works [actually a reissue of the THIRD EDICT of 24 September, 1525].

15-20 November, trial in The Hague, and death of Wendelmoet a widow of Monnikendam. [See proceedings of her trial, Appendix, # VII].

1528

18 January, the Emperor's SIXTH EDICT against works of Luther

1529

14 October, the Emperor's SEVENTH EDICT against works of Luther.

26 October, execution of Cornelis Wouterszoon of Dordrecht. He had been in prison in The Hague from 3 April, 1527 to 11 March, 1528, but his execution was delayed for many more months; they hoped he might recant.

1530

24 February, Emperor Charles V was crowned by Pope Clement VII in Bologna (the last Emperor so recognized by the pope)

1 December, death of Regent Margaret of Austria.

1531

Appointment of Mary of Hungary as Regent (1531-   )

Chapter 1

Charles (1500-1558),
King of Spain and Holy
Roman Emperor

Family Background

On 23 January, 1516, Ferdinand, King of Aragon, died after having ruled since 1479. His wife, Isabella, whom he had married in 1469, had been Queen of Castile since 1474. Their marriage had great political significance, not only in the Iberian Peninsula but in the rest of Europe as well. Their offspring were destined to begin the long process toward a united Spain. Upon Isabella's death in 1504, the title of Queen of Castille passed to her daughter Joanna. The latter had already married Philip the Handsome, who was Duke of Burgundy (this included The Netherlands) through his mother's (Mary of Burgundy) inheritance. Philip was also son of the Holy Roman Emperor, Maximillian (of Hapsburg). They lived in the inherited lands in a castle in Ghent/Gand, in the low countries, with headquarters in Brussels and Malines/Mechelen.

On 24 February, 1500, a son, Charles, was born to Philip and Joanna in the castle in Ghent/Gand/Gans. Charles would grow up knowing the Flemish/Dutch language, but in time he learned Spanish, French, and some German. In 1506 Philip the Handsome died, and since Joanna was mentally incompetent to rule, the Burgundian inheritance and The Netherlands especially, passed to her six-year old son, Charles, now Duke of Burgundy. The effective authority in The Netherlands, however, was Charles's Aunt Margaret of Savoy (and of Austria), who at age twenty-four had already been widowed twice. She functioned in that position until 1515 when the fifteen-year-old Charles was declared of age. Charles's mother, Joanna, lived in confinement in Spain until her death in 1555. (A genealogy diagramming these complicated dynastic relationships is included above, as Figure II, following the Introduction.)

When Ferdinand of Spain died in 1516 the titles King of both Aragon and Castile and ultimately King of a united Spain as well as ruler of The Netherlands was bestowed on the grandson of Ferdinand. Up to this time Charles had never set foot in the homeland of these grandparents. He assumed his new title at Brussels on 14 March of that year, yet it was not until one year later that he actually departed for Spain (8 September, 1517), and he would not return to The Netherlands until 1520; Margaret was again appointed regent when Charles sailed from Middleburg in Zeeland. In Spain his regent was Adrian of Utrecht, his former tutor in Flanders. Soon Adrian would be elected Pope Adrian VI (1522-1523). Margaret continued as regent in The Netherlands until her death on 30 November, 1530.

When Charles left his homeland it did not preclude his being regularly informed of the happenings in The Netherlands. To his dismay the communiqués he received brought regular notice of continuing blasphemy and disregard for religious tradition. Furthermore, since he thought that any critique of the church was also a critique of the state, he considered it imperative that he preserve order in both the religious and the political spheres of his territory.

Charles's first Edict against Blasphemy (30 November 1517)

On 30 November, 1517, the first edict against blasphemy was issued from Brussels in the name of Charles (who at the time was in Spain). While there is nothing in this document which would indicate that Charles had heard of Luther's work at this early date, the edict gives evidence of the ferocity with which this leader would continue to investigate and prosecute religious differences, especially in The Netherlands where he had more direct control than in areas of Germany which would become Lutheran. Blasphemy, so the document read, against God, the Virgin Mary "his glorious Mother," or the saints would be liable to strict punishment. The edict also noted that there had been blasphemy against Jesus, the saints, and the Roman Catholic faith. Since much of the local heresy seemed to come from unauthorized sermons, these were outlawed. For a first offense, the penalty would be a payment of money at the discretion of the judge--one third for the judge, one third for the accuser, and one third "for God through alms." The built-in possibility for corruption undoubtedly insured that the judge and the accuser would receive their share, regardless of whether God and alms were considered seriously. For a second offense the offender would have his tongue bored, and he would be placed in a public pillory. A third offense would earn a public flogging, and subsequent exile from the area. Should he/she return from exile, the gallows awaited. As Charles reasoned, swift punishment was necessary to avert God's ire, malediction and retribution—*i.e.* a national calamity of some type.[1] The publication of this all-inclusive condemnation did not, however, result in conformity. Consequently, it was issued in a modified form a little over a year later (19 January, 1519).

A note more suggestive of developments to come appeared on 8 March, 1518. Apparently, the Augustinian monks at Dordrecht were promoting some questionable theological ideas. The Magistrate of Dordrecht wrote to the provincial leader of the order, William of Alkmaar, (who at the moment was in Leiden). The magistrate accused four monks of erroneous teachings in their sermons and in their confessional advice: Pieter van Ferrewairde, Cornelis van Rijmmerswale, Gerryt de Man, and Symon van Mechelen. The magistrate added that if the officials of the order would not investigate the charges immediately, the city or provinciala authorities would do so instead.[2] Unfortunately, we do not know enough about the charges to evaluate the conflict. The monks, however, were a part of the same Observant branch of the Augustinians of which Luther was a member. This Augustinian monastery in Dordrecht will enter our story again in Chapter 7.

Undoubtedly, this is the problem which was referred to William of Alkmaar. After the complaint was filed on 8 March. William responded three days later, on 11 March in a letter to the magistrate. He gave a vague answer and said he would inquire into the situation before he left The Netherlands for business in Germany. Only then could he give a clear answer.[3]

A second, stronger threat came from the same magistrate about two weeks later. He warned that he must discipline his heretical brothers. They are a menace, he added, not only to Dordrecht but to Holland, Brabant, Flanders and other lands of "our Lord Charles." Again, he included a threat of secular intervention.[4]

Not only was there questionable teaching within the monastery, but "erroneous" ideas were discovered among the common people as well. On 2 March, 1517, Hendrik van Eemyck was accused of "un-Christian and horrible blasphemy" against God and ridiculed the state official in Friesland. He was pilloried, his tongue was "shortened the breadth of a finger;" and he was banned from all lands of King Charles, for "one hundred years and one day."[5] In Oudenaarde in the same year Torreken van der Perre was accused of "blasphemy against the holy sacrament." He was commanded to carry a wax candle in a procession.[6] In Leiden in 1518 a fine was levied against Daniel Jacopsz and Mees Symonsz because they had taken a picture of the Virgin Mary and had "insulted" it.[7] In Brussels, on 18 August, 1518, Lauken van Moeseke was accused of blasphemy and placed in a pillory. Evidently, he did not recant, because twelve days later the punishment continued. His tongue was bored with "a glowing awl," and he was beheaded with a sword at the Great Market in Brussels. His body was placed on a wheel outside the city.[8]

Charles' Second Edict against Blasphemy
(5 January, 1519)

A second edict against blasphemy was issued by Charles through his aunt and her court in Mechelen/Malines on 5 January, 1519. He reasoned that since his first order had not been put into operation as it should have been, it must, therefore have contained penalties which were too severe. To insure that the guilty blasphemers would not go unpunished, he softened the punishments. For the first offense a money payment was demanded; for the second offense, double the money was required. A third offense required a triple money payment and a six-day jail sentence on bread and water. The fourth offense would be punished by ridicule and mortification in a public pillory for two hours.[9] It hardly seems likely, however, that these reduced penalties would produce uniformity of belief.

In the meantime, on 12 January, 1519, the Emperor Maximilian, the paternal grandfather of Charles, died. Charles immediately became one of the candidates for the important position. After many secret negotiations, and a significant outlay of money, Charles was elected King of the Romans and Emperor designate on 28 June, 1519. He was crowned King of the Romans (German king) at Aachen on 23 October, in the cathedral of Charlemagne. He was not crowned Emperor by the pope for more than a decade, however, until 24 February, 1530.

In August, 1519, in Antwerp, another blasphemy was recorded. Kathelijne, wife of Nikolaas Janssens the innkeeper, was convicted of blaspheming the holy Eucharist and of spreading rumors. She was sentenced to leave Antwerp before sundown and begin a pilgrimage to the church of St. Peter and St. Paul in Rome. She was to be out of the province in three days. Upon her return, she was expected to bring a letter of proof of completion of her trip, at which time she would be required to pay a fine of twenty-four Burgundian guilders. She would then do her penance at St. Joris Church, and walk in the next procession of the Church of Our Beloved Lady (O. L. V. Kerk), in Antwerp. If she failed to follow these stipulations her hand was to be cut off.[10]

With his elevation as Emperor, Charles reigned over lands that rivaled the size of Charlemagne's kingdom, seven hundred years before. These areas were often loosely united with regional differences and divided loyalties. In the Netherlands, especially, there were ancient privileges enjoyed by various regions extending back before they became absorbed politically into the Burgundian inheritance. Unification of state and church would prove to be elusive. Humanist educational reforms, the emerging influence of Martin Luther, and the widening outbreaks of heterodoxy, blasphemy and heresy would severely challenge all secular and ecclesiastical efforts to secure a united realm and a common faith. All these cultural streams would be woven together in various ways to make the decade of the 1520s a rich kaleidoscopic collection of religious developments.

Notes for Chapter 1

1. *Corpus Documentorum Inquisitionorum (CDI)*, IV, 5, 30 November, 1517.
2. *CDI* , IV, 6f; 8 March, 1518.
3. *CDI,* IV, 7; 11 March, 1518.
4. *CDI,* IV, 8.
5. *CDI,* IV, 3.
6. *CDI*, IV, 6. Also *CDI,* I, 514-15.
7. *CDI*, IV, 190. See also *CDI*, II, 312, 313.
8. *CDI*, I, 515f, 18, 30 August, 1518; Also *CDI* , IV, 9.
9. *CDI*, I, 516, 5 January, 1519; Also *CDI* , IV, 10.
10. *CDI*, 1, 517 ff. dated Antwerp, 19, 20 August, 1519.

Chapter 2

Luther's Influence in The Netherlands

The border between The Netherlands and the Holy Roman Empire allowed travelers, business people and ideas to pass back and forth freely. The gradual infiltration of Luther's ideas into The Netherlands was a complex process. His writings were introduced by traders who disembarked at ports of commerce, especially Antwerp. As early as 1518 printed copies of several of Luther's works appeared, having been printed in Basel and various German centers. By 1519 Luther's works were printed in several cities in The Netherlands, although printers did so at considerable risk to their livelihoods or even their lives. This was especially true after Luther's works had been banned by the Papal Bull, *Exsurge Domine* (1520), and burned as early as 1520 in Antwerp and other cities.

Influences also came from Wittenberg through Luther's own order of Augustinian monks. Some students of Luther were leaders in monasteries in The Netherlands and the stream of students from The Netherlands who studied in Wittenberg continued throughout the next decade. In this chapter we shall follow some of these developments up to the excommunication of Luther in 1521, the imperial ban of Luther following the Diet of Worms also in 1521 and the establishment of the Inquisition in The Netherlands in 1522.

Luther's ideas and publications become known in The Netherlands

One of the earliest recorded references to the influence of Luther in The Netherlands was printed in the *Chronijcke van Zeelandt.* "Martin Luther and many of his sympathizers have begun to spread their teachings and print their works. These were sent into these lands [Zeeland]."[1] Jacobus Latomus (Jacques Masson), one of Luther's later antagonists, reported that Luther's works were known in Louvain/Leuven as early as 1518.[2] He reported in the same letter that the University of Louvain/Leuven decreed that although the works of Luther were strongly suspected [*vehementer suspectus*] of containing doctrinal errors [*rumores de mala doctrina*], the faculty would not make a decision now because they had not yet analyzed them [*Lutheri librum sibi non visum neque lectum*].

Erasmus was directly informed of the availability of Luther's works in The Netherlands when he received a letter from Lambertus Hollonius, a young scholar from Liege/Luik whom Erasmus had recommended for a publishing position in Basel. Hollonius's letter to Erasmus indicated that many people perceived little or no clear-cut distinction between Luther's work and that of the Humanists.

> I have taken a post with Froben the printer [line 13]. . . . Froben is sending you a book by Luther, a truly Christian theologian, but unpopular with our strict, not to say superstitions, characters who dress up as theologians. I cannot tell you how well it has been received by those who are keen on the subject; I at least, who am a mere nobody, have felt my mind set free from its former enslavement to all the most frigid details of ceremonial. How blessed we are to live in an age like this, in which with you to guide and lead us and bring us to perfection both literature and true Christianity are being born again [lines 20-27].[3]

Both interest in and opposition to Luther's ideas continued to grow. Ultimately, in 1519, the two universities in Louvain/Leuven and Cologne made official declarations against Luther's works. Luther's "heresy," however, was not evident to all. In particular, the Augustine monks of Antwerp, sharing his kindred concerns, criticized the selling of indulgences by Italian merchants in the port city. A later *A History of the Netherlands (1608)* reported:[4]

> In the meantime (1519 or 1520) many spirituals, and principally Augustinian monks, influenced by the books and pamphlets of Martin Luther, undertook to analyze several articles which they thought were being abused by the Roman church, principally in the case of indulgences.

So effective was this preaching to the people, this history continued, that "the church. . . could not hold the crowd."

Some time before "Luther" became a common name among the leaders, and before the government had a clear idea concerning Luther's teachings, the Governess [*landvoogdes*], Margaret of Austria (and of Savoy), was discussing the problems of the realm with the magistrates of Louvain/Leuven. They told her that Luther's writings were subverting the Christian cause, and she asked: "Who is this Luther?" They answered: "An unlearned monk." Her appropriate, and caustic, response was, "Therefore, all of you very learned men should write against this one unlearned one, for the whole world will surely put more faith in the work of many learned men than in that of one unlearned."[5]

Margaret's assumption that this was merely a set of new ideas put forth by an uneducated monk, and that they would ultimately have no results, is comparable with the supposed comment of Pope Leo X who thought that the Lutheran confusion came because this monk indulged in too much German beer. Others at this time, likewise, took the developments lightly, but some attempted to understand the issues more clearly. Some leaders in The Hague reportedly told Henry of Nassau, an official [*subregulus*] of Flanders, Brabant and Holland, that they suspected that Luther's writings were having great effects. In 1519 or 1520 Henry told them, "Go and preach the gospel of Christ sincerely, as Luther is doing, and offend no one; then you will have no occasion to complain about any adversary."[6] The Lord of Ravenstein, who held property in Zeeland, had heard some words critical of Luther at an imperial gathering. He responded: "Once in four hundred years a Christian man arises whom the Pope wishes to suppress [*occidere*]."[7] Nevertheless, although possibly an exaggeration, an English man stated at about the same time, "If there be three men that speak, the twain keep Luther's opinion."[8]

There were many printing presses in The Netherlands willing and anxious to print works by or about Luther. Sometimes these activities were done at great personal risk to the printers themselves. They often used various means to avoid censure or severe punishment. For example, several works of Luther were identified as printed "in Wittenberg," when upon closer analysis it is discovered that they were actually printed in Antwerp or some other location in The Netherlands.

This process of printing in the face of Roman Catholic opposition was analyzed by M. E. Kronenberg in 1948.[9] Her study analyzed the changing attitudes among printers after the publication of the Papal Bull, *Exsurge Domine.* She summarized several imperial edicts along with their punishments. She also listed many of the places where books were burned and printers endangered. Antwerp was second only to Paris as a printing center. Between 1500 and 1540 Antwerp had a total of 56 printers who published about 2480 works.[10] Among printers in the northern Netherlands the most important issuing works with reforming ideas were located in Leiden and Zwolle.[11]

A few years later, she wrote a further article listing the various editions of Luther which were available in The Netherlands from the beginning of the Reformation up to 1541.[12] Her preliminary count, for example, was: 14 publications in Latin, 47 in Dutch/Flemish, 5 in French (all in Antwerp), and 1 in Spanish. They numbered approximately seventy titles. In addition, there were 6 publications in Danish, all edited by Christiaan Pedersen in Antwerp. The appearance of Danish translations at this time gives an added dimension. King Christian II of Denmark attempted to introduce the Reformation in his own country in the early 1520s, but was forced to leave in 1523. He went into exile in The Netherlands, and his spiritual advisor, Christiaan Pedersen accompanied him. The King was welcomed into The Netherlands because he was married to Isabella, sister of Emperor Charles V. Differences in religion between these two rulers must have made for a potential conflict in the family, or at least some political tension.

An even more thorough study of Luther's works in The Netherlands appeared as a doctoral thesis in 1969. The author surveyed Luther's writings published in The Netherlands to 1546 (the date of Luther's death).[13] He attempted to assess the widespread influence of Luther not only by analyzing every publication, but also analyzing the printers themselves. His extensive study in the Dutch language is accompanied by a chapter-by-chapter summary in German.

Visser shows that the earliest works of Luther arrived in The Netherlands in 1518 from Froben, a printer in Basel. These became the basis of the condemnations by the universities of Cologne and of Leiden in 1519. We shall summarize these imported texts below (pp. 16-19) in relation to the actions of the two universities. We turn first, however, to works actually published in The Netherlands, some in Latin, some in German and some in Dutch/Flemish or French/Walloon. Some of the publications included more than one tract within their covers, and some had an accompanying edition in another language.

There are seventy-five works of Luther listed and annotated by Visser, almost all of them published before 1530. These included many of Luther's sermons and pastoral works. They concern the Lord's prayer (several editions), ten commandments (several editions), justification (several editions), indulgences, grace, penitence, marriage, prayer, baptism, Lord's Supper, Passion of Christ (several editions), and the preparation for death. There were some publications concerning Bible study. The three major theological tracts of 1520—*Address to the Christian Nobility of the German Nation, Babylonian Captivity of the Church* (2 editions), and *Freedom of a Christian* (in Latin, in German and possibly in Dutch/Flemish)—were all printed in The Netherlands. A few polemical writings were also included: the Bull of the Anti-Christ (his opposition to *Exsurge Domine*), his 30 articles justifying why the pope's Bull should be burned, his reaction against the condemnations of Louvain and Cologne, a summary of the Marburg articles, and one of Luther's tracts against the sacramental understandings of Zwingli and Oecolampadius. Luther's Smaller Catechism of 1529 was translated and published in 1530 in Antwerp,[14] and there is also evidence that his translated editions of the Bible were utilized.[15] The extent and availability of his works would suggest that they were read and used. Still, the influence of Luther was more strongly felt in certain parts of The Netherlands than in other areas. His works were best known in Humanist centers where education and analysis of new ideas were paramount.

Erasmus's Understanding of Luther

While Erasmus regularly stated that he did know of Luther's works but had not read them, he probably did know more of these developments at an early stage in the movement than he cared to admit. For example, (in October, 1518) he wrote to his friend Johann Lang, who had known Luther at both Erfurt and Wittenberg.

Elutherius [Luther sometimes used this Latin version of his name], I hear, is approved of by all the leading people; but they say that his writings are not what they were. I imagine that his Conclusions (*i.e.* the 95 theses) satisfied everyone, except for a few of them on purgatory (theses 10-25 especially), which that school of thought are loathe to lose because of its effects on their daily bread (lines 15-18).[16]

In an October, 1518, letter to Wolfgang Fabritius Capito, a close follower of Luther in Basel, Erasmus wrote that "someone writes to me that Martin Luther is in danger" (lines 11-12).[17] How much Erasmus understood about Luther's "danger" is not clear. Luther arrived Augsburg on 7 October, 1518, and had interviews with Cardinal Cajetan on 12, 13 and 14 October. The papal envoy had been instructed to extract a recantation from Luther or have him arrested and brought to Rome. In the discussion it was clear that Luther interpreted scripture differently from the Thomistic inquisitor who confronted him. Luther denied the idea of the treasury of merits, even though Cajetan reminded him of the papal document *Unigenitus* (1343), which established this very treasury. Cajetan asked Luther to do three things: 1) to repent of errors; 2) never to teach them again; and 3) not to disturb the peace of the church. Luther agreed to none of these stipulations and anticipated the worst. With the help of some supporters, however, he suddenly escaped out of Augsburg and returned to Wittenberg.

The Elector Frederick the Wise was regularly asked to have Luther deported to Rome. After much indecision, it was on 8 December, 1518, that Frederick wrote to Cajetan that he had decided he would not submit to that request.[18] Luther's "danger" was thus postponed, but there would be other challenges.

Luther's first correspondence with Erasmus, a few months later, was deferential. It began: "Erasmus my glory and my hope" (lines 1-2), and continued:

Who is there in whose heart Erasmus does not occupy a central place, to whom Erasmus is not the teacher who holds him in thrall? I speak of those who love learning as it should be loved (lines 4-7). . . .What a dolt I am to approach such a man as you with unwashed hands like this--no opening words of reverence and respect, as though you were a most familiar friend, when I do not know you, nor you me! . . . Having spent my life among scholastic philosophers, I have not even learnt enough to be able to write a letter of greeting to a learned man (lines 13-15, 17-19). . . .[H]aving heard from my worthy friend Fabritius Capito (in Basel) that my name is known to you through the slight piece I wrote about indulgences, and learning very recently from the preface to your *Enchiridion* that you have not only seen but approved the stuff [*sic*] [*fabulamenta*] I have written, I feel bound to acknowledge, even in a very barbarous letter, that wonderful spirit of yours which has so much enriched me and all of us; although I know that it can mean absolutely nothing to you if I show myself affectionate and grateful in a letter for you are quite content with the gratitude and Christian love, secret and laid up in God's keeping, that burn within my heart when I think of you, just as I too am satisfied because, although you know it not, I possess your spirit and all that you do for us in your books, without exchange of letters or converse with you in person. (lines 22-33). . . .[S]o, dear Erasmus kindest of men, if you see no objection, accept this younger brother of yours in Christ, who is at least much devoted to you and full of affection, although in his ignorance he has deserved nothing better than to bury himself in a corner and remain unknown even to the sky and sun which we all share (lines 36-40).[19]

Erasmus evidently received the letter from Luther, but before he answered Luther he wrote to Cardinal Wolsey in England. He evaluated Luther's ideas for Wolsey and reiterated the problems that Luther had caused concerning Erasmus's own literary objectives.

They confound the cause of the humanities with the business of Reuchlin and Luther, although there is no connection between them. . . . I know as little of Luther as I do of anyone, nor have I yet found the time to leaf through his books except for a page here and there; not that I despise him, but the pressure of my own work has not yet allowed me the leisure. Yet some people, they tell me, have a trumped up story that he has had help from me (lines 77-79, 86-91).[20]

When Erasmus finally answered Luther's letter at the end of May he made it clear that he did not want to be associated in thought with Luther. He insisted that he did not really know the content of Luther's writings. He had not had time to study them. Consequently, he reminded Luther that he was not happy to be thought of as the fountain-head of the German reformer's ideas.

No words of mine could describe the storm raised here by your books. Even now it is impossible to root out [evelli] from people's minds [animis illorum] the most groundless suspicion that your work is written with assistance from me and that I am, as they call it, a standard-bearer of the new movement. They supposed that this gave them an opening to suppress both humane studies--for which they have a burning hatred, as likely to stand in the way of her majesty queen Theology, whom they value more than they do Christ--and myself at the same time, under the impression that I contribute something of importance toward this outburst of zeal. In the whole business their weapons are clamor, audacity, subterfuge, misinterpretation, innuendo; if I had not seen it with my own eyes—felt it, rather—I would never have believed theologians could be such maniacs (lines 4-15).[21]

Despite the fact that Erasmus sought to distance himself from Luther and reiterated this idea many times, it remains difficult to discover exactly how well Erasmus knew Luther's work. He admitted that he knew that the works were circulating in the Low Countries, and alluded to some of the general ideas contained therein, but he repeatedly claimed not to have read or analyzed them thoroughly. The month before Erasmus wrote the above letters to Wolsey and Luther, however, he had defended Luther in a letter to Luther's prince, Frederick the Wise, Elector of Saxony. In this letter he asked for Frederick's support for the cause of good learning and liberal studies. He told him that some were using Luther's works as an excuse to criticize serious learning.

> There have recently appeared some pieces by Martin Luther, and at the same time rumor has reached us that he is persecuted beyond all reason by the authority of his eminence the cardinal of San Sisto, who is now papal legate in Swabia (*i.e.* Cardinal Cajetan). What instant rejoicing at this, what triumphant glee, as they think they see a perfect opportunity offered them to do harm to the humanities! (lines 46-51). . . . Immediately the pulpits, the lectures and committees, and the dinner tables were loud with nothing but cries of Heresy and Anti-Christ. In with this business, charged as it is with prejudice, especially among foolish women and the ignorant multitude, these cunning fellows mix allusions to the ancient tongues and good writing and human culture as though Luther trusted to these for his defense, or these were the sources whence heresies were born (lines 53-59).

He then defended Luther, while again insisting he was not familiar with his writings.

> I know as little of Luther as I do any man, so that I cannot be suspected of bias toward a friend. His work it is not for me to defend or criticize, as hitherto I have not read them except in snatches (lines 69-71). . . . How unsuitable to the mildness proper to a divine when insistently, and without even reading his book right through, they break out with such ferocity against the character and reputation of an excellent man, and do so moreover in front of the ignorant multitude, who are quite without judgment (lines 74-78) . . . . I write this to you freely, most illustrious Duke, because Luther's case has very little to do with me. Be that as it may, it is your highness's privilege to protect the Christian faith by your personal religion; and it is no less your business as a wise ruler not to allow any innocent, while you are the source of justice, to be delivered under the pretext of religion into the hands of the irreligious (lines 126-131). . . . What is thought of Luther in your part of the world, I do not know; here at any rate, I perceive that his books are read eagerly by all men of judgment, although I have not had leisure to read them through (lines 135-138).[22]

Erasmus knew of other Humanists and churchmen who were sympathetic with Luther's views. In fact, in his letter to Luther he revealed some sensitive and potentially dangerous information. "There are some here too, the bishop of Liege [Erard de la Marck] among them, who favor your views. As for me, I keep myself uncommitted, so far as I can, in hopes of being able to do more for the revival of good literature" (lines 42-44).[23]

Erard de la Marck, prince-bishop of Liege/Luik, attended the election of Charles of Spain as Emperor in Frankfurt in June, 1519. He was a significant political as well as religious official in the area. Why Erasmus made this suggestion that the bishop was sympathetic to Luther is not known. After a secretly-published copy of Erasmus's letter was shown to authorities at Louvain/Leuven, Erard de la Marck was investigated during a visit to Louvain in October, 1519. He denied the suggestion, and nevertheless, seemed to have remained on good terms with Erasmus. Erasmus was probably attracted to la Marck because of his interest in and support of the arts and good literature, and in church reforms, albeit not in the "Lutheran" manner. Several months earlier, in February, 1519, Erasmus dedicated his *Paraphrases* on I and II Corinthians to la Marck, and sent him a copy with a cover letter on 19 February.[24] Shortly after the discussion and/or inquiry between the bishop and the Louvain/Leuven theologians in October, Erasmus wrote another letter to la Marck, but neither mentioned the topic of Luther, nor the suspicions.[25] Evidently the case was closed, although the two seldom communicated thereafter.[26]

How Luther and Erasmus understood each other is a complicated puzzle. As the religious changes came to Europe, especially to the Netherlands, scholars and the common people were uncertain as to what Luther stood for, or what reaction they should have. Many thought that Luther and Erasmus were parts of the same movement. In fact, it was said that Erasmus laid the egg that Luther hatched. Erasmus protested "I laid a hen's egg; Luther hatched a bird of quite a different breed."[27] At about the same time (*ca.* 1520) at a meeting in Cologne involving Erasmus, Spalatin (Luther's confidant), and Frederick the Wise, Frederick asked about the situation. "When Elector Frederick asked him (Erasmus) in Cologne why Luther was condemned, what wrong he had done, Erasmus·reported, 'He has done much wrong who attacks the monks in their bellies and the pope in his crown.'"[28]

Initially Erasmus cautiously defended Luther. He, too, had often reflected on the abuses he saw in the Church, but he ultimately concluded that Luther's extreme views and actions would prove to be negative. Erasmus valued the humanist emphasis on good literary editions and academic excellence. Furthermore, he valued his continuing relation with the Roman Catholic Church in spite of its shortcomings.

Erasmus hoped to purify the church from within. Luther, on the other hand, was interested in a more thorough change within the church. Simply rectifying external practices would be insufficient. Luther insisted that more basic and thorough change in theological understanding was needed. Erasmus thought that selective modification could prove successful. Luther insisted that certain external practices of the church could not be modified sufficiently. The church must be reconstituted at all levels. This Reformation must be based on a total theological reorientation grounded in Luther's own scriptural understanding. Erasmus sought change in methodology; Luther sought change in theological understanding. Over time, the areas in which their interests overlapped became fewer and fewer. Erasmus thought that human nature was capable of cooperating with God in the process of reformation. Luther thought that human nature was impotent to cooperate with God, that the human condition could only change *sola gratia*.

In a letter written in 1523 Erasmus explained his dilemma with Luther to a Humanist sympathizer:

> I hate discord as the worst of all evils, not only in accordance with Christ's teaching and example but from some deep-rooted impulse in my nature (lines 774-776); . . .It is not even permissible to love those who richly deserve our feelings for them, nor is any quarter of the world free from the contagion of this plague. One party it is impossible to despise and the other will not let us despise it (lines 778-781); . . .I doubt whether either of them can be suppressed without the disastrous collapse of good causes at the same time. It cannot be denied that Luther has drawn attention to many abuses which it is in the interests of Christendom to rectify and which the world could endure no longer. It is in this world-wide tempest in human affairs that my unhappy lot is cast, at a time of life when I should as it were have retired long ago to a well-earned leisure, to enjoy, as I justly might, the fruits of my laborious research; or at least I might be allowed to be a spectator of this play, as I myself am so unfitted to be an actor and there are so many others on every side who crowd of their own accord upon the stage. Both sides, however, have taken special care to make this impossible; one party is eager to lure me on with their tricks until they can carry me off by force to join their camp, while in the other party there are some who strive by every means in their power to drive me into the ranks of the enemy, with no other motive except to use this way of destroying one who is a powerful supporter of the ancient tongues, of the humanities, and of classical theology, and whom they were not able to unseat from his position (lines 782-799). . . . In both parties there are certain people ill disposed toward me; on the one side there are those who interpret my silence as support for the party they hate, while among those who support Luther some are bitterly indignant because through cowardice, as they term it, I desert the gospel cause (lines 800-804).[29]

Many of their basic approaches presupposed different understandings of the faith, different presuppositions about human nature, and differences in methodology. Luther and Erasmus used the same scriptural references to prove conflicting approaches. It is probable that neither fully understood the reasons for their basic differences. These differences were eventually elaborated in Erasmus's *Diatribe De Libero Arbitrio* (1524), and in Luther's reply *De Servo Arbitrio* (1525). As Ozment has summarized, while Erasmus thought that sin was only an impediment to one's ability to turn to God, Luther thought sin actually brought about the destruction of this ability.[30]

Official Condemnations of Luther's Works: Cologne, 30 August, 1519; Louvain/Leuven, 7 November, 1519.

Several individual works of Luther were available in the Netherlands before and during the decade of the 1520s. The first analysis and condemnation of Luther's works came in response to a collection of his works printed in 1518 in Basel.[31] The publisher, Johann Froben, wrote to Luther that he had received many of Luther's works from a Leipzig printer, Blasius Salmonius, who had bought them at a recent book fair in Frankfurt.[32] Froben published the collection in October, 1518, and enlarged editions in February, 1519, August, 1519, and May, 1520. The collection was circulated widely and copies promptly arrived in Brabant. Froben wrote that he had also sent copies to France (even the Sorbonne), to Spain, Italy and England. The first collection contained three theological tracts, three sermons and two short letters. In addition, there were two works not by Luther. The theological tracts included: 1) Luther's "Resolutiones"[33] concerning errors of indulgences, with an analysis of each of the Ninety-five Theses. To this tract were appended two letters, one each to Johann von Staupitz and Pope Leo X. Very soon after he was aware of Luther's theses, Silvestri Prierias, the Dominican Master of the Sacred Palace in Rome and professor of Thomistic theology there, wrote a "*Dialogus against the presumptuous conclusions of Martin Luther*" in which he compared and contrasted each of the Ninety-five theses with the teachings of Thomas Aquinas.[34] 2) A second tract in the collection was the "*Responsio*"[35] to the challenge ["*Dialogus*"] of Silvester Prierias. 3) A third tract was Luther's extended analysis of the Ten Commandments.[36]

There were also three early sermons of Luther: on Penance (five pages),[37] the power of excommunication (ten pages),[38] and indulgences (four pages, a Latin translation of "*Vom Ablass und Gnade)*."[39] In addition to these Froben's collection included the tract of 109 theses against John Eck, by Andreas Karlstadt..

The edition of February, 1519, added a sermon concerning the preparation of the heart for receiving the sacrament of the Eucharist.[40] Noting the length of some of the tracts included, it is not difficult to imagine that there were 488 pages, which was the reported size of the collection sent from Louvain/Leuven to Cologne.

Academic leaders in the Netherlands took an immediate move toward official action against Luther and his works in the late summer of 1519. The faculty of Louvain/Leuven, the only University in The Netherlands at the time, had studied Froben's collection of Luther's writings, and while suspecting they were heretical, nevertheless, sought another opinion. They communicated their criticisms, along with the documents, to the faculty at Cologne, and awaited a reply. On 30 August, 1519 (actually the *Weimar Ausgabe* has the date as "*penultima die mensis Augusti,*" rather than August 29, which is used by some authors), the officials at Cologne sent a reply to Louvain/Leuven. The scholars at Cologne found the work contained elements of heresy and matters "alien to the teachings of the holy fathers." The works should be banned and burned, and the author should be required to make a public recantation.

The theologians at Cologne summarized Luther's supposed heretical ideas in eight points.

1) all human works are not meritorious, but sinful; it is impossible, by human actions alone, to perform works without guilt [*culpa*];
2) he perverts [*contorqueat*] the meaning of the sacred scriptures and of the sacred fathers in a dangerous way; he thinks the theology used by the "*Sentences*" perverts the meaning of the scripture;
3) the teachings about the sacrament of penance are pernicious;
4) ideas of contrition involve scandalous errors;
5) in Luther's teaching about confession, against the doctrine of the ancient and universal church he puts forth [*ingerendo*] perverse advice, claims that "good works" cannot remove mortal sin; there are erroneous doctrines concerning the practice of confession; only God remits sin, not the priest;
6) Luther rejects the treasury of merits [*indulgentiarum*];
7) souls do not suffer in purgatory because of mortal sins; therefore, to keep souls in purgatory if one has power to do otherwise, is contrary to Christian charity;
8) there are many errors concerning the Roman claim to dominion over the whole church; the papal chair [*sedes Apostolicam*] is treated disrespectfully; the pope has power to remit only those punishments he has decreed--not those according to divine law which he cannot arbitrarily change; the Pope is arbitrary; remission of sin is only from God. Furthermore, "Luther has many other scandals. . . even more grave and more pernicious [*immo graviora et perniciosiora*]."[41]

Cologne's ecclesiastical authority carried much weight in The Netherlands. Jacob Hoogstraten, the Domincan inquisitor in Cologne, who had been deeply involved in the trial of Johannes Reuchlin in 1514-1516, was one of the theologians involved in the Cologne review. After the university's decision it was he who took their conclusions to Louvain/Leuven where he arrived 12 October, 1519.

The theological faculty of Louvain/Leuven was not long in formulating its decision, guided by the decisions from Cologne. On 7 November, 1519, they decided that they must do all in their power to stop this growing heresy. They issued their own objections in 15 articles. They could not condone Luther's views in the following areas:

1) A good work, even well intentioned, is still venial sin.
2) The merits of the saints are not sufficient even for themselves, let alone for anyone else. No saint lived in this life without sin, hence had no extra merits. Luther was ready to declare anyone a heretic who believed

differently from his own conclusions, and was willing to suffer fire and death for his convictions.

3) Indulgences can remove only temporal penalties arbitrarily imposed by a priest or a canon.

4) In the sacrament of Penance, forgiveness comes only when the grace of God first remits guilt.

5) It is heretical to suggest that the Sacraments of the New Testament do not give justifying grace for those who do not place hindrance. Elsewhere he explained with reference to Baptism.

6) About contrition he gave advice: Even if you may wish to confess, if you are not in the spirit of confession you act not out of love of righteousness but out of habit or fear.

7) Faith believes the words of Christ "whatever you loose on earth will be loosed in heaven" (Matt. 16:19); [yet, the Roman Catholic Church insists] more is required in sacramental absolution than contrition. Luther said: 'Why is something more required than in contrition when the person believes himself/herself truly absolved?'

8) In his sermon on preparation for the Eucharist Luther said the same concerning the approval of the venerable sacrament. He disapproved the mode of examining the conscience, thus he wrote against certain chapters of councils concerning penitence and remission.

9) In confession one does not need to confess all mortal sins since it is impossible they could all be known. One must confess only the sins of the flesh which are easily known. Only God can reveal spiritual defects.

10) In penance a priest cannot affect one's righteousness before God, cannot remove or even diminish one's guilt or shortcomings in God's sight. These debts are part of divine justice and cannot be removed by human beings, because this would be to change the divine law.

11) There is no one in this life who is without sin because God has placed before us an impossible ideal [*Deus ligat hominem ad impossibile*]. Because we have a tendency to sin [*fomitem peccati*] we continue to break God's commandments. In this life it is not possible to be free from sin, therefore, we will always sin.

12) All descendants of Adam are sinful by nature; in this life no one is without sin because we continue to break God's commandments. We should acknowledge our sin [*hanc transgressionem*] and should not deny it or ignore it.

13) He said that moral virtue and speculative knowledge are errors and sinful because they necessarily come from an evil heart and not from the healing [*sanato*] through grace.

14) He introduced various suspect and dangerous propositions about purgatory, such as: souls in purgatory sin without intermission, they dread [*horrent*] punishment and long for rest [*requiem*].

15) In support of these erroneous assertions he misinterprets the Holy Scriptures. Similarly he corrupts and misinterprets the words of the Holy Fathers [*doctorum*] both ancient and modern.[42]

The condemnation continued, "Because of these errors we censor his books and all tracts of his in which these ideas appear. These are to be condemned, and burned and reduced to ashes. We require the author of the above articles to revoke and abjure these teachings against the pure doctrines."[43]

Despite these condemnations, however, Luther's tracts remained available and the number of followers grew. Some of the faculty at Louvain sent official notice to one of their former colleagues, the Cardinal Bishop of Tortossa, in Spain. He was Adrian of Utrecht, former tutor and confidant of Charles V. Adrian would be elected Pope Adrian VI in January, 1522. Thus the future pope, who knew The Netherlands well, had been informed of developments which would influence his short reign as Pope. He wrote a reply on 4 December, 1519, congratulating the Louvain/Leuven faculty on their swift action and "zealous faith" in counteracting these errors. He hoped they would be successful in combating this heresy filled with "pernicious errors."[44]

All these precautions taken by the imperial government, by universities or the Church as well as by the local magistrates, still did not result in conformity of belief and action. Consequently, on 29 January, 1520, Margaret issued her own command from Mechelen/Malines. She complained that the officials of Brabant had not been diligent enough in following through on the investigations since heresy and blasphemy were continuing as previously. She threatened to take stronger measures if they did not enforce the earlier decrees.[45]

Erasmus wrote to Martin Lips in Brussels, "As for Luther, this witch-hunt they are starting [against Luther] is both foolish and dangerous; they will realize later that what I am supporting is not Luther but the peace of Christendom" (lines 5-7).[46] When the condemnations were known, Luther immediately began to write his response to the condemnations. His rebuttal was published 25 March, 1520.[47]

Shortly after the rebuttal was published, Erasmus wrote to Melanchthon indicating he knew of Luther's response.

> I have greatly enjoyed this answer of Luther's to the condemnation by his enemies in Cologne and Louvain/Leuven. At last they begin to be ashamed of having passed judgment in such a hurry. I would rather my name had not been brought in; for that puts an onus on me and does not help Luther at all (lines 38-41).[48]

One of the major papal representatives who advanced the cause against Luther was Jerome Aleander (Girolomo Aleandro), head of the Vatican library. He was devoted to stamping out heresy and he presided in The Netherlands at various burnings of Luther's books. On 8 October, 1520, with the approval of the Emperor who was in Antwerp, more than eighty books of Luther were burned in

Louvain/Leuven. Aleander also presided with approval of the local bishop at the book-burnings at Luik/Liege on 17 October. The local bishop urged stronger punishments, including confiscation of property. Aleander wrote to the pope about these two incidents in a letter from Aachen, dated October 23.[49] In the next few years there were more book burnings in several other cities of The Netherlands.[50]

Ten days after Luther's books were burned at Louvain/Leuven Erasmus added his comment: "The burning of his (Luther's) books will perhaps banish Luther from our libraries; whether he can be plucked out of the people's hearts, I am not sure" (lines 179-180).[51] Erasmus directed this letter to Godschalk Rosemondt, theologian and rector of the University of Louvain/Leuven. Although much of the criticism of Erasmus's work was centered in the University of Louvain/Leuven, Rosemondt, for a time remained open to Humanistic learning. He would later, however, ally with the inquisitors. Erasmus feared the negative influences the book burnings might have on recent scholarship, but he also included a justification for himself.

Without knowing all that was involved the Emperor gave approval for the book burnings. Other book burnings that year occurred outside The Netherlands in the German lands at Cologne on 12 November, Mainz on 29 November, and on 29 October (led by Luther's rabid antagonist, John Eck). Concerning the burning of his works Luther had already planned to fight fire with fire. In a letter to Spalatin (7 July, 1520) he reasoned:

> For my part the die has been cast. I hold in contempt both the fury and favor of Rome. I will not be reconciled to them, nor will I ever hold communion with them. Let them condemn and burn my books. I will do that in return whenever I can use fire. I will publicly condemn and burn the whole papal law, that collection of heresies, and I will end the humility up to this time exhibited by me, and will no longer inflate the enemies of the gospel with this profession of obedience.[52]

In December, 1520 Erasmus reported to an unnamed correspondent,

> As for Luther, you will know, that there was some burning at Louvain, this being a favorite project of the theologians who produced the bull, and afterwards at Liege with the connivance of the bishop (Erard de la Marck), who has the eye on a cardinal's hat [de la Marck became a cardinal in 1520, although it was not announced immediately]; later with more bitter hostility in Cologne where Hoogstraten rules the roost. Although Luther's writings are not liked by everyone, everybody disapproved of the way it was done and of such savage and tyrannous behavior (lines 57-63).[53]

Exsurge Domine (1520)

Much of the popular opinion was exacerbated not only by the recent and on-going anti-clerical attitudes, but also by reports of condemnations by the two universities. It seemed only a matter of time until some official action would be taken in Luther's case. Indeed, on 15 June, 1520, the pope and his advisors completed their thorough, but pointed warnings against Luther. These discussions would take the form of the papal bull entitled *"Exsurge Domine"* [Rise Up, O Lord].

The Bull was meant to be a warning to Luther. It lifted forty-one assertions from his works which were deemed to be heretical. Luther was required to recant all these ideas within sixty days after receiving the document. The papal representative, Aleander, was sent to The Netherlands to enforce the papal decree and to do what he could to stir up hatred against Luther. He even presented a copy of the bull to the court of Emperor Charles V in Antwerp.

The Papal bull was printed in Antwerp even before Luther received a copy.[54] A portion of that well-known document with its graphic imagery is as follows:

> *Exsurge Domine* [Rise up, O Lord] and judge thy cause. Be mindful of the daily slander against thee by the foolish, incline thine ear to our supplication. Foxes have arisen which want to devastate thy vineyard, where you have worked at the wine-press. . . . A roaring sow of the woods has undertaken to destroy this vineyard, a wild beast wants to devour it. . . . Arise, O Peter, according to thy responsibility and care, bestowed upon thee by God . . . .Arise, O Paul, we pray, for thou hast enlightened the Church with thy teaching and the same martyrdom. . . . Finally, arise and lift yourself up, thou entire communion of the saints and thou entire Christian Church, whose truthful interpretation of the Sacred Scriptures is perturbed, some of whom the Father of Lies has blinded the senses so that they, according to the ancient custom of heretics, in their own wisdom, force, bend, and forge the Scriptures to have a meaning different from that dictated by the Holy Spirit. . . .
>
> We have unfortunately seen and heard with our own eyes many and various errors, some of which have already been condemned by the councils and definitions of our predecessors, since they incorporate the heresies of the Greeks and the Bohemians. . . .
>
> Prompted by the responsibility of our Episcopal office, which is entrusted to us, we can no longer suffer the deadly poison of the described errors to lead to the diminishing of the Christian faith. Therefore, we have enumerated some of these errors in this bull. . . .

Here the document listed the forty-one propositions taken from Luther's works, most of them in one sentence each. Then the document continued,

> Since these errors. . . are found in the writings or pamphlets of a certain Martin Luther, we condemn, reject and denounce these pamphlets and all writings and sermons of this Martin, be they in Latin or in other languages, in which one or more of these errors are found. . . .We order in the name of the

holy obedience and the danger of all punishment each and every Christian believer of either sex, under no circumstances to read, speak, preach, laud, consider, publish or defend such writings, sermons, or broadsides or anything contained therein. . . .

We prohibit this Martin from now on and henceforth to contrive any
preaching of the office of preaching. . . .We ask him earnestly that he and his
supporters, adherents and accomplices desist within sixty days. . . from
preaching, both expounding their views and denouncing others, from publishing books and pamphlets concerning some or all of these errors. . . .

If, however, this Martin. . . should stubbornly not comply with the mentioned stipulations within the mentioned period, we shall . . . condemn this
Martin.[55]

Although Luther did not receive the Papal bull until 20 October, he knew it
was being compiled. In the intervening months he prepared a justification for his
theology and a defense against the Papal charges. Altogether, he wrote four
documents, two in Latin and two in German. The first two were similar in that
the Latin original was soon issued in a considerably expanded German translation. The first two statements explicitly opposed the Pope's Bull.[56] The third was
written In Latin, and the fourth in German. In both Luther analyzed each of the
forty-one doctrines which were the main content of *Exsurge Domine*.[57] In the
fourth tract he had choice comments about those who burned his books,

Go ahead, pope, burn and condemn books! God shall overthrow you and give
you up to madness, and you will receive the reward which you have deserved
for always resisting divine truth. Let him who feels like it doubt that the pope,
who spreads all these errors throughout the world and receives in return the
wealth of the nations, is the true, chief, and final Antichrist. Thank God I know
him.[58]

After Luther received the bull, he was required to provide his answer in 60
days—by 20 December. Rather than recant, however, he had another plan. On
10 December the students of the University of Wittenberg gathered around a
bonfire into which Luther tossed not only the Papal Bull, but various books of
canon law as well. Luther composed still another document to explain why the
burning was necessary. He gave his rationale in thirty articles.[59] The book burnings in Louvain/Leuven and in Cologne were supposedly performed under the
authority of the Emperor, but Luther questioned this authority, and reiterated
what he considered a higher authority. He reasoned,

Since, then, through their kind of book burning great damage to truth and a
false delusion among the plain common people might result, to the destruction
of many souls, I have on the prompting of the Spirit (as I hope), in order to
strengthen and preserve the same, burned the books of the adversaries in turn,
since their improvement is not to be hoped for (p. 384 in the Spitz translation).

In his thirty articles he argued that the Pope tried to set himself up above God; the Pope refused to submit to Christian councils and regulations; the Pope claimed to set aside Conciliar decrees; the Pope allowed none to judge him—the Petrine theory of the origin of the papacy is faulty since the Pope claims that the Rock on which the church was built was himself, not the faithful people in general; the Pope claimed to depose kings; the Pope sets himself above God because he forbids married people to serve God, although presumably God instituted the office of marriage; the Pope interprets and applies the scriptures to suit himself. He explained his actions specifically with respect to canon law.

> If you want to know in a few words what the canon law contains, then listen. It is, to put it briefly, the following: The Pope is a god on earth over everything heavenly, earthly, spiritual, and secular, and all is his own. No one is permitted to say to him: 'What are you doing?' . . . Now the fact that no one or few people have been permitted to speak out to the pope about his abomination is not amazing, for it has been announced that he will have the consent of all the kings and princes.

Finally, Luther concluded:

> If they are allowed to burn my articles, in which there is more gospel and more of the true substance of Holy Scripture (which I can say truthfully without boasting, and prove also) than in all the Pope's books, then I am justified much more in burning their unchristian law books in which there is nothing good (p. 394).

As a final proof he quoted Sampson, (from Judges 15:11) "As they did to me, so have I done to them." Both the Roman Catholic officials and the Reformers sought to destroy what they considered poisonous books, as Luther referred to Acts 19:19, "A number of those who practiced magic collected their books and burned them publicly."[60]

Decet Romanum Pontificem [Excommunication of Luther, 3 January, 1521]

The official papal excommunication of Luther—*Decet Romanum Pontificem*—was issued on 3 January, 1521.[61] (The quotations in these paragraphs are from the translation which appears as Appendix I of this study). The Pope's preface began: "It is right for the Roman Pontiff [*decet Romanum Pontificem*] . . . to suppress the heinous efforts of the perverse. . . who are trying to rend the seamless tunic of the redeemer." To remind the readers or hearers of the gravity of the situation the Pope quoted the entire *Exsurge Domine* (Section I). The Pope came to his main point in Section 3. This set the stage for his emphatic declaration:

> We thus decree that excommunication and anathema, eternal malediction and
> interdict, have damnably come upon Martin Luther and the others who con-
> tinue obstinately in his perverse and condemned effort (Section 3).

The consequences of not changing their way of thinking would be loss of
dignity and honors, confiscation of goods and other censures. Churches which
would not renounce this heresy would be placed under interdict. This order was
to be proclaimed by all levels of church leaders to begin in three days. Indeed,
all church officials of whatever rank were to

> establish themselves as a wall for the Christian people, not being silent like
> mute dogs unable to bark, but crying out and lifting their voice incessantly, and
> preaching and causing to be preached the Word of God and the truth of the
> (Roman) catholic faith against these heretics and their condemned articles"
> (Section 5).

It was deemed unlawful for any one "to tear up this page of our constitution. . .
.or to oppose it by a rash deed" (Section 10). The pope did not mention that this
should not be burned, as was the fate of the earlier bull at the hands of Martin
Luther the previous December.[62]

Erasmus expressed his fears of the book burnings and promulgation of *Exsurge Domine* and *Decet Romanum* in a letter to Nicholaas Everaerts, president
of the Council of Holland with an office in The Hague.

> Two men are on their way to your part of the world to burn Luther's books,
> Nicholas Egmondanus (Baechem), an obstinate fool who is wonderfully
> pleased with himself, and Vincentius (Theoderici), a Domican who is said to
> have gotten himself into trouble in Dordrecht, one of nature's numbskulls, a
> man of no judgment and ignorant even by the standards of his own class, but a
> scandalous talker (lines 18-22).[63]

The book burnings continued. In Ghent books were burned on 25 June,
1521, under the supervision of Nicholas Baechem van Egmond[64] and at Antwerp
on 13 July, of the same year.[65] In Ammersfort, southeast of Amsterdam, burnings
also took place 19 August, 1521, and in Utrecht on the same day.[66]

Charles's Third Edict against Blasphemy
(17 February, 1521)

On 17 February, 1521, Charles issued his third edict against blasphemy in
The Netherlands. This edict was directed to the authorities of Flanders against
blasphemers, and those who swear in the name of God. It seems that his previous
decrees (*i. e.* the first issued 30 November, 1517, and the second 5 January,
1519, See Chapter 1) had been "thrown to the wind" because transgressions were
continuing to be more prevalent than ever, and the authorities did nothing to pre-

vent these occurrences. Henceforth, the prohibitions from previous edicts were renewed, and were to be carried through diligently [*diligemment*]. It is interesting to note that the name of Luther does not yet appear in the edict, although the Pope had already excommunicated Luther and the processes leading to Luther's appearance before the emperor at the Diet of Worms was already under way.[67]

Charles's first Edict directed against Luther's Works in The Netherlands

On 20 March, 1521, before Luther would appear before him in Worms, Charles issued his first edict in The Netherlands specifically against Luther's works. The document originated in Mechelen/Malines, although Charles was at the time at the Diet of Worms. The edict, published in French, catalogued many "false" ideas of Luther concerning the sacraments, baptism, confession, contrition and penance, sin, indulgences and pardon, the power of the pope, and other articles already used to condemn John Hus at the Council of Constance (1415). The edict reminded the readers that the opinions of Luther had already been condemned by the faculties of both Universities at Cologne and at Louvain/Leuven; therefore, neither schismatics nor heretics nor their writings nor their damnable opinions would be permitted in the territory—they cannot print, buy, sell, possess, read., etc. Immediately, therefore, the writings composed by the said Luther "shall be publicly destroyed, and at the sound of a trumpet, shall be reduced to ashes [*aboliz en mis en cendres*] because they are false, damnable and heretical."[68]

The Imperial Edicts of Worms against Luther, with respect to The Netherlands (8 May, 1521), and concerning the whole empire (also 8 May, 1521)

Luther appeared at the Diet of Worms on 17-18 April, 1521. On 8 May, two weeks later, the ban of the Empire was prepared and was promulgated against him. Actually, the Emperor issued two documents on May 8, the ban of the Empire written in Latin, and a parallel condemnation sent to leaders in The Netherlands. The latter was issued in both French/Walloon and Flemish/Dutch. Similar or even parallel language was used in both. The document written for the attention of The Netherlands began as Charles listed the areas of The Netherlands where his authority must prevail.[69] He then continued,

> It becomes us, and belongs to us to compel the enemies of our faith to the obedience of his divine majesty, by extending, as much as we can, the glory of the holy cross, and of our Savior's sufferings, to the utmost corners of the earth, and to maintain the Christian religion pure and unspotted from all suspicion of heresy (p. 62). . . . It seems to us that the person of the said Martin is not a human creature, but a Devil in the figure of a man, and cloaked with the habit of a

monk, to enable him so much the better and more easily to bring the race of mankind to everlasting death and destruction (p. 67).

There were warnings to those who were tempted to give serious thought to Luther's works:

> We expressly command, that no one hereafter be so bold or presumptuous, as to receive, protect, support, or encourage the said Luther, by word or deed, charging and commanding all people to seize and apprehend him, and bring him to condign punishment as an obdurate heretic (p. 72). . . . As for his abettors and accomplices, and the goods and estates of all such persons, the ordinary judges or magistrates, or the Parliaments, councils, and others to whom the cognizance of those matters belongs, shall proceed against them in such manner as their accusers, or the fiscals, attorneys and other officers shall think proper (p. 72). . . . Such prosecutions shall be set on foot and carried on at the request of any person whatever, against all that infringe and disobey these our commands, let them be of what state, condition, and quality soever, nor shall they be protected or screened by any kind of privileges (p. 73).

The familiar warnings were repeated:

> We further will and command, that all the estates of persons who shall be convicted of the said crimes or heresy, shall be forfeited and escheated, one half to our own use, and the rest to the benefit of the accusers and informers against the criminals (p. 73). . . .We do also mostly strictly order, upon the pains and penalties above-mentioned, that no person, of what state or condition, authority or dignity whatsoever, do buy or sell, keep, read, write, print, or maintain and defend any of the books, writings, or opinions of the said Luther, whether in Latin, Flemish, or other modern languages (p. 73).

Previous stipulations were summarized and repeated:

> Our will and pleasure therefore is, that all the said books shall be accounted everywhere as universally forbidden and as such burned and entirely destroyed (p. 73). . . . From thenceforth, on the forfeiture of life and estate, no bookseller, printer, or any other person whatsoever, should presume to print, or cause to be printed, any book or writing in which mention was made of the Holy Scriptures, or any interpretation of it, though ever so little, without leave first obtained (p. 75).

The second edict, the Imperial Ban in Latin, issued from the Diet of Worms, was very detailed covering approximately 30 pages. Toward the end of the document the Emperor centered his condemnation on Martin Luther,[70] with wording similar to the previous edict of the same day.

The Augustinian monk, Martin Luther, albeit exhorted by us, has rushed like a madman against the holy church, and has set himself to stifle it with books that are full of blasphemies. . . . In a word, and to say nothing of other malicious acts, this being, who is not a man so much as the evil fiend in human form, concealed under a monk's hood, has collected together in one putrid slough, all the most sinful heresies of times gone by, and to these has added new ones of his own. . . . Accordingly, we have dismissed from our presence this Luther, whom all pious and sensible men hold to be a fool, or one possessed by the devil; and our intention is, that on the expiration of his safe-conduct, recourse shall be had to the most effectual means for arresting his furious madness.

Therefore, it is, that under pain of incurring the punishments due to crimes of lese-majesty, we forbid you to give shelter to the said Luther, from the time that the fatal term be expired, to conceal him, give him food or drink, or furnish him, by word or deed, openly or secretly, with any kind of succor. We further enjoin you to seize him or cause him to be seized, wherever he may be found, and to bring him to us without any delay, or to retain him in sure custody, until you have learnt from us how you ought to act in regard to him, and until you shall have received the reward due to your exertions in so holy a cause.

As for his adherents, you will apprehend them, and confiscate their property.

As for his writings, . . . You will, therefore, burn them or utterly destroy them in some other way.

As for the authors, poets, printers, painters, sellers or purchasers of hand-bills, tracts, or pictures against the pope and against the church, you will seize them, body and goods, and treat them as you deem fit.

Should any one, whatever be his dignity, dare to act contrary to this decree of our imperial majesty, we ordain that he be put to the ban of the empire.

While both of these documents were dated 8 May, the emperor did not sign them until 26 May, 1521.

Erasmus's Problems with the Theologians of Louvain/Leuven

In the autumn of 1521, in the aftermath of the Edict of Worms, Erasmus gave serious consideration to his own position *vis-à-vis* Luther. He had not yet decided that he must oppose Luther, but his attempt to remain neutral in the growing conflict was made virtually impossible by the new law. For many months Erasmus had already been the target of attacks from his fellow theologians at Louvain/Leuven. His insistence on precise scriptural interpretation—even when changes modified previously-held concepts or practices—was interpreted as tantamount to agreement with Luther. He, of course, could not follow the logic of his opponents. Indeed, he insisted that correct understanding and careful interpretation were indispensable for the understanding and teaching of truth, even to the point of critical understanding of the scriptures themselves. To this end he had been very influential in founding the College Trilingua in Louvain/Leuven (made possible by a grant from Giles de Busleyden, in 1517).[71]

Erasmus was adamant that in the Trilingua Latin, Hebrew and Greek should be taught as the indispensable tools of good scholarship and good theology. He stated his objectives clearly in a letter dated 26 March, 1518. The new college "will recall students everywhere from muddy pools (the *Sententiae* and the *Summae*?) to the clear springs of Holy Scripture" (lines 38-39).[72] At the same time, Erasmus defended himself against critics of his New Testament editions, of 1516 and 1519.[73] He was especially harsh concerning one of his critics, the Carmelite, Nicholaas Baechem of Egmond, whom Erasmus called 'camelitus', in derision—a little camel. Their animosity had been continuing for several years.

> When the New Testament restored by me first appeared, a Carmelite divine, who is in his own opinion a wonderful scholar and a holy man, started clamoring that a great crisis threatened the Christian religion and that the coming of Antichrist was at hand; for they use this dramatic language to rouse the superstitious multitude. When it came to a discussion between us and I asked him with some urgency to produce what offended him in my New Testament, he replied in a simple-minded way that he had never read the book or even set eyes on it. This is what I usually find; none raise a more offensive clamor than those who do not read what I write (lines 141-149).[74]

In November 1518, Erasmus had his tract on theological method—*Ratio seu Methodus compendio*—printed at Louvain/Leuven.[75] He challenged a basic assumption of his associates in the University at Louvain/Leuven by arguing that theology should be based on an accurate knowledge of the Latin, Greek and Hebrew sources. Thus, so he argued, one could more adequately understand the text in its literal sense—letters, words, sentences. In addition, however, true scriptural knowledge required a spiritual knowledge, a metaphysical comprehension and an allegorical dimension. The focus of this scriptural knowledge was always Christ which would come clear only as one proceeded beyond the purely physical or human plane. Should one be tempted to use dialectic, analytic methods or emphasize other Scholastic procedures the result would be divisive and not clearly focused. The Scholastic method dealt too much in human reasoning or logic thus defeating or distorting the true meaning of God's word. With a thorough spiritual understanding the reader of scripture can grasp the meaning of the message of God and of Christ as developed in the early church.

In contrast to the linguistic methods of Erasmus, James Latomus (Jacques Masson), a theologian of Louvain/Leuven and a later opponent of Luther, insisted that language was not really necessary; he argued that Erasmus had introduced innovations into the study of theology. Latomus published a long treatise of his own.[76]

On 28 October, 1521, Erasmus left Louvain/Leuven for Basel, where he arrived two weeks later, 15 November, 1521.[77] Although he planned to stay only a few months, and although he was urged several times to return to The Netherlands, except for short visits, he seldom travelled out of Basel again until 1529.

When Basel became Protestant in 1529 under the leadership of Oecolampadius,[78] Erasmus retreated to south Germany, to Freiburg im Breisgau, where he remained for six years, returning to Basel only a short time before his death in 1536.

Establishing the Inquisition in The Netherlands (23 April, 1522)

There had been several attempts through edicts and decrees to suppress new religious ideas, or to forbid publishing of suspect theological documents. To reinforce those efforts, on 23 April, 1522, the Emperor finally made an "inquisition" official in The Netherlands. This repression was more specifically directed against Lutheran ideas, whereas, the earlier attempts at conformity were of a more general nature. One of Charles's council leaders—Frans van der Hulst—was appointed the inquisition leader, but only in Brabant.[79] Van der Hulst was a layman, a law graduate in both laws—*i.e.* ecclesiastical and secular law—from Louvain/Leuven, and was very much interested in enforcing religious uniformity. In a companion document the Emperor extended the authority of van der Hulst to all his lands [*alle onse landen*].[80] The Emperor reiterated that he had tried other measures to solve the problem of "unbelief" and Luther's heresy in the Netherlands; he had issued his edict of Worms (April/May, 1521), which was published in Louvain/Leuven, Antwerp and other places; Luther's books had been banned and burned in several places; and Luther had been declared a schismatic and a heretic.

"False sects," however, continued to develop. Van der Hulst was given very broad powers to pursue suspects and use law suits in keeping with the Emperor's previous edicts. Those persons who were contaminated by heresy were to be corrected "in all manner as though we ourselves were there in person."[81] Van der Hulst had been a member of the Council of Brabant for almost twenty years. In this position the newly-appointed inquisitor had participated in locating and prosecuting many suspected heretics Cornelis Grapheus, imprisoned 9 February, 1522 to 23 April (See Chapter 6). Another of his inquisitorial victims was Jacob Proost (Praepositus), also imprisoned in December, 1521 (See Chapter 7).

Two weeks after van der Hulst's appointment, on 7 May, 1522, the emperor elaborated the details of his duties, responsibilities and powers. A close associate Joost Lauwereyns, Chair of the High Council of Brabant in Mechelen/Malines, was appointed as overseer. The two were expected to coordinate their efforts, and van der Hulst was not to proceed in any trials or evaluations without the consent of Lauwereyns. They were allowed to appoint clergy members to assist them. Those who appeared before the two inquisitors within thirty days could be received in grace back into the church, according to stipulations which the inquisitors should impose. Those who "persisted in their errors" beyond the thirty days would be considered backsliding heretics and could be expelled from the realm, or even put to death. The inquisitors had wide authority concerning the life and the property of the accused. Special accusations and punishments would the imposed on those who possessed any writing by Luther. Their sentences could not be challenged except in strictly defined exceptions. Finally, at the end of the instructions there was a discussion of payments to be made to the inquisitors for their efforts.[82]

Not only was the Emperor concerned about the growing Lutheran movement, but Pope Adrian VI (elected, January, 1522) was also concerned—more than was his predecessor, Leo X. Adrian was interested in church reform, but completely within the confines of the Roman Catholic understanding. In December, 1522, the pope wrote to Erasmus with a broad hint that he should write against Luther in order to influence those who were undecided, but might respect the words of the great scholar. The Pope made this suggestion to Erasmus then in Basel:

> The affection. . .which we feel for you and the concern we have for our reputation and true glory prompt us to urge you to employ in an attack on these new heresies the literary skill with which a generous providence has endowed you so effectually; for there are many reasons why you ought properly to believe that the task has been reserved by God especially for you (lines 24-29). . . . Can you then refuse to sharpen the weapon of your pen against the madness of these men? (lines 92-93). . . . Remember that you are placed in such a position that through your labors and with God's help a great part of those who have been subverted by Luther can return to the true path, those who have not yet fallen may remain upright, and those who waver and are near to falling can be preserved from giving way (lines 100-104).[83]

We have no knowledge of any reply Erasmus might have made to the Pope's suggestion.

On 1 June, 1523, more than a year after the Emperor established the inquisition in The Netherlands and a half year after the pope's broad suggestion to Erasmus, the Pope also appointed his former close friend, Frans van der Hulst, to be the ecclesiastical inquisitor over the whole of the Netherlands. Thus van der Hulst had the Church's authority in addition to that of the empire. He was free to expand his activities widely. Under his leadership other scholars or religious thinkers were examined and/or tried. Very soon, however, the repressive policies of the inquisition came into conflict with the ancient and historic privileges of the courts in the Netherlands. It forced the Emperor and his Aunt Margaret to make some changes.

Charles's inquisition was not the first instance of inquisition in 16th century Netherlands, and earlier attempts at repression met with little success.[84] This newest inquisition did not go smoothly either. Barely a year later complaints were lodged against these jurists acting in the name of orthodoxy. On 19 September, 1523, Margaret, the Regent [*Landvoogdes*], was forced to withdraw inquisitional authority from Van der Hulst because of unwise or unjust actions with respect to the trials of Praepositus (See Chapter 7), of the Augustinian monks burned in Brussels (1 July, 1523, See Chapter 7); and the case against Cornelis Hoen, a lawyer from The Hague (See Chapter 5).

Cornelis Hoen had been a lawyer in the Court of Holland for many years. He was well respected as a lawyer and a scholar, but he was also suspected of heretical ideas [*propter sectam Lutheram*].[85] He was taken into custody at the insistence of van der Hulst in February, 1523, and was transferred illegally to a prison outside van der Hulst's jurisdiction. The local authorities were outraged and complained to Margaret. On 6 March she reported the details of the controversy to Charles, and said that she was returning Hoen to The Hague. Hoen was freed March, 1523. Erasmus, although in Basel, knew of this continuing controversy and wrote

> Cornelius Hoen, an excellent man they tell me, had been reinstated by the court. They dragged him back by a trick into some castle, and there would have convicted him of heresy (for in such a place Beachem's arguments carry much more weight than in the lecture room), but he was set free immediately by the chief men of Holland. What made him a heretic was his audacity in disputing with Baechem (lines 32-37).[86]

Erasmus continued his invective against Baechem: "to arm that Carmelite [Baechem] with such authority—I ask you, was it not simply to put a sword into a madman's hand?" (lines 43-44).

Hoen was soon imprisoned again in the same month, evidently on religious questions. He remained in prison to October, 1523. At the same time two other scholars, and friends of Erasmus, were imprisoned. They were Cornelis Grapheus, scholarly Secretary of the City of Antwerp (See Chapter 6), and Nicholas van Broeckhoven (or Buscoducensis), although van Broeckhoven was released a short time later (See Chapter 3).

Concerning Hoen's case Erasmus suggested that for these acts "the Camel" was stripped of his power. Van der Hulst narrowly escaped the death penalty because some friends protected him.[87] On 17 January, 1524, the Pope appointed Coppin de Montibus (*i.e.* of Mons), dean at Louvain/Leuven, as successor inquisitor.

Penalties for dissenting opinions

After 1522 and through the next decade, there were three options for those who, for academic reasons or personal convictions, dared to advocate religious views different from the prevailing imperial policies and Roman Catholic norms. **First,** they could recant and possibly live a relatively normal life in the good graces of the Roman Catholic Church. Several persons chose this alternative. **Second,** they could flee from their native land to a more sympathetic political regime. Many Netherlanders found positions in Lutheran organizations in Germanic lands, but some went even greater distances. **Third,** those who chose neither of these routes, or who were cast into prison, faced possible execution.

Before and even after the organization of the Anabaptists in approximately 1530 under the inspiration of Melchior Hoffman, The Netherlands provided many martyrs for their religious faith. Two Augustinians were burned in Brussels (1 July, 1523, Chapter 7), the first martyr in the northern Netherlands was burned in The Hague (1525, Chapter 10); the first woman martyr from the village of Monnikendam north of Amsterdam, and for whom we have extensive details, was burned (1527, Chapter 12). A law censoring printing was enacted in 1524 which affected both religious dissent and Humanist scholarship. (Chapters 8 and 9). Many writers, editors, Bible interpreters and printers were limited if not actually imprisoned according to requirements of this law. Despite these extreme measures, however, religious diversity persisted and even flourished in the decade of the 1520s. Some of the ideas reflected Luther's teachings, while other influences came from the educational programs of the Humanists, especially Erasmus.

From whatever sources, the dissension reflected many different emphases. No one "heretical" idea was dominant, and there was no figure to whom all could look as "leader." There were continuing anti-clerical and anti-Papal reactions. Some heretics made indulgences their main emphasis, others the Eucharist, others baptism or confession and penance. Biblical interpretation remained a flash point of contention, especially interpretation in vernacular languages. Translations and commentaries in sermons could be considered "heresy." Some political leaders, coveting their ancient privilege as petty nobles or counts, resented the tendencies toward the centralizing power in either church appointees or imperial consolidation.

Sometimes the traditions of "local autonomy," going back many decades or even centuries, became associated with and strengthened various dissenting religious ideas. Humanist lawyers, for example, were often supporters of education reforms and religious change; therefore, any attempt to separate religious change from education and humanist interests was virtually impossible. In the earliest part of the decade the boundaries between what were "Lutheran" doctrines and what represented the concerns of Humanist educators were not sharply drawn. Consequently, many people, and even the scholars, sometimes saw the two emphases as part of the same movement toward church or education reforms. We will look at this phenomenon in many different ways and illustrate it with several different individuals in the following chapter.

Notes for Chapter 2

1. Printed (1551) in *de Cronijcke van Zeeland* but referring to the year 1518; as printed in *Corpus documentorum inquisitionis haereticae Pravitatis Neerlandicae. Verzameling von stukken betreffende de pauslijke en bishoppelijke inquisitie in de Nederlanden.* Ed. Paul Fredericq, 5 vols. (Ghent and The Hague: 1889-1902); hereafter (*CDI*) IV, 10.

2. *CDI*, IV, 35. Latomus's letter is dated 31 December, 1520. He stated "*Ante duos annos (i.e.* 1518) *quum Lutheri liber impressus et undique divulgatus ad manus nostras venisset*"

3. *Collected Works of Erasmus* (hereafter *CWE*), VI, # 904, written from Basel 5 December, 1518. The editor of *CWE* suggested that the book was perhaps the tract "*Ad Leonem X. . . resolutions disputationum de virtute indulgentiarum*" printed in October, 1518. See Luther, *WA, Briefwechsel*, I, p. 146.

4. Van Meteren's *Nederlandsche Historie* (1608) as printed in *CDI*, IV, 36. Translated by the author.

5. Gerdes, *Historia Reformationis,* III (before 1521), as printed in *CDI*, IV, 36. Translated by the author.

6. Gerdes*, Ibid.*

7. Gerdes, *Ibid.*

8. Alastair Duke, *Reformation and Revolt in The Low Countries* (London: Hambledon Press, 1990), p. 80.

9. M. E. Kronenberg, *Verboeden Boeken en Opstandige Drukkers in de Hervormingstijd* (Amsterdam: P. N. Van Kampen & Zoon, 1948.)

10. *Ibid.*, p. 65.

11. *Ibid.*, p. 88.

12. M. E. Kronenberg, "Uitgaven van Luther in de Nederlanden verschenen tot 1541," *Archief voor Kerkgeschiedenis*, XL (1954), 1-25.

13. Dr. C. Ch. G. Visser, *Luther's Geschriften in de Nederlanden tot 1546* (Assen, The Netherlands: Van Gorcum and Comp. N. V., 1969).

14. *NK* 1422.

15. Paul Arblaster, "*Totius Mundi Emporium:* Antwerp as a Center for the Vernacular Bible translations: 1523-1545," in Arie-Jan Gelderblom, Jan L. De Jong, Marc van Vaeck, eds., *The Low Countries as a Crossroads of Religious Belief* (Leiden, Boston: Brill Publishers, 2004), pp. 9-31.

16. *CWE*, VI, # 872, Erasmus in Louvain/Leuven to Johann Lang in Erfurt, 17 October, 1518.

17. *CWE*, VI, # 877, Erasmus in Louvain/Leuven to Capito in Basel, 19 October, 1518.

18. *WA, BR*, I, 250, lines 22ff.

19. *CWE*, VI, # 933, Luther to Erasmus, 28 March ,1519.

20. *CWE*, VI, # 967, Erasmus from Antwerp to Wolsey, 18 May, 1519.

21. *CWE*, VI, # 980, 30 May, 1519, Erasmus in Louvain/Leuven to Luther.

22. *CWE*, VI, # 939, Erasmus in Antwerp to Frederick, Elector of Saxony, 14 April, 1519.

23. *CWE*, VI, # 980, Erasmus in Louvain/Leuven, to Luther, 30 May, 1519.

24. The long flattering letter which Erasmus wrote to the bishop about his dedication was dated 5 February, 1519 from Louvain/Leuven, *CWE*, VI, # 916. The cover letter

which accompanied the copies of the printed paraphrases was dated two weeks later, 19 February, *CWE*, VI, # 918.

25. *CWE*, VII, # 1038. Erasmus to Erard de la Marck, late October, 1519.

26. A summary of the career of Erard de la Marck is included in *Contemporaries of Erasmus*, II, 382-385.

27. Quoted in Preserved Smith, *Erasmus* (New York: Harper, 1923; reprint 1962), p. 209.

28. *LW*, vol. 54, "Table Talk," p. 19.

29. *CWE*, IX, #1342. Erasmus in Basel to Marcus Laurinus in Bruges, 1 February, 1523.

30. Steven Ozment, *The Age of Reform, 1250-1550: An Intellectual and Religious History of Late Medieval and Reformation Europe* (New Haven: Yale University Press, 1980), p. 295.

31. Hans Volz, "Die Ersten Sammelausgaben von Lutherschriften und ihre Drucker (1518-1520)," *Gutenberg Jahrbuch*, 1960, pp. 185-200.

32. Johan Froben in Basel to Luther, 14 February, 1519. English trans. in *Luther's correspondence and Other Contemporary Letters,* trans. and edited, Preserved Smith and Charles Jacobs (Philadelphia: The Luther Publication Society, 1918); vol. I, 161-163.

33. "Resolutiones disputationem de indulgentiarum virtute" (1518); *Weimar Ausgabe* (hereafter WA), I, 515-628. This writing includes short letters to Johann von Staupitz and Pope Leo X.

34. "Dialogus in praesumptuosos M. Lutheri Conclusiones," (June, 1518). Silvester Mazzolini was also known as "Prierias" from his birthplace. By virtue of his position in Rome he was not only the pope's theologian, but also censor of questionable works such as those of Martin Luther. *Contemporaries of Erasmus,* "Prierias," III, 120-121. See also Carter Lindberg, "Prierias and his Significance for Luther's development," *Sixteenth Century Journal*, 2 (October, 1972), 45-64.

35. "Ad dialogum Silvestri Prieratis de potestate papae responsio" (1518); *WA*, I, 647-686.

36. "Decem praecepta Wittenbergensi praedicta populo" (1518); *WA*, I, 398-521.

37. "Sermo de poenitentia" (1518); *WA*, I, 319-323.

38. "Sermo de virtute excommunicationis" (1518); *WA*, I, 634-643.

39. "De Indulgentiis," a translation of the sermon "Von Ablass und Gnade" (1517), which Latin translation appeared first in the Froben edition of Luther's works, Basel, October, 1518. The note concerning this Latin edition is in *WA*, I, 243.

40. "Sermo de digna praeparatio cordis pro suscipiendo sacramento eucharistiae" (1518), *WA*, I, 329-334.

41. *CDI*, IV, 12-13 (about Cologne). Also in *WA*, VI, 178-180, "Condemnatio Facultatis Theologiae Coloniensis adversus doctrinam F. Martini Lutherii." The condemnation in the *WA* is dated *"penultima die mensis Augusti,* [30August]" 1519, rather than 29 August which sometimes appears in scholarly writings.

42. *CDI*, IV, 14-16. *NK* 2227. Also printed in *WA*, VI, 175-178. "*Facultatis Theologiae Lovaniensis doctrinalis condemnatio doctrinae Martini Lutheri,"* printed 7 November, 1519.

43. *CDI*, IV, 16.

44. *CDI*, IV, 17-18.

45. *CDI*, IV, 20, 29 January,, 1520.

46. *CWE*, VII, #1070, to Marten Lips, from Louvain/Leuven, the last week of February, 1520.

47. "*Responsio Lutheriana ad Condemnationem Doctrinalem per Magistros Nostros Lovanienses et Colonienses factam*," *WA*, 6, 181-195. Luther's reaction to condemnations, [*NK* 4053], trans. of *WA*, 7, 884f.

48. *CWE*, VII, #1113, before 21 June, 1520.

49. *CDI*, IV, 33-34, 23 October, 1520.

50. Some examples of these activities were as follows: Antwerp, 13 July, 1521, 400 books were burned, *CDI*, IV, 78, and V, 402-403; the pope gave his approval in a response in July of the same year, *CDI*, V, 406-497; Gent/Gand/Gans, 25 July, 1521 (St. Jacob's day), when the Emperor, the King of Denmark and other political leaders attended, there were 300 books burned including some in both German and Dutch, *CDI*, V, 405; Gent/Gand/Gans, after 24 April, 1522, burning of Lutheran book confiscated from Lieven de Zomere, a baker, *CDI*, IV, 110, 113; The Hague and Amsterdam, 18 November, 1525, burning of heretical Lutheran books printed by Doen Pietersz., *CDI*, V, 63; Duinkerke/Dunkirk, 13 October, 1527, a fine of money and 3 months imprisonment for Jan Corbel for buying Lutheran books, and the books were burned, *CDI*, V, 267; Kortrijk/Courtrai, 14 October, 1527, banning of Pieter Notebaert, a Lutheran and his heretical books were burned, *CDI*, V, 96-97; Brugge/Bruges, 1527 or 1528, heretics burned along with their books, *CDI*, V, 354-355.

51. *CWE*, VIII, # 1153, from Louvain/Leuven, 18 October, 1520.

52. *WA Briefwechsel II*, 137. Luther to Spalatin, 10 July, 1520 (translated by the author).

53. *CWE*, VIII, # 1166. Erasmus wrote from Louvain/Leuven to an unnamed patron, probably in The Hague, December, 1520.

54. *NK*, 1342, published by Willem Vorsterman, Antwerp, 1520..

55.*Bullarum, diplomatum et privilegiorum Sanctorm Romanorum Pontificem,* Taurinensis Editio (1890), Vol. V, edited by Francisco Gaude. This document is found in Vol. V, 748-757. The translation used here is from: Hans J. Hillerbrand, *The Reformation in its own words*. London: S.C.M. Press, 1964; also New York: Harper and Row, 1964. The pagination is the same in both editions, pp. 80-84.

56. *Adversus execrabilem Antichristi bullam,* (November, 1520; in *WA*, VI, 597-612). The expanded German version appeared in the same month: *Wider die Bulle des Endchrists.* (in *WA*, VI, 615-629).

57. *Assertio omnium articulorum M. Lutheri per Bullam Leonis X novissimam damnatorum* (December, 1520; in *WA*, VII, 94-151). The German edition appeared only in March, 1521: *Grund und ursach aller Artikel D. Marti Lutheri sodurch Römische Bulle unrechtlich verdammt sind,* (in *WA*, VII, 308-357). The WA edition presented two German editions on opposing pages.

58. Perhaps the most accessible of these four responses is his "Defense and Explanation of all the Articles of Dr. Martin Luther which were unjustly condemned by the Roman Bull," trans. Charles M. Jacobs, revised by George W. Forrell, *LW,* vol. 32, "The Career of the Reformer" (Philadelphia: Muhlenberg Press, 1958), 3-99. This quotation is on p. 47.

59. "Why the Books of the Pope and his Disciples were burned by Doctor Martin Luther." *LW*, vol. 31, trans. Lewis Spitz, 383-395.

60. *Ibid*, p. 394.

61. The Latin version of this document is included in *CDI*, IV, 37-40. Since no printed English translation of this papal bull has been located, a recent unpublished translation by Dr. Michael Woodward, is used and this complete papal document is included as Appendix I of this study.

62. *Bullarum Diplomatum et Privilegiorum Sanctorum Romanorum Pontificem,* Taurinensis Editio (1890) vol. V, edited by Francisco Gaude. This bull is on pages 761-764. Dr. Michael Woodward used this edition for his translation located in Appendix I in this study.

63. *CWE*, VIII, # 1186, 25 February, 1521, from Louvain/Leuven.

64. *CDI*, IV, 76.

65. *CDI*, IV, 76.

66. *CDI*, IV, 78; *CDI*, IV, 80. Cf. *CDI*, V, 400-407.

67. *CDI*, IV, 41ff.

68. *CDI*, IV, 43-44.

69. This special version directed toward The Netherlands was published in both the French/Walloon, and the Dutch/Flemish languages. The Dutch/Flemish version is much longer and includes more detail. The two special documents for The Netherlands are published in parallel columns and parallel languages, in *CDI*, IV, 60-76. The English translation is from Gerard Brandt, *The History of the Reformation and other ecclesiastical transactions in and about the Low Countries*. 2 vols. (London: T. Wood, 1720-1732; reprint, London: A. M. S. Press, 1979), I, 40-41.

70. From J. A. Merle d'Aubigne, *History of the Reformation in the Sixteenth Century* (Lancaster, Pennsylvania: W. W. Freeman, [18??]), Vol. I, 356. There are several editions of d'Aubigne's work in French and in English with dates of publication not clearly indicated, and appearing in varying numbers of volumes. The copy used in this quotation was published in Lancaster, Pennsylvania, in two volumes [18??]. The Edict of Worms, dated 8 May, 1521, was published almost immediately in Latin in The Netherlands at Louvain/Leuven, and shortly thereafter, in Antwerp. The Latin text is printed in *CDI*, IV, 47-57.

71. Henry de Vocht analyzed in great detail the foundation of this school and most of its students and professors for the next thirty-five years. The name of Erasmus appears on many pages of the study, especially during the first several years of the school. *History of the Foundation and the Rise of the Collegium Trilinguae Lovaniense,* 1517-1550. Three volumes (Louvain: Publications Universitaires, 1953; reprinted Nedeln, Liechtenstein: Kraus reprint, 1976).

72. Erasmus's letter to John Robijns, in *CWE*, V, # 805, 26 March, 1518.

73. Ultimately there would be five editions of his Greek New Testament: 1516, 1519, 1522, 1527, and 1535.

74. *CWE*, VI, # 948, from Louvain/Leuven to Petrus Mosellanus, professor of Greek in Leipzig, 22 April, 1519.

75. *Ratio seu Methodus compendio perveniendi at Veram Theologicam, NK* 861 (Louvain, 1518); *NK* 862, (Deventer, 1520). A thorough analysis of this untranslated document can be found in Marjorie O'Rourke Boyle, *Erasmus on Language and Method*

in Theology (Toronto: University of Toronto Press, 1977), pp. 59-127. The translation of *Ratio* in the Toronto *CWE* edition is expected as part of vol. 41 in 2006.

76. Latomus, *De trium linguarum et studii theologici ratione dialogue*. This and other related documents are noted in the Introduction to Luther's tract "Against Latomus," *LW*. 32, 137-139.

77. *CWE*, VIII, # 1242 and 1243, to Stanislaus Thurzo, a bishop in Moravia.

78. He was urged to come to Flanders in 1529 (Allen, *E. E.*, VIII, 194, dated 9 June, 1529), and he even considered it. He was earlier urged to return to Louvain/Leuven. *(CWE*, X, # 1457, Jan Robbyns in Mechelen/Malines to Erasmus in Basel, 28 June, 1524). Neither of these alternatives, however, proved to have sufficient merit that he could leave Basel, and the proximity to his printers.

79. *CDI*, IV, 101.

80. *CDI*, IV, 104.

81. *CDI*, IV, 103.

82. *CDI*, IV, 123-127.

83. *CWE*, IX, # 1324, from "Pope Adrian VI to his beloved son Erasmus of Rotterdam," to Erasmus who was in Basel, 1 December, 1522. There is an alternate version of this letter in *CWE*, numbered 1324 A, with the same date, presumed to be in the hand of Aleander.

84. P. E. Valvekens, *De Inquisitie in de Nederlanden der zestiende eeuw.* (Brussels, Amsterdam: De Klinkhoren, 1949). Indeed, this author surveyed various examples of inquisiton three centuries back into the late middle ages.

85. *CDI*, IV, 181.

86. *CWE*, X, #1358, 17 April, 1523, from Basel, to Pierre Barbiere, chaplain to Pope Adrian VI.

87. *CWE*, X, # 1467 (lines 12-15), written from Basel to Johann van Vlatten, recently-appointed Councillor to the Duke of Cleves.

Chapter 3

Some Humanist Scholars and Dissenters
in the Early Modern Period

The scholars who were involved in education during the Renaissance period and who represented Biblical Humanism often taught in the Latin schools which could be found in many of the major towns of The Netherlands. They emphasized languages, literature, translations, and developing knowledge in many fields.[1] When new ideas in religion became available, the leaders in the schools were aware of these developments and often taught this new approach to their students. Although they were Humanist educators some became, knowingly or accidentally, reformers as well. They often discussed theological ideas in their classrooms, and periodically they gave lectures, which were often referred to as "sermons." There was ambiguity with respect to the jurisdiction of the church or the authorities of the inquisition when un-ordained schoolmasters spoke in their own classrooms and not in the churches. The division between these two functions became difficult to maintain when educated scholars became priests and the reforming ideas became part of their curricula. What for some were thought to be good educational practices, were thought by others to be subterfuge to undermine traditional religious understanding.

In addition to teaching, the Humanists also relied on the printed word. The printing presses, which had been available for more than a half century before the Reformation, were an indispensable method of spreading new ideas through monographs on various religious topics, new editions of earlier works, and through various translations—especially of the Bible. As a result, the control of printing became a paramount requirement for the Roman Catholic establishment seeking to maintain orthodoxy. Although an edict prohibiting printing of two specific books was issued in 1524 (See Chapters 8 and 9), the earlier papal bull, *Exsurge Domine*

(1520), contained a blanket statement against any questionable publications. The publishing did not stop, although many printers had to print secretly to avoid prosecution.[2]

We have a record of one association of like-minded scholars in Utrecht before 1520 and a second group in Delft and The Hague after 1520. Some of these persons became suspect, and their writings were scrutinized and condemned. Many of their publications appeared on the *Index of Prohibited books* of 1559.[3] At least one within this group was executed, and several found it expedient to escape from The Netherlands to Lutheran areas of Germany. Other scholars within the group ceased their scholarship or even disappeared from history.

In this present chapter we will survey more than a dozen of these persons. Concerning some of them, we have only limited documentation; while others left published records or, otherwise, provide us with sufficient information to form later chapters of this study. Many of them were related intellectually to Erasmus or to each other in various ways. Some of them studied in Wittenberg or had contact with Luther's ideas. In some cases, their published works were dedicated to others in the group.

The Dominican Wouter [or Gualterius] and his influence

While there were many individuals or groups who agitated for reforms or changes in the church before and during the early years of Luther's influence (*i.e.* back as far as 1510), perhaps the earliest who moved from a Humanist development to a reforming emphasis was the Dominican monk named Wouter (or Gualterius, Walter). While all studies of this earliest period of religious change refer to him, the primary sources are either sketchy or completely lacking. According to a source a century after the events,[4] Wouter may have been preaching questionable doctrines [*inculcavit reformationis igni*] in Utrecht as early as 1510. The historical record of M. Schoockius, who wrote in 1651, stated: "*hoc est septem annis ante Lutherum*" [this was seven years before Luther]. He elaborated:

> Before all others the accomplishments of the Dominican Wouter should be remembered. I will show from ancient tradition how at Utrecht in the 10th year of the 16th century (*i.e.*, 1510), this was seven years before Luther, he undertook to recommend truth more freely, and to point out various abuses. He became weak and consented to various revocations. This seemed to appease his adversaries.[5]

Unfortunately his activities at the earlier date are documented in only one source, and its date a century and more after the happenings gives us some concern. According to this same source, some of which was admittedly based on "*memorie*,"[6] Wouter preached freely in several places in The Netherlands where he pointed out many abuses in the church. Soon, however, he was called to account by the bishop of Utrecht. He quickly recanted his errors at that time and was released.

The "Evangelical" group in Utrecht, and Hinne [Johannes] Rode

Unfortunately, we do not know enough about Wouter. We do not know where he taught, nor who all of his associates were. We do know, however, that there was a small group of like-minded persons in Utrecht, who possibly owed some of their insights to his activities among them. Wouter was banned from the city of Utrecht in 1520, but evidently some of his followers continued their work for a time. The unofficial head of the group remaining in Utrecht after Wouter left seems to have been Hinne Rode (or Rodius), the rector of the School of St. Jerome [Hieronymus] at Utrecht (although R. R. Post argues that Rode was leader of the Brotherhouse and not actually Rector of the Hieronymus school).[7]

This school of the Brethren of the Common Life was organized in 1474. Named after the fourth century scholar and translator, it was closely associated with the Brethren House of the same name in Delft. As in other schools, this was a place for training young scholars, especially in the *trivium* and the *quadrivium*.[8] There evidently was little emphasis on philosophical questions, and the debate between the *via antiqua* and the *via moderna* within scholasticism was not prominent here. This school did, however, incorporate new Humanistic learning after the turn of the century (1500).

The date of the birth of Hinne Rode is unknown, but the form of his name indicates that he may have been born in Friesland.[9] On 5 March, 1476, he joined the Brethren of the Common Life and went to the Hieronymus School in Utrecht. We know nothing further of his career before he became leader of the school in about 1520. Rode was sympathetic with the theological works of Wessel Gansfort, and he emphasized serious Bible reading and study. He discounted legends of the medieval church, and he emphasized feast days but denied the necessity of celibacy.[10] His teachings evidently brought him into no difficulties at that time, however, because the Bishop of Utrecht was Philip of Burgundy, known for his lenient attitude toward theological questions. Philip died 7 April, 1524, and a different attitude toward theology—a rigid orthodoxy—prevailed thereafter.[11]

Before this time, however, Rode was gone from Utrecht. Arrangements were made for him to take certain theological documents of Wessel Gansfort and a letter on the Eucharist to Wittenberg to seek Luther's evaluation. The latter document was written, or perhaps compiled, by one of his humanist friends, Cornelius Hoen, and will be the subject of detailed inquiry in Chapter 5. At this point we are interested only in the travels of Hinne Rode, and there are even slight discrepancies in these dates. Otto Clemen, who studied the problem with care, concluded that Hinne Rode went to Wittenberg, arriving before Luther left for the Diet of Worms, early 1521.[12] This year seems to be indicated because one year later on 29 July, 1522, shortly after Luther left the Wartburg to return to Wittenberg, Luther published his preface to these works of Gansfort, in which he referred to his having received the documents recently. Hinne Rode returned to his school in Utrecht and arranged for the Zwolle edition of Gansfort's works (1522).[13]

We are not certain about the details concerning his situation in Utrecht in the year after he returned. Referring to a statement in the Chronicle from the Brotherhouse at Doesburg, we read that "Johannes Rode, rector of the house of clerics in Utrecht was deposed because of Luther (or perhaps because of Lutheran ideas)."[14] This happened in 1522. At this early date the name "Lutheran" referred to anyone who had broken from the medieval Roman Catholic Church and was interested in some aspects of the reforming ideas. These individuals were not unified with respect to any later "Lutheran" doctrine, but by the nature of affairs, they were a diverse group, with different concepts and emphasized different doctrinal ideas. Soon Hinne Rode went on a second journey, this time to Basel and to Zürich. Clemen concluded that Rode probably visited Oecolampadius late in 1522 and arrived in Zürich early in 1523.[15] The story of the influence of this visit on Zwingli and future discussions of the Eucharist will be analyzed in Chapter 5.

The career of Hinne Rode after his historic visit to Zwingli is not especially significant for later developments in The Netherlands. In 1524 he visited with Bucer in Strasbourg. The visit is indicated by a letter which Bucer wrote to Martin Frecht in Heidelberg "there came to me an unknown man, Johannes Rhodius. . . . This Rhodius was my guest [autumn 1524], and we discussed much concerning the Eucharist related to a writing he carried."[16] In 1525 he was in Deventer and then went to Norden in East Friesland where he was associated with former friends from the Hieronymus School. In East Friesland he married and took a position as a teacher. His opposition to some Lutheran teaching, however, led to his expulsion in 1530, whereupon he went to Wolthuizen, (Wolthusen, near Emden), also in East Friesland.[17] There is an undocumented suggestion that he later was an adherent of the Anabaptist movement.[18]

Evidently Hinne Rode left no theological writings. A suggestion that he was one of the translators of Luther's New Testament which appeared in 1525 in Amsterdam, while not impossible, is not documented.[19] We neither know the date nor place of his death, although his widow died in 1557.[20]

Some of these persons who continued in Utrecht are known only by name. We have limited information for others. We will meet Hinne Rode again in Chapter 5 as his traveled to Wittenberg, Basel, Zürich and Strasbourg with the famous letter concerning the Eucharist written or compiled by Cornelius Hoen.

Bartelt Laurens

Schoockius listed six persons in a group of dissenters in Utrecht, perhaps associated with Wouter or under his inspiration. The **first** person mentioned was Bartelt Laurens, a Carthusian, who talked with his brother monks about the new faith, only to be spurned by them. In fact, they expelled him from their cloister, and he was forced to beg and do hand labor on the outside. Evidently he was more determined to proclaim his new-found faith, and he continued to preach trust in the Scriptures alone.[21] No later references to him are known.

Bernard, a monk

The **second** associate was Bernard, a monk and preacher in the area. No more details are known.[22]

Gerrit van Wormer (or perhaps Gerryt Pietersz van Wormer)

The **third** person was Gerrit van Wormer, a priest from the region of Utrecht. De Hoop Scheffer suggested that Gerrit may have gathered a small congregation around him in Dordrecht.[23] He does not appear in our records again until he was imprisoned in The Hague. He was arrested September, 1525 and spent nine days in prison, "on beer and bread"[24]—19-27 September, 1525—because he "persisted in certain opinions which seemed to be of the sect of Lutherans."[25] He was to be confined until he "again came to his senses [resipisceerde=from Latin, resipisco]."[26] The new bishop of Utrecht (after the death of the lenient Philip of Burgundy in 1524) may have been a factor in this and other arrests in the year. We assume that Gerrit was released because he was returned to prison from 19 'November to 23 December, 1525 when he recanted and seemingly disappeared from the historical records.[27] Some time later, however, the same person, or perhaps another Gerrit (Geryt) van Wormer was imprisoned for heresy at Muiden and repented and paid his fine on 14 October, 1527.[28] His career may have continued in Enkhuizen even after this date.[29]

Willem Ottens (Ottonis)

The **fourth** person mentioned was Willem Ottens (Ottonis), a priest of Utrecht, who was imprisoned in The Hague in 1525. Later he appeared in Monnikendam, a few miles north of Amsterdam, where he had another bout with the inquisitorial authorities because he would not renounce his wife whom he had married in 1526 (See more detail in Chapter 12).

Dirk van Abcoude

The **fifth** person was Dirk van Abcoude (which was a small village near Utrecht), priest of St. Geert Church in Utrecht. In January, 1522 a newspaper article reported on some heretical activity in the region. The article referred to Dirk, and also Herman Gerrits who was vicar or assistant in St. Jacob Church, Utrecht. Both were drawing large crowds because of their teachings.[30] Dirk preached against misuses in the church, advocated other "evangelical" ideas, and questioned the traditional interpretation of the Eucharist. This was reported by a critical eye-witness account which referred to his "heresy" in 1520 or 1521. He was reprimanded, so we are told, and his preaching was periodically forbidden. He was popular, however, and learned men and interested persons came from all parts of the city to hear him. A critic once asked him, "Herr Pastor, you have had as good parents as I have; do you wish to appear wiser than they?" To this the minister responded: "They did not thirst to hear the truth preached."[31] As far as can be determined, Dirk remained in Utrecht until he was finally accused of heresy in 1540.[32]

Herman Gerrits

The **sixth** person was Hermann Gerrits [or Gherardi], who has already been mentioned. He was brought from Roermond to Utrecht to become Vice-Curate [*onder pastor*] at St. Jacob Church. Evidently he had to work for an unsympathetic head priest, but he continued to object to the shortcomings of the cloistered living and the arbitrary vows not commanded by God. He objected also to the sale of indulgences and meritorious reverence for the saints. In fact, a critic tells us that "the foolish hung onto every word that he spoke, and he preached heresy continually." Furthermore, such was his popularity that he gained strength from various sects, while learned people came to hear him or to criticize him.[33]

Finally, late in 1521 he was imprisoned in Brussels. On 9 February, 1522 Gerrits renounced nine points of theology which reflected many emphases of Luther (See Appendix II).[34] After his recantation he said

> I swear that I will remain for all time, and without doubt, within the truth of the Catholic church, and I declare that everything which is opposed to the faith and even these theses merit eternal condemnation.[35]

After he was condemned for his teachings the authorities threatened him with prison, but he chose, rather, to be banished from the Emperor's territory, never to return on pain of death. We know nothing more of this individual, nor do we have any indication of the source of his ideas.

The "evangelical" group at Delft and The Hague

With the recantation of Hermann Gerrits in 1522 and the expulsion of Hinne Rode (also in 1522) the brief "evangelical" circle in Utrecht appears to have come to its end. Evangelical preaching, however, sprouted elsewhere. Schoockius related, further, that at Delft the "first light of truth" again shone in 1520 when the same Wouter took off his clerical garb as a Dominican and preached in clothing of a layman. Indeed, it may have been at this time that he was called "the Lutheran Monk" (*de Luthersche Monick*).[36]

By 1520 Wouter seems to have been part of a group of Humanist scholars and priests in Delft. At least two doctrines were contained in his criticisms of current practice. **First**, concerning satisfaction through the sacrament of penance, "remission from purgatory could not be obtained for money." **Second**, he criticized the related practice of indulgences and asserted that

He did not believe that forgiveness of sin can be purchased for money, otherwise God, the Lord of heaven and earth, would not have sent his only begotten
son in the flesh in order to atone for our sins through his blood and his death[37]

The names of five persons in Delft who were probably influenced by
Wouter were listed by Schoockius. They were a diverse group comprised of
Humanist academicians, political figures, and at least one priest.[38] We can follow
the sketchy careers of a few of them through trustworthy documents, and we will
encounter others of these individuals in later portions of this study.

George Sylvanus (or probably Saganus)

The **first** person we encounter in this Delft/The Hague group is George Sylvanus (Saganus), who may have been the companion of Hinne Rode on his trip
to Zürich. (This story is related in Chapter 5). There are no further details concerning the activities of George Sylvanus (Saganus).

Johannes Sartorius (Jan Snijder)

The **second** person mentioned in this Delft/The Hague group was Johannes
Sartorius (Jan Snijder). The name of this evangelical-minded Humanist and
Latinist appears several times in the literature, but specific details are sketchy
and incomplete. He is mentioned as one of the associates of the Dominican
Wouter. Here he "first tasted the truth at Delft through association with Wouter,
but who confessed his faith elsewhere" (i.e. in Amsterdam and Noordwijk).[39]

This scholar was evidently born about 1500 in Amsterdam and received his
education in Louvain/Leuven. In 1525 he was imprisoned in the Voorpoort
prison near The Hague, where he was called "Jan Sartorius, rector of Amsterdam."[40] Evidently there had been complaints from other scholars in Amsterdam
who suspected his orthodoxy. Here he shared the prison with some other like-
minded scholars such as Wilhelmus Gnapheus (See Chapter 11), Frederick
Canirivus (Hondebeke, See later in this chapter) and Jan de Bakker (Pistorius,
See Chapter 10).[41] Apparently the charges against him were that he taught salvation by faith and published a tract on the Eucharist (alas, this is not extant), in
which he denied transubstantiation. His imprisonment lasted from 6 to 27 September, 1525.

After he recanted his "errors" he was allowed to go free. He is thought to
have continued his evangelical preaching and teaching, and in 1527 he became
schoolmaster at Noordwijk (Dutch: noord=north, wijk=district) near Leiden,
where he was sometimes known as "Aquilovicanus" (i.e., Latin: aquilo=north;
vicanus=villager).[42]

Around 1529 he again became a school teacher in Amsterdam, where he
was said to have taught that "all the people are seduced by monks and priests."[43]
At about the same time Wilhelmus Gnapheus, his fellow Humanist friend, dedicated one of his writings to him. This was a Humanist and Latin drama based on

the theme of The Prodigal Son, and entitled "*Acolastus*."[44] (We will analyze this in Chapter 11).

Sartorius' writings and publications reveal Humanist influence. Trapman summarized five extant works of Sartorius, although most of them appeared later than the period covered by this study.[45] The earliest was *De Grammatica*, probably completed in 1527 and dedicated to Wilhelmus Gnapheus. A related work was entitled *Syntaxis*, a teaching tool written in Noordwijk in 1528; later he wrote *Exercitus*, exercises to instill excellent Latin grammar with Dutch equivalents in opposition to "barbarian" or erroneous grammar in a sense similar to Erasmus's use of the word "Barbarian" *i.e.* those who do not know good Latin or Greek. His most extensive publication, on which he worked for thirty years, was an edition of Erasmus's *Adages* to which he added Dutch translations. This was published posthumously. His latest publications concerned paraphrases on Biblical works in which a Spiritualist tendency is obvious.[46]

It seems that Sartorius never left the Roman Catholic Church, although various suspicions concerning his orthodoxy led to his expulsion from Amsterdam in 1535.[47] He may have traveled to Zutphen, Emden, and Basel in 1545. Finally he returned to Delft about 1557 or 1558. There is uncertainty about the date and place of his death. He may have died as late as 1570.

Cornelis Hoen (Honius)

The **third** person listed by Schookius was Cornelis Hoen (or Honius). He was probably from Gouda, although this is not known for certain.[48] He attended the Hieronymus School near the turn of the century. By 1509 he was already a lawyer at the Court of Holland in The Hague. He was known to Erasmus, who said of him when Hoen was arrested, "an excellent man they tell me."[49]

In this same year he began the work which ultimately drew him into the orbit of developing reforming thought. A former associate at the Hieronymus School, Martin Dorp, invited him to look at some papers he had just found. Martin Dorp's uncle, Jacob Hoeck (Jacob Angularis), Deacon at Naaldwijk and Pastor at Wassenaar (two villages near The Hague), had willed that his nephew have access to his papers. Dorp, now Professor of Theology and Philosophy at Louvain/Leuven, invited Hoen to look at the papers with him. Among these were several works of the Dutch theologian, Wessel Gansfort (1420-1489), including his treatise on the Eucharist. Hoen decided to write a treatise of his own, or at least adapt a much earlier treatise on the Eucharist. Earlier scholarship thought the treatise to be an outgrowth of his reading of Gansfort's work, but now more recent discoveries suggest otherwise. Hoen wrote or compiled the letter, *Epistola Christiana admodum*, concerning a new interpretation of the Eucharist in a non-sacramental way [*i.e.* not *transubstantiation*]. This tract and its comparison with Gansfort's work will be analyzed in Chapter 5. These various friends decided that the new information—both the works of Gansfort and Hoen's letter—should be shared with Luther, whose writings had been known in The Netherlands for a few years. Hoen himself, because of his advanced age, could not go to Wittenberg, but the documents were taken in 1521 to Martin Luther and later to Zwingli. The messenger was Hinne Rode and others, as indicated above.[50]

Hoen was arrested and imprisoned in February, 1523, because he was suspected of sympathies for Lutheranism [*propter sectam Lutheram*].[51] He was imprisoned with his Humanist friend, Cornelis Gnapheus (See Chapter 11). Hoen was released in March, and then was taken back to prison until he was finally released on 29 October, 1523, but confined to the city of The Hague.[52] He died probably in 1524 at an advanced age.

Johannes Pistorius [Jan de Bakker]

The **fourth** person was Johannes Pistorius (Jan de Bakker) a priest who was sympathetic with reforming ideas, and who was married and defended his marriage during his trial. He was martyred, the first martyr for the Evangelical faith in the northern Netherlands (burned as a martyr in The Hague on 15 September, 1525). His career and confessions during his trial are analyzed in Chapter 10.

Gulielmus Gnapheus

The **fifth** person in this listing was Gulielmus Gnapheus, rector of the Latin School at The Hague. As rector he wrote a drama on the theme of the Prodigal Son, which was meant to be performed by his students. Before he fled The Netherlands he also wrote a defense concerning the trial of Pistorius and an evangelical tract of devotion and comfort. All his works were placed on the *Index of Prohibited Books* of 1559. He was imprisoned twice and finally fled to Germany. His works are analyzed in Chapter 11.

The twelve individuals named above seem to have had some contact with the mysterious "Lutheran Monk," Wouter, as summarized in the historical account of Schoockius. These persons worked either in Utrecht or farther west in the regions of Delft and The Hague. Whatever the permanent influence of Wouter might have been we cannot determine. It is interesting, however, that the listing of those associated with him includes several who wrote significant treatises in the period. By 1528 the inquisitorial process had became so strong that Wouter fled the Netherlands for Strasbourg where he remained the rest of his life.[53]

Other Humanist Scholars contemporary with those listed above

In addition to the names provided by Schoockius, there were several other Humanist scholars on the scene. Many of their scholarly works provide connections with the earliest dissenting ideas of 1520s. We will analyze some of these individuals and give samples of their theological idea, in so far as their writings have been preserved.

Frederick Hondebeke (Canirivus)

Another scholar related to this group in the early 1520s, although not included in the list which Schoockius provided us, was Frederick Hondebeke (Canirivus).[54] He was the rector of the Latin School in Delft. Little is known about him except a letter which he wrote to Kaspar Hedio the reformer in Mainz.[55] He expressed his concerns about the "Nicodemites" in his area who were sympathetic with the Reformation, but who did not dare to come out publicly for the new teachings of the faith. He disseminated his understanding of the faith in regular lessons or sermons on Sundays and feast days. On these occasions he attempted to clarify the gospels and epistles.[56] He preached in school buildings, but not in public places because of the intense hatred the monks had for the truth [*infestissimae sunt veritati*].[57] In his letter to Hedio he compared his devotion to the new faith with the more cautious approach of Erasmus. The latter, he stated, seemed to become cold [*frigescere*] or retreated from or revoked ideas which on other occasions he proclaimed, and he seemed to favor more the glory of the human than of God [*plus veretur hominum gloriam quam Dei*].[58] He suggested that Erasmus and other "Nicodemites" were driven by fear not to state publicly what they believed inwardly.

In May, 1523, two officials of the government in Delft sought information about Hondebeke who they thought had taught ideas contrary to the church teaching. The officials in Delft were informed concerning the questionable treatment of these heretical ideas in August, 1523. The local magistrates, however, opposed the attempt of the *landvoogdes* (the Regent Margaret) and inquisitor, Frans van der Hulst, to take Hondebeke and Cornelis Hoen to Gorinchem to inquire about their relation to the "Lutheran sect."

By August, 1523, however, Hondebeke was imprisoned in The Hague. More than a year later he was again in Delft but with restricted freedom. Although his arrest was protested by local authorities, he was taken again to The Hague. This second arrest and abduction resulted in a street demonstration in his favor. The imprisonment this time lasted three weeks, 1-25 September, 1525.[59] Thereafter, we have no further information concerning him.[60]

Nicholaas van Broeckhoven, or s'Hertogenbosch

Very shortly after Erasmus left the Netherlands, another of his close friends was taken into custody. Late in 1521 Nicholaas van s'Hertogenbosch (1478-*ca.*1553, also known as Nicolaus Buscoducensis or Broeckhoven)[61] was suspected of Lutheran ideas.[62] Born in 1478, he had been trained at the University in Louvain/Leuven and maintained close association with that University. In 1514 he was appointed rector of the school in Middelburg, in Zeeland. After 1517 he was a teacher in the Latin School in Antwerp and worked with Erasmus in editing some of his works. Nicholaas had also prepared several editions of theological works in medieval theology; some of which were published anonymously. At the same time, however, he had leanings toward Luther's ideas. This exemplifies the confusion not only among individual scholars but among the authorities, in that it proved difficult to distinguish between good scholarship and heretical teachings. Erasmus was quick to point out, however, that good scholarship and heretical teachings were not the same thing: the first did not necessarily lead to the second. Nicholaas had a Humanist education and was interested in classical Latin as was Erasmus. The details of his implication in "Lutheranism" are not known. In 1521, however, he was suspected of being a follower of Luther, and on 9 February, 1522, he was imprisoned with his fellow Humanist sympathizer, Cornelis Grapheus (See Chapter 6). Erasmus praised both of them for their scholarship and their role as teachers. The latter wrote to Joost Lauwereyns of Bruges, Chair of the High Court in Brabant in Mechelen/Malines, who was also soon to become officially involved with the inquisition. Defending Nicholaas, Erasmus continued:

> I am not now pleading for N.B. (Nicholaas Broeckhoven), for I do not know what he has admitted to. This I know, however, that there was no man in Antwerp of more unblemished character, more popular with his fellow-citizens, or of more value to the community in the education of the young. Nor do I express any opinion about his colleague (Cornelis Grapheus); for of his case, where it concerns Luther, I am ignorant. This I know, that he is a good scholar, versed in many languages, and his character is spotless, except that he is a rather unguarded talker. Baechem no doubt treated him with greater severity having suffered from his attacks in private. It is common knowledge that Hoogstraten and Baechem aim at the extinction of the ancient tongues and the humanities and seek above all a handle to attack those who teach them. In my opinion they would do better if they were content with their victory and did not arouse further tragic disturbances in this world of ours. The world will bear it somehow, if deprived of Luther; to be deprived of the tongues and the humanities, it will never bear (lines 100-114).[63]

In March or April, 1522, Nicholaas recanted publicly at Brussels and was released through the intervention of friends.[64] He made a short visit to Basel where he possibly carried some books to his friend Erasmus.[65] Shortly thereafter, he returned to his old position in Antwerp in 1523 where he lived several years without any suspicion of heretical religious ideas. In 1528, however, he left the Netherlands for Germany and married. He served the Lutheran cause first at Bremen, then in Denmark, and finally in Germany at Wesel until he was excluded by the Augsburg Interim (1548). He died *ca.* 1550.

Gerard Geldenhouwer (1482-1541)

Gerhard Geldenhouwer (sometimes Geldenhouer) of Nijmegen (Noviomagus) was trained in Deventer when it was a center of humanist studies under the highly respected teacher, Alexander Hegius (d. 1498).[66] He also studied in

Louvain/Leuven where he undoubtedly was acquainted with Erasmus. By 1514 he was employed at the court of the future Charles V. Geldenhouwer was best known in his early career as an author and editor. He published several historical works, including a detailed geographical study on Zeeland. He also edited some works of Erasmus, and several letters between them are preserved. In 1516 he edited Sir Thomas More's *Utopia* and had it published in Antwerp.[67]

Philip of Burgundy, a man with interests in Humanistic literature, was appointed Bishop of Utrecht in 1517. Geldenhouwer, as a staff member for the bishop, had responsibilities for correspondence on the bishop's behalf. Soon thereafter Geldenhouwer wrote the ceremony for the bishop's installation, [*Epistola. . . de triumphali ingressu*, 1517]. Erasmus wrote a warm letter to him commending him on the clarity of expression of the event, that it "has been described by you so clearly and so vividly, that I should have seen less had I been an actual spectator of all the ceremonies (lines 5-7)." He also expressed his pleasure that such a learned man was appointed to that position.[68] Later that year Erasmus dedicated his work *Querela Pacis* [Complaint on behalf of Peace] to Philip and sent him a copy.[69] Erasmus received responses both from the bishop[70] and from Geldenhouwer.[71] Signifying their close friendship, Erasmus signed one letter to Geldenhouwer, "sincerest of friends."[72]

When his patron, Bishop Philip, died in 1524, Geldenhouwer was forced to look elsewhere for employment. Evidently he had already developed sympathies for Reformation ideas, but these were not known until in 1525 when he left the Netherlands for Germany and attended lectures in Wittenberg.

In approximately 1526, Geldenhouwer wrote,

> eight years have passed since many books from Saxony were sent to our area [supposedly about 1518] which I bought and read because I had an interest in change and I had a great love for new books. These presented me with many incredible things, especially the truth which was presented in a direct manner.

He reported that there were also bundles and mountains of books [*stapels, ja bergen boeken*] which came from Italy, Rome, and two or three universities. These were directed against the writings from Saxony. In these books the "pride, the avarice and the greed of the priests and of the pope were made known to the people." He stated that he had diligently studied them and found "with God's help that the books from Saxony approximated more the Apostolic and Evangelical truth than the others."[73]

A Roman Catholic scholar has questioned the accuracy of these dates because the works of Luther and other reformers were not as readily available in The Netherlands in 1518 as the report suggested. Furthermore, he questioned the motivation for these seeming inaccuracies related to these early dates. In any case, we can discern no clear details of Geldenhouwer's shift to Protestant sympathies, which became public only after the death of the bishop in 1524, and probably in part as a result of his visit to Wittenberg in 1525.

During the last decade of Erasmus's life the two old friends drifted apart not only because of the Reformation itself, but also with respect to ideas concerning toleration for those suspected of heresy. After Geldenhouwer sided with the Reformation he wrote many other works. One was a letter to Emperor Charles V urging him to work for peace and, especially, to cease persecuting heretics.[74] He used Deuteronomy 13 to distinguish between two types of persons. **First**, there were the true and rigid heretics—worshippers of other gods—treasonous against "our God who brought you out of Egypt." **Second**, he suggested that not all who are called heretics in their own times are necessarily false prophets or blasphemers against God. He used the parable of the wheat and the weeds of Matthew 13—leave the two plants to grow up together, and the decision could be made later by God. Furthermore, he argued that the early church shunned those they thought went astray, but they did not kill them. The admonition to kill came from bishops and Popes at a later time. The only way to judge is to sit on the seat of Moses or of Christ, and earthly powers hardly occupy that position.

This Latin letter was quickly printed in four different editions in German. What influence it might have had on the Emperor is not known, but it reflected the Humanist admonition for peace in the church and in the society.

Up to this point Geldenhouwer and Erasmus were in general agreement in the treatment of heretics—rejection of the church's position of extermination.[75] Geldenhouwer concluded that the taking of life for wrong belief was always wrong. When he quoted some of Erasmus's writings which he thought supported his ideas, he ignited a controversy. Erasmus qualified his own argument with more rigid observations.

> There is heresy which is manifest blasphemy, and there is heresy. . . which makes for sedition. Shall we sheath the sword of the magistrate against this? To kill blasphemous and seditious heretics is necessary for the maintenance of the state.[76]

Erasmus abandoned absolute toleration when it seemed the state or the order of society might be at stake. In principle, however, Geldenhouwer followed the idea of absolute toleration, letting the law of Christ—as in the parable of the wheat and the weeds—be the final judge.

As one sympathetic with the Reformation, he traveled widely, meeting reformers especially in Strasbourg and Augsburg, and wrote other works on history. He was married in Worms. In 1532 he became Professor of History and Theology at Marburg, where he died ten years later.

Gerard Listrius (b. *ca.* before 1490- d. unknown)

Gerardus Listrius, a younger contemporary of Erasmus, at times also a close associate in editing and printing,[77] was born in the vicinity of Utrecht about 1490 (perhaps a few years earlier). He studied at Deventer where he was probably first introduced to Humanist methodology. He continued his studies at Louvain/Leuven and Cologne where he became proficient in the three languages of Humanist scholarship, Greek, Hebrew and Latin. There are also suggestions that he studied medicine at Pavia and later at Basel.

In Basel he became a friend and associate of Erasmus. There in 1514 they collaborated on various projects including a 1514 edition of the *Adages*. Perhaps his most significant work as a Humanist scholar was his commentary on Erasmus's *Praise of Folly*, published by the Froben press in March, 1515. While Erasmus wrote some sections of this work, the major credit evidently must be given to Listrius.[78] Erasmus appreciated the clarification the commentary made with respect to certain classical allusions where "Folly" may have been misunderstood,[79] and Listrius did a great service to Erasmus in emphasizing the moral and spiritual dimension which Erasmus had in mind. This commentary was the standard analysis of the *Praise of Folly* for many years.

In 1516 Listrius left Basel to become rector of a school in Zwolle. From his new position he wrote a letter to Erasmus, in which he expressed his great admiration for his older contemporary.

> Jupiter strike me with his thunderbolt, if there is anything in the world dearer to me than you are, for whom it would be a pleasure to sacrifice my life, not to mention those external things which are exposed to the caprice of fortune. . . . You know your friend Listrius to be too sincere to bring himself to any flattery. . . .My living conditions here [in Zwolle] are not particularly attractive, partly because of my unremitting labours hard as iron, partly for my great loss in the way of reading; for I scarcely have time to glance even sideways at a book. . . .You started me on the path of learning, you published my name to the world, you were the founder of my fortunes; would that some day you might finish the work. What could a man like me have achieved or even attempted without you? Everything I have, such as it is, I owe to you[80] (lines 9-12, 28-30, 36-40).

In Zwolle his major work was publishing scholarly books to be used in his classes. In the next few years he became suspect and was criticized by the Dominicans there, probably because he was associated with the printer, Corver, who published certain works of Luther and Wessel Gansfort. Listrius wrote against his critics in his *Epistola theologica. . . adversus Dominicanos Suollenses*. B.J.Spruyt analyzed this work and discovered that Listrius was moving from strictly Erasmian Humanism to some ideas associated more strictly with Luther. He singled out such ideas as justification by faith, contrition as an act following faith, and confession. Other doctrines associated with the Dominicans were thought by Listrius to be constructed as "human precepts."[81] This conflict may explain in part Listrius's move in 1522 from Zwolle to be rector of a school in Amersfoort. Shortly after this he disappeared from our historical records.

Some scholars have suggested that Listrius was the author of the *Lamentations of Peter*, written in 1521 in the style of an Erasmian satire (See Chapter 4). Listrius could be a possibility as the author of the tract. He was thoroughly familiar with Erasmus's satirical style, having assisted him with various scholarly editions as well as producing the Commentary on "Folly." He was also familiar with Erasmus's criticisms of many monastic practices. Furthermore, he had assisted Erasmus in editing and publishing Biblical documents. For these reasons it is not surprising that some have suggested he might be the author of the satirical tract of 1521.

As noted above, however, this was the very period when Listrius was moving to more noticeably Lutheran ideas. His reflection of more strictly doctrinal positions would not automatically preclude his writing a satire such as *Lamentations*, but it would seem to make it unlikely. For various reasons, however, other scholars of the period have not followed this suggestion. Consequently, until more research is completed, or new evidence surfaces, the authorship of the *Lamentations* must remain unknown.

Conclusions

In the previous discussion in Chapter 2 we summarized some details concerning Luther's influence in The Netherlands, not only through his published works but also through travels of his students in the Augustinian order. In this chapter we have discovered several humanist educators who were developing divergent religious ideas as well. We have names of twelve persons who supposedly were influenced by the Dominican Wouter in Utrecht or in Delft/The Hague. Three of these left sufficient writings to form later chapters in this study while the remainder we know only by name. A few other scholars have some relation to the developing study through their work in editing or their correspondence.

To attempt to summarize the various ideas expressed by this diverse group of scholars would be presumptuous. Furthermore, to suggest any systematic theological organization of this period would also be impossible. While some of these scholars knew each other, undoubtedly some ideas or documents mentioned here were not known by even a majority of these scholars. They came to their understanding through diverse paths, and they expressed their concerns in their own way in their own circumstances. In addition, they emphasized different theological concerns, whether these were related to baptism, the Eucharist, indulgences, or the authority of the pope and the medieval church. There was thus no unifying theological thread, and consequently, it would be an exaggeration to suggest they formed a "movement," whether Protestant or otherwise. They represented different levels of dissent, and their works contributed to a period which was in a state of constant flux, that is, diversity as compared with each other as well as dissent from the presumed Roman Catholic standards for belief and action.[82]

In spite of their differences, however, there were certain similar understandings—stated or implied—which give us some insight into the changes which were under way. A major difference is noted in similar assumptions as to the authority of the Bible—however interpreted—as contrast to the authority of the Roman Catholic Church, its pope, its decrees and its political involvement. There was an assumption that the Roman Catholic practices were "human laws" or "earthly requirements." By contrast, the true law and precepts of God were to be found in a careful reading of certain portions of the Old and New Testaments. To be sure, those who wished to use Biblical authority exclusively brought their own presuppositions to their study no less than Roman Catholic authorities who also brought their own tradition and centuries-long practices to their understanding.

Prior to these dissenting opinions, however, there was a rather general shift of attitude and innovative educational methods that influenced the scholars. The shift came in part through careful study of religious literature, including the Bible and Church Fathers, and a need to apply their results to human concerns—*studia humanitatis*—, not the traditional concerns of the Roman Church with such supra-human topics as purgatory, after life, or the doctrine of sainthood. This change of perspective led scholars to question the sale of indulgences, to question the efficacy of the doctrine of *ex opera operato* with respect to the Eucharist, to question merits of the saints which could be transferred to humans through the hierarchy of the church. For example, Jan de Bakker (Pistorius), met his fiery fate because he would not renounce his wife (See chapter 10). He opposed the church's unwarranted limitation on the very human institution of marriage and pitted his personal understanding of the medieval sacrament against the external authority of the church.

Those who knew of Luther's teaching "by faith alone" [*sola fide*] understood it as replacing reliance on the authority of the institution church. Those who were committed to the new learning likewise substituted   reliance on improved documents and translations for a reliance on what some called the "dead" creeds or the "humanly constituted" requirements of the Roman Catholic establishment. Whether they were relying on Luther's multi-faceted sources—Bible and the Church Fathers—or the equally multi-faceted sources of the Humanist scholars, they were involved in a shift of loyalties. Erasmus was a prime example of this shift in that he was critical of the medieval church and emphasized a more inward understanding of the faith, although he never wavered in his loyalty to the institution of the Church of the ages. Erasmus, and his loyal colleagues emphasized a new climate within the old church, on the one hand. On the other hand, Luther and those who were drawn toward him asserted the necessity of a new Church and new loyalties.

These evolving and differing understandings of the relationship between the faith of the past and of the present could only lead to manifold dissent. There would, however, be no clear solution to these cultural growing pains in The Netherlands during the 1520s. The documents analyzed in the following chapters, and the individuals responsible for their composition, each in their own way, will provide an elaboration on these varied dissenting ideas, and the theological struggles they inspired.

Notes for Chapter 3

1. The widespread phenomenon of Humanist education in early 16th century Netherlands was thoroughly analyzed by Josef Ijsewijn in his article: "Humanism in the Low Countries," in Albert Rabil, ed., *Renaissance Humanism: Foundations, Forms, and Legacy*, vol. 2, *Humanism beyond Italy* (Philadelphia: University of Pennsylvania Press, 1988), pp. 156-215. Indeed, The Netherlands was a major crossroads for education and educators from all of western Europe from approximately 1450 and for two hundred years. Those Humanist scholars analyzed in this chapter are only a small sampling of the educators of the period, and represent only scholars who touched on theological dogmas of the Roman Catholic Church or the early Dissenters of the 1520s.

2. M. E. Kronenberg, *Verboden Boeken en opstandige Drukkers in de Hervormingstijd* (Amsterdam: P. N. van Kampen & Zoon, 1948).

3. *Index Librorum Prohibitorum (Romae: Ex officina Salviana, XV Mens* Feb. 1559), (reprinted, 1980).

4. M. Schoockius, *Ultrajectenis* [*i.e.* of Utrecht] *Liber de bonis vulgo ecclesiasticis dictis,* (Groningen, 1651), as quoted in *CDI*, IV, 19. The book by M. Schoockius is rare, but valuable because it was based on sources no longer unavailable. The suspected Wouter was called *Gualterius dominicanus Ultrajectenis* [*i.e.* from Utrecht], *CDI*, IV, 19.

5. Schoockius, as duplicated in *CDI*, I, 498.

6. J. G. de Hoop Scheffer, *Geschiedenis der Kerkhervorming in Nederland, van haar ontstaan tot 1531* (Amsterdam: G. L. Funke, 1873), p. 62. See also his footnote reference back to the writing by M. Schoockius

7. A. Ekker, in his *De Hieronymusschool te Utrecht* (Utrecht: Bosch and Son, 1863), pp. 23ff., listed Rode as the third rector. R. R. Post, on the contrary, argued that Hoen was leader of the Brotherhouse and not actually rector of Hieronymusschool. R. R. Post, *The Modern Devotion* (Leiden: E. J. Brill, 1968), p. 571.

8. A. Ekker, *Ibid.*, p. 7.

9. "Rode," *Realencyklopädie für protestantische Theologie und Kirche* (Leipzig: J. C. Hinrich'sche Buchhandlung, 1906), XVII, 62.

10. "Rode," *Realencyklopädie*, XVII, 62.

11. Conradus Eubel, ed., *Hierarchia Catholica* (Münster: 1923), III, 316.

12. Otto Clemen, "Hinne Rode in Wittenberg, Basel, Zürich und die frühesten Ausgabe Wesselscher Schriften," *Zeitschrift für Kirchengeschichte*, XVIII (1898), 346-371. A recent review of all known references to the thought and the travels of Hinne Rode was written by Bastian J. Spruyt, "Hinne Rode (*c.*1480-*c.*1539): Het Leven en de Ontwikkeling van de Dissidente Rector van het Utrechtse Fraternhuis" in H. ten Boom, E. Geudeke, H.L.Ph. Leeuwenberg, P.H.A.M. Abels, Eds., *Utrechters Entre-Deux: Stad en Sticht in de Eeuw van de Reformatie, 1520-1620* (Delft, The Netherlands: Eburon, 1992), pp. 21-42.

13. Details concerning this Zwolle edition are in The Weimar edition of Luther's works (Weimar: Bohlaus, 1910), vol. X, part 2, 312.

14. "*Rector autem domus clericorum in Traiecto* (Utrecht), *D. Johannes Roy, propter Luterum depositus est.*" This portion of the *Doesburg Chronicle* is published in *Kerkhistorisch Archief*, III (1862), 108-115. It is reprinted in *CDI*, IV, 162.

15. "Rode," *Realencyklopädie*, XVII, 65.

16. *Ibid.*, XVII, 65. *"kam ein fremder man zu mir, Johannes Rhodius. . . . Dieser Rhodius war mein gast* (autumn 1524)."

17. *Ibid.*, XVII, 65.

18. J. A. Toorenenbergen, "Hinne Rode (John Rhodius), rector van de Hieronymusschool te Utrecht (? -1522), predikant te Norden (? -1530), in betrekking tot de Anabaptisten." *Archief van Nederlandsche Kerkgeschiedenis,* III (1889), 90-101. This suggestion is on pp. 99-100.

19. H. J. Royards, "Proeve eener Geschiedenis der Hervorming in de Stad en province Utrecht," *Archief voor Kerkgeschiedenis*, XVI, (1845), 360-363.

20. "Rode," *Realencyklopädie*, XVII, 67.

21. De Hoop Scheffer, *Geskiedenis*, pp. 317-318. He summarized information from the record of Schoockius.

22. De Hoop Scheffer, *Ibid.*, pp. 317-318.

23. De Hoop Scheffer, *Geskiedenis*, p. 81.

24. *CDI*, V, 10.

25. *CDI*, V, 88.

26. De Hoop Scheffer, *Geskiedenis*, p. 391.

27. *CDI*, V, 77.

28. *CDI*, V, 267.

29. De Hoop Scheffer, *Geskiedenis*, p. 570.

30. *CDI*, IV, 85-86.

31. *Gedenkschriften van Jhr. Herberen van Mijnden*, as printed in *CDI*, IV, 85.

32. De Hoop Scheffer, *Geskiedenis*, p. 325.

33. *Gedenkschriften van Jhr. Herberen van Mijnden*, as printed in *CDI*, IV, 86.

34. *CDI*, IV, 86-87. These nine theological principles are translated in Appendix II of this study.

35. De Hoop Scheffer, *Geskiedenis*, p. 323-324.

36. Reported by Schoockius, as printed in *CDI*, IV, 19.

37. J. G. de Hoop Scheffer, *Geschiedenis der Kerkhervorming in Nederland van haar onstaan tot 1531*. Amsterdam: G. L. Funke, 1873; p. 83. De Hoop Scheffer is dependent on the one source of Schoockius as printed in *CDI*, IV, 19. The section is translated in Cornelius Krahn, *Dutch Anabaptism: Origin, Spread, Life and Thought* (1450-1600) (The Hague: Martinus Nijhoff, 1968); p. 57. See also "Wouter" in *Nieuw Nederlandsch Biografisch Woordenboek*, ed. L. Knappert and P. J. Blok (Leiden: A. W. Sijthoff's Uitgevers, 1921), vol V, 1147.

38. These names are listed in the source from Schoockius, as printed in *CDI*, IV, 19.

39. Schoockius, *Liber de bonis vulgo ecclesiasticis dictis* (Groningen, 1651); as printed in *CDI*, IV, 19. Schoockius related some details about Sartorius: "*qui Delphis per Gualterum se primum veritatis gustum percepisse alibi fatetur.*" Four other brief references to this man have been used in this study.

    1. N. van der Zijpp, "Sartorius," *Mennonite Encyclopedia* (4 vols., Scottdale, Pennsylvania: The Mennonite Publishing House, 1959), IV, 424f.

    2. Alastair Duke, "Sartorius," *Oxford Encyclopedia of theReformation*, ed.Hans J. Hillerbrand (4 vols., New York: Oxford University Press, 1996), III, 484-485.

    3. The most extensive, Johannes Trapman, "Johannes Sartorius (*ca.* 1500-1557) *Gymnasiarch te Amsterdam en Noordwijk, als Erasmiaan en Spiritualist*," *Nederlandsche Archief voor Kerkgeschiedenis*, 70 (1990), 30-51. The author kindly provided me with a copy of this article.

    4. A sketch of the life and influence of Sartorius is also found in Bastian Jan Spruyt, *Cornelius Henrici Hoen (Honius) and his Epistle on the Eucharist* (1525) (Houten, The Netherlands: 1996), pp. 93-94.

40. *CDI*, V, 10.

41. Frederick Canirivus (Hondebeke), was rector of the school in Delft (see later in this chapter); Wilhelmus Gnapheus was rector in The Hague (See Chapter 11 of this study); Jan de Bakker was the priest of the nearby town of Woerden who was burned to death 15 September, 1525 (See chapter 10 of this study).

42. Noord-wijk in the Dutch translates as "North District." Likewise, the Latin term *Aquilo-vicanus* translates *aquilo*= "north", *vicanus*="villager."

43. Van der Zijpp, in *Mennonite Encyclopedia*, IV, 423.

44. This drama is analyzed in Chapter 11 in connection with its author, Guilhelmus Gnapheus.

45. The extensive and thorough summary of these publications appears in Trapman's article, pp. 38-48.

46. Trapman argues that Sartorius was familiar with some of the works of the German Spiritualist reformer, Sebastian Franck (1499-1543), a writer otherwise unknown in The Netherlands in this period.

47. The name of "Sartorius" appears in the *Index of Prohibited Books* of 1559, indicating that all writings are prohibited. Unfortunately, individual titles are not listed.

48. Otto Clemen, "Honius," in *Realencyklopädie*, VIII, 312-313.

49. *CWE*, X, # 1358, 17 April, 1523, Erasmus in Basel to Pierre Barbier, chaplain to pope Adrian VI.

50. Otto Clemen, "Hinne Rode in Wittenberg, Basel, Zürich und die frühesten Ausgaben Wesslescher Schriften," *Zeitschrift für Kirchengeschichte*, 18 (1898), 346-373.

51. *CDI*, IV, 181.

52. *CDI*, IV, 237.

53. De Hoop Scheffer, *Geschiedenis*. . . . p. 538.

54. A brief mention of Hondebeke is included in Bastian J. Spruyt, *Cornelius Henrici Hoen (Honius) and his epistle on the Eucharist (1525)* (Houten, The Netherlands: 1996), pp. 90-92.

55. *CDI*, IV, 115. Dated before 29 April, 1522.

56. De Hoop Scheffer, *Geschiedenis*. . . . p. 84.

57. His letter to Hedio, *CDI*, IV, 115.

58. *Ibid.*, letter to Hedio.

59. *CDI*, IV, 215-216; *CDI*, V, 10.

60. There are minimal sources for a study of this individual. The materials in the last few footnotes are summarized in B. J. Spruyt's thesis *Cornelius Henrici Hoen (Honius) and his Epistle on the Eucharist* (1525) (Houten, The Netherlands: 1996), pp. 90-92, and in his later *Ketter aan het Binnenhof: Cornelis Hoen en zijn tractaat tegen de transubstantieleer* (1525) (Heerenveen: J. J. Groen en Zoon, 1997), pp. 18-19.

61. *Contemporaries of Erasmus*, "Broeckhoven," I, 204-205.

62. *Diercxsens Antwerpia*, as printed in *CDI*, IV, 83.

63. *CWE*, IX, # 1299. Erasmus wrote to Joost Lauwereyns, Councilor of Mechelen/Malines in Brabant. The letter from Basel was dated 14 July, 1522, eight months after Erasmus left Louvain/Leuven. He was regularly informed, however, of the developments in his own country.

64. G. Geldenhouwer, *Collectiana*, as printed in *CDI*, IV, 114. J. Prinsen collected many works of Gerard Geldenhouwer as *Collectiana van Gerardus Geldenhouwer Noviomagus* (Amsterdam: Johannes Müller, 1901). In this collection there are references to several scholars of the region, including Nicholaas Buscoducensis.

65. *CWE*, X, # 1431. Erasmus wrote from Basel to Guy Morillon, 15 March, 1524.

66. "Geldenhouwer," J. P. de Bie, J. Loosjes, *Biographisch Woordenboek van Protestantische Godgeleerde in Nederland* (The Hague: Martin Nijhoff, 1901-1937), III, 195-198. A doctoral thesis concerning Geldenhouwer was published as: Jacob Prinsen, *Gerardus Geldenhouwer Noviomagus: Bijdrage tot de kennis van zijn Leven en Werken* (The Hague: Martin Nijhoff, 1898).

67. "Gerard Geldenhouwer," *Contemporaries of Erasmus*, II, 82-84.

68. *CWE*, V, # 645, from Louvain/Leuven, 31 August, 1517

69. *CWE*, V, # 682, from Louvain/Leuven, 5 October, 1517.

70. *CWE*, V, # 728, from Vollenhove, the bishop's castle, 6 December, 1517.

71. *CWE*, V, # 727, # 727, 5 December, 1517.

72. *CWE*, V, # 759, 10 January, 1518, from Louvain/Leuven.

73. Olof Hendriks, "Gerardus Geldenhauwer Noviomagus (1484-1542)" in *Studia Catholica*, 31 (1956), pp. 129-139 and 176-196. This discussion is on pp. 142-144.

74. *CDI*, IV, 292-295.

75. An extensive study analyzing religious toleration of the period, especially with reference to Geldenhouwer, is Cornelis Augustijn, "Gerard Geldenhauwer und die religiöse Toleranz," *Archiv für Reformationsgeschichte*, 69 (1978), 132-156.

76. Erasmus's understanding concerning the limits of toleration are quoted from materials which Sebastian Castellio compiled in his *De Haereticis, an sint persequendi* (1554), as translated by Roland Bainton in *Concerning Heretics, whether they are to be persecuted...* (New York: Columbia University Press, 1935), p. 41.

77. A brief summary of most of the known details are included in C. G. van Leijenhorst, "Gerardus Listius," in *Contemporaries of Erasmus*, II, pp. 335-336. J. Lindeboom summarized Listrius's place in scholar pursuits in his work on Biblical Humanism: Lindeboom, *Het Biblisch Humanisme in Nederland* (Leiden: A.H. Adriani, 1913), pp. 145-152.

78. This commentary is analyzed by J. Austin Gavin and Thomas M. Walsh, "The Praise of Folly in Context: The Commentary of Gerardus Listrius," *The Renaissance Quarterly*, 24 (1971), pp. 193-209. Two years later (1973) Gavin completed his Ph. D. thesis at St. Louis University, *The Commentary of Gerardus Listrius on Erasmus' "Praise of Folly" A Critical Edition and Translation with Introduction and Commentary*.

79. *CWE*, vol. V, # 641, from Louvain/Leuven, 29 August 1517. Erasmus wrote to Joris van Halewijn, in the French portion of the Southern Netherlands: "To begin with, few people understood it [*Folly*] until Listrius added his notes; but once Folly began to talk French as well, thanks to you, she is understood even by these men who cannot understand their psalter" (lines 5-8).

80. *CWE*, IV, # 495, Listrius in Zwolle to Erasmus, end of November, 1516.

81. Bastian (Bart) J. Spruyt, "*Listrius lutherizans: His Epistola theologica adversus Dominicanos Suollenses*" (written in 1520, first published in 1733), in *Sixteenth Century Journal*, XXII, 4 (1991), 727-751. The thesis on the Commentary on "Folly" by Gavin and Walsh (1973), in which they included a listing of Listrius's writings (p. xlvi), does not mention this tract against the Dominicans.

82. This emphasis on "diversity" of approach is a major presupposition and emphasis of the article "Reformatie in meervoud," [Reformation in its plurality] by B. J. Spruyt.

Chapter 4

Lamentations of Peter,
(anonymous, written before
23 September, 1521)

Many of the foregoing leaders [in Chapter 3] were accused of being "Lutheran" when their works were questioned, although as we have seen, there was no clear understanding of what could be called "Lutheran" at this early date. Many of them were probably as much Humanist scholars as religious reformers, even perhaps more so. While surveying resources in The Netherlands a number of years ago, I happened to be talking about these ideas with the late C.C. de Bruin at the University of Leiden. He had done considerable work in this period of history and it was he who called my attention to a little-known work called *Lamentationes Petri*. He was speculating about the authorship, which is still a mystery, but I was especially interested in the content and how it might lend insight into developing religious ideas in that part of Europe.

Recently (1997) one of de Bruin's former students, J. Trapman, published a brief summary of this satire. He asserted that it is probably more in the Erasmian style of reform than that of Luther,[1] despite the fact that Luther plays a much larger place in the tract than does Erasmus. The scholarly world, especially students of religious developments within The Netherlands, would be much enriched by a modern translation and edition of this work, including annotations indicating its references to the larger Humanist/Erasmian influence.

Using the Nijhoff-Kronenberg bibliography of early printed books in the Netherlands (from the beginning of printing to 1540).[2] I located some material concerning the work. It was published, we assume, in Zwolle with neither the author's name nor publishing date. The actual date was probably 1521, but this must be deduced from internal analysis of the document itself. It was written in Latin, and I have located no evidence it has ever appeared in any other edition, nor has it been translated. The bibliography listed a copy available at the

Bibliothéque Nationale in Paris. I, therefore, arranged to have a copy sent from Paris, and have used that version in this study. In intervening years I have found that there are copies also at three German Universities.[3] The publication was placed, by title, on the *Index of Prohibited books* in 1559 and thereafter.[4]

The document is printed with no page numbers, which we take for granted in works this old. Rather, each double page is marked Ai, Aii, Aiii, Aiiii, or eight pages for the A designation. We will designate the pages with the numbers as Ai-a, and the following page without a number as Ai-b, and so on through the work. Then there are eight pages for B, eight for C and so on through H. There are thus eight letters and eight pages each totalling sixty-four pages. Finally, there are three pages in the "I" designation, for a sixty-seven-page document. The document is further organized as follows:

> Title page and one blank page: 2 pages [Ai-a and Ai-b]
> Dedication to Willem Frederiks: 6 pages [Aii-a to Aiiii-b]
> Prologue: 7 pages [Bi-a to Biiii-a]
> A paragraph concerning Luther's
>   *Assertio omnium articulorum:* 1 page [Biiii-b]
> A paragraph each for a "statement" to the reader, and a
>   summary of the argument on the top half of the first
>   page of the document: 1 page [Ci-a]
> The remainder of the text: 50 pages [Ci-a to Ii-b]
> Total: 67 pages

A clue to dating the document involves a letter which Erasmus wrote on 23 September, 1521. In that letter he stated:

> Aleander gave me to understand that two pamphlets are attributed to me, one called *Eubulus* and the other the *Lamentationes Petri*. My life upon it if I had ever heard either title before he produced them (lines 165-168).[5]

This date of 23 September 1521 is the *terminus ad quem*.

The *terminus a quo* relates to the works of Luther. On the page before the text began [Biii-b] our unknown author referred to Luther's *Assertio omnium articulorum M. Lutheri per bullam Leonis X novissimam damnatorum*, using this complete title.[6] This was one of four pamphlets which Luther wrote to defend himself against the bull, *Exsurge Domine*. In this papal bull, written in June, 1520, the authorities had extracted forty-one supposed errors from Luther's works. Luther received it on October, 20 of the same year and had sixty days to recant his errors. On 10 December, 1520, instead of recanting he publicly burned the bull along with a copy of canon law. His four defenses, including the *Assertio* formed a justification, or at least an explanation, of his actions. Our author referred especially to the last (or the forty-first) article which the bull discussed, and to which Luther reacted. Thus Luther's defenses of December,

1520 had to be known by our Netherlands author. He could have secured a copy early in 1521. This then becomes the *terminus a quo*. Based on these considerations we may assume that the *Lamentationes* was written between early 1521 and 23 September of the same year.

Preliminary Considerations

The main point to which our author referred in Luther's *Assertio* was the bull's criticism that Luther had advocated abolishing all mendicant orders. Luther had only said that he wished there were none and, as we shall see, the *Lamentationes* is extremely antagonistic toward the mendicant orders. The author wrote following his reference to Luther's *assertio*, "Whoever wishes to know more about certain problems in which the mendicants are involved, study the little work of this Esdras" [Biiii-b].

The author wrote a dedicatory letter to Willem (Guilhelm) Frederiks, one of two priests at St. Martin's church in Groningen [Aii-a to Aiiii-b]. Frederiks was evidently slightly older than Erasmus and had studied at Cologne and Ferrara.[7] He was appointed to the church in Groningen in 1485 where he remained for forty years. Evidently he had regular association with Wessel Gansfort near Groningen up until the latter's death in 1489. We know little about Frederiks or why the *Lamentationes* was dedicated to him.[8] Perhaps our author saw in Frederiks a companion in the broader theological emphases that inform his work. Frederiks was known to Erasmus since Erasmus wrote at least one letter to him.[9] Gozewin van Halen, head of the house of the Brethren of the Common Life at Groningen, had brought a gift from Frederiks to Erasmus, and Erasmus's letter expressed thanks for the gift and included praise for the devotion to spiritual concerns which Erasmus knew was a part of the community in Groningen. Erasmus praised the leader in Groningen because he was faithful to the Gospel and was concerned about furthering sacred learning. Furthermore, he praised Frederiks for collecting a library of books from the ancient church fathers and continued to be inspired by the Holy Scriptures. Erasmus concluded by commending Frederiks for taking the side of Erasmus in a dispute in Groningen (where Erasmus was criticized by two men who had not read his works). Erasmus thanked Frederiks for trying to "constrain the blockheads" [line 57]. By his tone in this letter alone Erasmus suggested that Frederiks was of a Humanistic frame of mind and purpose similar to that of Erasmus. We are left to wonder, however, about the author of *Lamentationes'* relation with Frederiks.

Indeed, it has recently been suggested that the author of the work may have been Nicholaus Lesdorpius, rector of the Latin school at Groningen, and well acquainted with all the leaders there.[10] Akkerman includes extensive argument that the rector may have been the same author for the *Lamentationes* as well as the Groningen *Disputatio*.

The dedicatory letter to Frederiks covers six pages of the document [Aii-a to Aiiii-b]. The author congratulated certain Germanic peoples who were reintroducing ancient and important authors and bringing them again to the light. In place of the worn out Aristotle, Jerome is enlightening the world. In place of the dead Plato, the apostolic heroes are joyfully returning from exile. "Everywhere songs, exultations and thanksgivings rise as one voice. . . . These things I, Esdras, announce to you noblest priest [*optime Antistes*] in my Lamentation" [Aii-a]. The author went on to note that there have of late been two major problems. First, there are those who have sought to destroy evangelical literature, their authors, and the whole apostolic influence. Second, the authority of Aristotle's writings supersedes the Apostolic faith. In both cases the high God cannot be contemplated by the people [*homine*] [Aii-a], and, consequently, God ceases to be the true subject of religious concerns.

> What value is it for theology, yes, for evangelical man [*virum*], that is to say a good Christian, to discuss material, infinity, place, motion, time, emptiness, quiddities and formalities as one hears in the contemporary academic world? One should, rather, read Paul, Peter, or John [Aii-b].

"If one should study these sources he/she would discover that neither chastity nor excessive abstinence from food would produce a religious attitude at any time" [Aiii-a]. "There is nothing which is rightly spoken in Cicero or Plato or by many other authors which was not already stated better by Moses or the prophets or in the Apostolic writings" [Aiii-a].

After discussing these problems thoroughly, he included praise for Frederiks himself,

> you champion of the fatherland, glory of Frisia,[11] instructor of the priesthood, authority of the people, understanding of the senate, hope of orphans, sanctuary of the needy, tutor of widows, honest liberator of all living" [Aiii-a to Aiii-b].

He compared Frederiks with Augustine because of his complete devotion to the people in his charge. "Indeed, what is there of good literature which arises there which is not promoted by your sincerity" [Aiiii-a]?

> I believe you will receive my *Lamentation* favorably, and if all hoods and cowls be thrown into the lake and if all persons devote themselves seriously to the scriptures, that is the apostolic way [Aiiii-b]. I urge you to free all Frisia from barbarity. Turn all Franciscans and Thomists toward the true studies, and your people as well. In the meantime Jerome will be smiling quietly. You have other distinguished persons with you; if all serious souls might be turned toward this learning I do not know what would be possible. Farewell, most erudite Priest, and those with you [Aiiii-b].

Following the dedicatory letter our author included a seven-page "Prologue" to his main work [Bi-a to Biiii-a]. He complained that people are willing to read nothing except Scotus or Aquinas. By their methods they have sought to suffocate [*offocare*] good literature. They neglect Latin literature and have even more contempt for Greek or Hebrew learning. The philosophy of Aristotle was taken to be completely true, and since Thomas Aquinas tested and compared his philosophy with that of Aristotle, it was assumed that Aquinas also did not err.

If the opponents cannot be restrained and good literature be allowed to flourish again, the author will name names and announce to the world. "Indeed, I would see Aristotle, Plato, Socrates, Demosthenes, Prophyry and other philosophers be cast into the midst of the flames" [Biii-b]. We must not overlook their impudence and inexperience, he added. The earthly should not emphasize what is not in harmony with the heavenly.

> For this purpose this Lamentation is prepared. I will relate, in the mode of a satire, all things which the heavens will proclaim. Read this our writing carefully, most erudite Pastor. Farewell, this epistle was written by my hand, for the purpose of revealing what has been hidden, for the year of new redemption, for restoring the ancient ones, for eternal good fortune [Biiii-a].

After the "Prologue" he added a short paragraph directed "To the Reader" [Ci-a]. The writer asked all the readers to scrutinize his claims. If he has overstated his case with respect to the works of Aquinas or Francis, or with reference to the monastic institutions, he retracts it. In this spirit he asks the reader to read carefully.

In a further paragraph he summarized the "Argument of the tract" [Ci-a]. The Lamentations of Peter reports to all readers that God and all sects are to be consulted with respect to the Lutheran question. He summarized the problem of the church since the origin of the monastic movements. He related how all brilliant authors are eclipsed, and prudent writings no longer merit readers. These problems are derived from the strong support for Aristotelian and Platonic writings. The Lamentations claims that evangelical sincerity and Christian liberty are in decline because of the monastic orders.

The Lamentations of Peter

The document claims to have been written by Esdras, a scribe, but this is surely a pseudonym. In addition, there were added notations by Johann Andrae, undoubtedly not an authentic name either. The *Lamentations* began:

> I Esdras, for a long time, was a scribe after the manner of a public notary of the holy ones [*sanctorum*]. Some time ago I was admonished by an oracle from above, and I brought together five men to whom God gave understanding or perception [*intellectum*]" [Ci-a].

The five men were named Saream, Sabriam, Selemiam, Echanum and Asiel, but

I have not yet discovered if they are from Greek mythology, or are fictitious for this document. At any rate, these five wrote for many nights, about things they did not understand. During forty days two hundred and four books were written.

Esdras continued, "while I was surveying this collection of works of unknown content, I reflected on Paul and Peter, in deep discussion in the midst of heaven" [Ci-a].

Now the scene shifted from the author to a conversation between the heavenly companions. Paul engaged Peter in the conversation.

"What is the situation, Peter? Do you introduce poison in your writings, or unpleasantness in your letters? Why do you not attract readers?"

Peter replied, "Why do you weary me with this unpleasantness? I am gentle, and never harsh; I set forth in my writings nothing unpleasant. In addition, my epistles themselves give evidence that in them everything is most in harmony with human nature" [Ci-a].

Paul, "You are wrong, Peter, you err. I want you to tell me why your writings do not merit or bring forth more attention."

They discussed various reasons why their writings no longer received the attention they deserve. They also noted that the writings of John do not receive adequate attention either. What illustrious writing [of John] could narrate piety more pleasing and more modestly [Cii-a]?

Peter said, "You state it correctly, Paul."

After discussing this problem further, Paul stated, "Don't you know, Peter, that the whole world gives great attention to the books of Aristotle? The extra attention to his works frustrates adequate attention to our works."

Peter replied

> You increase my astonishment. For a long time now, I have not feared to believe my God, and accept the promise from Him [Luke 21:15] 'I will give you words and a wisdom that none of your opponents will be able to withstand or contradict.' You have truly explained these promises of God to me in a very different way.

Paul concluded that John's works were really more read because he, like Aristotle, got his idea from Plato.

Peter: "He borrowed from Plato?"

Paul: "Yes, the son of Zebedee."

Peter: "I am not persuaded this is true, because since the family were fishers, the son could not have had enough time to study such philosophy."

Then Paul stated that the works of James, Matthew, Jude, Luke and Mark are also neglected. Peter remarked that it is not surprising in the case of Mark and Luke because neither was taught by Jesus in person [*non tamen e Christi ore dicere*] [Ciii-b], and their writings were given at a later time. Peter wondered, however, why the works of James, Matthew, and Jude were not valued because all of these persons knew Jesus the Christ in the flesh. Why is this so?

Paul answered, "Take James for example, he taught what was disparaging to the people, even not pleasing to them."

Peter responded, "What do you mean Paul?"

Paul replied, "I mean he taught that tribulations were important to endure when he said 'My brethren and sisters, whenever you face trials of any kind, consider it nothing but joy' (James 1:2). Matthew suggested that only those would be elevated who were the least, or the most humble. [Paul continued] For example, 'blessed are the poor in spirit' (Matt.5:3), or 'Unless you change and become like little children' (Matt. 18:3), or 'whoever wishes to be great among you must be your servant'" (Matt. 20:26). Peter's and Paul's remarks seem to be a criticism of the presumptions of the rich or the proud [Ciii-b].

To investigate further knowledge Peter called for the accused persons to come forward. There appeared John, James, Matthew, Jude, Mark and Luke. Peter then asked them, "Beloved and apostolic men, our brother Paul has said a surprising thing, namely that in all ages and among all kinds of people our writings are not often deemed worthy of reading. Is it possible that one or another of you has mixed in your writing something of poison or malice?"

After some discussion James suggested that there are orders of monks under whose pressing tyranny the church moans.

Peter: "Are they are so holy?"

James: "They are not so much holy [*sanctus*] as superstitious [*superstitiosa*]."

Peter: "What do you mean by that, good James?"

James: "The first of their rules is that they should shun all wealth, they should fall upon that which belongs to another, so far as all their laws are concerned, and whichever one of them is most outwardly observant, that one will be most effective and most holy."

Peter asked, "What kind of life is this that one should relinquish all his own wealth and beg from others?. . . . In all my life I have never heard anything so astounding" [Di-a].

The conversation continued and the group decided to see how others have dealt with the apostolic writings. They called Ambrose, Augustine, Gregory, Jerome, Chrysostom, Cyprian, Hilary and Ignatius [Di-b]. When they appeared, Luke sought their opinion.

He stated, "O true brothers [*germana*] and apostolic cohorts, I have a question concerning my writings and those of our brothers."

Ambrose: "What are you saying, Luke?"

Luke: "Apostolic brothers [*viri*], I can explain it simply. There is a new order of life which has been established whose objective is contempt for self, and with avarice and begging from others. They claim that they find their defense in my writings" [Di-b].

Ambrose: "What do you mean?"
Luke:

> They are saying that I have stated dogmatically that 'He will be most blessed who neglects his fields and all his own possessions for the sake of Christ' [Di-b]. Furthermore, they are not satisfied but report in addition that I said, 'Blessed are the mendicants, the poor.' I confess [*fateor*] these are my words, but I did not mean they should be interpreted as they are [Dii-a].

The conversation continued for several pages until the various participants, Augustine, Ambrose, Cyprian, Jerome, all convinced Luke of a different interpretation.

Luke finally asserted

> [*Coram Deo*, and *Coram terra*] Before God and earth I really meant 'blessed are the poor *in spirit*,' humble and modest souls, those who want piety with respect to the supreme God and those with inclinations toward moderation; I did not mean unrestrained and uncontrolled begging and weak or lax preaching [Diii-a].

Then Luke continued, "Let me ask you, Jerome, why are your writings or at least those of Ambrose not widely known among the people. Is it because they are lay persons?"

Jerome:

> It is not because they are lay, but because they are simple [*rustica*] and not erudite [*inerudita*]. . . .In fact, my works would already be almost totally cut asunder if it were not for my Erasmus who saved me from destruction. This is the case with Ambrose and Augustine and other renowned writers [Diiii-a].

Luke: "Are there really those who have not read Peter or Paul or James" [Diiii-a]?

Jerome: "There are."

Luke: "Again, I ask, are they lay persons or clergy?"

Jerome: "They are clergy because they have been consecrated by the holy papal office, and consecrated as ministers of the sacraments" [Diiii-a].

Luke: "Even if they administer the sacraments of Christ, I do not believe the people are so entirely simple that they would not be influenced by good literature."

Jerome: "They know literature, but I do not know if it is good."

Luke: "If they have literature, why do they not have good literature?"

Jerome: "Because authors of good literature were thrown out altogether a long time ago. To be sure this is why Peter is complaining, why Paul laments, and why John is weeping" [Diiii-a].

Luke: "I am stunned [*stupeo*], Jerome, by what you say."

Jerome:

> This astonishes [*stupes*] you, good Luke? More to be wondered at is what is bound to it. Among many ways of life there is one new group, however, which emulates the birth and the infancy of the church, and in their lives they bring together what you, Luke, have commended in your writings. They call themselves the Brethren of the Common Life [Diiii-b].

Then they discussed the shortcomings of various mendicant orders.

> There are four factions living a similar mendicant life. The FIRST are the followers of Saint Dominic. They have many writings, and it is difficult to suggest others. Most important among these is Thomas who produced so many tracts that our own writings are no longer read often [Ei-a].

The SECOND are the minorites who follow the most saintly and most worthy Francis [Eii-a]. Their main writers include Bonaventure, and they accept no other opinions. They have departed from the ideals of poverty of the founder of the order. The THIRD sect, the Augustinians, have nothing in common with their founder [Eiii-a]. The FOURTH group,

> the Carmelites, are those who took their name from Mount Carmel. They falsely claim that their teaching is ancient and based on the teachings of the great and distinguished Basil the Great (430-479) [Eiii-a].

They observed that the four mendicant orders have control over all our destiny. "These four factions have divided the total world into certain areas for themselves, and there is no part so rich or poor which they do not control, even to the shores of the oceans" [Eiii-b].

The heavenly participants then discussed how they can break the hold of these orders. Paul concluded: "We must try to win someone from one of the parties over to our side and incite his opposition to his associates, one who is a well-recognized leader in his group" [Fiii-b]. ·

Then Augustine spoke up:

> There is one in the sect which falsely claims me as the founder, Martin Luther by name. This person embraces the order, that is the Augustinian, in the right spirit [Fiii-b]. . . .He interpreted Ambrose and Jerome and Gregory well [*integre*]. Furthermore, he has for a long time cried a torrent of tears concerning the lack of devotion of his people. . . . As an erudite leader among his followers he is certainly of first rank. In addition, he brings a life of clarity, of integrity and of blameless character" [Fiiii-a].

The apostolic group quickly decided that Jerome and Augustine should go to a certain town, Wittenberg, to talk with Luther. Rapidly they made their way to the designated city. Luther was asleep.

Jerome called him: "Martin, Martin."

Luther: "Here I am, who asks for me?"

Jerome: "Martin, don't you know me?"

Luther: "There is really no way that I could know you."

Jerome: "Martin, look, I am your Jerome, whose codices you held back and hid in your room, whose books you secretly and eagerly examine."

Luther: "If you are Jerome, then whom do you have with you?"

Jerome: "This is the bishop of Hippo, Aurelius Augustine, whose works you know well."

Luther wondered if he had died, and said in reply: "Great and true apostolic men (if I may be allowed to call you that) it is very beneficial to me that you visit here. If I deserved death, then I do not fear death."

Jerome continued:

> Oh, don't concern yourself, Luther, with those who oppose you and cry out against you. While you were secretly scrutinizing our codices, you were doing nothing bad. You stood absolutely for the most agreeable way with respect to the apostolic message. Do not fear, good Luther. All the heavens [or Gods, *dei*] and the company of Peter and Paul owe a debt to you, the man to whom [renewal of] erudition and the purity of Augustine is principally attributed [Fiiii-b].

Martin: "See! I thank God because he heard your concerns."

Jerome explained:

> All people in these groups have already made it known that the privileges of the mendicants are to be praised, and a chorus of the saints applauded loudly. At the same time, however, all authors who were both evangelical and apostolic were met with hostility, and by no means moderately. On account of the wickedness of their impiety they [mendicants] rejected all good literature from the whole region, and these same persons determined that no authority should be attributed to either Peter or Paul.

Martin: "I know what you say, Jerome, for the injustices to your communities torture my soul, and by no means moderately."

Jerome: "Our delegation makes a request that you may restore to us what they have taken away."

Martin Luther then gave his explanation:

> I hardly know where to begin. The evil is directed not only toward these men of ours, but rather in the whole world good literature is rejected; it is clear that they reject these authors. It is most rare, indeed, in such a case that your works, Jerome, or certainly yours, Augustine, would be considered worthy to be read. These injustices to you have been increasing for 300 years. I assume these

monastic orders were constituted with pure motives, but they acquired unworthy tendencies toward you and for these three hundred years they have been on the attack. I don't know how they will be able easily to pull back. I do know where I experience the situation—totally in my own person. As a gang [*agmine*] they shout at me, and they brand me with charges of heresy and wish me a thousand deaths. They have many scholastic disputations and sophisticated arguments in which they assault me. They bring up various philosophical summaries [*summi*], codices of their God Aristotle, which accuse me of rejecting the tradition. Above all they have laws, and have collected monstrous canons which support themselves and discredit me [Fiiii-b].

Jerome said that Peter, Paul, Cyprian, Hilary, Ambrose and Gregory are all fully prepared to support Luther if he would write evangelical literature.

Luther acknowledged their encouragement with some hesitation. "I accept that which you urge upon me; but you may have given me gifts related to death, for I will have enemies" [Gi-a].

Jerome did not take him seriously. "Now, first you should study to have the life of integrity and through proven means to mold the apostolic man. Then, at a later time, shake up the whole world with violence" [Gi-a].

Luther: "What should I emphasize first?"

Jerome made a suggestion:

Evangelical Liberty for the Christian people, and release them from the weight of all canon law. As a herald you will cry out for a new kind of salvation; the Christians of the whole world have long been pressing for such a settlement. They want release also from the uneducated scholastic arguments and from other things required by the mendicants' institutions [Gi-b].

Jerome spoke of such things as "tyranny" and said further:

reject all summaries, and little lists with respect to the Christian life which have as many tortures as they have pages. . . . The Christian life is not formed by these writings of the Thomists or the Franciscans which are needed for maintaining their institutions, but the Christian life is formed by the apostolic literature [Gi-b].

They discussed a long list of writings which should be burned. The collection was long and included many well-known persons and their writings, many lesser-known and even unknown writers. The writers fell into three categories: Thomists, Franciscans, and Carmelites. Among the Thomists was "all the Philosophy of Thomas Aquinas, most pernicious for the church" [all these are listed on pages Giiii-a and Giiii-b]. Also included was the well-known Albertus Magnus [1200?-1280], along with eight others who are obscure. "Writings of these and obscure authors of the Dominican family should be thrust out [*exige*]."

Among the Franciscans the author listed Alexander of Hales [ca. 1185-1245]; Bonaventure [1217?-1274]; Duns Scotus [1265-1308], "to be totally burned [totus exuratur]"; and William of Occam [ca 1280-1349], especially his sentences and his quodlibet. There are eight more names of obscure writers. "These and however many others known to be of this sect, must be totally destroyed [prorsus abjicito] [Giiii-a]." Following these Jerome listed eight names under the category of "Carmelites." In addition, "All books of Aristotle and his doctrines with their authors are to be rejected [abjiciat] [Giiii-b]."

Jerome: "None of these many writings [summulis] can be attributed to faith. . . . Now if you wish all errors of the church to be corrected, all these summaries [summulas] must be committed to the flames and burned up" [Hiii-b]. Jerome suggested that Luther was the one to lead in this project of burning.

Luther said he was surprised that such a task was assigned to him. Weren't there many others, well-educated men to whom you might delegate this task? What about Erasmus, erudite and enjoying high respect in the Christian world?

Jerome:

> When it comes to bringing monks back to the truth you are better prepared. You know their tricks and craftiness [astum]. Let nothing dissuade you from complying with our request, because it is time that we should return to him [eum] who sent us [presumably to return to the heavenly realm] [Hiiii-a].

Martin: "Behold, place my hands in fire! I know that for my own good I would hesitate. . . .I fear the authority of the supreme pope [summi pontificis]."
Jerome: "What do you mean?"
Luther tried to explain the seriousness of the contemporary situation:

> The Roman called Pope whose word is truth, whose authority is gospel. He pressures me with authority. He has a good number of assistants or informants, those are my mendicant brothers. You see we have these most dangerous or aggressive ones [infestissimos]. These will be on guard with the God of this our world, the pope. There is no moderation in the situation, Jerome.

Jerome tried to understand Luther's concerns, though reflecting on an earlier age:

> What is this God of this world? I do not know the man. There was in my day Damasus [366-383], there was Liberius [352-366] but they were only Roman bishops. The eastern churches had their own authorities. I know of no Roman pretenders who ruled in the east. Carthage had Cyprian who wrote many letters to Cornelius [251-253], the bishop of Rome. Cyprian called him 'brother' not 'pope' [Hiiii-a].

Luther: "You speak well, Jerome. Do you mean then that all bishops had the same authority and the same power?"
Jerome:

Not exactly. Compare yourself with your prior. You both have consecration, but in certain ways your authorities differ. . . . Thus all the apostles shared one power, but Peter had greater authority. Christ gave nothing to Peter that he did not give to all. Truly they were united around Peter their head. It makes no difference in the church if the Roman pope is more revered, or if he is the successor of Peter himself, or if he is elected to a more famous seat, and if he is consecrated as prince of the apostles, you esteem his power differently, but no greater than any other [Hiiii-b].

Luther: "Yet I *do* fear the pope" [Ii-a].
Jerome: "Who is this Roman pope today?"
Luther: "He is called Leo."
Jerome seemed not to understand:

Yes I know him. You will have nothing to fear from him. He is a man most gracious who having heard your opinions will support you candidly and openly. He will oppose you in no way, he will do nothing which is against the evangelical writings [Ii-a]. . . . Hereafter, do nothing about changing the great ones of the earth, or even the pope. This, as I said, will happen easily. Be governed by the example of the first Christians [Ii-b].

Luther: "I beseech you earnestly, tell me what path to follow."
Jerome:

The pope, clerks, and whatever groups of nobles or common people, of whatever condition, rich and poor in the same group, wherever these see the Christian life which you exemplify, they will turn away from the institutions which they do not find abounding in piety, where spiritual nourishment and Christian hospitality are not in evidence. The exception will be the mendicants who persist in their own insane opinions [Ii-b].

Jerome then concluded with one final warning and encouragement. The Thomists will undoubtedly continue to attack, and in fact, are doing so now in the person of Thomas Radini of Placentinus [Piacenza, north Italy].[12]

One like this incites to battle, he is not erudite but tends to audacity and impudence [*procax*]. You must condemn such shameless men, and agitate them thoroughly with your reproach. After all, he is seeking fame while you are seeking glory! Whoever disapproves of what you are doing negates the gospel of Christ. You should further this theology of the cross [*crucis theologiam*] as Paul did, and as a public crier [*preco*] announce it to the whole world. Such was always the situation of the church which through the cross, through persecution, through denunciations always reflected more gloriously [Ii-b].

Here the discussion ended.

The Context of this Writing

While Erasmus did not mention this document until September 1521, it seems probable that it may have been written several months before. The author made no reference to the Diet of Worms where Luther appeared in April (1521), nor did he refer to Luther's subsequent stay at the Wartburg (May, 1521-March, 1522). Surely these situations would have convinced the author that the Luther question was being drawn into a sphere larger than that of a quarrel among stubborn mendicants. By that time Luther would have had more than the pope to fear.

The author reflected the humanist concern for returning to the devotion of the early church, its literature and the early church fathers. He naively thought that if Luther would continue his evangelical writing that the "powers that be" in the church would see their errors, and as a consequence, minimize the stifling influence of the medicants on evangelical learning. Indeed, even Luther may have believed this at first. This document evidently reflected the impression of many within the humanist movement, at least in The Netherlands at this time. If we are surprised at what the author concluded, perhaps we should not be overly critical of his naiveté. We must consider the viewpoint which seemed possible for him.

Since the author wrote early in 1521 it is possible that he knew or could remember Luther's recent major writings: *Address to the Christian Nobility of the German Nation* (August, 1520); *The Babylonian Captivity of the Church* (October, 1520); *Freedom of the Christian Man* (November, 1520); and the burning of the papal bull *Exsurge Domine* (December, 1520). Yet, the author seems to reflect none of the major ideas of Luther contained in these documents of 1520 nor the content of the Papal Bull. The author likewise did not reflect a knowledge of the bull of excommunication against Luther (*Decet Romanum Pontificem,* 3 January, 1521), the outcome of the Diet of Worms (April/May, 1521), the Edict of Worms (Luther's being banned by the empire, 6 May, 1521). Indeed, by then the world had become more complicated than the world of the *Lamentationes.*

Two years after the writing of the Lamentations, hence two years after its dedication to Willem Frederiks of Groningen, a theological disputation [*Religionsgespräch*] was held in Groningen, 12 March, 1523. Willem Frederiks was involved in the discussion between several humanist scholars and leaders of the Dominican order in Groningen. Earlier scholarship has presumed that this was an early evidence of Reformation ideas in the northern part of The Netherlands.[13] Since Willem Frederiks was a leader or even organizer of the discussion, it was assumed that he was sympathetic to the reforming arguments.

More recent scholarship, however, has discovered that the content of this discussion pitted scholastic arguments of the late Middle Ages against Humanist scholarship. The discussion reflected none of the major Lutheran doctrines which were becoming well known by this time. This discussion was analyzed by R. R. Post.[14] He produced conclusive evidence to support his assertions. His conclusions were substantiated a few years later in a doctoral thesis at the University of Nijmegen in The Netherlands by Petrus Franciscus Wolfs, O. P., who provided a comprehensive and convincing argument that the discussion was really a Humanist/Scholastic academic exercise.[15] As a part of his analysis of the context [*Umwelt*] of the Groningen discussion, Wolfs analyzed the *Lamentationes* along with other contemporary Humanist scholarship.[16] Both Post and Wolfs denied that the discussion had any relation to early Reformation doctrines, an assertion more recently affirmed by F. Akkerman[17] who suggested that these discussions were of a general religious nature, not specifically in relation to any doctrine advocated by Luther.

While the discussion in 1523 does not imply that Frederiks was a proponent of the Reformation in Groningen, it nevertheless confirms the suggestion that he was a supporter of good literature, humanist learning, and accurate textual analysis. For these attributes Erasmus was undoubtedly correct in praising him for his scholarly activities in this northern area. For the same reasons the author of the *Lamentationes Petri* recognized Frederiks as an ally in their common cause for rejuvenating Humanist learning and scholarship.

Notes for Chapter 4

1. J. Trapman, "Erasmianism in the Early Reformation in The Netherlands," in M.E.H.N. Mout, H. Smolinsky and J. Trapman, eds., *Erasmianism: Idea and Reality* (Amsterdam, Oxford, New York, Tokyo: Koninklijke Nederlandse Akademie van Weten-schappen Verhandeling, Niew Reeks, deel 174, Colloquium held 1997, published 1997), pp. 169-176. See especially pp. 173-175.

2. Wouter Nijhoff and M.E. Kronenberg, *Nederlandsche Bibliographie van 1500 tot 1540*, vols. 1-3, (The Hague, 1923-1966) [referred to as *NK*]. The entry concerning the *Lamentationes Petri* is # 2985 [*i.e.* NK 2985]. The document was last analyzed extensively by Otto Clemen, "Die Lamentationes Petri," *Zeitschrift für Kirchengeschichte*, XIX (1899), pp. 431-448.

3. In Hamburg, Wolfenbüttel, and Zwickau. In the latter library the *Lamentationes* is bound with several other contemporary works, including some by Wessel Gansfort. From this library, thanks to their librarian, Herr L. Mahnke, I have been able to secure a second copy of the section on the Lamentations. I was informed that the copy in Wolfenbüttel

was "*zu eng gebunden*" so that duplication was impossible without damaging the binding or losing extensive parts of the text.

4. *Index Librorum Prohibitorum, Romae: Ex Officina Salviam*, February 1559. Listed alphabetically: *Lamentationes Petri, auctore Esdra* [under the heading *Incertorum auctor libri prohibiti*], no page numbers.

5. *CWE*, Vol. VIII, Letter # 1236, 23 September, 1521 (Toronto: University of Toronto Press, 1988), pp. 307f.

6. *LW, Career of the Reformer II*, vol. 32. (Philadelphia: Fortress Press, 1958), p. 98ff.

7. "Willem Frederiks," in *Contemporaries of Erasmus*, 3 vols., (Toronto: University of Toronto Press, 1985-1987), II, 56.

8. One doctoral thesis gave some information concerning this man and his work. Willem Zuidema, *Wilhelm Frederici, persona van Sint-Marten te Groningen* (1489-1525), *en de Groninger staatkunde van zijn tijd:* (University of Groningen, 1888).

9. *CWE*, VIII, # 1200, from Louvain, 30 April, 1521, 199-200.

10. F. Akkerman, "The Early Reformation in Groningen. On Two Latin Disputations," in F. Akkerman, A. J. Vanderjagt, A. H. van der Laan. *Northern Humanism in European Context, 1469-1625* (Leiden, Boston, Cologne: Brill, 1999), pp. 1-42, especially pp. 12-13.

11. He used "Frisia" as a general designation, common at the time, to refer to the northern Netherlands. In later years, however, Friesland and Groningen were divided to become two different provinces.

12. Thomaso Radini Tedeschi (d. 1527), a Dominican originally from Germany, but lately of Piacenza (north Italy), and closely associated with the Vatican. In 1520 he published an attack on Luther because the latter had rejected scholasticism. The next year Melanchthon wrote a reply to Radini outlining a thorough summary of Protestant principles. *Contemporaries of Erasmus*, III, p. 131.

13. For example, J. G. de Hoop Scheffer, *Geschiedenis der Kerkhervorming in Nederland van haar ontstaan tot 1531* (Amsterdam: G. L. Funke, 1873), pp. 283-309.

14. R. R. Post, *"Het Groningsche Godsdienstgesprek van 1523," Studia Catholica*, XX (1944), 113-124.

15. Petrus Franciscus Wolfs, O.P., *Das Groninger "Religionsgespräch" (1523) und seiner Hintergründe,"* (a thesis presented in July, 1959 and published at Centrale Drukkerij, Nijmegen), 1959.

16. Wolfs, Thesis, *Ibid.*, pp. 40-41.

17. F. Akkerman, "The Early Reformation in Groningen. On two Latin disputations." Note especially pp. 2-5.

Chapter 5

A New Interpretation of the Eucharist

The understanding of the Eucharist had been a major point of dissent and contention throughout the Late Middle Ages. There were many who objected to, or flatly denied, the assumptions concerning *transubstantiation* which was made a dogma during the IV Lateran Council (1215). The controversy was well known in The Netherlands during the 15th century, although there was not a clearly developed alternative theory or understanding. In the earliest period of reforms immediately following Luther's emergence a new understanding was developed within the circle of Humanist scholars in The Netherlands. The brief letter "A Most Christian Letter" which contained this new analysis was probably written, or at least compiled, by Cornelius Hoen. The letter was published in 1525 by Zwingli, although anonymously. There remain questions about its sources, its relation to other scholars of the period, and many details of how it came to Zwingli's attention.

An often-repeated, but now questionable, explanation suggested that Hoen came upon some of the theological writings of Wessel Gansfort (1420-1489), including a treatise on the Eucharist. It had been suggested that Hoen modified the basic assumptions of the document on the Eucharist and arranged to have several works of Gansfort, as well as his own letter on the Eucharist, carried to Luther and Zwingli. As the story goes, Luther accepted many of the ideas of Gansfort, and, indeed, arranged for their publication. Luther rejected, however, the ideas in Hoen's document on the Eucharist. Yet when Zwingli read Hoen's letter a few years later he accepted the propositions apparently clarifying ideas that Zwingli had been struggling with for quite some time.

Before we can affirm this construction of historical developments as an accurate story we must look at several related parts of this theological puzzle. Important questions need to be asked: What place did Wessel Gansfort and his thought play in this period? How did this set of ideas affect Luther? How did Zwingli use these newly-discovered ideas? What are the contents of Hoen's document, and what are the major emphases of Gansfort's document on the Eucharist? Perhaps crucial to all the above is an analysis of the sources for these ideas, and how they were incorporated into Late Medieval as well as Reformation theology.

Wessel Gansfort (1420-1489)

An interesting example of the relation between the theology of the Late Middle Ages and the earliest dissent had its complicated origin in The Netherlands. It concerns Wessel Gansfort (1420-1489), a theologian who studied and taught at many places in Europe, including Paris and Heidelberg. Toward the end of his life he returned to his home in the northern Netherlands at Groningen. He was closely associated with schools of the Brethren of the Common Life, and there are suggestions that he may have had contacts with Thomas à Kempis in this part of the Netherlands shortly before Thomas died in 1471. He wrote many more works than are now extant, because after Gansfort died some of his papers were destroyed by hostile groups, while others were hidden and preserved.

Wessel Gansfort indeed has been called a "Reformer before the Reformation."[1] This terminology of a previous era presupposes that there was a sharp break between the Reformation and all that went before. Consequently, so the assumptions continue, since he wrote about some of the same ideas which would be analyzed again by one or more of the figures in the Reformation period, he was thus a "reformer" before there as a Reformation. It is more accurate now to think that the Late Middle Ages and the Reformation periods were actually part of a continuum.

The problem of the "Forerunner" of the Reformation, as indicated above, was thoroughly analyzed by Heiko A. Oberman[2] where he argued for continuity on many theological fronts. One argument against the earlier "forerunner" concept is that the idea arose in Protestant circles and was arbitrarily applied to earlier periods in an artificial or dogmatic, hence misleading way. A related and second argument is that the superficial use of the "forerunner" fails to let the concepts arise out of their own context, and rather presupposes an evaluation from a context several decades in the future.

Cornelis Hoen (d. 1524) and Hinne (Johannes) Rode (d. ca. 1535)

Having noted these qualifications and cautions, we can proceed to an analysis of how the series of writings by Wessel Gansfort in the middle of the 15th century may have informed the developing Reformation in the 16th century, more than thirty years after his death. According to a long-established tradition, some of Gansfort's writings were discovered in Jacob Hoeck's library near The Hague. Jacob Hoeck (d. 11 November, 1509) had been Canon and Deacon in Naaldewijk and Priest at Wassenaar—two villages near The Hague. The library had been entrusted to Martin Dorp, Hoeck's nephew, who had been professor of Theology at

Leuven/Louvain since 1504. Dorp invited Cornelius Hoen, a Humanist lawyer and his former classmate at the Hieronymus School in Utrecht, to help evaluate the papers with him (See Chapter 3).

The earliest biography of Gansfort was by Albert Hardenberg, written in the 1560s, more than 70 years after Gansfort's death. He stated that among the tracts in Jacob Hoeck's collection there were some writings of Gansfort and some from other sources. As they were analyzing the writings, Hoen

> found an old treatise on the Lord's supper, which seemed to condemn the crude, Capernaitic eating of Christ's body and to establish it as a spiritual act, true indeed and essential, but only perceptible and appropriate to faith. . . . [Hardenberg then qualified his comments, not confirming or denying that this treatise was by Gansfort] I have heard that this manuscript of Hoeck's was exceedingly old, having been circulated among pious men and transmitted from one to another for more than two hundred years.[3]

We have no idea what source Hardenberg may have used to construct this story. Consequently, while some of the details may reflect reality, probably other details are not trustworthy. Complications arise, however, since we are not certain if the "old" document was not perhaps another writing on the Eucharist which Hoen may have used—not Gansfort's at all. This ambiguity continues, because in the collection there is extant an authentic document by Wessel Gansfort on the Eucharist ("Concerning the Blessed Sacrament of the Eucharist; and the hearing of the Mass"), which will be analyzed below. It has not generally been recognized that we may be dealing with two different documents on the Eucharist, both of which were in Jacob Hoeck's library, but if this is true, we should not be surprised that their contents differ in many ways.

When Gansfort's works were gathered together six of the writings became known as the *Farrago* (*i.e.,* a miscellaneous assortment).[4] In addition, in the collection there was a seventh, the authentic tract of Gansfort on the Eucharist. Hoen recognized the importance of these documents and decided to send them to Martin Luther for his evaluation, and perhaps so they could receive wider exposure in the religious world. Furthermore, as the story goes, Hoen was so impressed with some ideas he found in these theological documents that he decided to write his own tract, *Epistola christiana admodum* [A Most Christian Letter]. This tract on the Supper of the Lord by Hoen was undoubtedly in the collection which was sent to Luther. Because of its inclusion in the collection sent to Luther, it has often been assumed that Hoen's tract reflected the ideas of Gansfort on the Eucharist. As we shall see below, this assumption undoubtedly is not correct.

Luther's reaction to the theological works he received from The Netherlands

Since Hoen was elderly, he arranged for Hinne (Johannes) Rode, teacher of the Latin School in Utrecht, to take the documents to Luther.[5] Evidently Rode arrived in Wittenberg shortly before Luther left for the Diet of Worms (2 April, 1521). Included in the works which were taken to Luther were the Farrago consisting of six writings: Providence of God, Incarnation, Ecclesiastical Dignity and Power, Sacrament of Penance, Communion of the Saints, and Purgatory. In addition, there were copies of Gansfort's and Hoen's tracts on the Eucharist.

How thoroughly Luther studied the documents we do not know. At the first reading he seemed impressed with the tracts of Gansfort, perhaps feeling an affinity with the mystic or spiritual overtones of Gansfort's writings as well. In fact, soon after he arrived back in Wittenberg, after his ten-month stay in the Wartburg Castle, he arranged for publication of *The Farrago* at Wittenberg (1522).[6] Probably without analyzing the works thoroughly, Luther wrote a preface praising them:

> Word comes to me that the Lord has saved a remnant even at this time, and that his prophets are safe in hiding. This is not only told me, but to my joy it is proven to me. Behold! a Wessel has appeared, whom they call Basil, a Frisian from Groningen, a man of remarkable ability and of rare and great spirit; and it is evident that he has been truly taught of the Lord, even as Isaiah (54:13) prophesied the Christians would be. No one could think that he received these doctrines from men, any more than I mine. If I had read his works earlier, my enemies might think that Luther had absorbed everything from Wessel, his spirit is so in accord with mine. . . . I wonder, however, what ill fortune has prevented this most Christian author from being widely read.[7]

Luther's quick reading of these tracts surely reminded him of theological concepts which were uppermost in his mind. To suggest, however, that they were of the same spirit is rather an exaggeration, since some of Luther's ideas would ultimately differ significantly from those of Gansfort.

Wessel Gansfort had many theological opponents during the last decades of his life, and indeed, upon his death in 1489 many of his writings were burned. In addition to the collection Luther had printed there are three more extant works, all untranslated: 1) A "Tract concerning prayer and the mode for praying" (192 pages in the Latin *Opera*),[8] 2) "The Ladder [*scala*] of Meditation" (220 pages in the Latin *Opera* dedicated to the brothers of St. Agnietenberg at Zwolle, the monastery in which Thomas à Kempis lived until his death in 1471), and 3) "Concerning reasons [*causis*] of the incarnation and the magnitude and bitterness [*amaritudine*] of the Passion of the Lord" (241 pages in the Latin *Opera*). All works of Wessel Gansfort were placed on the *Index of Prohibited Books* in the next century. All page numbers in the following section refer to the collection in the Miller/Scudder

English translation.[9]

The six documents, briefly summarized, are 1) "Concerning the sure and benign Providence of God which operates in and graciously orders all things" (consisting of 33 pages). Gansfort exemplified his nominalist understanding by insisting that God is always active; nothing happens by chance or by automatic outcome. "Truly it is not by natural causes that anything exists, but by the will of God" (p. 80).

2) "Concerning the Cause, mysteries and effects of the Incarnation and Passion of our Lord" (consisting of 41 pages).

> When we meditate on the suffering and death of Christ, and when these become our own, we are no longer observers, but participators. After knowing of the life of Christ and having appropriated it for ourselves, we must *imitate the life of Christ* [italics mine].

3) "Concerning Ecclesiastical Dignity and Power. The true and right obedience, and how far those who are subject to prelates are bound by their mandates and statutes" (consisting of 35 pages).

> Although it may be assumed that the pope and prelates, in view of the high station of dignity to which they have been raised, walk in the truth of the gospel more nearly than all others, and that therefore, other things being equal, they should be believed rather than any of those subject to them, nevertheless their subjects are not bound to believe them without reserve (p. 151). . . . Indeed, the life of the just would be greatly imperiled if it depended upon the life of the pope, for many of the highest pontiffs have erred harmfully (p. 152).

4) "Concerning the Sacrament of Penance; and what the Keys of the Church are; Concerning the power of binding and loosing" (consisting of 31 pages).

> What is this key of the Kingdom of Heaven? . . . The key, as Augustine explains, is love diffused through the Holy spirit in the hearts of the children of the Kingdom. . . . He defines the keys of the Kingdom as being: 1) love diffused through the Holy Spirit in the hearts of the children of God, and 2) the Holy Spirit (p. 188).

5) "Concerning the Communion of Saints" (consisting of 25 pages).
Gansfort asserted that true believers are a part of the Communion of Saints, no matter where they live, or if they live under unworthy or feuding prelates. The unity under one pope is not necessary, merely accidental or convenient. The real mark of our participation in the Church is the strength of our continuing love.

If, therefore, anyone truly wishes to share in the treasure of the church, let the participant become a partaker of love. . . . Each one in the degree of his/her own love and calling in God and the Lord Jesus has his/her own measure of communion or exclusion, and it is through no decree of the pope that one has more or less communion with the saints or is excluded from it (p. 251).

6) "Dr. Wessel concerning Purgatory: what the fire of purgatory is, and its nature; concerning the state and progress of souls after this life" (consisting of 42 pages). He interpreted Purgatory and purgation in way more positive than simply as punishment.

The fire of purgatory is a fire which does not torment, but rather cleanses the inward person of the impurity which accompanies one even when released from the flesh. A fire, I say, that devours the filth, *i.e.* the sins; for the inward person [*homo*] can have no other stains (p. 281).

I believe that the fire of purgatory is not primarily material, yet I think it is principally a purifying fire, because. . . it purifies; for the more it grows, the more it assimilates and unites one to God. Hence, I say, to be made like God and to be united to God through love is to be purified. I call a soul impure, if it does not love perfectly. To grow in love, this indeed is to be purified (p. 292).

He suggested, as well, that only God knows how pure a person is, and will judge accordingly. It is, therefore, irrelevant for pope or priest to judge how many days or years one should spend in purgatory.

Many of these writings in the *Farrago* seem to presage later Reformation ideas. Because of these similarities, Gansfort has sometimes been referred to as a "Reformer before the Reformation," as noted above. This is perhaps an exaggeration, since in many other aspects of his thinking, Gansfort wrote like a typical Late Medieval theologian, influenced by organizations such as the *Devotio Moderna*. A comprehensive analysis of this question is not germane, however, to the analysis of Hoen's document concerning the Eucharist.

We do not know of Luther's reaction to Hoen's tract on the Eucharist—or if he even analyzed it. We have only a possible reference in the title of the document which stated that it was sent "to someone with whom stood the final judgment of Holy Scripture" [was Luther the person mentioned?] Later the explanation continued: "*sed spreta*" [but spurned by him].

Thus far we have analyzed a complicated connection between Gansfort, Hoen, and Luther. Martin Luther received the documents in the *Farrago* and was struck by some kindered ideas. We will analyze Gansfort's authentic tract on the Eucharist below.[10] How many of Gansfort's ideas influenced Luther's writings of the period, however, would require an extensive analysis of this question.

The Documents from The Netherlands are taken to Zwingli

Hinne Rode returned from Wittenberg to Utrecht in 1521 and became involved with another publication of Wessel's *Farrago* (Zwolle, 1522). Soon after his return to The Netherlands, however, he was expelled (1522) from his position in Utrecht because of possible association with Luther's ideas, or perhaps because of divergent teachings.[11] He abandoned the city of Utrecht and traveled to several places in Europe.[12] He arrived in Basel early in September, 1522, where he showed Gansfort and Hoen's works to Oecolampadius, the future reformer at Basel. Also, while in Basel, he arranged for still another publication of the *Farrago* (Basel,1522). To make this publication possible, he had evidently brought with him a copy of the Zwolle edition. Oecolampadius was impressed with Hoen's letter especially and suggested it be taken to Zürich. There the Dutch travelers met Zwingli in the summer of 1523.

When Zwingli read the documents, he seemed pleased, especially with Hoen's tract, because it contained a formula he had been seeking—a concise explanation of "this is my body." Before Zwingli had a chance to publicize his enthusiasm for this new expression, Rode and Saganus departed for Strassburg, where they met Martin Bucer in November, 1524. Bucer was impressed with Hoen's ideas as well. Following this visit, Rode and Saganus evidently returned to their home country.

In the meantime in The Netherlands, Cornelius Hoen was arrested (February 1523)[13] and briefly imprisoned, along with his friends Frederick Hondebeke (Canirivus) (See Chapter 3), and Gulielmus Gnapheus (See Chapter 11). Shortly thereafter, all were released, but Hoen was confined to the city of The Hague. By 1524 he had died.

To understand this interrelation between the theology of the Late Middle Ages and the early Reformation, especially the new understanding of the Eucharist, we must analyze three different phases of the complex relationship: **First**, how Hoen's tract was received by Zwingli, and how it influenced his thought; **Second**, how Hoen's tract compares with the treatise on the Eucharist which Gansfort had composed a half century before; and **Third**, other sources of the Late Middle Ages that address Eucharistic theology.

Huldrych Zwingli's New Insight as a Reflection of Cornelius Hoen's Writing

As often happens in history, chance relationships and unusual circuitous connections can lead to significant changes and modifications in both theological understanding and ecclesiastical practices. Such is the case concerning the new interpretation of the Eucharist in the early sixteenth century. Zwingli had already expressed his misgivings with the traditional Roman Catholic doctrine in the 18th article of his 67 theses of 1523: "The Mass is not a sacrifice but is a remembrance of the sacrifice and assurance of the salvation which Christ has given us."[14] In this and other early writings, he had already rejected the idea that the Eucharist was a re-sacrificing of Jesus on the altar; he argued that one sacrifice 1500 years ago was sufficient.

Hoen's letter which Zwingli probably read in 1523, was enthusiastically embraced and led to his enthusiastic evaluation. He had found the explanatory formula he needed: "is" [*est*] is to be interpreted as "signifies" [*significat*]. In fact, as early as November, 1524, Zwingli wrote to Matthew Alber, the reformer in Reutlingen,[15] using this new wording.

> Now take up Christ's words in Matthew 26:26, Jesus took bread, etc., saying 'Take eat; this is my body, which is given for you' [actually Luke 22:19]. Put 'signifies' for 'is' here and you have 'take, eat; this signifies my body which is given for you.' Then the meaning will certainly be 'take, eat, for this which I bid you do will signify [*significabit*] to you or remind [*memorabit*] you of my body which presently is to be given for you'.

The tract by Cornelis Hoen, was compiled in its latest form in 1520. Before it reached Zwingli, however, it had traveled by way of Luther in Wittenberg and Oecolampadius in Basel. Because of his enthusiasm concerning Hoen's insights, Zwingli arranged to have the document published in 1525, although without the name of the author. The title as published in Zürich was

> A Most Christian Letter, sent four years ago from the Netherlands to someone with whom stood the final judgment of holy Scripture, but spurned [*spreta*] by him. This letter presents the Lord's Supper in a very different fashion from that which was hitherto the case.[16]

Erasmus, in Basel, had already heard of Zwingli's publication of Hoen's document before 3 October, 1525. On that date Erasmus wrote

> When Karlstadt was in hiding in these parts, he distributed some pamphlets, written in German, in which he maintained that nothing was involved in the Eucharist except bread and wine. Several people were persuaded at once. His views have now been supported by Zwingli in a series of publications. Four years ago a Dutchman made the same point in a letter which has now been published, though without the author's name.[17]

Zwingli later acknowledged his indebtedness to Hoen. On 23 October, 1525, he wrote to Johann Bugenhagen, an associate of Luther:

> It came to pass by the goodness of God that two pious and learned men whose names I will not yet mention came to Leo [Jud] and me to confer upon this theme, and when they heard our opinion in this matter, they gave thanks to God (for they kept their own view secret [*celabant*], because it was not safe then to tell everybody what one thought [*sentiret*] in this matter), and untying their bundle [*sarcina*] they gave us to read that letter of a certain learned and pious man of

Holland, which had been published anonymously. In that [tract] I found this blessed pearl of wisdom, that 'is' in our passage is to be taken in the sense of 'signifies.'[18]

Two years later, writing directly to Luther, Zwingli again acknowledged his debt using the names of his visitors. "This conclusion that *'est'* stands for *'significat'* I adopted from the Dutchman Hoen, whose letter John Rode and George Saganus, men distinguished both for piety and erudition, carried with them."[19]

An Analysis of Hoen's Document: A Most Christian Letter

Hoen's analysis of the Eucharist was not systematic, but included many complementary ideas in a rather random order. There are emphases which are positive or proto-Protestant, as well as specific negative criticisms of contemporary Roman Catholic practice and understanding.

Hoen based his understanding of the sacrament largely on John 6:48-50, which he reiterated several times. In John, Hoen says, we read: "I am the bread of Life. Your fathers ate manna in the desert and died. This is the bread which came down from heaven, he who eats this bread will live forever." His reference to "This is my body", and "This do in remembrance of me" (I Corinthians 11:24-25) must be seen only in this context of the Gospel of John. In this he presupposed that "to eat" is an activity which must be done in true faith. When the believer "remembers" he/she participates in the larger meaning of the heavenly bread, is incorporated into the benefits of the life and death of Jesus Christ already available through faith and remembering. With this Biblical understanding Hoen began his summary of the sacrament.

In the Eucharist Jesus promised forgiveness of sins and sought to strengthen the faith of the believers. To do this he provided a pledge [*pignus*] so there would be no uncertainty. Hence the believer who takes the Eucharist should "believe Christ now to be his, given for him, and His blood shed for him." This is similar to the bridegroom who says to his bride, "I give myself to you; here is the ring." Because the bridegroom is not contained in the ring, the bride must see it as a symbol or sign of the larger meanings promised. B. J. Spruyt noted that the symbol of the "ring" is the only concept used in common by both Gansfort and Hoen, but with differing meanings. Since the symbol of the "ring" was widespread in Late Medieval thought, Spruyt assumed that this parallel usage was not sufficient to prove a close relationship between Hoen and Gansfort.[20]

Then Hoen came to the best-known aspect of his letter, namely that the "*est*" [is] in the phrase "*hoc est corpus meum*" [this is my body] really should be understood as "this signifies [*significat*] my body." Hence the body of Christ is present not "corporeally" but "sacramentally." Hoen gave some examples which he thought should prove his point. We do not understand that John the Baptist literally became Elijah when we read "He [John the Baptist] is Elijah" (Matthew 11:14).

Likewise, when Jesus on the cross said to Mary "woman behold your son" (John 19:26) John was not transformed into her son [Jesus]. Similarly, when Jesus said, "Upon this rock [*petram*] I will build my church" (Matthew 16:18); and the rock "is" Christ is to be interpreted as the rock represents or signifies Christ. In these three examples no transformation of form is understood and in all cases the "*est*" is to be interpreted as "*significat*" [signifies]. Other examples are given: Christ **is** the Way; Christ **is** the cornerstone; Christ **is** the true vine. These should never be understood literally. Hoen argued that it is because of Papal authority that the "*est*" is often misunderstood and is taken literally rather than figuratively.

There is a voluntary aspect to this faith and in the Eucharist. The believer who realizes its significance "turns his heart away from all whom he used to love and clings to Christ alone;" he "places all cares on Christ" [268].[21] Hoen suggested that those who partake of the pledge [*pignus*] of the Eucharist in faith reflect the scripture in John 6:57 ("Whoever eats me will live because of me.") The pledge [*pignus*] of the Eucharist does not in and of itself provide or produce the faith, but it serves as a constant reminder. The intention of the believer, and his/her faith, is thus more important than both the institutional hierarchy of the church, and the physical elements of the sacrament.

Not all who partake of the Eucharist will have eternal life, but those who later fall from the faith will not be spared [272]. This was what it means to eat Christ and drink his blood. The faith of the believers is crucial. Those who take the Eucharist without living faith partake only in the outward aspects of the sacrament but do not receive any benefit from it.

Hoen evaluated the Roman Catholic faith of his day as one which ignored the need for a living faith and emphasized instead, a "dead faith" which sought to confine Christ to the consecrated bread as the True Body of Christ. Hoen evaluated his opponents by writing that "there are many subtle theories but no scriptural proofs" (268) of how this interpretation can be explained. If faith is lacking, the Eucharist becomes as "historical facts" or spiritless manna on the desert. He insisted that "the objective presence [alone] cannot justify" [269]. He suggested that the adoration of the bread is no different from worshipping "wood and stone," because those who do "arbitrarily assumed that the stones were gods" [269].

Hoen also suggested why priests could have assumed so much power surrounding the words "this do in remembrance of me." This could be taken two ways: "this do"—meaning priests should consecrate the bread; or "this do"—meaning lay people should participate in the Eucharist. After the time of Jesus there was no one to do "this" [*i.e.* consecrate], so the church empowered certain persons (priests) to do it. They consecrate the elements and preside over the transubstantiation—in place of the Jesus. Yet, "these assertions are foggy and unclear" [273]. The Roman Catholic Church claimed that through the process of *ex opera operato* the Eucharist was the real body of Christ; but can the worshipper be certain of that? Hoen reiterated the suggestion from John (6:46-51) that the real

Eucharist—the real body of Christ—should be eaten by faith and not by mouth. Because of this, Hoen could hardly agree with any *ex opere operato* understanding.

Against the literal, physical interpretation of "This IS my body" [hence Christ is IN the bread, or more precisely, Christ has BECOME the bread], Hoen argued that the words written in Matthew—"'Look here is the Christ,' or 'There he is' do not believe it" (Matthew 24:23)—must be understood as a warning against this type of literalness.

Hoen further elaborated the Biblical reference: "I am the bread of life. Your fathers ate the manna in the wilderness and they died. This is the bread which comes down from heaven, so that one may eat of it and not die" (John 6:48-50). This important difference is that the manna in the desert may have sustained physical life but provided no spiritual presence, hence did not lead to faith. Christ the living word [or bread] which came down from heaven made all the difference. Merely to participate in the external elements of the Eucharist is no guarantee that its value has come to the individual. Hoen used I Corinthians 10:1-5 to show how some persons in the days of Moses, even passing through the Red Sea [baptism], did not benefit from the physical elements they took because they did not have the faith which is also requisite. According to Hoen's understanding of Paul, the spiritual presence is the determining factor. As Paul further stated , "The cup of blessing which we bless, is it not a participation in the blood of Christ? The bread which we break, is it not a participation in the body of Christ" (I Corinthians 10:16). The spiritual presence leads to faith and saves from death those who eat in the faith of Christ. The physical elements of the Eucharist are not, by themselves, efficacious. The Eucharist signifies the spiritual presence and the faith, both of which are indispensable. "Faith active in true love" is the only way we can "receive the things signified by the sign" concluded Hoen [272].

He added another argument against the bread as "real" body. Since the bread, even though consecrated is temporal, and can and does become corrupt—or may be eaten by a mouse—, this indeed cannot be the body of Christ. Even if it may be supposed that Christ with his extensive miraculous powers did transubstantiate the bread—which he did not, as evidenced by the lack of scriptural references—even so, we must not assume that "a mere priest" [272] could do so.

Hoen gave his own interpretation of the traditional words of consecration "Jesus on the night that he was betrayed took a loaf of bread, and when he had given thanks he broke it, and gave it to his disciples and said 'This is my body'" (I Corinthians 11:24). When the consecrating priest, according to the Roman Catholic doctrine, repeats these words, he speaks as though speaking for Christ, as if he were a surrogate Christ performing the same consecration [and presiding over transubstantiation] as in the upper room. Actually, according to Hoen, when the consecrating priest, with a more correct understanding, uses these words, he is not speaking for himself. Rather, he speaks as one REMEMBERING that Jesus spoke these words, "do this in remembrance of me." Hoen concluded that the Roman

Catholic interpretation cannot stand unless upheld by "human props" [274]. In short, the Roman Catholic Church had "materialized" the main symbols of the faith, thus deadening them or making the faithful guilty of worshipping a molten calf [276]. Hoen again admonished, "If anyone says 'here is Christ,' do not believe" (Matthew 24:23).

The emphasis on transubstantiation is further suspect because ordinarily we would expect that it should have prominence in the early tradition, but it is neither referred to in the Apostles' Creed, nor the early church. It appears, rather, in decrees of popes. This absence from the creed, and its appearance at a later time, led Hoen to claim it is a "papal and Satanic invention" [274]. Actually, Christ withdrew from the earthly scene in favor of the "Comforter," the spiritual presence; consequently, it would be erroneous to look for Christ in the physical bread. Instead, we are now better able to find the spiritual reality, since without a physical presence it is easier for us to serve Christ "in the spirit through faith" [274].

According to Hoen, it is Satan who has attempted to lead us astray by suggesting that if Christ is no longer physically present in the form of a man then he is at least physically present in the bread. To the end that the bread—supposed to be God—may be glorified, the Roman Catholic Church has created "extravagant churches," "sumptuous decorations of temples," "torches and candles," "sacred vestments woven of linen and gold," "the bellowing of monks in the choir," and "anointings and purification of priests" [275]. These practices distance the true sacrament from the people.

The supposed miracles of the pope are of such a character that the senses cannot observe, such as the substance of bread changed while the accidents [appearance] remain the same. Many other miracles of the pope are of less consequence: "liberating souls from purgatory," "remitting. . . punishment imposed for sins—or for money" [276]. Hoen continually reminded the believers, however, that the bread received by the mouth must always be accompanied by faith (which is the presence of Christ).

Hoen concluded that "the entire religion of the pope would collapse" if "the physical presence were eliminated" [275]. The papal formulation is a "human contrivance" [275] and not "built on a rock;" otherwise, it would not be vulnerable when subjected to close analysis.

Jesus did not want the bread to be transubstantiated, but wanted to give Himself through the bread. Hoen illustrated this by comparing it to when someone wants to sell land, the seller gives some token [although there is no word to be translated "token" in the Latin original] of the sale—a staff, straw or stone" [275].[22] In the same manner the transfer of ownership of a house is symbolized by giving over the keys. In like manner Jesus gave a token or pledge with the sacrament. Jesus

gave himself to us by means of bread, as if to say, 'take and eat. Do not regard the bread as unimportant; that which I give you signifies My Body which I give you by giving you this bread. When it has been given over and hung on the cross it will be for you; indeed, everything I have done or shall do is yours' [275].

The purpose of Jesus when he gave this command "this do," was not to suggest a physical transformation of the elements—*i.e.* as though the presence of his corporeal body had any significance in and of itself. Rather, it was for the purpose of strengthening the faith of the believer. Faith of this type, according to Hoen, could not be instilled through a physical presence in the sacrament. The Gospel of John refers to eating not by mouth, but by faith; a strengthening of faith is the end purpose for the "eating." Furthermore, faith is not simply a pious wish, but must be made active in love.

Hoen's letter can be characterized as analytic, linguistic, legalistic in its close reasoning, and certainly polemical against certain Roman Catholic practices as he understood them. We still ask, however, was his letter really informed by Gansfort?

The Document on the Eucharist by Wessel Gansfort [De Sacramento Eucharistiae et Audienda Missa]

In contrast to Hoen's letter, the tract on the Eucharist by Wessel Gansfort portrayed a strikingly different approach. It is not strictly theological but is more devotional and meditative. There is nothing polemical in it, and the key phrase which Hoen used, "*est*" understood as "*significat,*" does not appear in Gansfort's writing. Gansfort did not deny transubstantiation (but he does not specifically affirm it either). The only obvious comparison between the two documents is that they both urge the believer to seek a spiritual reality beyond the physical bread. To exemplify these differences we include a brief summary of Gansfort's document on the Eucharist.[23]

In his thought concerning the Eucharist, Gansfort made many assertions similar to other Humanists such as Erasmus, but he developed their theological context more fully. The key word in this whole tract is "remembrance." When we understand the full implications Gansfort had in mind with that key phrase, we understand his approach to the sacrament. He stated simply: "To eat [of the sacrament] is to remember, to esteem, to love."[24] To eat, however, does not mean simply to eat. "Eat" must be taken symbolically to be understood in its fullest sense. Therefore, the important thing was to *remember*, to have Christ in one's mind—and not to eat bread only physically. Gansfort also asserted that this experience can and does take place apart from physical bread, and apart from the Mass of the church. In these assertions he transformed the medieval meaning drastically. He stated that "it is this remembrance of Him that constitutes the true Eucharist" (p. 4). Let us look at several related concepts in more detail.

Gansfort related the process of "remembering" on the part of human beings, to the process of "generating" a Word on the part of God. God was involved in deep thought concerning his purposes for the world, when the Word came forth.

Consequently, if we seriously meditate about our lives and about the sufferings of Christ for us, we are involved in a God-like process. The process of remembering and of rationality is the part of human nature which is most like God; therefore, it is logical that God's supreme act, the suffering and death of Christ for us, or at least the re-enactment through remembering and rethinking, should be lodged in that part of our nature. The end result of this remembering is that we might become more nearly perfect, or more nearly God-like. Gansfort then asserted that we have no other means of retaining the Word of God than by remembering it. "How then can anyone retain the Word that was sent except by remembering it? Unless one remembers, it escapes" (p. 16).

> Meditation, therefore, in its origin is very close to the origin of the Word. The same wisdom was necessary to originate meditation as to beget the Word. Surely then, if by virtue of its noble birth our meditation courts a proud and exalted marriage with the Word of eternal wisdom, our mind must contract this marriage by remembrance (pp. 16-17).

Gansfort reflected his deep Augustinian or Pauline context of thought as he distinguished between the "outer" and the "inner" being. The latter is spiritual and closely related to God, while the former is the physical element, more closely related to the world.

> Now just as there is the outer person [homo] and the life of the outer person [hominis] and the nourishment of the outer life, so there is the inner person [homo], the life of the inner person [hominis], and the nourishment of the inner life (p. 21).

In this sense he related eating the Eucharist with the stomach—i.e. physically only—and eating the Eucharist with the heart and mind—i.e. spiritually. Unless the physical eating results in spiritual awareness, it is of no value to the Christian believer.

> Even as this inner person [homo] is invisible, so also that person lives [vivit] an invisible life and is nourished and strengthened by an invisible bread, and just as in the nourishment of the body the stomach does not exist for the food but food for the stomach, so that not only is grain sought for humans [hominem] and hay for cattle, but it is known to be salutary; so if we closely examine and clearly apprehend the inner person [hominem], we shall more nearly conjecture what this spiritual nourishment is (p. 21).

The real Eucharist is a spiritual food—either in addition to, or in place of any physical bread or wine.

> However much therefore one may eat and drink the visible Eucharist with one's teeth and mouth, if the inner person does not live after God, that person does

not eat. . . . Whoever therefore eats visibly, does not eat, unless that person eats [*manducat*] spiritually (p. 25)

To summarize the ideas presented thus far concerning memory and the Eucharist, we quote from him again.

'Except you eat the flesh of the Son of Man and drink his blood, you have not life in yourselves.' Manifestly it must be admitted that the life, of which he speaks is the life of the inner person [*hominis*], *i.e.* life in the Holy Spirit. Necessarily, therefore, it must also be admitted that when he says, 'Except you eat of the flesh of the Son of Man and drink his blood,' we are to understand that it is an inward eating and drinking, *i.e.* of the inner person [*hominis*] (p. 25)

Here Gansfort reflected Augustine again as he distinguished three trinitarian aspects within the inner self: memory, intellect and will.

How does the inner person eat the flesh and drink the blood, when he/she is nothing but mind, intelligence? The inner person [*homo*] *i.e.*, the memory, intellect and will, should be occupied with the Word that became flesh, with God who became human, with times, desires, doctrines, examples, precepts, benefits and promises, just as the mouth, throat and stomach of the outer person are employed with a feast (p. 25).

Thus, as Augustine argued, if humanity is made in the image of God, that image which is "Trinitarian-ness" must be observed in the human race. Gansfort also argued that if this three-fold interpretation is true for us, the sacrament must also have some relation to each of these three aspects.

Attention, meditation, reflection are functions of the memory; for one reflects in order to discern. Argumentation, assent, discernment belong to the intellect. Exertion in confidence [*intentio fiducia*], impulse or desire belong to the will. It is only in this wise that this food is thrust before us [*minatur*] and is eaten, *i.e.* by the mental acts of the three faculties of the soul (p. 49).

Gansfort had anticipated Luther on at least two points. **First**, one who eats the physical bread and wine, but eats unworthily without faith, brings on one's own destruction—it is a negative influence for that life. Thus the sacraments have a spiritual power—either negative or positive—depending on the good intention of the believer, or the lack of intention of the non-believer as the case may be. At the same time, however, he did not state the later Lutheran position, namely that the teeth of the believer actually tore apart the spiritual body. Gansfort located the spiritual aspect in a place other than between the believer's teeth.

To all the faithful . . . He is food to be eaten by seeing with the inward eye, by remembering, considering, desiring and loving; but He is not food to be torn with the teeth (p. 43).

Gansfort's spiritual interpretation, likewise, anticipated Luther on a **second** point. He argued that when Christ is physically and spiritually present in each celebration of the Eucharist, he nevertheless remained in heaven. The "everywhereness" of the Spiritual Christ was Luther's concept (*ubiquity*) which Gansfort stated two generations earlier.

> I do say that to one who remembers his name, the Lord Jesus is truly present, not only in his deity, but also in his flesh and blood and entire humanity. Who can doubt that the Lord Jesus is often bodily present with his faithful disciples in their last agonies—although he does not on that account forsake his seat at the right hand of God in heaven? Who can doubt that this may simultaneously occur apart from the Eucharist as well as in it? (pp. 57-58).

In this last statement he introduced another aspect of his thought, namely that the presence of the spiritual Christ can come outside the Eucharistic celebration as well as through it. He referred to the spiritual presence within the Eucharist as a "sacramental" presence which is not physical and does not involve transubstantiation. He contrasted these two ideas, *i.e.* spiritual and physical presence:

> To the spiritually faithful He is also given—even in bodily presence— outside of the Eucharist and apart from the forms of bread and wine, since he is given to those who believe in him. If none has life except that person eats his flesh and drink his blood, and on the other hand, the one that believes on him has eternal life, it must obviously be admitted that everyone that believes eats his flesh and drinks his blood (p. 56).

Gansfort indicated further that spiritual communion may be more important than physical or liturgical ingesting.

> Indeed, in some respects spiritual [or according to the spirit, *pietatis*] communion is more fruitful than sacramental [*ordinis*], at least in this respect, that in the former [spiritual] so far as the laity are concerned they both eat and drink, while in the latter [*ordinis,* sacramentally or liturgically] they only eat-- unless by a blessed draught they are filled with spiritual peace. The latter [sacramental or liturgical] is bound down by time and place, is permitted to certain persons only, and is compelled to observe a particular form; the former [spiritual], springing from a pious heart in faith unfeigned rejects no age, no sex, no race, and is adapted to all places and all times. The latter [sacramental or liturgical] is often harmful: the former [spiritual] is always fruitful and salutary (p. 56).

He then turned to the benefits or the outcomes which result from the "eating" or meditation upon the life, teaching, death, and resurrection of Christ. **First**, through meditation, and remembering the sacrifice of Christ, the believer realizes, more and more, that Jesus's suffering was really the believer's own. The more vividly the believer can remember or imagine the stories of the suffering, the clearer it becomes for him/her.

> Gladly therefore, Lord Jesus, will I remember that thy flesh suffered for me, thy body was broken for me, thy life was relinquished for me, knowing that remembrance, if it be frequent, will not be unfruitful. In remembering Thee, not only by thy promise but also—which is sweeter—by Thy condescension, I have Thee present with me. How shall I truly eat of Thy body broken for me, without having Thee present as the guest of my soul? (pp. 6-7).

Thus through memory and reflection the sufferings of Christ become the believer's own, vicariously, as it were; they become more vivid.

This leads to a **second** aspect. The more Christ's sufferings become a part of the believer the more perfectly love is restored within him/her. Perfect Communion with the Spiritual Christ results, theoretically, in perfect love on the part of the believer. "Of those who eat it is the degree of their love that determines the degree of their perfection" (p. 31).

Third, remembering the passion, which leads to perfected love, results finally in Christ living wholly in the believer; and the believer, in turn will live wholly in Him. This is a mysticism of love.

> Moreover, in partaking of the Eucharist we not only eat but also are eaten. We take of it and are strengthened just as when we take and eat food; yet because this strengthening is effected not by any power of ours, but by the power of the bread we take, it transforms us into itself; and hence we say we are eaten. It is just as when iron is made red hot, the iron absorbs the fire and yet is entirely possessed thereby. Hence the fire eats the iron and is also eaten by it. Mental changes are even more to the point; *e.g.* the pupil's faithful belief eats, so to speak, the teacher's wisdom; and the love of two lovers is fed by love (p. 50).

Gansfort argued that since it was by Adam and Eve's eating that the human race fell, so it is by eating that humanity is restored to the position occupied before having fallen. Consequently, the Eucharist became extremely important in the medieval Church but too often the Eucharist was wrongly interpreted. The real meaning of the sacrament for the individual can be restored only when it is interpreted in its true spiritual meaning.

This concept of the Eucharist has mystical, devotional, and meditative tendencies. While it recognized the physical side of the Eucharist and the physical aspects of humankind, nevertheless, these are of little significance. It is the inner and spiritual person who eats (or really meditates upon) the sacrificed bread. The food is spiritual food and nourishes in a spiritual way.

> If we had open eyes, we would not merely eat the flesh and drink the blood of the Son of Man, which with regard to the great works of God consists in

worthy remembrance, reflection, discernment, comparison, meditation, seeing, tasting and desiring; but by philosophizing upon these works we would be fed (p. 69).

Recent attempts to re-evaluate Hoen's document with relation to the work of John Wyclif and Jan Hus

One recent study of Gansfort interpreted the Hoen/Gansfort relationship differently from Albert Hardenberg's mid-sixteenth century understanding. Maartin van Rhijn spent a large part of his academic study concerning Wessel Gansfort.[25] He suggested that Hoen may actually have constructed his ideas from Gansfort's sharp distinction between the spiritual aspect of the Sacrament and the literal or physical body and blood. Hoen's interpretation may be a more radical conclusion from Gansfort's thought that the spiritual "communion" can take place without being connected with the physical partaking.[26] Both Hoen and Gansfort, however, emphasized the necessity of the physical, liturgical, sacramental participation in addition to the spiritual communion.

Cornelis Hoen's document, especially the sources he used in his tract, needs further analysis. Our question is what inspiration or new ideas did Hoen receive? A careful analysis and comparison as noted above shows very little, if any, comparison with Gansfort. The formula which Hoen used regularly—*"est"* = *"significat"*—does not appear in Wessel's document. Furthermore, Hoen's is a humanist and legalistic analysis; the document of Gansfort is a devotional tract, encouraging a mystic or felt relationship with the living (spiritual) Christ. If we pose questions as to how, or if, Hoen used Gansfort's document, then where must we look?

The key to this complex development seems to have been provided by a doctoral study completed in Leiden in 1996, by Bastiaan Jan Spruyt.[27] He presented a sharply different alternative from all previous interpretations. His studies are now the definitive analysis of the relationships between Cornelius Hoen's writing and the thought of Late Medieval Theology. In these studies Spruyt traced Hoen's sources to the works of John Wyclif (1328-1384) and Jan Hus (1371-1415), instead of Gansfort. Both these Late Medieval scholars wrote on the Eucharist, and both were critical of the "realistic" interpretation as promulgated at the IV Lateran Council (1215). Both theologians used figurative, symbolic, or metaphorical language with regard to the Eucharist. The works of Wycliff and Hus were widely known in England and Bohemia but were circulated also in the Burgundian Netherlands. Indeed, some works of Wyclif or Hus may have been included in the "old" document which Hardenburg suggested was among Gansfort's works as discovered in the library of Jacob Hoeck. Or, on the other hand, perhaps the "old" document among these papers was actually a tract by someone else, reflecting writings going back to Jan Hus or even John Wyclif. In either case, surely Humanist educators would have been acquainted with documents such as these.

Spruyt analyzed three works of Wyclif: *De Apostasia* (1380); *De Eucharistia* (1380) and *Trialogus, a Summa (1382-1383)*. Wyclif's assertions may be summarized in at least four points which parallel assertions in Hoen's letter, although Spruyt's analysis is much more extensive. **First,** the doctrine of Transubstantiation is a recent addition to the doctrines of the Church. As Wyclif analyzed this doctrine, he noted that the idea was a recent addition because it did not appear in earlier formulations or creeds. For this reason he thought it was suspect, even a trick of the devil or of the anti-Christ.[28]

Second, Wyclif's philosophical realism prohibited him from conceiving the possibility of accidents remaining after the inner substance was changed—hence there could be no transubstantiation (changing the substance) in a medieval sense. He thought rather that Body of Christ and Bread of the Eucharist, which are two different substances, could exist in juxtaposition, as God and Man existed in Christ according to the Chalcedonian formula (451 A.D.). Thus Wyclif rejected the idea of the annihilation of the substance of bread in the Eucharist. Furthermore, he denied that the earthly bread could be equated with the body of Christ. With this logic, to adore the host, the earthly bread, as in transubstantiation, was idolatry. The earthly substance of bread cannot be equated with Christ.

Third, Wyclif used a figurative understanding of many passages of scripture. When one refers to the bread as the Body of Christ, Wyclif thought it was a figurative way of speaking—a *predicatio habitudinalis*. In addition, Wyclif interpreted figures of speech such as "the Rock is Christ" (I Cor. 10:4), the "seven ears of wheat are seven fertile years" (Gen. 41:26) or "the bread is the body of Christ," as a figurative way of speaking. The "est" was not meant to be taken literally as "is."

Fourth, on one further point Wyclif seems to be the source for Hoen's thought. Wyclif denied the idea that Christ would be a product of "impanation" [*impanitur*], in any way similar to the "incarnation" [*incarnatio*]—if in fact there were a word "*im-panatio*" (Divine substance in bread) parallel with *in-carnatio* (Divine substance in flesh). It was sacrilegious, he insisted, to suggest that the priest could call down the divine power into the bread in a way similar to the once-and-for-all incarnation into the womb of Mary. Furthermore, if a mouse ate the consecrated bread, it was eating real earthly bread, according to the senses—not the true body of Christ. In addition, Wyclif's argument is an elaboration of Psalm 16:10, "You will not leave my soul in hell; neither will you suffer your Holy One to see corruption." The implication is that since the bread could be eaten by a mouse (*i.e.* corruption), the consecrated bread is not the Holy One. This is stated more clearly by Hoen, as we will note below.[29]

Hoen's letter reflects all four of these emphases, using the same scriptures and the same Latin terminology. **First,** he argued that transubstantiation as a doctrine is a late addition. He suspected it was a Romanist invention or even an invention of Satan because he found that it does not appear in the earliest creeds.[30] **Second,** Hoen contrast partaking the sacrament with true faith to taking the manna of the Jews. The latter did not give satisfaction because it was an emphasis on a dead faith. He argued, therefore, that the Roman Catholic scholastics taught a dead faith without scriptural basis. **Third,** Hoen used several biblical references which obviously should be taken in a figurative manner—not literally. He quoted "three branches **are** three days" (Gen. 40:12) and "seven good cows and the seven full ears **are** seven prosperous years" (Gen 41:26). Furthermore, about John the Baptist, he said "He **is** Elijah" (from Matt 11:14), as well as citing "the Rock **was** Christ" (I Cor 10:14); or "I **am** the true vine" (John 15:1). He concluded that "*est*" should be used in the sense of "*significat.*"[31] **Fourth,** Hoen's used the expression "impanation" (p. 270 in the English translation)[32] and referred to the mouse which might eat the Eucharistic bread (English trans., p. 272).[33]

Wyclif's concepts found welcome soil in Bohemia during the reign of Emperor Charles IV (1346-1378). These ideas were spread in the earliest national reform movement, which began a few decades before Jan Hus (1371-1415) came to prominence and reflected similar ideas.

Hus's treatise on the Eucharist [*de Sanguine Christi*] grew out of a controversy about the ruins of a church which the pious believed contained remains of the True Body of Christ. The situation was exploited as a site to which pilgrimages could be made. A committee from the University of Prague, including Jan Hus in their number, was appointed to investigate. Hus argued **first** that at the time of the crucifixion Christ glorified all his blood, and none remained on earth. Instead, All his blood remains at the right hand of God, and those who insisted otherwise were furthering a clever deceit. Both Hus and Hoen used Matthew 24:32 ("'Look, here is the Messiah': or 'There is the Messiah,' do not believe them"). Then Hus followed Matthew in warning against false prophets who will lead the faithful astray, who urged the people to venerate a false Christ as though he were present in the consecrated bread.[34]

Second, Hus argued that although visible body and blood might more easily convince believers, still Christ chose to withdraw—*i.e.* to hide his blood. Hus used the scripture John 16:7: "It is to your advantage that I go away, for if I do not go away the Advocate (Comforter) will not come to you."[35] He argued that not only the blood of Christ, but indeed the whole body had gone away. It is, therefore, futile for priests to claim that the body is really present in the form of bread.

Third, even a small amount of blood could not have been left behind in an earthly, non glorified (hence corruptible) state because of the statement—"you will not give (up) your Holy One to see corruption" (*KJV*, Psalm 16:10).[36]

Fourth, in his tract, *De sex erroribus*, Hus singled out the error that priests erroneously believed that they could produce the body of Christ repeatedly and at will, and think they are more worthy than Mary who brought forth the body of Christ only once.

The letter of Cornelis Hoen contains ideas paralleling these four points and more. **First,** he suggested that Satan has attempted to persuade believers that the real presence is before, us not in the form of a man but in bread. He also used John 16:7 in insisting that the whole body of Christ had been removed from the earthly scene.

Second, Hoen insisted that the presence of the physical was no guarantee, and perhaps elaborate accoutrements were even a detriment to true faith. Some examples were "extravagant churches," "sumptuous decorations," "torches," "candles," sacred vestments woven of linen and gold," "bellowing monks in the choir," and "anointings and purifications of priests." Indeed, as noted above, Hoen asserted "if the physical presence were eliminated the entire religion of the Pope would collapse."[37]

Third, Hoen also used Psalm 16:10 to suggest that the body would not be corrupted. The fact that the mouse could eat the bread proved that it was not really the body of Jesus. **Fourth,** Hoen argued that the body could not be produced at will, but even if that were possible, it would not be meaningful. It is unnecessary to argue for real body in the bread because the gospel of John "refers not to eating by the mouth but by faith."[38] These parallel ideas and scripture references point rather clearly to an influence on Hoen coming from Wyclif, Hus and even to scholars before that time.

Following a careful analysis of the works of Wyclif and Hus, Spruyt summarized considerable research into the earlier Medieval history of the doctrine of the Eucharist. Wyclif's approach is traced back to Berengar of Tours (1000-1088) and, ultimately, to Ratramnus, the monk of Corbie (d. 868). In a contrasting approach, which seemed to justify transubstantiation, Spruyt moved backward from the IV Lateran Council to Lanfranc, Archbishop of Canterbury (d. 1089) and Paschasius Radbertus, another monk of Corbie (d. 860). He followed this by analyzing many contacts between The Netherlands and Bohemia in the fifteenth century. He also summarized many documents and presented evidence of scholarly exchange between the two countries throughout the fifteenth century, including specific examples of the availability of Wyclif and Hus' writings available in The Netherlands. It seems rather likely that the Humanist scholars, especially Cornelis Hoen, would have been conversant with many of these documents. That he used these ideas in compiling his own work seems beyond question, and corrects, or actually expands, suggestions which have been presupposed for centuries.

The Larger influence

Zwingli made no reference to Gansfort's document on the Eucharist, if in fact he had even seen it. He expressed his enthusiasm, however, for Hoen's document and reflected this new understanding in many subsequent writings. Zwingli's thought, hence the thought also of Hoen, had great influence on the sixteenth century and beyond. Several groups within the Radical Reformation adopted the ideas that the bread signifies the body, and "do this in Remembrance of me." This was especially true for Melchior Hoffman and the Mennonite groups in The Netherlands beginning in the next decade. Furthermore, Zwinglil's wording this wording was included in the Second Prayer Book of Edward VI (1551), and was incorporated into the Dissenting movement within the Church of England, influencing especially denominations of the Americas which developed from this dissent: the Congregationalists, the Baptists, the Presbyterians and finally, the Methodists In these groups the phrase is reiterated: "this do in REMEMBRANCE of me," with even stronger emphasis than in I Corinthians 11:24-25.

Notes for Chapter 5

1. Karl C. Ullmann, *Reformers Before the Reformation: principally in Germany and The Netherlands* (Trans. Robert Menzies, 2 vols., Edinburgh: T. and T. Clark, 1855). The extensive material on Gansfort's life and his theological tracts is found in II, 263-615.

2. Heiko A. Oberman, ed., *Forerunners of the Reformation: The Shape of Late Medieval Thought* (New York: Holt, Rinehart and Winston, 1966); especially "The Case of the Forerunner," pp. 3-49.

3. "Life of Wessel of Groningen" by Albert Hardenberg. English trans. in Edward Waite Miller and Jared Waterbury Scudder, *Wessel Gansfort: Life and Writings* (2 vols., New York: G. P. Putnam's Sons, 1917), II, 334-335.

4. From Latin: *Farrago,-inis*, a mixture.

5. Otto Clemen, "Hinne Rode in Wittenberg, Basel, Zürich und die frühesten Ausgaben Wesselscher Schriften," *Zeitschrift für Kirchengeschichte*, Vol 18 (1898), 346-373. Otto Clemen analyzed not only the travels of Hinne Rode but included also some information on the earliest editions of Gansfort's works, *The Farrago*. See also, Bastian Spruyt, "Hinne Rode (*c*.1480-*c*.1539): Het Leven en de Ontwikkeling van de Dissidente Rector van het Utrechtse Fraternhuis" in H. ten Boom, E. Geudeke, H.L.Ph.Leeuwenberg, P.H.A.M. Abels, eds., *Utrechters Entre-Deux: Stad en Sticht in de Eeuw van de Reformatie, 1520-1620* (Delft, The Netherlands: Eburon, 1992).

6. See *WA*, vol. 10, section 2, p. 312, where this edition is listed among the publications in Wittenberg.

7. Luther's preface to the works of Gansfort is in *WA*, Vol. X, section 2, 316-317. It is also included in the *Opera* of Wessel Gansfort (Facsimile of the Edition of Groningen, 1614), (Nieuwkoop: B. de Graaf, 1966). Luther's preface is on p. 854. The English translation is in Edward Waite Miller and Jared Waterbury Scudder, *Wessel Gansfort: Life and Writings* (2 vols. New York: G. P. Putnam's Sons, 1917), I, 231-233, dated in Wittenberg IV before the *Kalends* of August, 29 July 1522. This date is duplicated from the Wessel Gansfort, *Opera*, p. 854. The *WA*, however lists the date as III before the *Kalends* of August, or 30 July, 1522, (vol. 10, pt. 2, p. 317).

8. M. Wesseli Gansfort Groningensis, *Opera* (Groningen: Johannes Sassius Typographus, 1614.) Facsimile reprint, 1966.

9. Edward Waite Miller and Jared Waterbury Scudder, *Wessel Gansfort: Life and Works.* Vol. II, Principal Works in translation (New York: G. P. Putnam Sons, 1917).

10. The tract is *De Sacramento Eucharistiae*, in Wessel's *Opera*, 658-705. It is translated in the Miller/Scudder volume, II, 3-70.

11. *"Propter Lutherum depositus est,"* CDI, IV, 162. This was some time during the year 1522.

12. As noted above, Otto Clemen, "Hinne Rode in Wittenberg. . . " *Zeitschrift für Kirchengeschichte*, 18 (1898), 346-373.

13. *"propter sectam Lutheram,"* CDI, IV, 181.

14. "The Acts of the First Zürich Disputation, January, 1523" in Samuel Macauley Jackson, *Huldrych Zwingli: Selected works* (Philadelphia: University of Pennsylvania Press, 1901, 1972), p. 112.

15. "Letter to Matthew Alber Concerning the Lord's Supper" [November, 1524], *ZW*, III, 335-354. This reference is on p. 345. An unpublished, typed, early twentieth century translation of this letter by Henry Preble is bound in the Library of The Iliff School of Theology. This quotation is on p. 21. The more recent version in *Huldrych Zwingli Writings, II*, translations and revisions by H. Wayne Pipkin is based on Henry Preble's translation. This reference is on p. 139 in the Pipkin edition.

16. This English title is from the translation of Paul Nyhus in Heiko Oberman, ed. *Forerunners of the Reformation: the Shape of Late Medieval Thought* (New York: Holt, Rinehart and Winston, 1966), pp. 268-278. The Latin title as published by Zwingli in 1525 is: *Epistola Christiana admodum ab annis quatuor ad quendam, apud quem omne judicium sacrae scripturis fuit, ex Bathavis missa, sed spreta, longe aliter tractans coenam dominicam quam hactenus tractata est. Zwinglis Werke*, IV (Leipzig, 1927) [=CR 91], 512-519. The tract was published in Zurich in August/September, 1525.

17. *CWE*, Vol. XI, 3 October, 1525, written from Basel.

18. Zwingli's reply to a letter of Johann Bugenhagen of Pomerania (23 October, 1525), as translated in the early Twentieth Century by Henry Preble. An unpublished, typed and bound translation is in the library of The Iliff School of Theology in Denver. This statement is found on pp. 5-6 of this unpublished material. The Latin original is found in *ZW*, IV [=CR 91], 558-576. This citation is on p. 560.

19. *Amica Exegesis, id est: espositio eucharistiae negocii ad Martinum Lutherum*, (February 1527) printed in Zwingli's works *Huldrych Zwinglis Sämtliche Werke* (Leipzig: M. Heinsius, 1934), V [=CR 92], 562-758. *"Ipse ex Honio Batavo (cuius epistolam Johannes Rhodius et Georgius Saganus, viri tum pietate, tum eruditione insignes, attulerunt), per 'est' pro 'significat' expedivi."* This reference is in *ZW*, V, 738. An English translation from the early Twentieth Century is in the library of The Iliff School of Theology, translated by Henry Preble, pp. 1-253. This reference is on p. 231. The Preble translation was used as the basis of Wayne Pipkin, *Huldrych Zwingli Writings, II* (Allison Park, Pennsylvania: Pickwick Publications, 1984), pp. 238-369. This citation in Pipkin's translation is on p. 357.

20. B. J. Spruyt, "Wessel Gansfort and Cornelius Hoen's *Epistola Christiana*: 'The Ring as a pledge of my love,'" in Ackerman, F, Hinsman, G. C., and vanderJacht, A. J., eds., *Wessel Gansfort (1419-1489) and Northern Humanism* (Leiden, New York, Köln: E. J. Brill, 1993). Spruyt's article is on pages 122-141. The discussion concerning the

ring with reference to Hoen and Gansfort is on pp. 137-140.

21. All page numbers in this section refer to the translation by Paul Nyhus in Ober-man, *Forerunners*. . . , pp. 268-278.

22. This discussion is on page 517 of Zwingli's edition of Hoen's document.

23. The Latin *De Sacramento Eucharistiae* is in *M. Wesselli Gansfort Groningensis, Opera* (Groningen: Johannes Sassius Typographus, 1614), pp. 658-705. The English translation is in Edward Waite Miller and Jared Waterbury Scudder, *Wessel Gansfort: Life and Writings* (2 vols., New York: G.P. Putnam's Sons, 1917), II, 3-70.

24. Miller-Scudder edition, II, 30. Hereafter, unless otherwise noted, the page numbers inserted in this section refer to this collection of translations.

25. Maartin van Rhijn, *Wessel Gansfort* (The Hague: 1917); and M. van Rhijn, *Studiën over Wessel Gansfort en zijn Tijd* (Utrecht: Kemink en Zoon n.v., 1933).

26. This discussion is in van Rhijn, *Wessel Gansfort*, pp. 213-215.

27. B. J. Spruyt, *Cornelius Henrici Hoen (Honius) and his Epistle on the Eucharist* (Houten, The Netherlands: 1996). This study was published in English. A prelimary study on this subject by the same author was published in 1993 as: *"Laat middeleeuwse Ketterijen en de vroege hervorming in de Nederlanden: Cornelis Hendricxz Hoen en zijn Epistola Christiana (1525)," Doopsgezinde Bijdragen*, Vol 19 (1993), 115-128. A shorter version, seemingly a summary, appeared in Dutch the next year: *Ketter aan het Binnenhof: Cornelis Hoen en zijn tractaat tegen de transubstantieleer* (Heerenbeen: J. J. Groen en Zoon, 1997). We will refer to pagination as contained in the more extensive 1996 thesis.

28. This suggestion is in Spruyt's thesis (1996), pp. 161-162. As we compare the ideas of Wyclif and Hus, and as we find them reflected in Hoen's document, we will use not only the 1996 Leiden thesis, but also the Latin and the English version of Hoen's let-ter as follows: The Latin version, as published by Zwingli, is found in *ZW*, IV, 512-519. The English version is that of Paul Nyhus, trans., in Heiko Oberman, *Forerunners of the Reformation: The Shape of Late Medieval Thought* (Philadelphia: Fortress Press, 1966, 1981), pp. 268-278.

29. Spruyt's discussion of this point with reference to Wyclif is on pp. 164-165 in his thesis.

30. Hoen's letter, English trans., pp. 274, 268, 270.

31. *Ibid.*, p. 274.

32. The Latin reference is "*quod autem Christus quotidie impanatur (ut ita loquar) in manibus cuiusvis sacrificuli, neque a prophetis est predicatum nequa ab apostolis predica-tum* (from *ZW*, IV, 513, lines 29-30). .

33. The Latin statement of Hoen is: *Sed panis consecratus corrumpitur et a muribus comeditur, ut patet experientia: ergo panis consecratus non est Christus," ZW*, IV, 515, lines 3-4.

34. Spruyt thesis, pp. 166-168.

35 Latin, Nestle text: "*Expedit vobis ut ego vadam: si enim non abiero, paraclitus non veniet ad vos.*"

36. The Hebrew text is quoted in Latin translation, "*non dabis sanctum tuum videre corruptionem.*"

37. Hoen's letter, English trans. p. 273.   38. *Ibid.*, p. 273

Chapter 6

Cornelis Grapheus (1482-1558)
A Humanist Scholar who recanted

Prohibition of Printing in The Netherlands (8 May, 1521)
    Although the Emperor had directed various decrees against "blaspheming" toward The Netherlands, in 1521 he became more specific. By then the universities of Louvain/Leuven and Cologne had condemned the works of Luther, and many of these works had already been committed to the flames throughout the Empire. Emperor Charles' edict against The Netherlands—coming on the heels of his famous Edict of Worms[1]—not only forbad reading, writing, buying and selling works of Luther, but

> no bookseller, printer, or any other person whosoever shall presume to print or cause to be printed, any book or writing in which mention was made of the Holy Scriptures, or any interpretation of it, though ever so little, without permission first obtained.[2]

This edict obviously compromised the scholars of the region who prized good learning and accurate texts no matter what their source might be.
An early Humanist and editor who was affected by this decree was Cornelis Grapheus (the Greek form of his name)[3] also known by the Latin form as "Scribonius." He was secretary of the city of Antwerp, having held that position since 1520. He was well acquainted with the Humanists and their literature. On 5 February, 1522, he was arrested and imprisoned in Brussels.[4] His main crime was that almost one year earlier he had arranged for the first printing of the theological work *de Libertate Christiana* by John Pupper of Goch. Grapheus evaluated the work with glowing praise for the author and his significant theological ideas. It was evidently this preface which came under

suspicion because the remainder of the work was almost a half century old. The relationship between the ideas of John Pupper and Cornelis Grapheus is interesting and sheds light on further developments in this region of Brabant.

John Pupper of Goch (1420-1475)

John Pupper had been born shortly after the year 1400 (*ca.* 1420?), in the town of Goch, and was usually known as John of Goch rather than by his family name.[5] In the mid-15th century the town of Goch was a part of the Duchy of Gelres (Gelderland, most of which is now a part of The Netherlands). In 1473, however, the area around Goch became part of the Duchy of Cleves, (now a part of Westphalia, in western Germany). We know little of the education of John Pupper, but he may have been trained in the schools of the Brethren of the Common Life, perhaps in Zwolle. Some advanced education is indicated, and his name appeared on the matriculation records of Cologne for 19 December, 1454.[6] In 1459 he founded an Augustinian cloister, "The Tabor," in Mechelen/Malines a few miles north of Brussels. He became its prior and remained in this position to his death in 1475.[7] It was here that he wrote all his theological works, which were only published for the first time in the decade of the 1520s. Yet, none caused as much controversy as the *Libertate Christiana*, especially the preface (1521) written by Grapheus.[8]

Three other major works of John Pupper are preserved,[9] including some fragments on other topics: 1) e*pistola apologetica adversus quendam praedicaterii ordinii declarans*; 2) *dialogus de quatuor erroribus circa legem evangelicam exortis*; and 3) *Fragmenta aliquot*, which consisted of several fragments on monastic vows, grace and merits, faith and works, and on the perfection of evangelical religion.[10] As a scholar Grapheus became acquainted with these works. He edited one other work of Goch, the *Epistola Apologetica* in 1520.[11] It did not become a subject for the inquisitors, probably because the repression was not yet organized.

The main thrust of *de Libertate Christiana* is of interest to us, however, because this work is directly related to our analysis of developing religious ideas and consequent persecutions against printers in the southern Netherlands. There were supposed to be six sections to this book on liberty, but only three and a portion of the fourth were completed.[12]

The *first* section affirmed the scriptures as the only sure source of the Christian faith. He distinguished two "scriptures," the natural and the supernatural. The former included human knowledge such as philosophy, while the latter, the canonical scriptures, especially when interpreted, more literally, lead to the highest truth and faith. Philosophical knowledge is human, fallible, and divisive whether one is Albertist, or Thomist, or Scotist.

Scripture, however, the source of infallible truth, liberates from inadequate and divisive knowledge. Outside of Scripture, the works of the ancient fathers are more valuable than the "modern" doctors.

The *second* section concerned the human will, and the origin of sin. John of Goch was thoroughly Augustinian, emphasizing a strong doctrine of original sin which removed original righteousness, and caused a strong inclination toward evil. Only through God's grace can the human being be restored—however, not grace that works thorough faith alone, but grace active in love

The *third* portion of his writing condemned the merit system of the medieval church. He criticized merits of worthiness, of congruity, and condignity as being all, or in part, Pelagian. Cooperative grace was also rejected. The only merits of value are the merits of Christ.

The fragments we have of the *fourth* section referred to vows. Rather than an outer law or a new Mosaic law such as a vow, the Christian should aspire to the inner law, the evangelical law. As he summarily observed,

> The essential object of the Gospel law is to emancipate man from all bondage and constraint, and to exalt him to the full liberty of the children of God, and, therefore, all that it requires of him is, with genuine and holy affection, to love God and his neighbor, as it is by this one thing, embracing every other, that he is delivered from coercion, and conducted to the glory of the children of God.[13]

Cornelis Grapheus as a humanist scholar, writer and editor

Cornelis Grapheus was a Humanist scholar; therefore, it was not unusual that he should be knowledgeable about literature of the period, including theological tracts. He related in an autobiographical letter: "On my own I learned poetry, music, and the art of drawing or painting. I acquired some taste of Greek and Latin as far as time and fortune will permit."[14]

He was born in Aalst, Flanders, in 1482.[15] We know nothing of his early life, but to enhance his learning of language and literature he traveled widely in Italy.[16] He was a close friend of Erasmus, and several letters between them have been preserved. Other humanist scholars who were his friends included Willibald Pirckheimer in Nürnberg, the painter Albrecht Dürer, and Gerhard Geldenhouwer, private secretary to Bishop Philip of Burgundy.[17] Although Grapheus became Secretary of Antwerp only in 1520, he lived there some years earlier. Indeed, he was a spokesman for the city when he organized the celebration honoring Charles' election as Emperor in 1519.

The next year (1520) when Charles came from Spain to The Netherlands on his way to assume authority in the Empire, Grapheus wrote a long poem [338 lines] for the occasion.[18] He extolled the virtues of Charles, as the new hero of learning who will bring a golden age and eternal peace to the whole world. The Pope will again be a true Christian leader and will have no aspirations toward world domination; he will be a shepherd of people.

To you, great priest [*Antistes magnus*];
You will follow in the steps of Peter of your own accord;
He will discreetly restore one sword to you;
Your oath required you to be content to assist in the holy services of the Gods [*Deorum*];
To exercise the office of pastor and of father piously,
To protect from treachery of wolves,
To scatter the seeds of the divine word everywhere,
To teach the uninstructed, to make firm the wavering ones,
To chastise the evil ones, to extend Christ to all.
The offices of priest are most glorious;
These are the arms and the sword which tames rebellious spirits.

The Emperor on the other hand, will be the glorious king of all lands.

To you, however, (never doubt) is due another sword, And other authorities:
You should be the greatest one of all.
At one time the hero of Tiryntha [*i.e.*, Hercules] carried the world on his shoulders;
Hercules was great, but you are greater, you are braver;
You do not have such shoulders as he, nor such a strong back;
You have no help from Atlas;
But you convince by means of your own virtue,
Or as in one hand you bring together all peoples of the world;
You will be called `Great Lord of the whole world'."[19]

We do not know what led Grapheus the next year to John of Goch's *Libertate Christiana*, but it is suggested that his friend, Nicholas van s'Hertogenbosch (also known as Nicholas Buscoducensis), teacher of the Latin School in Antwerp, sent him a copy.[20] Unfortunately, within a year of his publication of this work, he was arrested for suspicion of "Lutheranism."[21] Not only did the title of this work sound strangely similar to one of Luther's recent writings,[22] but Grapheus evidently had spoken favorably about some Luther's ideas. Indeed, he may even have been a promoter or salesman of recent publications of Luther. Albrecht Dürer, who was in Antwerp in June 1521, wrote[23] that Grapheus gave him a copy of Luther's *Babylonian Captivity of the Church*—quite illegal according to the edict of the Emperor issued one month earlier. What other works of Luther he may have had we can only surmise. He remained in prison in Brussels from 5 February, 1522, until his trial two and a half months later on 23 April.[24]

The preface to *Liberate* included some common criticisms by the Humanists which were consistent with Luther and the later Reformers' complaints.[25] As we have seen, the distinctions between the Humanists and the early Reformers were not always clear at this time. Grapheus undoubtedly thought that he was giving a true interpretation which no thinking Christian could deny; he meant to enlighten his readers, rather than become a heretic. He began the preface by affirming that Jesus Christ purchased our freedom when he took away sin and made it possible for us to be adopted as sons and daughters. Alas, however, we have sunk back into slavery more than the Egyptians, into superstition more than the Pharisees. "We have regressed from Christ to Moses and backslidden from Moses to Pharaoh."[26] Instead of the promises of the Savior, we have begun to trust in "human fables" (*fabulis hominum*).

> For the Gospel we have substituted decrees [of the Pope]; for Christ, a certain [*quendam*] Aristotle; for piety, ceremonies; for truth, deception and division; fearing all things we do nothing because of faith or love.[27]

These problems have plagued the church for 800 years so that almost all the church's activity has become less adequate and worthy than in ages past.

Once all were people of God, a chosen generation, a royal priesthood (I Peter 2:9). Now, rather than being heirs of Christ we are "sons of the earthly Adam, or of St. Francis, others of St. Dominic, others of Augustine or Bernard."[28] In place of the simple gospel we now are confronted with "jest, sophistry, conclusions and distinctions." In place of Jesus Christ, our heavenly foundation, we have set up an earthly head, an "idol" [*idolum quasi*].[29] Once the services of the church were performed freely, but now "there is nothing that cannot be purchased with money." "All things, no matter how holy, are objects for sale," and even a burial place for a Christian is not available without a fee. Once Christians could choose their own pastors, but now "ambitious men, with tyrannical power, by gifts and menaces . . . intrude into the spiritual office. . . .Ignorant hirelings, men living with concubines or profligates are generally chosen."[30]

Unworthy priests, who are ignorant of the gospel and more enamored with the schoolmen than with Jesus Christ, cannot teach the true faith. Furthermore, the hierarchy demands that only the learned and those trained in scholastic methodologies should be allowed to interpret scriptures. Others do not know logic nor anything about theology, we are told. Yet, according to Grapheus, the scriptures and sound theological works should be available for all to read. His highest regard for the capabilities of humanity is obvious.

> I very much wish, in so far as the philosophy of Christ is common to all, that it were carefully translated into the vulgar tongues by erudite and good interpreters. Then every professor of the Christian religion, at least those who can read, can buy a book and, prompted by the spirit, might be led to a knowledge of evangelical philosophy.[31]

In this way the people again can be conducted along the "royal road directly to Christ."

> This, I well know, will be opposed by those gluttonous monks (I always except the good ones) who with pleasure pervert the work of God to their own gain. I shall not, however, be restrained by them, for there is need that the truth should at some time be set in its rightful place.[32]

The truth of Christ is being restored, he suggested, and Paul is being brought back to life. Among those involved in this new development

> I introduce you to John of Goch, a man of singular erudition and second to none in his own time. He is a zealous defender of Christian liberty, a diligent interpreter of evangelical law. Turn to him day and night, especially when you have leisure from reading the sacred literature and the epistles of Paul, for the latter should be your major study. Farewell in Christ Jesus.[33]

Then follows the date: "In the years from Christ's birth 1521, 4 before the calends of April" [29 March, 1521].[34]

Grapheus recanted on 23 April, 1522[35] in Brussels, after examination by the inquisitors Frans van der Hulst and Nicolaus Baechem [van Egmond]. Selections of his writings were excerpted by the authorities and formed into propositions which he was then asked to deny. We note, however, that these statements are much more specific, and contain many more seemingly "reformed" ideas than can be documented in his extant writings. Since he swore to the articles, we are assured that they were probably representative not only of his extant writings, but other statements which he may have discussed. His recantation is in three parts.

In the *first* part he made the statement which was demanded.

> I, Cornelius Grapheus, anathematize all heresy and precepts being promulgated by brother Martin Luther as taught in his books and sermons. . . . Especially I reject certain articles among those written in a certain preface to a certain book entitled *de libertate Christiana*, edited from John Pupper of Goch. . . which [preface] I wrote with my own hand.

He affirmed that he believed whatever the Holy Roman Church confessed.

Then he related to us the process against him. "I was interrogated and examined by the Commissioners of the Emperor's Majesty designated for this purpose, about the contents in the previously-mentioned preface, including those which follow."

The *second* portion of the trial document included 18 propositions drawn from his work. These are translated as an Appendix IV in this study and are only summarized here.[36]

(1) He was critical of the Church because of its increasing emphasis on laws and requirements. Examples of this legalism which he cites are: confessions once per year, monastic vows, fasting, food laws, canonical hours, rosaries, frequent prayers, and worship limited to churches or certain supposedly more holy places. He called these restrictions superstition or a return to Jewish ceremonialism.

(2) He criticized the power and presumption of the Pope, indicating correctly that the term "supreme pontiff" was assumed first in the time of Boniface III (*A.D.* 607). All successors have arrogated to themselves the privilege of making laws, as though by divine decree, and have required certain practices which, if the believers did not follow through, would condemn them as guilty of mortal sin. He doubted the superiority of Peter among the apostles, and he suggested that the office of the papacy is merely idolatry

(3) He denied the strict separation between priest and laity and, by implication, questioned the validity of ordination as a sacrament confirming this separation. Indeed, all lay *men* [*sic*], (he explicitly denied the privilege to women and children) are priests and are able to consecrate the "venerable" sacraments of the communion if given permission to do so. (This assumption implied a non sacramental understanding of the Eucharist). Likewise, since lay *men* [*sic*] were originally allowed to teach and interpret the scriptures in public, the present practice of limiting this to masters, bachelors or licentiates (*i.e.* those within the ecclesiastical hierarchy), reflected a limitation or a "slavery" which he could not accept.

(4) He gave precedence to the Bible, especially the writings of Paul, in opposition to the practice of giving prime authority to "subtleties" of the scholastics.

(5) He denied merit of our own works, denied the meritorious nature of confession, and stated that indulgences have no benefits.

(6) He condemned certain financial arrangements in which priests expected extra money for performing the rites of the church such as administration of sacraments, conducting funerals, and preaching.

(7) The writings of Luther were commended to be read because they were biblical and rejected scholastic ideas. The Pope's condemnation of Luther and

his teachings was unjust because it was based neither on scripture nor reason.

(8) The work of John of Goch is the most important theological work of the recent past, and more valuable than works of the scholastics.

The *third* section of the trial document was an expansion of the 18 articles, giving the Roman Catholic explanation as to why the propositions were in error. We suspect that these summaries, as well as the 18 propositions, were written by the authorities and not by Grapheus himself, despite what he said at the conclusion of this third part.

> These above statements I, Cornelius Grapheus, freely and wilfully have written; and in the form as written, I am content and prepared to revoke and deny as has been required of me. Witnessed by my own hand, 23 April, 1522.[37]

At the conclusion of the hasty trial his sentence was pronounced in six parts: 1) His goods were confiscated (although he reiterated that he had little); 2) he was deprived of his office and forever forbidden to assume another; 3) he must make another recantation in the City of Antwerp; 4) he would be brought back to Brussels to be confined in prison for two months; 5) thereafter, he would be confined within the city walls of Brussels perpetually; and 6) he must wear a mark of scandal on his clothing.[38] A few days later (29 April, 1522)[39] he repeated his recantation in the market place in Brussels, and there publicly burned his preface to John of Goch's book. Shortly after his trial in Brussels, he was taken to Antwerp where on 6 May of the same year in Our Lady's [O.L.V.—*Onse Lieve Vrouw*] Church he confessed once again.[40] On that same day Luther's books were burned in Antwerp while the Emperor was visiting in the city.[41]

Erasmus followed the proceedings and was well aware of the fate of his friend, Grapheus. On 14 July, 1522, from Basel he wrote a very sharp criticism of his treatment. The letter was directed to Pierre Barbier, who was in Rome as chaplain to Pope Adrian VI.[42] Erasmus did not miss an opportunity to express his disgust also against his constant opponent, the inquisitor, Nicholas Baechem of Egmond.

> X, [Cornelius Schrijver, Grapheus], an excellent young man and a good scholar, was treated by him [Baechem] with a tyranny worthy of Phalaris [a tyrant in ancient history, 6th Century, *B.C.*] because he called Baechem a fool [lines 97-102].[43]

Erasmus had many times expressed his disdain for Baechem in words equally inflammatory.

Despite his recantation, Grapheus was returned to prison in Brussels, where we know nothing about him for several months. His wife and small children remained in Antwerp with no means of supporting themselves. Their poverty became a growing concern for him. Finally, later that same year, so he related, his wife wrote a plea to the Chancellor of Brabant to ask that her husband at least be imprisoned in his home area of Antwerp rather than in Brussels where all people were strangers to him. We have a long autobiographical letter which Grapheus wrote (18 November, 1522) to the same Chancellor of Brabant, John [or Jean] Carondelet (who was at the same time Archbishop, in absentia, of Palermo, where he never visited).[44] Grapheus emphasized that he had written the preface "long before the Emperor's placard came out."[45] He admitted that he may have written "rashly," but it "was only for the exercise of my mind without design of giving the least offense." He was a scholar and should have been allowed to pursue his studies.

> Whatever evil has been committed by me is the result of an active mind, but not a malicious one. If the human mind, exposed in any respect to error, purely from a desire of exercise, without any ill intention, without perverseness or obstinacy, but with submission to the correction of better judgments; I say, if a mind so disposed should be the occasion of our ruin, how much better were it that we should be brute beasts, or inanimate creatures, than men.

He then compared his situation with that of Ovid. If that "sweetest of poets" should suffer banishment for his work, it would have been better if Ovid had never been created with such a mind but rather a recluse or a man-hater. About himself, Grapheus wrote,

> In case an understanding neither obstinate nor perverse, but always disposed to amend itself upon even the least admonition, has involved me in these troubles, which overwhelm me on all sides, how much more advantageous had it been to me, to have been deprived of my senses, or to have been a fool, a buffoon, a comedian, or a parasite and flatterer, or any such despicable creature. . . .

He argued the case for good letters against bigotry in religious thought:

> Certainly then, a good genius, especially such as is tractable, and ready to listen to good advice, ought not to be immediately oppressed but handled gently; not terrified by force and severity, but allured with rewards and promises, and helped forward by all possible means, even though it should chance to have done amiss through ignorance or imprudence, which is the common effect of human frailty.[46]

He then related his reaction to the trial.

> I acknowledged my indiscretion, and testified my sorrow; and was ready to
> retract my errors, to detest my obstinacy, and to ask pardon of my rashness;
> when suddenly I was thrust into a dungeon like a heretic.

He complained that he did not really have a fair trial either by the laws of the
state or of the church (Matthew 18:15-18) which ordered him to retract all the
articles drawn from his works and to burn the preface he had written.
Following this the six sections of his sentence were reiterated as noted
above.[47]

He was appalled at the methods of the inquisitors who conducted their
activities according neither to church nor state laws. Indeed, even Jews who
leave Judaism or heathens who give up heathenism are welcomed as
Christians. Yet his situation is less serious than theirs, even though in the New
Testament there is rejoicing over the one sinner who repents rather than the
ninety-nine who are upright. He unjustly received "a certain mark of
unbearable scandal, unworthy of a Christian man with a pious name from an
upright family, and not from the dregs [*heffe*] of the people."[48]

The prisoner then turned in his letter to more pressing present problems.
His goods were confiscated. Thus his wife, still in Antwerp, had no means of
supporting herself and her children. She had petitioned several times that he be
allowed to be imprisoned in Antwerp where he at least had friends, but Frans
van der Hulst, the inquisitor, had not bothered to answer her request. "That
gentleman has delayed giving it [answer], to my great prejudice, even to this
very day, after using several evasions. . . ."[49]

There was common concern in The Netherlands about the degree to which
the inquisitors were forcing decisions and promulgating opinions contrary to
the ancient rights of the people of The Netherlands. Was not the inquisitor
really assuming prerogatives over which the political authorities should have
control? Grapheus appealed to the greater concern, he hoped, of the
Chancellor of Brabant.

> Certainly it cannot be thought, that the Council in which you preside, should
> ever have required his advice, if that same Council, according to its wonted
> discretion, had not known before-hand, what power he had in these matters.
> Perhaps he defers giving his advice, that he may weigh the matter more
> maturely. He has fed us poor wretches now almost these three months with
> doubtful hopes. . . . We most humbly beseech and conjure you, for Christ's
> sake. . .that by your means, that most illustrious and most gracious princess,

the regent, together with the Council, may vouchsafe to require Master van der Hulst at last, without further delay or subterfuge, to communicate his opinion.[50]

He did not fail to remind the Chancellor of his previous loyalty to the Emperor.

Nor will you, I hope, think this to be an unreasonable request, when you consider how great my inclination and desires have been to serve the Emperor to the best of my power; for which purpose I send you some little tracts which I have published just before my imprisonment, in honor of his majesty, such as a welcome from Spain [*i.e.* when Charles had returned in 1520].[51]

Indeed, the prisoner stated that he planned to write even more tracts concerning the Emperor, but his imprisonment had made that impossible.

As far as we can determine, this letter to the Chancellor of Brabant did not have any immediate effects. Indeed, very soon thereafter Grapheus expressed himself again, this time in Latin poetry to one of his Humanist friends.[52] The 180 line poem was sent to Gerhard Geldenhouwer of Nijmegen (or Noviomagus), Secretary to the Bishop of Utrecht.[53] He told about the bad conditions in the prison, bad health conditions, darkness, and dampness. Evidently, the administrators of the prison did not lack for methods of agitating and tormenting their prisoners.

In every respect we are made the objects of blame, we are talked about, joked about, victims of insensitivity, of desecration, horrible hissing and what else? What, alas, should be done next? Should we despair? Oh, no, we will not despair; for if we forsake the world, the best of all is that Christ will in no way forsake us. Look! Christ is present; the walls tremble, the columns of the prison shake and twist, and a glorious light reveals the bending of the arches. In the midst of the light stands Christ approaching the melancholy ones; and on the right human illnesses are soothed by the heavenly; sadness of the soul is cured by divine salve [*unguine*] and the weak are lifted up sound. . . .Such is the honey and sweetness of the presence of Christ. . . .If Christ is with us, all fear is empty, and it is not able to touch one who is turned toward Christ with a spirit of courage.[54]

Whatever response Grapheus may have received from his friend at the Bishop's headquarters in Utrecht is unknown.

How long the imprisonment lasted is also unknown. The experience was evidently so shattering for Grapheus that he ceased being a creative or aggressive scholar, and he became very cautious about what he wrote.[55] In later years he did edit and publish various tracts, but none having anything to do with the church or with theology except a book condemning Anabaptists.[56] The close association with Erasmus, however, continued to the end of the latter's life. The London edition of his letters suggested that in his last will (1536) he provided for Cornelis Grapheus: "Let 50 golden florins and 46 Rhenish be given to Cornelius Grapheus, whom I suspect to be in need. He is a man worthy of a better fate."[57] While only the London edition of his letters included these words, we are not sure how they were incorporated into the later will. They were undoubtedly erroneously transferred from a letter written twelve years earlier.

In 1524 Erasmus wrote to Conrad Goclenius, professor of Latin at Louvain/Leuven: "It remains for me to commend to you, the most reliable of friends, the thing I hold most dear, which is my posthumous reputation" (lines 126-128). Erasmus sent him his *compendium vitae*, knowing that opponents might try to vilify his character or modify the details.

> If anything should happen to me in the way of mortality, I want you to have 400 gold florins. . . [meant for various named people]; 50 gold florins and 46 and a half Rhenish to Cornelis Schrijver [Grapheus], whom I suspect to be in need though he is a man who deserved a better position [lines 132-136].[58]

Grapheus lived with his family in Antwerp the remainder of his life. In 1540 he was restored to his position as secretary of the city.[59] He died there on 19 December, 1558, as we are told, in the good graces of the Roman Catholic Church.

Notes for Chapter 6

1. The Edict of Worms, dated 8 May, 1521, [but there is uncertainty if this date was really inserted later to give the impressison that it was issued on this early date]. It was published shortly thereafter in Latin in the Netherlands at Louvain/Leuven, and still later at Antwerp [*NK* 1261, Antwerp]. The Latin text is printed in *CDI*, IV, 47-57. The special edict incorporating much of the wording from the Latin text, but expanding certain sections with special reference to The Netherlands, carries the same date. The second version was published in both the French/Walloon, and the Dutch/Flemish languages. The last of these is much longer and includes more detail. The two special documents for The Netherlands are published in parallel columns and parallel languages, in *CDI*, IV, 60-76.

2. *Ibid.*, p. 75.

3. A biographical sketch of Grapheus appears in P.S. Allen, *Erasmi Epistolae* (hereafter Allen *Epistolae)*, IV, 225, in relation to a letter Eramus wrote to him. C. Ullmann, in *Reformers before the Reformation*, has some biographical material in so far as Grapheus was related to John Pupper of Goch. Cf. C. Ullmann, *Reformers before the Reformation*, trans. Robert Menzies (2 vols. Edinburgh: T. and T. Clark, 1855), I, 397-416. Otto Clemen, who wrote a definitive study on John Pupper of Goch (see note 4, *infra*) included some information on Grapheus summarized in his article in *Realencyklopaedia für protestantische Theologie und Kirche*, VII, 61f.

4. *CDI*, IV, 88, as reprinted from the *Annales Antverpienses.*

5. The most complete study of the life and work of John Pupper of Goch is by Otto Clemen, *Johann Pupper von Goch* (Leipzig: Duncker and Humbolt, 1896). The same author summarized his work in the article "Goch" in *Realencyklopaedia für protestantische Theologie und Kirche*, VI, 740-743.

6. Otto Clemen discovered this reference in the records of the University of Cologne. Cf. his *John Pupper von Goch*, p. 27.

7. Some of the problems concerning this date are discussed by Clemen in his work on Goch, p. 39. One of the earliest references to the date of Goch's death is by Grapheus himself.

8. *NK* 3111, as edited and published by Grapheus in Antwerp, March, 1521.

9. These writing are discussed and analyzed by Clemen in his study on Goch, pp. 43-72.

10. 1) *NK* 1011, Epistola Apologetica super doctrina doctorum scholasticorum, ed. Grapheus, Antwerp, August 23, 1520; and *NK* 3110, Epistola apologetica declarans quid de scholasticorum scripturis, probably The Netherlands, 1521, also ed. Grapheus. 2) *NK* 3109, *Dialogus de quatuor erroribus circa evangelicam legem exhortis*, Zwolle, 1521. 3) *NK* 1012, *Fragmenta aliquot*, (Several Fragments on monastic vows, grace and merits, faith and works, and on the perfection of evangelical religion), Zwolle, 1521.

11. Otto Clemen discussed this *Epistola Apologetica* (published 1521) and the preface by Grapheus, in his *John Pupper of Goch*, pp. 50-54.

12. The complete *Libertate* of Goch has been printed in the original Latin in *Bibliotheca Reformatoria Neerlandica* (hereafter *BRN*), VI, 33-225. Clemen discussed this major work in *John Pupper of Goch*, pp. 43-50.

13. This summary appears in C. Ullmann *Reformers before the Reformation*, I, 81.

14. This statement is included in his autobiographical letter written to Johann Carondelet, the Chancellor of Brabant and bishop of Palermo, on 18 November, 1522. The letter is printed in *BRN*, VI, 256-263. The English translation is in Gerard Brandt, *History of the Reformation and other ecclesiastical transactions in and about the Low countries* (London: T. Wood, 1720-1723); reprinted (New York: AMS Press, 1979), I, 43.

15. Otto Clemen has included a biography of Grapheus in his work, *John Pupper von Goch*, pp. 269-275.

16. This biographical material appears in his autobiographical letter of November 18, 1522, as noted above, written to the chancellor of Brabant. His complete letter to Carondelet is on pp. 42-45.

17. Cf. biographical section of Clemen's work on Goch.

18. The poem [*NK* 1026, Antwerp, 1520] was printed in *CDI*, IV, 152-156.

19. The section of this poem translated here appears in *BRN*, ed. F. Pijper, vol VI, "Geschriften van Johann Pupper van Goch en Corn. Grapheus" [1520], 603-604.

20. Nicholas van s'Hertogenbosch (1478-1550), also known as Nicholas Buscoducensis, was a humanist scholar and schoolmaster in Antwerp. He was in regular correspondence with Erasmus. As early as 1521 he was suspected of the "Lutheran" heresy, and was familiar with Luther's writings. He was imprisoned, then released in May, 1522. Later the same year he stayed a short time at Basel where Erasmus had arrived one year previously. He served the cause of the Reformation in Denmark and Bremen, Germany, until the Augsburg Interim in 1548. This Nicholas was first introduced above in Chapter 3.

21. *CDI*, IV, 88, 5 February, 1522.

22. Luther's recent work was entitled also *de libertate Christiana*. It was printed in Germany in November, 1520, and the Latin text was printed four times within a year in the Netherlands: Antwerp, 1520, 1520, 1521 and Zwolle, 1521 (according to C. Ch. G. Visser, *Luther's Geschriften in de Nederlande tot 1546*, pp. 51f). Perhaps the identical titles of Luther's work and the earlier tract caused extra concern for the inquisitors, although the content and major emphases of the two are quite different.

23. This is quoted from the collection of Dürer's letters, and reprinted in *CDI*, IV, 77. The *Babylonian Captivity* had been published in Antwerp in 1521 [*NK* 3450], and in Leiden [*NK* 3451] the same year. The latter carries a camouflage statement to delude the censors--"printed in Wittenberg." Undoubtedly Grapheus' copy was the version as printed in Antwerp. The next year, 1522, a Dutch/Flemish translation appeared, but it is not known where it was printed, or who translated it.

24. *CDI*, IV, 105.

25. The preface to *Libertate* in the original Latin is printed in *BRN*, VI, 33ff; and in Otto Clemen, *John Pupper of Goch*, pp. 255-260. An English translation of some of this is included in Ullmann, *Reformers Before the Reformation*, I, 138-141. The latter has been modified as seemed necessary when compared with the Latin, and references are to the Latin edition of the preface in Clemen, *Goch*, pp. 255-260. The page numbers in these references relate to Clemen's edition of the Preface.

26. Preface to *Libertate*, as printed in Clemen, *Goch*, p. 255;; also in *BRN*, VI, 35-36.

27. *Ibid.*, Preface to *Libertate*, p. 256.

28. *Ibid.*, p. 256.

29. *Ibid.*, p. 257.

30. *Ibid.*, p. 257.

31. *Ibid.*, pp. 258-259.

32. *Ibid.*, p. 259.

33. *Ibid.*, p. 259.

34. *Ibid.*, p. 260.

35. The recantation is printed in Fredericq, *CDI*, IV, 105. It is a copy from Gerdes, *Scrininum Antiquarium* (1764).

36. These 18 propositions are printed in *CDI*, IV, 105ff. They contain basic theological concerns of the period, and for this reason are translated in full, and appear as Appendix IV of this study.

37. The longer explanation to each of the 18 propositions gave the official Roman Catholic position on each point. For our purposes it has not seemed necessary to translate them in the text of this study.

38. The punishment is explained by the prisoner in his long autobiographical letter to Carondelet. The sentence itself is printed in *CDI* IV, 147.

39. Clemen thought this public recantation was separate, and a few days later than the trial and recantation noted above.

40. From the *Annales Antverpienses*, as printed in *CDI*, IV 122. The facts are substantiated also by a report of J.C. Diercxsens, *Antverpia Christo nasens et crescens*, as printed in 1747-1763, and reprinted in *CDI*, IV 122f.

41. From the *Chronycke van Antwerp*, as printed in *CDI*, IV 121. The visit of Charles on the same day was reported in *Die excellente cronike van Vlaenderen*, as reprinted in *CDI*, IV, 121. This was actually the second burning of books, for the first such conflagration was held on 13 July, 1521 (*CDI*, IV, 17).

42. Barbier was from The Netherlands [Arras] and was associated with Adrian before his papal election. He accompanied him to Rome. See *CWE*, IX, # 1294, dated 14 July 1522, introduction.

43. *CWE*, # 1302, 14 July, 1522, Erasmus wrote from Basel to Barbier in Rome.

44. This information about his wife is a part of the autobiographical letter written to John [or Jean] Carondelet, Chancellor of Brabant, *CDI*, IV, 145-151. This letter also included the long autobiographical section which Grapheus dated 18 November 1522, from his prison in Brussels. The English version of Gerard Brandt's, *The History of the Reformation. . .in and about the Low Countries*, contained translations of parts of the letter, pp. 42-45. Although the letter was originally written in Latin, *CDI* included only a Flemish/Dutch translation.

45. Depending on which of the Emperor's edicts is meant, this can be either true or merely rationalization. The first edict from the Emperor was dated 20 March, 1521, nine days before the date of the preface. The revised and translated Edict of Worms was dated 8 May, one and one half months later than the date of the preface.

46. G. Brandt, *History of the Reformation. . . .* I, 43.

47. *Ibid.*, p. 43.

48. *Ibid.*, p. 44.

49. *Ibid.*, p. 44.

50. *Ibid.*, pp. 44-45.

51. *Ibid.*, p. 45.

52. This long poem, entitled "Querimonia in carceris angustia" [Complaints concerning difficulties in prison], is printed in *CDI*, IV, 152-156.

53. Gerhard Geldenhouwer (or Gerhardus Noviomagus after his birthplace of Nijmegen) (1482-1542), a humanist and friend of Grapheus, was secretary of the lenient Bishop of Utrecht, Philip of Burgundy, until the latter died in 1524. Thereafter, Gerhard went to Germany where he became an avowed Protestant and lived in Strasbourg, Augsburg and Marburg to his death in 1542. We introduced more complete information concerning him in chapter 3, above.

54. The section of the poem which is here translated touches most closely some of the theological questions raised in the trial and imprisonment of Grapheus. This portion appears in *CDI*, IV, 153f.

55. Letter written by Grapheus to Albrecht Dürer, 23 February, 1524, noted in Allen, *Epistolae*, IV, 225.

56. *NK* 1024, Antwerp, 1535.

57. Erasmus wrote to a close friend, Conrad Goclenius, concerning the details of how to carry out the wishes of his will. This appears in the London edition of Erasmus' letters. Reported by C. Ullmann, *Reformers before the Reformation*, I, 415. When we begin to discuss Erasmus's wills we are faced with confusion. There were three, of which only two have been preserved. We are concerned only with the last, dated 12 February, 1536, five months before Erasmus died (see Allen, XI, Appendix XXV, pp. 362-365). In that letter he mentioned a gift to Conrad Goclenius, an old friend of Erasmus, and a long-time professor of Latin in Louvain (see *Contemporaries of Erasmus*, I, 42-46). Evidently Erasmus left money in trust to Goclenius at various times after he left Louvain/Leuven in 1521, but details as to how Erasmus wanted it distributed were not established until later. The last will merely mentions the funds which Goclenius had, but no details for distribution. The details concerning the gift to Grapheus appear only in the London edition of Erasmus's Works, which unfortunately I have not seen. The chapter on "Erasmus's Last Will," by P.P.J. L. van Peteghem, published in J. Sperna Weiland and W. Th. M. Frijhoff, *Erasmus of Rotterdam: The Man and The Scholar* (Leiden and New York: Brill Publishers, 1988), pp. 88-97, does not result in complete clarification because research is still continuing.

58. *CWE*, X, # 1437, 2 April, 1524, from Basel.

59. Otto Clemen, writing in *Realencyklopaedia für protestantische Theologie und Kirche*, VII, 61f.

Chapter 7

Lutheran Ideas, Dissenters and Martyrdoms

Like the Latin schools and the intellectuals, some of the monasteries were also abuzz with the new theological ideas. . There were four cloisters of the Observant (strict) branch of the Augustinian order in The Netherlands in this period, a part of the over-all Saxon Congregation. The first cloister in Haarlem was founded in 1493 by monks of the Saxon Congregation. By the turn of the century a second congregation was organized in Dordrecht, where an early prior was Henry of Zutphen (to be analyzed later in this chapter).

A third house was developed at Enkhuizen, 30 miles north of Amsterdam. The prior in this monastery early in the century was the well-respected Johannes van Mechelen, who was sent by his superior, Johannes von Staupitz, to Rome on a five-month business trip concerning the order. A companion on this trip (1510-1511) was a young monk from Erfurt named Martin Luther.[1]

Soon after they returned from Rome, Mechelen led several monks in establishing a fourth house in Antwerp (1513). They constructed their building in Antwerp that same year; but the first decade of this monastery proved to be turbulent and it was finally destroyed in 1523.

In 1503 Staupitz, Luther's confidant in his formative years, was chosen Vicar-General of the Observant Augustinians, with supervision over the houses in Saxony and the four in The Netherlands. Because of his office he made official visits to The Netherlands before the Luther question was raised. For this reason the connection between the cloisters in The Netherlands and the Augustinian leaders in Wittenberg was very close. Many monks from The Netherlands studied in Wittenberg, and several formed close personal contacts with Martin Luther. Indeed, Otto Clemen estimated that during the time of Luther perhaps one hundred Augustinians from The Netherlands studied in Wittenberg.[2] Staupitz himself had supported Luther at first. After the publication of Luther's 1520 documents, however, he began to have second thoughts. He finally severed his relation with Luther, and accepted an invitation to go to Salzburg and join the Benedictine order.[3]

Let us follow the careers of three of the priors in the Antwerp monastery: **first**, the second prior, Jacobus Praepositus, who chose to escape to Germany in 1522; **second**, the third prior, Henry of Zutphen, who also escaped to Germany in 1522 only to be martyred there in 1524; and **third**, the last prior, Lambert de Thoren who was imprisoned for several years while two of his brother monks became the first martyrs for the Reformation cause in The Netherlands (perhaps the first in all Europe). In addition, we will follow the career of a shoe-maker in Dordrecht who may have been influenced by the monastery there, or specifically by Henry of Zutphen who was prior in Dordrecht for five years (1515-1520).

Praepositus of Antwerp

Gradually, a growing suspicion of heresy centered on Jacob Praepositus (the name, Praepositus, is the Latinized form for Jacob Proost [Dutch] or Propst [German])[4] the second prior of the new Augustinian Observant monastery in Antwerp. Praepositus, who became the second prior in 1518 or 1519, was evidently among the first persons in The Netherlands to preach Lutheran doctrines openly at this early date, 1518 or 1519. He was born toward the end of the 15th century, probably in Ypres/Ieper, Flanders.[5]

That Praepositus's activities were not secret can be noted from a letter which Erasmus wrote to Luther, 30 May, 1519. He stated:

> There is a man in Antwerp, the prior of the monastery there, a genuine Christian, who is most devoted to you and was once your pupil, or so he says. He is almost the only one among them all who preaches Christ; the others as a rule preach the inventions of men or their own advantage [lines 61-65].[6]

It is not clear how extensive Praepositus's knowledge of Luther's thought and activities was at this early date, although he advocated many ideas similar to Luther's. Janssen has preserved the letter in which Praepositus evaluated his work. "[I] preached at Antwerp with all diligence with considerable modesty and attempted to counteract the vile lies which were being spread against the Christian Doctor Martin Luther."[7]

In 1520 Praepositus travelled to Wittenberg to study, where he received his degree Baccalaureus Biblicus on 13 May, 1521, and the Licentiate in Theology on 12 July of the same year. Since he studied at Wittenberg during the time of the Diet of Worms and Luther's later confinement at the Wartburg, we do not know how close their association could have been. Yet they evidently met and began a long friendship.

After Praepositus returned to Antwerp, he advocated the theology he had learned. The authorities became suspicious and in the autumn of 1521 Nicholas Baechem of Egmond, acting as an inquisitor, was sent by the government of Margaret and her councilors to hear the preaching of Praepositus and report back to them.[8] Praepositus summarized some of the happenings at the time. "God hindered this work," so he stated, "when his [the inquisitor's] horse threw him off, injuring one of his legs."[9] On 5 December, 1521, the eve of St. Nicholaas Day, Baechem returned with other representatives of the inquisition to ask Praepositus to come to Brussels for a disputation.[10] The accused was told "you have nothing to fear, nothing to doubt, nothing evil stands against you. You are called for your own good, and if you wish, you may stay in my house and be my guest."[11] When they got to Brussels, however, the prior was immediately imprisoned on the charge that he had preached against the Pope and his spiritual authority—that Praepositus had preached, instead, the evangelical teachings.[12] Not completely certain what his fate might be, since there was no precedent for martyrdom in the Netherlands at this time, Praepositus wrote a letter from prison to a friend, Casper, expressing his faith. "Didn't Paul say that all who want to live piously in Christ must suffer persecution?" (II Cor. 2:10; II Tim. 3:12). In January, 1522, Erasmus in Basel received word of Praepositus's imprisonment from his Humanist friend, Juan Luis Vives, who wrote from Louvain/Leuven.

> There is an Augustinian who has been haled from Antwerp to Brussels to stand his trial; the cripple [Latomus] and the Camel [*i.e.* the Carmelite, Baechem] have come post-haste to the scene. These men, I fear, have been spreading wicked falsehoods about you; but they were already doing that before Luther was born (lines 25-29).[13]

This indicated again the close relationship between Erasmus and Luther's sympathizers in the earliest years of the reforming movements.

During more than a month, while he was in prison, Praepositus was visited by the inquisitors. Each of his inquisitorial guests tried to convince him to change his mind and agree to recantation. For some time Praepositus continued reaffirming his theological views concerning fasting and limiting the sacraments to only three. He insisted that God's law was more important than human (and papal) law, and he emphasized the importance of faith alone giving evidence in love.[14] The inquisitorial visitors continued coming, raising in Praepositus's mind false hopes that they really heard his suggestions and understood them. Some time shortly after Christmas (1521), so Praepositus related, they told him very bluntly that he must either recant or die. The prisoner, realizing they meant what they said, succumbed to their threats. "I agreed to follow through with the revocation according to their wishes, with my mouth—but God knows, not with my heart."[15]

The day of his recantation was 9 February, 1522. Before St. Goedele
Church in Brussels he took his stand and recanted , "loud and clear" (as he was
told), so the inquisitors could hear every word.[16] The thirty statements that he renounced, reflected many of Luther's ideas. He recanted his teaching that: (1)
there are only three sacraments; (2-5) indulgences and merits are of no value; (6-
7) all works of the saints are sin, and the treasury of merits contains only the
merits of Christ; (8) Luther and his teaching are not to be judged by the Apostolic See; (9-11) works of free will are sin, all one does for his or her own justification is sin; (12-15) fasts are of no value; (16-18) papal power has no authority
to condemn one to death; (19) the papal command that believers confess only
once a year is unreasonable; (20-22) the pope is not head of the church by God's
law; Peter was chosen by humans, and his followers must be so chosen; all bishops are ultimately equal; (23) a council alone can determine the meaning of
scripture; (24) lust, supposedly erased in baptism, is still sin against God's law—
"do not lust" (Matt. 5:28); (I Thess. 4:5); (25) flesh, corrupted by lust, makes all
human works sinful; (26) the martyr deaths of Peter or others must be revered in
themselves, and not as merits for others; (27) all lay persons are priests; (28)
anyone who remains in original sin cannot be worthy of baptism, of the priesthood, of a bishopric, or of the papacy; (29) repentance for sin is not the way to
justifying grace, rather, justifying grace is the only way to true repentance; (30)
repentance for one sin, without repentance for all, is still sin.[17]   These thirty
statements are translated in Appendix III.

He spoke first in Latin, and then in the Flemish/Dutch of many of his hearers. Luther was terribly disturbed when he heard of his friend's recantation under
pressure. He wrote from the Wartburg to John Lang in Erfurt, "Satan attacks us,
one and all. The enemy produced a letter glorifying in the recantation of two Lutherans, our Jacob and Hermann." This "Hermann" may refer to Hermann Gerrits, mentioned in Chapter 3. Luther called this a "terrible recantation."[18]

After the recantation Praepositus was set free, but the officials were uncertain where to assign him. They did not want him again leading the monastery in
Antwerp for he had too many former associates there. Instead, they sent him to
the cloister of Augustinians at Ypres/Ieper, Flanders, near his own home town.[19]
The authorities hoped the monks there would not be familiar with his earlier
teaching, and he would be able to live a new life in the good graces of the
church.

His convictions, however, were such that he could not deny his true beliefs
very long. Officials began to complain that he was continuing his former preaching, and they prepared to investigate.[20] Praepositus reported:

> I began again to preach the Word of God to Christian folk who were so thirsty
> and anxious to hear. I did not preach the human ways nor affirm the papal au-
> thority. I said 'Christ is our true bishop. To him we must go with perfect open-

ness, for he knows how to be compassionate with us as he has previously shown'.[21]

Again the authorities proceeded against him, but they were frustrated for a time by one city official in Ypres/Ieper who said, "so long as he does not preach against the Gospel of the Holy Scriptures, his preaching will never be forbidden by me."[22] Not to be continually frustrated the opponents appealed to Frans van der Hulst, who one month previous had been officially named the Inquisitor General. He took the necessary steps to place Praepositus in prison once more in Brussels, May, 1522.[23] This time Praepositus could only expect death by fire. He was impatient at the slowness of the inquisition and said,

> Why do you wait so long. My body is in your power. The flesh you can kill, but the soul you are not able to kill. I am prepared to suffer all the punishment you have decided to mete out to me.[24]

Again, Luther knew of the happenings in Brussels, and on 27 June, 1522 he wrote to Staupitz,

> James, prior of Antwerp, has been taken prisoner again. It is thought that he has been burned at the stake. . . it was certain that he would be put to death because he recanted his recantation.[25]

Many assumed that Praepositus was certain to die, or had already been martyred. That was not the case, however, for, as he wrote, without any detail, "God helped me escape from prison with the help of a brother in the order, and that without any danger."[26] Who helped Praepositus escape, and where he went next is not known. In a letter, however, dated 11 August, 1522, Luther wrote to Spalatin, "Jacob, prior of Antwerp, liberated by a miracle of God, is here with us,"[27] and Luther listed some of the monks he brought from The Netherlands. Praepositus visited the Augustinian cloister in Nürnberg in September.[28] He soon married a woman known to Luther,[29] and in 1524 went to be the Lutheran minister in Bremen where he remained to his death, 30 June, 1562.[30]

Henry of Zutphen

Another interesting connection with the monastery in Antwerp concerns Henry of Zutphen, his monastic experience, his education in Wittenberg, his leadership as prior in Antwerp following the departure of Praepositus, and his arrest, escape and later martyr death in North Germany. The only knowledge of his earlier life (b. ca. 1488-1489) is contained in the name by which he has been known "of Zutphen." This refers to a town in Gelderland in the eastern Netherlands, near two centers of the Brethren of the Common Life, namely Deventer and Zwolle. What influence the Brethren of Common Life may have had on him, if any, is not known. How he came to be involved in monastic life is obscure, but in the summer of 1508 he was enrolled in the University of Wittenberg, a few months before Luther arrived there.

Evidently, he was an Augustinian brother in his early life, influenced by one of the three Augustinian monasteries which at that time were active in the Netherlands: Enkhuizen, Dordrecht and Haarlem.[31] These Observant Augustinian houses, as noted above, had strong personal and jurisdictional connections to German monastic centers. Which of these might have been his home for a time is not known.[32]

While many details are lacking, we do know that in the summer of 1508 he was a student at the University of Wittenberg a few months before Luther arrived. He developed a friendship with Luther over the next several years, studying in Wittenberg on two different occasions: 1508-1514, and 1520-1521. During the first period he completed his Baccalaureate degree (autumn of 1509), and a Master of Arts (February, 1511).

In 1514 he became sub-prior of the Augustinian monastery in Cologne. By the next year he was prior in his home country at Dordrecht. In 1516 Luther reported that his former classmate was prior at Dordrecht, having recently gone there from Cologne.[33] We may assume that he furthered many of the ideas of Luther during his five years in Dordrecht. We have little information concerning his career there, but in the summer or fall of 1520 he went back to study in Wittenberg. In January, 1521 he completed his requirements for the degree Bachelor in Theology by defending his theses in Biblical study. We can glean some of his emphasis by analyzing his extant theses, as summarized by Friedrich Iken.[34]

The theses were on four topics. **First**, "human nature." The human race [*der Mensch*] is dead because all are deprived of the living word of God. Aristotle and the blind teachers of the *Sentences* called this "life," but this leads us only into deeper depravity. **Second**, "the law." The law is good in itself but its use by humanity is only evil and makes all things worse, just as the sun awakens the evil smell in a dead body. Compared with the law of God, how can human law be of any value. **Third**, "gospel and faith." God has provided a different "promised Seed" through which all creatures can be made new. The promised one subjugated the human law, and through the Lord of the law all persons can come to fulfillment. For this, faith is necessary, and our own works are unnecessary. **Fourth**, "love." This realization of the lack of value of our own works provides impetus for our renewal. Faith without love is unthinkable, and the Aristotelian idea of the *habitus* doctrine is also not meaningful. The individual must be instructed by the spirit concerning Christ, and made free from the law.

By October, 1521, he had completed requirements for his degree as *Sententiarius*. He made his way back immediately to his home country. Soon after Praepositus was taken from his monastery to prison on 5 December, 1521, Henry began his new position as prior at the beleaguered monastery. Within a few months, however, on 29 September, 1522, Henry himself was imprisoned in Brussels. He did not have to recant, however, because an uprising among the people led to his release. He had hoped to return to Wittenberg, but he went by way of Bremen, where he arrived November, 1522. His work reflected strong Lutheran persuasion and continued along with his popularity. In the spring, 1524, his predecessor as prior at Antwerp, Praepositus, also arrived in Bremen. Nevertheless, in Bremen opposition continued, especially from Dominican leaders, who did what they could to disrupt the Augustinians' efforts.

Late in 1524, however, messengers came from the neighboring village of Dithmarschen, in western Holstein, begging Henry to come to their town. He felt compelled to accept this invitation. So on 4 December, 1524, he began preaching in the village. Opposition quickly organized and plans were made to capture him and execute him by night. A drunken mob pulled him from his bed and dragged him into the street. The accusation, according to Praepositus, was that "[t]his malefactor blasphemed God and his Mother, let him be burned!" Henry responded, "I did not do this." The crowd, however, clamored "Burn him, Burn him."[35] He went to his fiery death on 10 December, 1524. Many details of the last few weeks of life were related by Praepositus in a letter he wrote to Luther in late December. The letter was printed many times and had wide circulation.

Within two months learning of this tragedy concerning his former friend and colleague Luther wrote a long treatise entitled "The Burning of Brother Henry."[36] He praised Henry "who suffered such shameful martyrdom in Dithmarschen for the sake of God's word and who so effectively confirmed the gospel with his blood."[37]

First Martyrs in Brussels: 1 July, 1523

Slightly over a week after Henry of Zutphen was removed from his position in Antwerp, the authorities, fearing the spread of heresy, took drastic measures. Sixteen Augustinian brothers from the cloister in Antwerp, including the new prior, Lambert de Thoren, were arrested and imprisoned in the Vilvoord prison (8 October, 1522).[38] Thirteen quickly recanted and were set free later the same year.[39] The other three—the prior, and two monks Hendrik Voes and Johann van den Esschen—however, were "recalcitrant" and refused to recant. They were taken to Brussels for further questioning and punishment. As a precaution against further heresy in Antwerp, the Emperor gave his approval that the remaining monks should be transferred elsewhere, and ordered that the cloister should be razed to the ground because it seemed to be a focus of Lutheran propaganda. The demolition took place on 16 January, 1523.[40]

The three Augustinians who had been arrested and imprisoned in October 1522, were required to stand trial in Brussels a few months later. During their trial sixty-two articles of heresy were recorded.[41] Part of these were written in the form of dialogue between the inquisitors and the accused. Most of them probably reflect the wording of the condemned men or summaries by the inquisitors.

It has been assumed that because the inquisitors said the victims were "Lutheran" that they, in fact, reflected Lutheran teachings. Indeed, they probably were conversant with many writings Luther for Luther's works were regularly printed in Antwerp, as we have seen, and their last two priors had studied in Wittenberg. The key points of their condemnation follow.

1. Support for the use of Luther's works

They strongly affirmed their right to read the works of Luther. Indeed, the first of the sixty-two articles they affirmed was: "[1] No one is obligated, because of a mandate from either Pontiff or Emperor, to abstain from reading books of Luther." They used Luther's works not only because these writings were considered an authority in themselves, but because they seemed to reflect the Spirit of God more clearly. [2] The spirit of God was thus the judge of their worth; the precepts of the Roman Catholic church were not an authoritative guide, and those who would prohibit the reading of Luther's works were acting from ulterior motives. [3] They introduced two different scripture proofs supporting analysis of the works before they are condemned. ["Test the Spirits to see whether they are of God," I (John 4:10)]; and ["Test all things" (I Thess. 5:21)]. These are repeated in article [10]. [5] In fact, "the books of Luther shed more light on the sacred scripture than other doctors one can read"; and [6] "Luther leads one nearer to the Gospel of Christ than does Augustine or Jerome".

2. Centrality of the Scriptures

The centrality of Scriptures was basic to this whole argument. "[19] Nothing ought to be believed, under danger of conscience, except what is stated in the Divine Word, or can be drawn out [*illici potest*] from the Divine Word." [48] Therefore, since Christian teachings and practice should be based on the scriptures only, Christians should dispense with all ceremonies which are not based on Scriptural warrant.

3. Questions concerning the scope and authority of the hierarchy of the church

Many general criticisms concerned the hierarchy of the Roman Catholic church and its close relation with secular powers. This was obviously opposed to the scriptural test. The prisoners did not deny that earthly government possessed certain necessary authority. They did, however, insist on a clear understanding as to what powers earthly authorities had and what they did not have. "[9] The secular authority has power to prescribe and prohibit such things as relate to the body [*corpori*], but not those pertaining to the conscience". Among the former were surely the maintenance of order and forbidding unruly individuals or groups from disrupting society. The mixing of authority, however, was condemned.[42] They insisted that only the divine power [8] should be supreme over matters of conscience. Therefore, the political authorities (including in this instance the political pretensions of the Roman Catholic hierarchy) should not presume to require or to prohibit what God does not command or prohibit. Likewise, [20] councils have no authority to legislate anything not commanded in Scripture.

The true calling of a Christian leader is ministry to real human concerns. Consequently, "[35] The Roman Pope, Peter's successor, is not vicar of Christ over the church in the whole world. . . for Christ instituted the office not to be vicar [*vicarium, i.e.* taking the place of Christ], but for a ministry." "[7] From Sacred Scripture it is not possible to prove that the pope or any prelates have any more authority than for ministry of the Word of Christ alone." As a consequence, [59] even the pope's true calling should be to a ministry through "feeding his sheep by preaching the word of God."

They thought that legislation of the Church, much of it based on non-scriptural arguments, counteracted the God-given freedom of humanity" [36, 37]. All perpetual vows, issued beyond the precepts of Christ, such as the vows of the religious, are imprudently issued through ignorance of Christian liberty, and thus are not obligatory." Grace could not be derived from observing vows based on humanly constituted requirements. The Spirit of Christ, or of God, speaking to the individual person through faith, was the source of grace, in contradistinction to vows and the sacramental system advocated by the Roman church. Again, the Christian task should be ministry in Christ's name, and there are no divisions and no hierarchy for this calling. "[12] All persons [*homines*] are priests [*sacerdotes*] before God."

4. Only Three sacraments are affirmed

They affirmed three sacraments: baptism, the Eucharist, and penance (as truly understood). "[28] Baptism, Eucharist and Penance initiate the promises of Christ which are aroused by faith; for that reason he believes they confer faith and grace." The sacraments confer grace because of one's faith, not because they are related to any human works.

Baptism and Eucharist

Baptism was affirmed as a sacrament, but it was only mentioned and not analyzed. The Eucharist was elaborated in several articles. [43] The major importance of the Eucharist was not as an oblation or renewed sacrifice on the altar. Its significance comes from the one and only sacrifice of Christ on the cross. Thus its value in the present age requires a recollection or memory of the benefits of that once-accomplished sacrifice.

When the prisoners were asked if they believed that the bread remained after the consecration, they said, "[18] If it is contained in the Scriptures, then I believe, otherwise I do not believe it." This was an indirect denial of the idea of transubstantiation. More important than the elements themselves, whatever their reality, was memory of the sacrifice on the cross. "[16] In the Mass the body of Christ is not offered by a human person [*ab homine*] because what is given in remedy or cure [*remedium*] and commemoration is not offered." The articles continued: "[17] The body of Christ is not offered in the Mass, but they (words of the Mass) are taken up [*sumitur*] only in his (Jesus's) memory." The inquisitors suspected the prisoners thought that the words of the canon of the Mass were false.

Penance

They thought that the common understanding of Penance emphasized the wrong things. They insisted that love is a fruit of which comes only from Christ, not from the works of a contrite sinner trying to satisfy God. They sought to distinguish between the "true, Christian and catholic faith" from the present "Roman Catholic" usage. "[38] It is not possible for the true, Christian and catholic faith to be separated from love for love is the fruit of faith, and Christian faith without love is dead." "[52] If a person believes himself/herself [*se*] truly absolved, the sins are forgiven." [44] There are only two parts to the sacrament of penance: contrition and confession. After all, [40] it is God who remits sin, and all sins, through the death of Christ, hence satisfaction is of no further value. Furthermore, [41] they did not know if there was a purgatory, nor did they know [45] whether the help of the living benefited the dead.

With respect to this sacrament of penance the articles were very specific. "[27] It is not a divine law, nor a precept of God, that all mortal sins are to be confessed to a human person [*homini*], because no one among humans [*hominum*] is able to know all sins, much less to confess them." There is much more emphasis on the communal concept of forgiveness than on the priest who supposedly forgives, which is in sharp contrast to the medieval practice of the confessional. The prisoners expanded on these ideas, by using Matthew 18:15-17 [13]. The articles argued that one must be confronted with sin directly, and if repentance does not result, he or she then must be approached by two persons, or if necessary, by the whole community. Also, "[15] It is a power of the community of all persons to remit sins," reflecting perhaps John 20:23 where we read: "If you forgive the sins of any, they are forgiven; if you retain the sins of any they are retained." Thus [33] it followed that the church does not have the power to require confession once a year, to require celebration of feasts, or to require fasts in Lent.

The articles affirmed a true penance which rejected the benefits of indulgences. They reiterated that there are only two parts to penitence: contrition and confession. Satisfaction is not necessary, for forgiveness is by faith alone—not by works: "[52] If the sinner believes he or she is truly absolved, the sins are removed." The satisfaction for all one's sins was made by Christ himself: "[40] God remits sins of the sinner through the death of Christ and remits all penalty." [41] On the other hand, purgatory is neither affirmed nor denied. The articles are also inconclusive with respect to [45] prayers for the dead. No special merit is attained from reciting the canonical hours, [49, 50] especially since this is not prayer to the Father in Spirit and in Truth. Likewise [56], they neither confirmed nor denied adoration for saints.

5. Rejection of four Roman Catholic sacraments

The Medieval sacramental system was strongly criticized. Four of the sacraments were denied. [29, 32] Confirmation, extreme unction, marriage and ordination do not confer grace because they do not contain the promise of the Scriptures. Furthermore, "[25] In the Episcopal consecration we do not understand that any new power is attained through the consecration."

6. Denial of Good works

Suggesting further Lutheran influences, the monks were accused of denying good works. "[34] Christ performs all good works in and through human beings [*hominibus, homines*], such that humans [*homines*] do nothing [*i.e.*, works] actively, but only passively, for Christ works in them as if they were an instrument."

7. Priesthood of all believers, and importance of lay persons

In addition to these evaluations concerning the sacramental system, there was a strong emphasis on lay persons. The artificial boundary between priests and the remainder of the believers is non-existent in the sight of God. We have already noted the insistence that "[12] all persons [*homines*] are priests before God." This was, in turn, immediately qualified by another article. While "[31] priesthood [*sacerdotium*] is not a sacrament, it is nonetheless necessary." This evidently was seen as a function of ministry in the community rather than of a higher level of holiness implied in the Medieval sacramental system. The report indicated that the prisoners did not know if there "[22] was a difference between priests and lay persons [*laicos*] in consecration of elements [on the one hand] and the consecration pertaining to the priesthood of Christ and the priesthood of the New Testament [on the other hand]." We assume that this evasive answer implied that while they had no clear thought as to the different functions, the sacramental authority of the priesthood was not affirmed in the Biblical account. These 62 articles are translated in Appendix V.

After analyzing these statements, the authorities prepared to burn the offenders. One of the accused affirmed his faith, and argued that the inquisitors had no authority to do this. When assured by his persecutor that they did have authority to do this, one prisoner said "This is the Word of Pilate, and you have no power over me which is not given to you from above."[43] This statement, in a letter sent to Luther affirmed their insistence that power comes only from God, not through human initiative.

An eye-witness reported:[44] "There was exhibited to us today a spectacle, miserable to talk about, fearful to spectators, and wretched in itself, and not blessed to be observed." The sacred procession to the Great Market Square, site of the executions, was elaborately described including a report of the mitred hats of the abbots, the academic dress of the Louvain/Leuven theologians, and other ecclesiastical finery. The prisoners were led to the place of execution in full clerical garb. Ceremoniously one portion was removed at a time while an official revoked the consecration of the prisoner. This complete ceremony took an hour, after which the victim was turned over to the civil authorities for the burning. After this was completed for one person, they repeated the same ceremony for the second victim.

Especially noteworthy in the mind of the eye-witness was the composure of the prisoners "not in a manner of one contemplating death." They recited the Creed and sang the *Te Deum Laudamus*.[45] Finally, having been convicted of the errors of "Lutheranism," on 1 July, 1523, Johann Esch and Hendrik Vos, the first two martyrs for "Lutheranism" in The Netherlands, went to their deaths.[46]

Lambertus de Thoren was not burned with the two monks. For reasons unknown he remained in prison until he died—or perhaps was murdered—in September, 1528.[47] There were stories which circulated at the time insisting that he had recanted at the last minute, but these are not substantiated by any documentation. There were also those who insisted that the two who were burned recanted at the last minute as well. These rumors are undocumented and probably reflect wishful thinking on the part of the accusers.[48]

As soon as the news reached Luther, he was deeply disturbed and wrote his well-known letter, around 28 August, 1523 to

> all beloved brothers in Christ, who are in Holland, Brabant and Flanders.[49]
> . . . . It has been your lot, before all the world, not only to hear the Gospel and to know Christ; but you are also the first to suffer shame and injury, anxiety and difficulty, imprisonment and a dangerous situation [*ferligkeyt=Gefährlichkeit*] for the cause of Christ. Now you have become so full of fruits and have become so strong [in your faith] that you have nurtured it and confirmed it with your own blood. In your presence the two noble brothers in Christ, Henry and Johannes at Brussels, have considered their [earthly] lives trifling [*geringe*], through which means Christ and his Word are blessed. . . . May God be praised and in eternity be blessed, that we have been permitted to see and to hear such real saints and true martyrs since up to now we have exalted and worshipped so many false saints. Over here (Saxony) we have until now not been worthy to become such valued and worthy offerings for Christ. . . . My beloved, be confident, therefore, and joyful in Christ, and let us give thanks for his great signs and wonders which He has begun among us. He has constructed a fresh new example of his life or us.

At about the same time Luther wrote a hymn in which he praised these two martyrs. It consisted of 12 verses, telling much of their story.[50] It is entitled "A New Song Shall Here Be Begun."

> (Verse 1) The Lord God help our singing!
> Of what our God himself hath done,
> Praise, honor to him bringing.
> At Brussels in The Netherlands

By two boys, martyrs youthful
He showed the wonders of his hands,
Whom he with favor truthful
So richly hath adorned.

The two are named:

(Verse 2) The first right fitly John was named,
So rich he in God's favor;
His brother, Henry—one unblamed,
Whose salt lost not its savor. . . .

Some authorities sought to dissuade them from their beliefs.

(Verse 3) The old arch-fiend did them immure
With terrors did enwrap them.
He bade them God's dear Word abjure,
With cunning he would trap them;
From Louvain many sophists came, . . .

Since they wanted to serve God in a different way, they renounced their monastic life.

(Verse 5) Their cloister garments off they tore,
Took off their consecrations;
All this the boys were ready for,
They said Amen with patience. . . .

They were forced to restate their basic theological ("heretical") beliefs, and were condemned for affirming obedience primarily to God rather than to Roman Catholic [*i.e.* human] authority.

(Verse 7) They wrote for them a paper small,
And made them read it over,
The parts they showed them therein all
Which their belief did cover.
Their greatest fault was saying this:
"In God we should trust solely;
For man is always full of lies,
We should distrust him wholly:"
So they must burn to ashes.
(Verse 8) Two huge great fires they kindled then,
The boys they carried to them; . . .

Although they had been burned to ashes, their influence yet remained.

(Verse 10) Leave off their ashes never will;
Into all lands they scatter;
Streams, hole, ditch, grave—nought keeps them still
With shame the foe they spatter.

The suggestion that they had recanted at the last minute was denied as a "lie" by Luther, and he said as much in the 12th verse.

Cornelis Wouterszoon of Dordrecht

The mention of the Dordrecht cloister and its prior, Henry of Zutphen, in connection with early Lutheran developments, brings us to several problems, most of them insoluble. For example, how much Lutheran influence did the various priors exert? For how long? Furthermore, were the Lutheran teachings preached or taught outside this monastery? Was the activity of Henry of Zutphen, for example, known by the parishioners in the area? These questions lead us to the interesting career of Cornelis Wouterszoon whose example may have been typical of others who neither wrote nor published, or who for other reasons do not appear in our records.

Cornelis Wouterszoon was a shoemaker in Dordrecht. Why he was usually referred to also as "*Koperen-potje*" [copper pot] is unknown.[51] It was evidently late in the year 1524 when he translated and arranged to publish a tract associated with the name of Luther. This tract was at first thought to be "The seven Psalms, translated and printed by Cornelis Woutersz, alias Coperpotgen."[52] De Hoop Scheffer, however, discovered that the "heretical" translation was not a work by Luther but referred instead to an anonymous mystical text of the Late Middle Ages written a century and a half before Luther, now known as *Theologia Deutsch*, or *Theologia Germanica*.[53] A partial version of the *Theologia Deutsch* was edited by Luther in 1516 (a more complete version in 1518) and printed simultaneously in Wittenberg, Leipzig and Augsburg.[54] Luther's title, in translation is "A German Theology [*Theologia Deutsch*], that is a noble little book, explaining the relation between the old Adam and the new Adam, which is Christ. . . how the old Adam within us must die so that the new Christ may be born in us." How Cornelis came to have access to this Lutheran edition, and how his interest in this "heresy" was aroused is unknown. At any rate, since the printing of Luther's works—or even writings associated with him—had already been prohibited, this shoemaker quickly came under suspicion.[55]

In 1525 he was imprisoned. After being threatened in various ways, he weakened and recanted his actions. His penance was to go on a pilgrimage, and burn the required candles in the church after walking barefoot and bareheaded in a procession.[56] Hardly had he been released from prison on the promise that he would perform his required penitence, when he began to have misgivings about his recantation, and he regretted his cowardice and his weakness. His orthodox wife helped matters very little when she continually criticized his "errors" and "heresy."[57]

Sometime afterwards, when his conscience would not let him rest, he left Dordrecht, traveled to Leiden, Amsterdam, Kampen and out of The Netherlands perhaps to Wittenberg,[58] and finally settling in Bremen where Henry of Zutphen had been working before his martyrdom in 1524.[59] Again, whether the two had earlier been acquainted in Dordrecht, we do not know. It would not, however, be unlikely if in the small town of Dordrecht they had shared their common interest in Luther's 'heresy.' In Bremen he worked at his trade of making shoes.

He remained in Germany approximately six months, so he wrote, until he had a strong desire to return to his own area. He did return to Delft, about twenty miles from his home.[60] Here he sought information about the advisability of his returning to Dordrecht. The information he received was negative, so he wandered instead as far as Antwerp.[61]

In January, 1527, Cornelis sent a message to his wife urging her to join him in Antwerp. She refused, however, to leave Dordrecht, since she was not convinced he had returned to the orthodox faith.[62] When he received word of her refusal, Cornelis was, as he said, moved by the Spirit—and, we are sure, moved by disappointment at his wife's answer—to write and to print two letters.[63] He interpreted his difficulties as punishment for his earlier weakness in his faith, and he determined to reverse his recantation and reaffirm his faith. To this end he composed the letters with this information, printed them in Antwerp, and took hundreds of copies with him to Dordrecht.[64] The first letter was to the city leaders; the second was directed to the people.[65] By early April he was distributing these in the town, and on 6 April the authorities reported they already had him in custody in Dordrecht.[66] It is from the document of this later trial that many of the details of his earlier arrest and recantation are known. When the representative of the inquisitors, Aernt Sandelin, asked about Cornelis's activities, the prisoner freely admitted he had not followed through on his earlier required penance, that he had traveled abroad to Lutheran areas, and that a few days before he had printed letters on a press in Antwerp without permission. He was, however, always cautious never to reveal with whom he had stayed on his trips or where the printing press was located.[67] When asked why he left Dordrecht after his recantation, he replied that he had "scandalized the truth"[68] by his revocation, and his shame drove him to take this step.

Authorities from The Hague went to Dordrecht late in April, 1527, and brought him back to the prison in The Hague.[69] Two weeks later, in a further trial in The Hague, it was evident that the prisoner was now adamant about his views, even if it might mean death. The authorities assumed that his errors indicated a strong relationship to Lutheran thought, although the evidence for this does not appear in the discussion. Only general non-Roman Catholic ideas, which could have been affirmed by many critics of the Roman Church, were expressed.

Five emphases highlighted the discussion.[70] **First**, he criticized the authority of the Roman Catholic hierarchy. Cornelis probably said that the hierarchy was of men only and not of God; **second**, he questioned confession and was accused of confessing in secret to God only—not to a priest; **third**, he objected to the idea of purification through penance, presumably insisting that purification comes only from God; and **fourth**, he questioned purgatory. A **fifth** idea caused him the most difficulty. He had not participated in the communion service for over a year, and the last communion was in the Lutheran congregation in Bremen. Because of the apparent strength of his faith the authorities feared that to punish him publicly would be to elevate his cause in the minds of his sympathizers. The prisoner said that he was ready to die soon, but, preferably, he wanted an opportunity to suffer a long time to witness publicly for his faith.[71] The questioners suggested, rather than immediate death, that he be secretly punished.

In May, 1527, Margaret wrote that the officials in The Hague had her authority to proceed as they thought best.[72] The decision was not to execute him immediately but to subject him to a long imprisonment.[73] A financial note sent on 22 March, 1528, indicated that by then he had already been imprisoned 329 days (3 April, 1527-11 March, 1528).[74] He was not to die for his faith for another year and a half. The final sentence read that he was

> to be placed on the scaffold which was standing on the square in The Hague, and there the sentence to be carried out with the sword. His body was to be tied to a wheel and his head put on a stake. All his goods were to be confiscated.[75]

The grim conclusion read: "Done in The Hague. . . 26th day of October, 1529."[76]

Notes for Chapter 7

1. Regnerus Richardus Post, *Kerkelijke verhoudingen in Nederland voor de Reformatie: van 1500 tot 1580* (Utrecht, Antwerp: Het Spectrum), 1954, p. 347-348.

2. "Staupitz," *Realencyklopädie für protestantische Theologie und Kirche* (Leipzig: J. C. Hinrichs'sche Buchhandlung, 1906), 18:783.

3. David C. Steinmetz, *Misericordia Dei: The Theology of Johannes von Staupitz in its Late Medieval Setting* (Leiden: E. J. Brill, 1968).

4. "*Praepositus*" is Latin for one in authority, such as a prior; "*Propst*" in German and "*Proost*" in Dutch carry the same meaning. Cf. English: provost.

5. The only full-length study of the career of Praepositus, either while he was in Antwerp or in Germany, is H. Q. Janssen, *Jacob Praepositus: Luther's Leerling en Vriend* (Amsterdam: G. L. Funke, 1866). This author included most of the known writings of Praepositus concerning his Netherlands career as appendices in this book. Brief references are also found in *Realencyclopaedia für protestantische Theologie und Kirche* (hereafter *RE*) under "Propst," XVI, 110-112; in *Die Religion in Geschichte und Gegenwart* (hereafter, RGG) under "Propst," V, 639. In an introductory note to the letter from Erasmus to Luther the date of his birth is given as 1486, although there is no reference to justify this assertion (*CWE*, VI, # 980, Erasmus in Louvain/Leuven to Luther, 30 May, 1519). Jansen, p. 23, suggested "at the end of the 15th century."

6. *CWE*, VI, 980, Erasmus in Louvain/Leuven to Luther, 30 May, 1519.

7. Janssen, *Jacob Praepositus*, p. 290.

8. From the Royal Archives in Brussels, as printed in *CDI*, IV, 84f.

9. Praepositus's letter, as printed in Janssen, *Praepositus*, p. 291.

10. *Die excellente cronicke van Vlanderen* (Antwerp, 1531), as printed in *CDI*, IV, 99-100. See also Janssen, *Praepositus*, p. 31

11. Praepositus elaborated in his letter, Janssen, *Praepositus*, p. 291.

12. *CDI*, IV, 86.

13. *CWE*, IX, # 1256, to Erasmus in Basel from Juan Louis Vives in Louvain/Leuven, 19 January, 1522.

14. Praepositus's letter in Janssen, *Praepositus*, pp. 292-296.

15. Praepositus states it thus: "Ergab mich mit mund und (als Got weisz) nit mit hertzen, die revocation zu thun nach jrem willen." Janssen, *Praepositus*, pp. 292-296.

16. There was indeed a large representation of inquisitors to hear the answers, and the "recantation;" Hieronymus Aleander, apostolic *nuntius*, representing the Pope; Hieronymus van der Noote, Chancellor of Brabant, representing the emperor; Suffragan bishop Adriaan Herbouts of Kamerijk/Cambrai and his vicar Romerus Stoops; Lodewijk Carolen and Jan Quintana, both professors of theology; Jan Glapion, confessor to the Emperor; Nicholaas Baechem of Egmond and Jacob Latomus, both doctors of theology from Louvain; Frans van der Hulst, licensed in both laws, member of the Raad [Court] of Brabant, and head inquisitor; and there were others. *CDI*, IV, 89.

17. These thirty statements are printed in Latin in *CDI*, *IV*, 88-95; and in Dutch/Flemish translation in Janssen, pp. 69-71. A complete English translation appears in Appendices III of this study.

18. Luther's letter is dated 12 April, 1522, in *D. Martin Luthers Werke, Briefwechsel*, *II* (Weimar Ausgabe), 494f.

19. Praepositus's letter in Janssen, *Praepositus*, p. 302.

20. *CDI*, IV, 129.

21. Praepositus's letter in Janssen, p. 302.

22. Janssen, *Ibid.*, p. 303.

23. Janssen, *Ibid.*, p. 304.

24. *Ibid.*, p. 304.

25. *LW*, vol. 49:12, dated 2 June, 1522.

26. Praepositus's letter in Janssen, p. 305.

27. *Luthers Werke, Briefwechsel*, II, 586, under the date 11 August, 1522.

28. *CDI*, IV, 136.

29. Luther stated in a letter to Wenceslaus Link, the superior of the order in Altenburg, 8 April, 1523, *"Deinde an uxores Praepositi et Hieronymus simul veniant."* *Luther's Werke, Briefwechsel,* III, 53.

30. Allen, *E. E.*, III, 606-607, n. 54.

31. Friedrich Iken, "Heinrich von Zütphen," *Schriften des Vereins für Reformationsgeschichte,* No. 12, Halle, 1886. Iken mentions three monasteries in The Netherlands before 1513, pp. 4-5. Otto Clemen mentioned only the first two in his study of the Antwerp cloister. Otto Clemen, "Das Antwerper Augustiner-Kloster bei Beginn der Reformation (1513-1523)," *Monatshefte der Comenius-Gesellschaft,* X (1901), 306-313.

32. Otto Clemen, "Das Antwerpener Augustiner-Kloster," *Ibid.,* p. 306.

33. *LW*, 48, Letter to John Lang, October 26 1516, p. 31.

34. Friedrich Iken, "Heinrich von Zütphen," *Ibid.* pp. 3ff.

35. From a letter Praepositus wrote to Luther late in December 1524. *WA Briefwechsel* III, 401-403. This quotation is on p. 402. A German translation of the letter appears in *WA* 18: 217-218.

36. *LW*, 32: 265-285, "The Burning of Brother Henry" (Philadelphia: Muhlenberg Press). *WA* 18:224-240, first published February/March, 1525.

37. *Ibid.,* p. 266.

38. Statement from the Royal Archives, Brussels, printed in *CDI*, IV, 173, where the date of 8 October appears.

39. From "Die excellente cronike van Vlanderen" (1531), as printed in *CDI*, IV, 191.

40. A letter noting that this demolition was approved is dated 10 January, 1523, as printed in *CDI*, IV, 176. A statement reporting that it had been accomplished on 16 January, 1523 appears in *CDI*, IV, 177. See also, Otto Clemens, "Das Antwerper Augustiner-Kloster bei Beginn der Reformation (1513-1523)." *Monatshefte der Comenius-Gesellschaft,* 10 (1901), 312.

41. "Articuli Asserti per fratrem Henricum &c," printed in *BRN*, VIII, 39-43. They are also printed in both German and Latin in *CDI*, IV; the German, pp. 195-198; the Latin pp. 210-213. An elaborate analysis of these articles, written by Martinus Reckenhofer from Ingolstadt in the Tirol, appears also in *BRN*, VIII, 65-114. The numbers in square brackets [ ] refer to the 62 articles as translated in Appendix V of this study.

42. Interestingly, this emphasis also became a major point of the Anabaptist movement, to be organized within a decade. One well-known example of this idea is contained in the Schleitheim Confession (1527) which represented many Anabaptists in south Germany and Switzerland.

43. From a letter written to Luther at the time, as printed in *CDI*, IV, 203.

44. "Historia de duobus Augustinen," printed in *BRN*, VIII, 35-37.

45. *Ibid.,* pp. 36f.

46. *Ibid.,* p. 37.

47. The death of Thoren is noted in *CDI*, V, 360, under the date 15 September 1528, where it is stated that he did not receive penance before his death.

48. A letter to this effect was written by Frans van der Hulst, a major leader of this inquisition, printed in *CDI*, IV, p. 204, and dated 1 July, 1523.

49. This Latin letter appears in *WA, D. Martin Luther's Werke* (Weimar: Hermann Bohlau, 1891), XII, 77-79. Luther did not date this letter but the editor suggested that it was written about 28 August, 1523.

50. The hymn, consisting of 12 stanzas, is printed in *WA*, 35, pp. 411-415, although there is some discussion as to the order of the last few verses. It first appeared in 1523, and the next year was incorporated into a Lutheran hymnal. The English translation is printed in *LW*, 53, pp. 211-216, including the tune used in the early Lutheran hymnal. It is this *LW* version used here.

51. Documents concerning correspondence at the time of the trials are collected in *CDI*, IV, 299; V, 198-204, 224-226. A summary of his life was written, using this documentation, by J. G. de Hoop Scheffer, "*Cornelis Woutersz, van Dordrecht, een Martelaar der Hervorming (1525-1529)*," *Kerkhistorisch Archief*, IV (1866), 1-22.

52. De Hoop Scheffer discovered this title referred to in a letter written by the inquisitors in The Hague in 1531. See his article on "Cornelis ," *Ibid.*, p. 6, n. 2. He at first assumed the "seven psalms" referred to Luther's "*Die Sieben Buszpsalmen*" written in 1517, but he later discovered his error and determined that the translation of the supposed Lutheran publication was actually *Den Ouden Adam, een excellente, devote, godlijke theologie, dat es een leeringhe ende verclaringhe hoe dat een kerstenmensche sal leeren kennen ende crighen een recht verstant"* (Antwerp, 13 March, 1521, *NK* 2228). De Hoop Scheffer, *Geschiedenis der Kerkhervorming in Nederland*, p. 404, n.2. The German edition of Luther in 1518 was entitled: *Eyn Deutsch Theologia: das ist eyn edeles Buchleyn, von rechtem Vorstand* [or *Verstannd*], *was Adam und Christus sey, und wie Adam yn uns sterben, und Christus ersteen sali* [or *soll*]." *WA*, I, 376.

53. A recent edition is a translation by Bengt Hoffman, *The Theologia Germanica of Martin Luther* in the series *The Classics of Western Spirituality* (New York: The Paulist Press, 1980).

54. *WA*, I, 376.

55. Cf. *CDI*, IV, 299, where we note that some time before this letter of 31 December, 1524, officials at Dordrecht had become suspicious of Cornelis. By early January, 1525, the authorities in The Hague prepared to conduct an investigation in Dordrecht to analyze the situation first-hand. *CDI*, IV, 305, where the letter is dated 2 January, 1525.

56. His penance, not yet completed, is referred to in *CDI*, V, 224.

57. *CDI*, V, 200.

58. *CDI*, V, 224.

59. *CDI*, V. 199; dated 5-7 April, 1527.

60. *Ibid.*, p. 199.

61. *Ibid.*, pp. 199f.

62. *CDI*, V, 198; dated 5-7 April, 1527.

63. *Ibid.*, p. 198.

64. *Ibid.*

65. *CDI*, V, 198, dated 5-7 April, 1527.

66. *CDI*, IV, 202.

67. Report by Inquisitor, A. Sandelin, on 9 April, 1527, *CDI*, V, 203f.

68. *CDI*, V, 199-201.

69. *CDI*, V, 212; dated 27 April, 1527.

70. *CDI*, V, 224; discussion dated 12 May, 1527.

71. Report written 12 May, 1527, by A Sandelin, representing the inquisition; located in the Royal Archives, Brussels; printed in *CDI*, V, 224-226. This statement appears on p. 225.

72. Margaret answered on 25 May, 1527; printed in *CDI*, V. 232.

73. The record of this trial and the subsequent decision was written on 1 February, 1528. Printed in *CDI*, V, 322f.

74. *CDI*, V, 387; report of 11 March, 1528.

75. Reported in the *Criminal Sentence 's Hofs van Hollant*, and quoted in de Hoop Scheffer's article, "Cornelis Woutersz," pp. 21f.

76. *Ibid.*, p. 22.

Chapter 8

The Gospel of Matthew
Translated (1522) by Johannes van Pelt

On 23 March, 1524, Emperor Charles V issued a special edict against certain printers in the Netherlands because they had issued two books suspected to be unorthodox.[1] The edict was directed not only against the printers, but also against anyone selling or possessing the two books. Furthermore, following the requirements of the Edict of Worms, the suspected books were to be burned. These two texts were, **first**, a Dutch translation of the Gospel of Matthew with explanatory glosses or commentaries and, **second**, to be analyzed in Chapter 9, *De Summa der Godliker Scrifturen* [A Summary of the teachings of scripture], (or *Oeconomica Christiana* in the Latin original).

The Translation of the Gospel of Matthew

The Dutch translation of the Gospel of Matthew had glosses or short commentaries following each of its twenty-eight chapters, and a concluding summary. The imperial edict referred to it as "The Gospel of St. Matthew, with glosses written therein; although poorly translated, the glosses contain certain errors." The whole title of the actual translation, covering most of a page, suggests some of its basic content.

> Here begins the Gospel of our Lord Jesus Christ, which contains the good news of the forgiveness of sins, and of eternal salvation, translated into the Dutch [*duytscher*] language. This St. Matthew, the apostle and evangelist of Jesus Christ, has written, with short glosses in order that we might understand it better, and so that we should make it known that every Christian person is required to read the Gospel of Christ and to carry this gospel in his/her heart above all other writings, and therein freely, lovingly, and trustingly to live and to die.

The text was printed in Amsterdam in 1522 by Doen Pietersz, who had alaready printed other materials of questionable orthodoxy. According to Charles' edict the text was "poorly translated" [*qualijcken=kwalijk getranslateert*] and unauthorized, but even more serious in the glosses there were errors.[2] (I am indebted to the Library of the University of Utrecht for permission to purchase an offprint of this rare [and likely unique] copy of this 1522 publication).[3]

The identity of the author first became known almost 20 years later, in March 1539, during the trial of Jan Hubrechtsz, a former sheriff of Amsterdam. He admitted that in the early 1520s he had sympathy for Luther's ideas and had often heard the sermons of Jan van Pelt, the prior in the Amsterdam Franciscan monastery. The defendant stated that Pelt was likely of the sect of Luther and often preached Luther's doctrines in the hall of the cloister.[4] It is interesting to note that this translation was published the same year (1522) as Erasmus's *Paraphrase of the Gospel of Matthew.*

What actual dependence, if any, he may have had on Erasmus's work is not known, but a few interesting parallels have been indicated. Pelt planned to translate the remaining three gospels as well, but after a brief detention, he fled the Netherlands in 1524. The remaining three gospels were printed shortly thereafter in Antwerp in Dutch by Jacob van Liesveldt. These were not original translations but earlier translations of the late fourteenth century from the school of Jan van Ruysbroeck (1293-1381).[5] They were bound together with Pelt's document in 1523. Later publications by van Liesveldt were of a Protestant nature, and we are told they "cost him his head."[6] Pelt's career, however, continued for almost four decades. He fled first to Braunschweig (Brunswick). Then he went to Bremen where he became a Lutheran minister. In exile he was often associated with other refugees from The Netherlands such as Henry of Zutphen and Jacob Praepositus. He died as minister in Bremen in 1562.[7]

To attempt to understand the specific theological interpretations to which the emperor, and especially his advisors, were opposed, we shall analyze the work, especially the glosses following each chapter as well as the translator's concluding summary statement. The methods of the commentator were diverse. He often compared the Old Text (Latin Vulgate) with the Greek text (of Erasmus) or a Hebrew text. Periodically, he contrasted a Greek reading with the Latin, usually siding with meaning of the former. He regularly used commentaries of Origen, Chrysostom, Augustine, or Jerome to support his arguments.

Throughout the commentary he included interesting political or geographical information in a sermonic form. There are many references to Old Testament prophecies, which Matthew's text purports to fulfill, but at one point he indicated, correctly, that Matthew's reference to Jeremiah actually does not appear in Jeremiah. He often exposed the subtle differences in meaning between the Greek and Latin texts. For example, referring to Matthew 27:33, he stated that "Golgotha" [skull] is not a Hebrew term, but rather is Syriac (perhaps he would have been more correct to say Aramaic). He conflated similar names, especially in the genealogy material in Matthew 1. To elaborate or in an attempt to complete several stories, he borrowed from the other gospels to explain materials or situations which do not actually appear in the Matthew text. His main historical source outside the Bible or the Church Fathers seems to have been the writings of Flavius Josephus. We will mention key sections from each of the chapter glosses.

Chapter 1

The genealogical material in Matthew Chapter 1, Pelt suggested, was included so that we might know that Jesus is the son of David, the heir of Abraham. He elaborated the text so that we may know that Jesus, Son of God, came to release us from original sin, and that through him we may be anointed and made holy. He analyzed differences in names, conflated names that are similar, and, as a consequence wondered whether the fourteen generations each, between Abraham and David, to the Babylonian Exile and to Joseph were exact. Finally, he asked "Why be concerned about the genealogy of Joseph if he is not the father of Jesus?" He concluded that the genealogy of Joseph and of Mary were similar because they were of the same lineage or "tribe" [geslacht]. A comment by John of Damascus (675-749) was used to justify this argument. The birth of Jesus was summarized with no special theological differences from the biblical text, although he elaborated on various Old Testament prophecies not referred to in Matthew, which were supposedly fulfilled at this time.

Chapter 2

In commenting on Chapter 2, Pelt related the story of the wise men, the flight into Egypt, and the return to Nazareth. He gave some geographical background of Bethlehem, the ("house of bread"). He explained that Herod was from Idumea, hence a "stranger" [vreem] to Israel, and, consequently, his hostility to the announced birth can be explained in part. The return from Egypt after the death of Herod the Great sets the context for a brief excursus about Herod the Great's family. Pelt based his analysis on Josephus, moving well beyond the Matthew text. He explained "tetrarchy" and hinted at the complex rivalry between various members of the family of Herod the Great—Archelaus, Herod Antipas, Philip and Herodius, Philip Tetrarch of Iturea. The culmination of this, according to Pelt, was that the area of Galilee, ruled by Herod Antipas was more peaceful than was Judah, ruled by Archelaeus. Thus Joseph was able to take his family to Nazareth to fulfill prophecy that Jesus would be called a "Nazarene."

Chapter 3

He analyzed the words "Repent for the Kingdom of Heaven has come near" (Matt: 3:2). His translation reads *"Bekeert u luyden doet penitencie"* from the Latin *"agite poenitentiam"* [do penance]. He continued:

> The words 'do penance' are not to be understood like many people assume: a pain to suffer for our misdeeds, which persons falsely call penance. Rather, it means that everyone should recognize his/her misdeeds, and because of love should refrain from them and should return to the right way.

The verse meant, further, that "one should receive a good heart and a good will, and that he/she should be transformed from the old person into a new person." The baptism by John was a preparation for faith so that the believers could better understand the coming faith in Christ and willingly lay their sins aside—and, reported Pelt, "Mister Erasmus" said the same. We do not know if Pelt had access to Erasmus's *Paraphrases on Matthew* or if he had a general knowledge of Erasmus's ideas from other sources. He may have had reference to Chapter 3 in the *Paraphrases on Matthew* when Erasmus commented on the wheat and the chaff.

> Hereafter there shall be no meane, either ye muste thoroughly be good, or thoroughly evil. . . . He (God) seeth also your inward secretes of the hartes. Before him either ye must be chaffe or fyne wheate. But in the meane season whether of both ye wyll be, he has partly put in your choyce.[8]

Some Jews came saying they were sons of Abraham, but that was not sufficient justification. John's baptism and the confession of sins were the only sufficient preparation for the forgiveness of sin. John washed the body while the Christ, who is to come, will wash away sins.

Chapter 4

Pelt highlighted three themes in Matthew's fourth chapter: fasting, temptation and calling the first disciples. First he emphasized Jesus' two crucial statements: "we are not to live by bread alone," and "we should not tempt the Lord our God." Passing by the Sea of Galilee, Jesus called the disciples three times. (Pelt noted the parallels to Mark and Luke's gospels). From Luke Pelt interpolated the story about Peter's falling down on his knees before Jesus. He referred to people who came to Jesus from far away, from the Decapolis region (he explained for the reader the meaning of the ten cities east of the Jordan River), and the Pentapolis, which supposed region does not appear in the Matthew text, nor is this region specifically located.

Chapter 5

With respect to "the poor in spirit," Pelt suggested they are those who do not put their trust in earthly goods. Likewise, as he examined the Beatitudes, Pelt surmised that Christians must not only be peaceful, but must be peacemakers. Furthermore, he added, "blessed are those who believe in Christ, but more blessed are those who for the sake of truth endure persecution for His sake." Concerning "salt of the earth," many doctors asserted that Christ said that "they were the wisdom of the world," but he meant that like salt which preserves, we were protected or saved from corruption, so that we would not be tasteless and worthless.

Concerning human laws, we should respect both their positive and negative aspects. He explained that the "jot" (KJV, 5:18) or "yodh" (in Hebrew) is the smallest letter of the Hebrew alphabet. Hence, the smallest part of the law should be maintained. The law of Moses had to do not only with one's works, but more with one's will and one's consent. According to God's will we must love our enemies sincerely.

Chapter 6

The gloss to Chapter 6 included two major homiletical suggestions. First, we must pray not with external show, but from the heart, with the understanding. Second, when we as Christian people put our trust in Christ, we need not be anxious about the future.

Chapter 7

Jesus stated that our blessedness does not rest with prophecies or miracles. It is only concerned with right belief and doing the will of God. Then he introduced material extraneous to the Matthean text, indicating that even Baalam (Numbers 22-23), and "many others," although outside the faith, still spoke the word of God.

Interpreting Matthew 7:15-20, Pelt revealed some of his own attitudes about his fellow Christians.

> Christ taught us that we should beware of and recognize false prophets. That refers to false monks and individuals in religious orders who suck out (*uit suygen*) and milk dry (*uit melken*) the sweat and blood of the common folk who are taught to do many good works for the profit of the monks, without having love and right belief in Christ. When these have an evil root and an evil or stingy attitude then all their works and fruits are evil. All these with all their works, but done without God, shall be burned in eternal fire.

An interesting parallel with this is in Erasmus's *Paraphrase on Matthew*. Referring to the same verses, Erasmus wrote,

They that shewe themselves to be prophetes and boaste themselves of this tytle, they that feyne themselves by religiouse apparel to be shepe whereas in hearte and affection they be wolves, they must be esteemed and judged by their fruites.[9]

Chapter 8

After relating that the Centurion's son was healed, Pelt explained that the Centurion was not a Jew but a heathen captain sent to them from Rome. Returning to the story of the evil spirits of the Gaderene demoniacs, Pelt made a comparison with people who live like pigs when the devil is in control. Similarly, he identified Matthew's story of the fig-less fig tree (Chapter 21) with people who had no "good fruit" *i.e.* no beliefs and trust in Christ. It is interesting to notice his parallel imagery, although strained—devil-filled pigs and barren fig tree. Again he emphasized an inner belief or spiritual dimension as more important than external aspects.

Many heathen were baptized because of their good will and their belief, who would come into the Kingdom of heaven before the 'Christian persons' who were baptized with water, but who merely bore the Christian name without right belief.

Chapter 9

Jesus then took a boat from the land of the Gadarenes to Caphernaum, which the translator stated was the main city in Galilee. Again, Pelt emphasized internal rather than outward spirituality. He quoted Hosea 6:6, " I desire mercy not sacrifice," in connection with Matthew 9:13, "Go and learn what this means, 'I desire mercy, not sacrifice;' for I have come to call not the righteous but sinners."

Without commenting on the leader of the synagogue (Matt 9:18-19), whose daughter was healed, Pelt explained the meaning of synagogue while pointint out that Jerusalem had more than one. Likewise, without commenting on many other stories in this chapter Pelt summarized: "Then he taught openly in cities and towns, and not like the hypocrites and false preachers who were more concerned about their own profit."

Chapter 10

Pelt alluded to Jerome who stated that, despite Simon Peter's primacy in the list of the apostles, no one should think that Peter was first in authority. Indeed, Jerome wrote that all apostles were equal in worthiness and power.

Moving on to the human predicament, Pelt affirmed that all persons, however sinful, can come to Christ. Using Matthew 10:39 he argued,

Those who find their soul shall lose it, and this is not to be understood as some monks understand it that we must mortify our own self; but rather that we must pay attention to our own life, and that we must, for Christ's sake, consider our own life lesser and should disdain or despise our life, and that we should accept tribulation willingly, and we should not, on our own, proceed to punish our own self.

Chapter 11

Jesus proclaimed woes to unrepentant cities. Bethsaida was supposedly the home of Philip, Andrew and Peter (John 1:44), therefore, it was a surprise that it did not repent. Likewise Pelt condemned the towns of Chorazim and Capernaum because they did not follow the teachings of Jesus. He added that these towns were all near each other at the north end of the Sea of Galilee.

Chapter 12

The commentator thought that three parts of this chapter needed clarification. First, with respect to the man who had a withered hand, he suggested a reason for Jesus's healing. The person was a worker in metal and stone, and he needed his hands to make his living. For this reason, he asked Jesus to make him whole. Second, Pelt quoted the long passage from Isaiah (Matthew 12:18-21) concerning God's chosen servant. As long as the chosen one is on earth, truth will prevail and God's law will be obeyed. Third, the sin of blasphemy against the Holy Spirit will not be forgiven here or in the future.

Chapter 13

Pelt centered his whole commentary concerning this chapter on the parable of the wheat and the weeds growing together, and he developed this idea extensively—i.e. the relationship between good and evil people. All people will follow their own good or evil nature. To illustrate, he referred to Jesus's statement to Judas: "What you do, do it quickly" (i.e. follow your own evil nature). He concluded that the interpretation meant by Jesus was (and he used the Latin: sinite utrasque crescere) to allow both to grow up together that after the plants (or the people) were grown it was God who would separate the good grain from the weeds, or the righteous people from the unbelievers.

Chapter 14

Setting the stage for Herod's order to behead John the Baptist, Pelt introduced several geographical references. Again, he explained the meaning of Tetrarchy to emphasize the complicated relations, even rivalries, within the families of Herod the Great's descendants. Herod Antipas was ruler of one of these political jurisdictions. A brother, Philip, whose wife was Herodias ruled another of the four regions. Their daughter was Salome. John the Baptist's moral and legal criticisms of the political and family relationships led to his death.

Pelt had no comment concerning the feeding of the 5,000 or Jesus's walking on the water.

Chapter 15

Pelt's homiletic conclusion to "Honor your father and your mother" was that we should honor them by staying with them, helping them with worldly concerns, and supporting them with the power of our soul. He was critical of those who spoke with their lips but not from their hearts, or of those who adhered to human institutions and laws and yet let God's commands go unheeded.

After the feeding of the 4,000 in Matthew 15:39 Jesus went to the Magadan, and Pelt compared the same story in Mark (8:10) where the name of the town was Dalmanutha. Chrysostom and Jerome had suggested that Jesus went to the end of the land of Magalorum. Pelt followed up these geographical discrepancies in detail, concluding that they referred to the same place.

Chapter 16

The commentator thought it necessary to give some information concerning sects of Judaism. There were, he said, three: the Pharisees, the Sadducees, and the Essenes. The Pharisees often lead a stiff and sober life, concentrating on the law. They studied astronomy and other worldly matters. They seemed to be separated and acted as though they were better than the other Jews. The Sadducees respected only the law of Moses, but not the prophets. They did not believe in resurrection of the flesh, angels, or Spirit.

When Matthesw 16:13 mentioned the district of Caesarea Philippi, an explanation seemed necessary. We are told that this was the city built by Herod Antipas, son of Herod the Great. It is at the headwaters of the Jordan River which itself originates from two springs. Then Jesus referred in 16:17 to Peter "Bar Jonah," which Pelt explained means "Son of Jonah."

Pelt clearly betrayed his heretical leanings when he interpreted Matthew 16:18. *The paraphrase of Erasmus* on 16:18 follows:

> Thou arte very Peter, that is to say, a sound and sure stone, not wavering hither or thither with sundrie opinions of the vulgare sort: upon this stone of thy professyon will I builde my churche, that is to saye, my house and my palace: whiche being set on a sure foundacion, I will so fortifie that no power or strengthe of the Kingdome of hell shall be noble to beate it downe."[10]

The Pelt commentary on the same verse is as follows:

You are Peter, which means strong in faith, not as the common people lightly believe. On this strong confession of faith I will build my church, where the gates of hell cannot oppose it. Augustine said that Jesus proved and stated that he himself was a strong stone on which he would build his church. Christ builds us on himself and not on any human person; therefore, it is a great marvel that some want to interpret this scripture referring to the Pope, and with this want to elevate him. No holy doctors have ever wanted to suggest that the foundation of the church of Christ stands on a human being [*mensche*].

Chapter 17

Concerning the transfiguration, he stated that Elijah and Moses really were with Jesus—*i.e.* this was not a fantasy—and their clothes were like light. That Elijah was there literally, Pelt supposedly proved from Malachi 4:5.

Chapter 18

The Scripture reports that the one who tempts anyone toward sin should have a great millstone tied around his/her neck and be drowned in the sea. Pelt countered this with the suggestion that we should hold all people in honor for God's sake. Forgiveness seventy times seven really means consistent acts of forgiveness without number, according to Pelt—a truly heart-felt forgiveness.

Chapter 19

The Hebrews had a lenient attitude toward divorce, although the husband had to give the wife a letter explaining reasons for the separation (Deuteronomy 24:14). The wife was usually the victim of hate in such a situation; Pelt attributed this problem to the strong sinful nature of the Jews. As a contrast, Jesus made the stipulations stronger. There should be no divorce at all.

Pelt referred to both Ambrose and Chrysostom concerning the rich man and the difficulty of going through the eye of a needle. He referred to a commentary of Jerome's which said that Jesus meant a "real" living [*levenden*] camel. Then Pelt referred to other commentators who attempted to ameliorate the impossibility by referring to a gate in the wall of Jerusalem, through which a camel might go but with difficulty.

Chapter 20

The parable of the unequal pay for the vineyard workers is told in a straight-forward manner—the owner said that he would distribute wages to his workers as he decided.

Furthermore, following "are you able to drink the cup that I am about to drink?"(20:22), Pelt added that in some editions the following words are missing "or to be baptized with the baptism that I am baptized with." This means, he continued, "Are you able to bear the suffering and the pain which I must endure?" This undoubtedly referred back to the statement earlier in this chapter where Jesus predicted his death and resurrection.

The discussion about who should sit at Jesus' right and left hand is not answered in the commentary, but Jesus compared rulers of the Gentiles, probably political leaders, with his own mission. The prince of the Gentiles (*heydene=heiden*) takes command against the rest of the people without their approval. In contrast to this tyranny, Jesus explained that he must give his life as redemption of many.

Chapter 21

Pelt commented on some of the geographical and historical elements of the chapter. The Mount of Olives is near Jerusalem; Bethphage is a small village nearby, perhaps a village of many priests near the Mount of Olives. When Jesus rode on the "donkey, the foal of a donkey" he did not ride on both animals at the same time, but one after the other. In this he failed to understand the Hebrew or Greek parallelism that actually meant only one animals. Pelt also noted the parallels of this story in Mark and Luke.

He modified the story of the fig tree in an interesting way and used it to condemn fellow monastics: the fig tree is meant all monks and spiritual persons who have great holy titles and holiness in their clothes and their being and outward show, and have nothing but miserliness, unchastity and haughtiness in their hearts. These will remain, as the fig tree, without fruits into eternity.

Pelt observed that Hosanna, from the Hebrew, is from two words. It means "to make Holy or blessed." When spoken to God it is a prayer meaning, "Make us holy, we ask."

Chapter 22

At the wedding banquet after the invited guests did not come, the servants were sent out to bring a variety of people—evil and good—to the banquet. By this we are to understand that it was the Jews who were the evil ones, even though they let it be thought that they were good at least outwardly.

Commenting on to the section concerning paying taxes, he noted that Caesar Augustus required the whole world to be taxed, and every one went to the place of his/her birth to pay taxes. Actually he incorporated Luke 2:1-7, and used it to complete the story of the taxes. These details are not part of the Matthew text. Attempting to locate in time Jesus' discussion about taxes, "give to the Emperor the things that are the Emperor's and to God the things that are God's" (Matt. 22:21), Pelt suggested that it happened on the Wednesday before the passion of Jesus. The Pharisees tried to trick Jesus with their question to see if Jesus would deny the law of Moses or the law of the Emperor. Yet Jesus straddled the issue to avoid their trick.

Chapter 23

In the gloss on this chapter Pelt included an extended criticism of Scribes and Pharisees, especially because of their public display of broadly embroidered shawls and clothing. He added that "rabbi" in Hebrew meant simply "teacher" not Master or overlord. He then observed that many Pharisees traveled over sea and land to proselytize for Judaism, and he explained that "proselytize" meant to convince outsiders to become adherents of the Jewish law. Metaphorically he concluded that the Pharisees made sure their pots and dishes were clean outside, although inwardly they were filled with plunder and deceit.

Pelt referred to the example of Zechariah (Matt 23:35) son of Barachiah, who spoke against the officials who transgressed the law and was, subsequently, killed in the temple. He conflated this with the story of Zechariah, son of the priest Jehoiada who was stoned in the "court of the house of the Lord" (II Chronicles 24:21, centuries before the time of Jesus). Another story of Zechariah (or Zachariah) appears in Josephus[11] which death occurred at the time of the destruction of Jerusalem (70 A. D.). This reference in Josephus, is to another Zechariah, son of Baris (Baruch). Pelt noticed the confusion among those named "Zechariah." He also found that Origen thought that this was the father of John the Baptist (Luke Chapter 1). Pelt rejected this idea accepting Jerome's assumption that this Zechariah was the son of a priest named Joades, also known as Barachiah (23:35), but this is possibly a mistake in copying which Jerome took to be authentic. In a convoluted way this set the context of the statement "Jerusalem, Jerusalem, the city that kills the prophets and stones those who are sent to it" (Matt 23:37). It is also impressive how many sources Pelt must have had at his disposal to make these comparisons.

Chapter 24

Pelt located the discussion about the destruction of the temple and the last judgment on the Mount of Olives near Jerusalem. He called to our attention that Josephus wrote that the destruction would be accompanied by many strange happenings; such as a beast of inhuman proportions appearing in the days of Emperor Claudius. The commentator then referred to Acts 11:28 where the prophet Agabus traveled from Jerusalem to Antioch and predicted famine. Since a famine actually occurred in the reign of Claudius in A. D. 46 or 47, Pelt interpreted the two as predictions of the end, although neither Agabus nor Claudius is mentioned in the Matthew text. With respect to false prophets who will appear, Pelt referred to another sign in Daniel Chapter 9: the abomination of Desolation (See Matthew 24:15), where an anti-God or an idol is set up in the holiest place in the temple. Despite all these possible signs, however, no one knows the day of Judgment. We should all be watchful, warned Pelt, and some will remain faithful during the trials of the last days.

Chapter 25
In the parable of the ten bridesmaids, five had sufficient oil while five were lacking oil. Pelt explained that by "oil" is meant "spiritual gladness," which the wise maidens possessed. On the other hand, members of the religious orders are like the foolish maidens who did not act with love and good intentions willingly. Furthermore, for all, religious or secular, Pelt wrote that those who buried their treasure in the earth trust only in temporary and worldly things.

Chapter 26
In the house of Simon the Leper, the woman poured costly oil on Jesus. She was reprimanded by some of the onlookers. During this episode, according to Pelt, Simon ceased being leprous (which is not in the Matthew text). Furthermore, he added, the woman with the jar of perfume (borrowing from John 12:1-8) was Mary, sister of Martha and Lazarus.
Pelt explained that the day of unleavened bread (Passover) lasted seven days [as in the Gospel of John, but not as in Matthew]. When Jesus was arrested he was, as predicted (Isaiah 53:7), "led as a lamb to the slaughter." Again, Pelt's elaboration of Isaiah's story, however, is not in the Matthew text.
Finally, he discussed the meal the disciples had together. He related the Passover meal between Jesus and the disciples (Matt. 26:17-25), to the last supper (Matt. 26:26-30). He observed that the first meal reflected Jewish Passover usage, while the second was parallel with Mark 14:22-26, as a modification of the meal for special theological reasons—a heavenly banquet and the need for shed blood. While Jesus was still seated at the table, he took bread and spoke concerning the sacrament of the bread and of the wine of the New Testament, truly the Paschal Lamb, "but to be seen as a figure or a symbol." He concluded with the liturgical interpretation: "Then Jesus performed the first mass and consecrated his disciples to be priests."

Chapter 27.
Pelt suggested that Judas who hanged himself did so because he realized he had sinned against innocent divinity. He elaborated on the details of the narrative. The Greek text names the potter's field "Acheldemach" [or "field of blood"]. The coins which Judas left lying on the ground were used to buy the field as a burial place of strangers. The Matthew text states that it was Jeremiah's prophecy that this would be fulfilled. Pelt, however, noticed, correctly, that this text does not appear in Jeremiah, but actually comes from Zechariah 11:13.

Chapter 28
In a limited commentary on the resurrection, Pelt reported that when Jesus said, "Lo, I am with you always" he actually meant, "See, I am with all you

people as your head and your comforter. No one else is your head. Hence, as Reformers would emphasize, Christ is the only head of the Church.

The commentary ended with these words: "all peoples ought to know the Word of the Lord so they could live therein freely and would be enabled faithfully therein to die."

The Translator/Commentator's Conclusion

In his conclusion to the Gospel Commentary, Pelt outlined the theological principles which guided his exegesis. He opposed the idea of works righteousness and argued that salvation is brought to us only through the Grace of Jesus Christ. Salvation comes when the believer is washed through baptism, reborn and regenerated through renewal by the Holy Spirit. Through the Grace of God alone we will be made heirs and have hope of eternal life. It is more than we broken, sinful persons can conceive, but because of His great love for us, our God and Creator brought salvation to us through his own flesh and blood. Because of this, Jesus was an example to us that our life, our body and our blood, should be spent for the faith and love of Jesus, so that others might also receive salvation. Our own nature and efforts can only produce evil. Yet, for the love of Jesus we can put our evil works behind, and not because of fear or control by anyone. In this way we can fulfill all that God desires and wills for us. In order that we may accomplish this perfectly, God has provided for us four Gospels written by the Holy Spirit.

Pelt then described some of his sources and the personal reasons for his efforts. He stated that he has compared the old text (Vulgate edition) with the new Greek text of Erasmus. (Sometimes the Greek text was used where the old Latin text was unclear; sometimes he expanded the text and used both versions). He also used the commentaries of Jerome, Augustine and Erasmus for brief glosses (commentaries) where the Greek or Hebrew was difficult to understand. He added that he made this translation not as an idle exercise, but for people who spend more time with human statutes than they do with the Word of God. He also planned to translate the three remaining gospels into Dutch. In this way he hoped that he could lead others to live and die in the faith as contained in the other Gospels. Thus, he hoped, he could bring honor to the Father, the Son and the Holy Ghost. Amen.

Unfortunately, he did not complete the other translations because in 1524 he fled from Amsterdam. He became was minister in a Lutheran church in Bremen, and died in Germany in 1562.

Theological Conclusions we may deduce from Pelt's glosses

After analyzing the glosses following each of the chapters of the commentary we can only surmise which sections were the basis of the Emperor's condemnation. Some ideas expressed were obviously in opposition to common Roman Catholic doctrines of the time. Many other suggestions, however, seem less controversial and were much more educational, explanatory, or pastoral. We will analyze his major emphasizes in seven parts.

First, judgment against monastic presumptions and shortcomings

Even though he was a Franciscan, Pelt harshly criticized his fellow monks. In Chapter 7 he suggested that monks were false prophets who take advantage of the people, for profit, and, consequently, they do not have correct motivation. They have an evil and stingy attitude, and, therefore, their fruits are evil. In Chapter 10 he criticized those within the monastic orders who emphasized punishing the body so that the spirit might be strengthened. Pelt considered the outward disciplinary measures as external show which failed to produce true inner substance. In Chapter 21 he compared those in monastic orders with the fig trees without figs. They emphasized their titles and fine liturgical clothing, whereas in their hearts they were miserly, haughty, and filthy. In Chapter 25 he compared monastics with the virgins who did not have sufficient oil in their lamps. By this he meant that they did not have sufficient love and good intention, that their spiritual depth was virtually non-existent.

In general, he thought that the shortcomings of the monastics gave evidence of little or no spiritual integrity. Rather, the external aspects of their lives, to be observed by others, seemed to be their main emphasis. Hence true Christian convictions were lacking.

Second, The need for internalizing the faith as contrast to both Jewish usage and Roman Catholic practice

While Pelt emphasized the need for a strong internal faith ("in the heart") in many places in the commentary, some illustrations were more vivid than others. For example, in Chapter 5 he used the example of salt. We must be saved from corruption as salt preserves food. Our "saltiness" is therefore related to our inner integrity. Furthermore, the smallest part of the law of Moses, which we should maintain, concerns not our external works but our inner will and consent. In Chapter 8 he assumed that those whose inner self is controlled by the devil will be as the pigs into which the evil demons were cast. They rush to their deaths. The internal disciplines which characterized a true Christian are, rather, true belief and trust in Christ. Baptism with water alone is not adequate without a person's good will, strong faith, and steadfast belief. In Chapter 9 he argued that sacrifice is not as important as mercy, using the teachings of Hosea. Many persons who lack this mercy or inner integrity are more concerned with profit than with service.

The sharp criticism against the Pharisees and Scribes in Chapter 23 concerned their tendency to be pure on the outside (as the dishes) but inside (as related to the cups) corrupt. Their emphasis on prayer shawl decoration seemed to be more important than their inner spiritual life. Titles and appearance were of more importance to them than substance. We achieve an inner Christian value and conscience not by our own efforts, but only as we rely on the Grace of God, which makes us true heirs of the Kingdom of God and life in the presence of Christ.

Third, Criticism of the Roman Catholic doctrine and practice of penance

Whereas contemporary Roman Catholic practice emphasized that penance was something one does—contrition, confession, satisfaction—, Pelt looked in another direction. He paralleled Luther's later doctrine which emphasized penance more as a state of being. In his gloss on Chapter 3 he suggested that a result of true penitence would be a change in the inner person; the believer was really regenerated. This, however, went beyond Luther's concept of *"simul justus et peccator"* [at the same time justified and a sinner]. The "new creation" (II Corinthians 5:17) or "new nature" (Colossians 3:19) could become a reality; the old person could truly be made new and not merely "declared" to be new.

Thus it was that he concluded (with Erasmus) that "do penance" (Matthew 3:2) really should be translated as "be penitent," or "repent." Following this idea he interpreted Chapter 6 to mean that our heart-felt prayer should reflect our new understanding. The believing Christian is washed by baptism and made new when the Holy Spirit brings rebirth and regeneration. Penance thus referred not to an outward act but an internal change of the heart; the old person had indeed been made new.

Fourth, The Grace of God

The Grace of God, not human effort, was basic to human change. This was interpreted, however, with an emphasis on human cooperation—synergism. Sin did not permanently warp the human person (in a Lutheran sense). Rather, the grace of God made it possible for individuals to put their sins behind them and begin a new life in God's grace. Throughout his conclusion, Pelt noted that we must be washed by baptism, and renewed and regenerated through the Holy Spirit. Then through faith in Christ we can put our evil works behind us, not because of fear but because of love. The four Gospels guide us along our journey. If we attempt to do anything on our own, only evil will result. Yet through the Grace of God, mediated to us directly through the scriptures and the Holy Spirit, and the examples of Christ who gave his own flesh and blood as an example for us we can prevail. Grace is not available through monastic vows, the power of the Papacy, the confessional, or the doctrine of penance. Furthermore, he remained highly critical of the notion that punishing the body enhanced the Spirit. He stated that instead of mortifying our bodies we should pay attention to our own life, that we might actually live for the sake of Christ.

Fifth, Evaluation of Papal power

The classic Roman Catholic teaching concerning the authority and power of the Pope came through a particular interpretation of Matthew 16:18. This understanding stated that Peter was the "rock" on which the church was built, and all of Peter's successors in the "See of Peter" are God's vicars on earth. From the interpretive sermons concerning papal theory by Leo I (440-461) and certain interpretations in the previous century, this became the Church's position. Pelt argued that this doctrine was a misplaced emphasis concerning a specific human being, and he repudiated it. His gloss on this verse was translated above and is repeated here in its entirety:

> You are Peter, which means strong in faith, not as the common people lightly believe. On this strong confession of faith I will build my church, where the gates of hell cannot oppose it. Augustine said that Jesus proved and stated that he himself was a strong stone on which he would build his church. Christ builds us on himself and not on any humans; therefore, it is a great marvel that some want to interpret this scripture referring to the Pope, and with this want to elevate him. No holy doctors have ever wanted to suggest that the foundation of the church of Christ stands on a human being [*mensche*].

He analyzed the idea again in Chapter 10 where he recognized Peter as first-named apostle, but denied that this was to be interpreted as first in authority. Furthermore, he found that in a fourth century commentary of Jerome (331-420), hence before the interpretations of Leo I (440-451), it was stated that all apostles were equal in worthiness and power. Likewise, in Chapter 28 concerning the resurrection Pelt had Jesus say, "See, I am with you people as your head and your comforter. No one else is your head." The implication seems clear that Christ is the only head of the church; there is no authoritative earthly head.

Sixth, Good people versus evil people

The comments on Chapter 13, concerning wheat and weeds growing together, gave him occasion to indicate both that there were individuals with an evil nature, such as Judas, and that the ultimate separation between the good and the evil would be according to God's judgment. He did not elaborate whether he thought those with an evil nature were inherently so, or simply that they were evil because they acted on personal or limited motives and did not allow themselves to be regenerated by the Holy Spirit. The extensive discussion in Chapter 22 about those chosen to come to the banquet—the evil and the good together—gave him another chance to indicate that the evil persons were the Jews. He criticized their outward piety and lack of inward sanctity.

Seventh, Pastoral Concerns

Since we know that Pelt was accustomed to preach sermons within his Amsterdam monastery, we are not surprised to recognize many pastoral concerns in his commentary. We have already noted his many explanatory comments concerning geography and other descriptive matters of interest to his hearers. In commenting on Chapter 18 he dealt with forgiveness. Forgiveness, he stated, meant not merely words spoken, but forgiveness from the heart. The same chapter gave him a chance to warn against those persons who tempted another. The punishment would be severe (drowning). We should, instead, refrain from temptation and hold all people in honor for God's sake.

In Chapter 19 he approached the question of divorce, surely a pastoral concern in his day. He assumed that many divorces arose from hatred against the wives. Rather than allow a written statement of reasons for separation, as the Jews did according to Deuteronomy (24:14), he stated that Jesus argued against divorce at all times.

His pastoral concern for the hearers is reflected in the section "Honor your father and mother." He insisted that specific things should be done to put this "honoring" into real and concrete practice.

In Chapter 26 he stated that the Passover meal (Matthew 26: 17-25) and the Last Supper (Matthew 26:26-30) were the origin of "the first Mass." The Paschal Lamb was to be seen as a figure or a symbol (not as transubstantiated elements). When Jesus performed this "first Mass" he then consecrated his disciples as priests to continue the practice.

Finally, Pelt had a pastoral concern when he translated the Gospel for the people so they could spend more time in understanding the scriptures (in their own language) and would thus, he assumed, be less tempted to spend time at secular pursuits.

The place of the Matthew translation in the religio-political developments in The Netherlands is difficult to discern. There are many interpretations in the glosses of this gospel which would have raised much caution and concern among Roman Catholic officials—questions concerning the Papacy, criticism of monastic orders, criticism of external practices of the Roman Catholic church, criticism of the doctrine of penance, emphasis on the Grace of God in place of Roman Catholic practices and assumptions.

While the interpretations are not orthodox Roman Catholic teachings, many are also not clearly influenced by Luther. Surely Luther would have agreed with the interpretation of Matthew 16:18, but he would have been horrified at the suggestion that a human being can cooperate with the Grace of God. He thought that any hint of synergy robbed the transcendent God of His place as God the Creator and Sustainer.

The strong emphasis on internal faith in opposition to external practices reflects Erasmus and Humanist thought. It may also reflect the widespread anti-clerical attitude in much of the region in The Netherlands. The suggestion that the interpretation of the Eucharist should be taken spiritually or symbolically rather than literally, was to be thoroughly developed within a short time. Such interpretations would highlight some of the differences between later Reformers.

There are many theological questions for which Pelt does not provide clear answers. Nor do we have information as to how these ideas were incorporated and used in the culture of The Netherlands of the 1520s, both inside and outside the monasteries. We are thankful, however, for the insights he does provide for us, especially as they are preserved in only one remaining original copy of his work almost five hundred years later.

Notes for Chapter 8

1. Paul Fredericq, *Corpus Documentorum Inquisitionis* (5 vols,: Ghent: Université, 1889-1902), IV, 265f. The Emperor noted that some printers thought the publishing of these documents would be permissible because they did not have the name of Martin Luther on the cover. They contain false doctrine, nevertheless, and the edict declared that after eight days from the issuing of this decree, prosecution and punishment would begin.

2. *(I)nde glosen zekere dwalingen bevonden zijn geweest.*" *CDI*, IV, 266.

3. The *NK* lists this as #369, published in 1522. Furthermore this bibliography indicated that the only known copy of the work is in the library of the University of Utrecht where I purchased my microfilm copy.

4. Wolfgang Schmitz, O.F.M. *Het Aandeel der Minderbroeders in onze Middeleeuwse Literatuur: Inleiding tot een Bibliograpfie der Nederlandse Franciscanen* (Nijmegen/Utrecht: Dekker & van de Vegt en J. W. van Leeuwen, 1936), p. 140.

5. C. C. de Bruin, *De Statenbijbel en Zijne Voorgangers* (Leiden: A. W. Sijthoff's Uitgeversmaatshappij, 1937), p. 136.

6. C. C. de Bruin, *De Statenbijbel en Zijne Voorgangers*, p. 138.

7. C. C. de Bruin, *Ibid.*, p. 135.

8. Taken from *Paraphrases of Erasmus on Matthew* Chapter 3, translated in England, and presented to King Edward VI, London, 31 January, 1548. The Toronto edition of the *Paraphrases on Matthew* in English is expected to be published in 2006 or 2007.

9. Erasmus's *Paraphrase on Matthew*, *Ibid.*

10. *Ibid.*

11. Josephus, *Jewish Wars*, Whiston version IV, 5.4; Penguin Classics translation (1959) by G. A. Williamson, p. 240.

Chapter 9

Summa der Godliker Scrifturen: (1523) An Unauthorized Translation

In Chapter 8 we considered the first of two printings specifically condemned by the Emperor on 23 March, 1524.[1] In this chapter we turn to the second book condemned by that special edict. While it is more extensive, it also has a more complex history. In 1973 I was discussing early Protestant developments in The Netherlands with Dr. C. C. de Bruin, late professor in the University of Leiden. He called my attention to the a little-known text of the period called *Summa der godliker scrifturen oft een Duytsche theologie*, or in the Latin original, *Oeconomica Christiana* [*i.e.*, a summary of the teachings of the Scriptures]. I secured a copy of the document and filed it away among my documents for future reference.[2] In preparation for a lecture at the Sixteenth Century Studies Conference/American Society of Reformation Research in Kalamazoo, Michigan, in May, 1981, I began an analysis of the *Summa*. This lecture was subsequently published in its original form in the *Mennonite Quarterly Review*, June, 1982.[3]

Shortly after this publication I was informed that a parallel study of the same document was available in Dutch as a published doctoral dissertation written under the direction of Dr. C. C. de Bruin in Leiden.[4] An even more interesting coincidence is that on my extended study tour in The Netherlands in 1973-1974 I had met Johannes Trapman at Leiden when he was engaged in his graduate education. At the time we did not discuss his future thesis plans. In the intervening years I have benefited from his writings and his very extensive analysis of this document. As a consequence, and after discussions with him, I have made several changes to my original 1981 lecture, especially in the discussion of terms such as "sacramentarians" or "sacramentists" to describe early evangelical movements which advocated a non-sacramental understanding of the Eucharist or baptism. Whereas the Roman Catholic doctrine assumed that sacramental acts are "bearers of grace," the early reform movements interpreted the traditional sacraments in several different ways from the medieval Roman Catholic sense.

The longer title of this document is *Summa der godliker scrifturen, oft een duytsche theologie, leerende ende onderwijsende alle menschen wat dat christen gholove is.*[5] It was a Dutch translation, printed in Leiden in 1523. Since the publication was issued without the author's name, the government authorities proceeded against the printer Jan Seversz. In 1523 legal authorities were sent to Leiden to summon him.[6] In February, 1524 another official went to Leiden[7] to determine the extent of his possessions for possible confiscation. In April two more trips were made to Leiden.[8] On 13 July, 1524 he was banned perpetually from Holland, Zeeland and Friesland, and all his goods were confiscated.[9] Unknown to the authorities, Seversz had printed other works of a reforming nature. A most glaring example was Luther's *Babylonian Captivity* in 1521, printed with the city identified as "Wittenberge."[10] Careful analysis of the type used in the printing, however, showed that it was actually printed in Leiden by Seversz, although not discovered by the censors at the time.

A year after he was banned a note appeared indicating that Seversz was seen in Utrecht, and he was allowed to come again into Leiden.[11] There is some confusion in names at this time because references to Jan Seversz de Croepel [the crippled] appeared in Amsterdam. Kronenberg argued that there might have been two individuals with similar names, but that they were both "*besmet*" [infected] with the ideas of Luther seems unlikely. The conclusion to the problem is not neatly solved, yet Jan Seversz evidently printed other works in Leiden after 1527.[12]

The Latin title of the original was *Oeconomica Christiana in rem christianam instituens*, written probably in 1520 or 1521, but not published until 7 August, 1527, perhaps in Strasbourg.[13] In 1523, while the Dutch translation was being printed, a French edition was issued from Basel, soon to be banned by the Sorbonne;[14] and in 1529, an English edition was issued, to be banned by the Archbishop of Canterbury both in 1530 and 1531.[15] In the next decade several editions appeared in Italian.[16] Many of these found their way to various *Indices of Forbidden Books*, including the main index of 1559. No 16th century German edition has been discovered. Some analysis of the theological assumptions of this work will give us information as to why it was condemned so swiftly in The Netherlands.

Many early "protestant" developments in The Netherlands were called "Lutheran," and many were indeed influenced by Luther. In addition, however, they were also deeply molded by an Erasmian Humanism which often reflected an understanding of the sacraments different both from Luther and medieval Roman Catholic usage. This document fits this pattern, in that it included a long section on the symbol [*teken*] of baptism, and an alternate interpretation of the Eucharist. The author also insisted on a moral and ethical life, while rejecting the value of monastics and hierarchical vows. He denied any distinction between priests and the laity.

I have used both the Dutch edition of 1523 and the Latin original. That the Dutch is a translation from the Latin seems indicated by the addition of a three-page prologue in the Dutch, summarizing the main emphasis of the work. The prologue ends with these words: "My intention was not to circulate this book (the Latin original) but because this was urged upon me, I have translated it, and brought together the principal chapters out of the Holy Scriptures for the profit of all Christian persons [*alle kersten menschen*]."[17] The Latin edition comprised 143 pages in 1527, printed in 109 pages in 1882. The Dutch edition, printed on much larger pages, covered 81 pages in 1523, and 78 pages in 1882. The Dutch edition included 31 chapters, of which there are 15 on baptism, and 16 on the remainder of his theology. The Latin included 29 chapters, again with 15 on baptism, and only 14 on the remainder of his theology. Some of the chapters are divided slightly differently, and there are several pages in the Dutch which have no parallel in the original Latin.

While the work does not include the name of the author, many scholars seem convinced it was written by Henry Bomelius, or Henry van Bommel, prior of a convent in Utrecht.[18] Other scholars, however, doubt that the authorship can be determined. Henry was from the town of Bommel, on the Maas River in Gelderland, and matriculated at the University of Cologne in 1520. He became a priest in 1522 and worked in Utrecht until after 1525. Thereafter, he disappeared from history until he reappeared as a Lutheran minister in Germany in the 1540s where he was active until his death in 1570.[19] Karl Benrath, who studied this literature extensively at the end of the 19th century, concluded that Henry of Bommel was influenced first by the writings of Wessel Gansfort and Erasmus, and in later years by Martin Luther. If this is true, this work of the *Oeconomica Christiana*, or *Summa*, in the Dutch translation, came at a juncture between Biblical Humanist influence in The Netherlands and developing Lutheranism in Germany. Let us analyze the theology contained in this work to test our assumption.

The Latin and the Dutch versions are substantially the same through the first fifteen chapters. These chapters constitute the First Part of the Latin version. The content concerns baptism and faith. At this point the Latin version began the numbering of the chapters again, from Chapter 1 (Second Part) through Chapter 14. There is an error in Toorenenbergen's Latin edition of the Second Part in that Chapter 12 is followed by Chapter 14. The Dutch version numbered the chapters continuously from Chapter 1 through Chapter 31. The second half of the work, in the Dutch translation, does not follow the same order as the Latin for all chapters. In addition, the Dutch version has four added chapters for which there is no Latin original.

Christianity is based on Faith

The author's main assertion was that Christianity must be based on faith.[20] Because there are too few people who understand this fundamental principle, there are many erroneous practices and false understandings which pass under the name of Christianity. The major thrust of the treatise, therefore, is to interpret the Scripture so that Christian faith can be understood according to God's clearly revealed plan.

His discussion of faith, however, presupposed a dichotomy within the human person and within the world. He contrasted inner faith and outer works. There is an inner, spiritual aspect of the human creature which can and does respond with faith. He called this the "new" man. On the other hand, there is an outer dimension as well, which we might call the physical or the "old man." If the inner, spiritual nature holds sway, we become new through Christ. Faith is a response only of the inner, spiritual person.

He used another symbol for the contrast between the old person and the new. When the physical, the old, has control of our life, we are as the first Adam.[21] When the inner, or spiritual, dimension holds sway, however, we are made new beings in Christ—the second Adam. To allow the spiritual dimension to be in control, or at least to assist it, is the main lesson we should learn from the Scriptures. Hence, to instill faith—or to control the old man by the new—is the goal of the Christian message and the purpose of the Scriptures.

When we ask how it is possible to be changed from children of the old Adam to children of the new Adam—to change from the old physical self to a new spiritual being—the Christological dimension arises. Our chance to be born anew comes only because of the shed blood of the new Adam. Only thus can we become other than sinners and property of the devil. There is, however, nothing automatic about this possibility of change. The passion and the death of Christ—blood—makes such deliverance possible, not assured.[22] We ourselves must appropriate the benefits by faith.

What does he mean by faith? "That one places all his hope, all his reliance and all his trust in God as his only salvation and his only refuge, and does not rely on his own merits or his good works."[23] This is a faith which is based on inner conviction of the whole person without reservation. It comes only from a complete trust in God at the expense of previous worldly, fleshly or personal concerns.

Baptism is a confirmation

Faith is thus the foundation of Christianity, but faith is confirmed by baptism. Only one who has appropriated the benefits of the blood through faith, and who has confirmed his faith through the water of baptism can achieve salvation. Only he/she can become a true associate of the second Adam, a true son/daughter of God, one who can say with all its meaning "Our Father." Baptism, moreover, is given an alternate interpretation—for the power to become sons/daughters of God comes to us not because of any power within the water, but because of faith. The water is merely a sign of what God alone can do.

He summarized his concept of baptism as follows:

> The water of baptism in itself does not take our sin away, otherwise it would be a glorious water indeed, and we would spend all day there washing ourselves. The water of the font has no more power within itself than the water that flows in the Rhine. Therefore, one could as well be baptized in the Rhine as in the font. When Philip baptized the Eunuch, he had no consecrated water, nor candles, nor salt, nor honey, nor consecrated vestments, but he simply baptized him in the water running beside the road. Here you must note carefully that the power of the baptism lies not in consecrated water, or other objects which one has at the font, but in what then? The power resides in your faith.[24]

Our faith, confirmed in baptism, makes us participants in the passion of Christ.

The water of baptism is only a sign, a symbol of something else. As a sign it was prefigured among the Jewish people at the Red Sea. "The baptism was prefigured when the children of Israel went out from the land of Egypt, through the Red Sea, and when Pharaoh sank in the sea with all his followers."[25] The children of Israel, on the contrary, survived the waters because of their faith, "and, so to speak, came from death to life." Thus, as one is being baptized he/she puts off Pharaoh (*i.e.*, the devil) because of faith, and takes on a new master, becoming a new being. Likewise, as the Christian goes into the sea (baptismal font) he/she goes to death, not of the body but of sin. As the person comes out of the font, faith leads him/her from spiritual death to the dry land (*i.e.*, to eternal life).

That the water of baptism is only a sign is expressed in another way. The Jews used the sign of circumcision so that people would know whether they were Jews or heathen. Christians have the sign of baptism to show that they have God as their Lord.[26]

The emphasis on baptism as a sign which one can recognize and relate to biblical symbols would seem to imply an adult understanding, hence adult baptism, and would reflect a forerunner of Anabaptist developments in The Netherlands. This, however, is not to be the case, since the author also included the Augustinian concept of baptism "for fear a child may become ill." One must not wait until he/she can of his/her own volition reject the devil and confirm this won faith. "Concerning baptism no one should say, as was strongly affirmed in previous times, that none should be baptized before he/she comes to the age of understanding, or that he/she should believe, forsake the devil, and should be old enough to know what he/she believes." If one should die as a child, can it then be said that this person has salvation in this manner? The author said "Yes! You know that the faith of your godparents was so strong that you were able to receive salvation thereby."[27]

How the strongly symbolic understanding of baptism, with its implied responsibility for adult interpretation, can be reconciled with this Augustinian concept of faith developed by one's godparents is not clear. One impression, however, is that the symbolic interpretation is the author's real assumption. The more "orthodox" or medieval concept was introduced briefly only as homage to tradition. Evidently, godparents influence children like parents influence their children through education. In any case, there appears to be no grace or power contained within the baptismal water.

The Lord's Supper

The author also made some modifications in his understanding of the Lord's Supper, or the Eucharist. There is no real presence in the elements, physical or spiritual, and no mention of change in the elements because of priestly practice. The Lord's Supper evidently does not play a significant part in his theological understanding, for while he has fifteen chapters analyzing baptism, he has one paragraph concerning the Lord's Supper. The Latin original of Chapter 7 does not describe the establishment of the Lord's supper, but refers to the body and blood as pledges or tokens [*pignora*=pledges or tokens] of Christ's exceptional love for us.

> This is his testament that he has made for us, and for this he died. So that we would certainly believe, he has provided for us a certain sign of his holy body for food, and a sign of his blood for drink. As St. Luke wrote in his 22nd chapter, "When the Lord sat in the Last Supper with his disciples, he gave them bread saying, take and eat, this is my body which will be given for you, and the cup: Drink of it all together, this is the cup of the New Testament in my blood, that for you and for many people will be shed for the forgiveness of sins." That body is a tangible pledge [*pant*=*pand*=pledge or pawn] of his love toward us. Even beyond this he has left his Spirit in our hearts as a comfort for us who in this world are confident even in our tribulations.[28] [It is interesting to note that he referred to Luke but did not quote Luke 22:19-20 exactly. More often he reflected Matthew 17:26-28 in establishing the Eucharist.]

Human Responsibility is presupposed, and an actual change occurs

Faith has a transforming power within the believers. Faith confirms human responsibility, or at least energizes it within the individual. The author assumes that the new believer will have the inner power, or free will, to respond to the things which faith demands.

The inheritance which one receives by becoming a child of faith can be related functionally to the doctrine of salvation or justification. The means of salvation is *sola fide*, as Paul and later Luther affirmed. This assertion is as basic to the theology of the *Summa* as it was for Luther. The content of salvation, however, and the way this is worked out in the individual life, shows that the author was not conversant with Luther's concept of forensic justification. The human through his/her faith and baptism does not merely "appear" justified in the sight of God, as Luther's concept implies. Through faith and baptism the sinner becomes actually a child of God—not a son/or daughter by declaration only, but in reality. "As a person is baptized, so will he/she believe with certainty his/her sins are forgiven, and that he/she becomes a child of God; and God becomes his/her father."[29] This is what is accomplished at the font, an actual change is given to us through faith,[30] although this was obviously not Luther's teaching. In a similar way the author was hardly Lutheran when he stated that "we have as much claim to heaven as Christ himself has, for while Christ is a Son of God, so are we also."[31]

Necessity of Evidence of Faith (Works)

If we actually become children of God through faith and baptism, we must give evidence of faith. We must act in a new way. "There is no more certain sign of salvation than that the person [*mensche*] lives a godly life."[32] True belief, and thanksgiving for what God has done for us, results in love, and love produces good work. The Epistle of James is quoted approvingly in a non-Lutheran sense with respect to the passage, "Faith without works is dead" (James 2:17). "He does not say that his faith is small or sick, but that it is *dead*. What is dead is nothing."[33] The author suggested that faith must be related to works, "for when the Spirit of God comes into our heart with belief and with love it cannot remain empty."[34] The one who has faith in God and Christ must be an imitator of Christ, a doer of ethical works. He summarizes: Works without faith are sin, (with which Luther would agree). Yet faith without works of faith reflects no true faith at all; consequently, the true believer is only known by the life he/she lives, with which Luther would disagree. "Only those who through love serve their neighbors will remain children of God; only they will be preserved in the faith."[35]

What are the good works which the faithful will accomplish through faith and love? The author constructs a list modeled after Colossians 3:5 similar to Galatians 5:19-21. "We should put to death in ourselves all covetousness and works of the flesh such as impurity, avarice, wrath, blasphemy, backbiting, or presumption."[36] In place of these one must rather "serve one another with love, comfort the poor with alms, help them, advise them, and do similar things." One must seek not one's own good, but that of the neighbor. Above all, one must do all for the glory of God.

Flesh/Spirit, a Dichotomy among Life-styles

The dichotomy between flesh and spirit, adopted from Paul was used in several ways to distinguish among people and ways of life. The ways of God are of the Spirit, while the ways of the world and the devil are flesh. The inner and the outer person are often contrasted, as we have seen; but the two are not mutually exclusive. The way of God must be made evident in the fleshly world, and the spiritual or inner person must give evidence of faith in outward and worldly acts. What is important, however, is the interrelation between the two. The inner spirit must be enlightened and related to God by faith in order for outer works have religious validity. One's outer acts must be a reflection of one's inner faith, or they are of no value.

Consequently, one's outer action or appearance is no guarantee that his/her life is lived according to the Spirit. A monk, for example, is no holier than any other person just because outwardly he has taken a vow.[37] One must emphasize faith more than orders and vows. The author uses the contrast between the two murderers who were crucified with "God."[38] (He actually calls them murderers.) The one asked Jesus to remember him in Paradise (Luke 23:42), and to be sure, the man on the cross had no good works to prove his faith—he had faith only that Jesus had the power to save him. His inner self received salvation while his body was crucified. The other thief on the cross wanted an external miracle, not an inner faith; he merely wanted Jesus to come down from the cross and save the two of them.

The unbeliever on the cross was compared with many people who trust in outer works. "They go to church every day, they celebrate all the holy days, they fast regularly, they hear mass every day. They shall die because they trust only their good works."[39] The author, however, was not so much interested in eliminating these aspects of the contemporary church, but rather, he made a plea to use prayer and fasting in a true spiritual sense as a proof of faith, not as bargaining for favor because of one's good works. "Our God desires our heart. What does God care if we celebrate fasts, or hear mass, or whether our coat is gray or blue if God does not have our hearts?"[40] All ceremonies, therefore, which are performed for their own sake are fruitless, they are as works only of the law based on an unfaithful heart.

Education, Especially Concerning the Bible

The strong biblical emphasis in this tract was further exemplified when the author discussed the necessity for teaching the Bible so that all may learn its truths. "God has commanded that the holy gospel should be proclaimed, not to priests [as intermediaries] only, but to all people."[41] This is important for two reasons. First, this is the only source of faith for the Christian; and second, only through this universal proclamation will all parents and all godparents be prepared to rear their children in the faith. It should be possible for "the burghers to read the Bible in their own homes with their children. For this reason it is important either that we have a Dutch translation, or that all children learn Latin."[42] There were several Dutch versions at this time.

The emphasis on learning was indicated in other ways. Many adults do not understand the Lord's Prayer or the creed when they hear it. Many cannot repeat it, and hence have not internalized it. It is important that we have more schools for our people. This would solve two serious problems of our day. First, "we would not then have so many unlearned priests and monks in the church. . . . Because of unlearned priests and monks many great errors have come into the world."[43] Second,

> If more people were learned they could understand the preacher better, for they would have already read the history or the gospels for themselves. Then all burghers could relate incidents from the gospels, or the Psalms or other parts of the Scriptures, to their work with their servants or with their children.[44]

All the foregoing argument is included in the first fifteen (out of a total of thirty-one) chapters in his book (the Dutch *Summa*).

The Monastic Life

Beginning in Chapter 16 (in the Dutch *Summa*) our author devoted the next six chapters to the question of monastic orders. Because of the length of this section, we may be assured that this represented one of his major concerns. He had earlier criticized monks and their devotion to outer vows and ceremonies. Here he developed his analysis of monastic orders more thoroughly. He did not condemn the orders as such, but analyzed why and how they went astray and diverged from their original goals. They became too worldly, relied too much on external forms and rules. He suggested that their real goal should be an inner faith.

He sketched a history of monasticism and identified the probable cause of the monks' deviation from their ideals. Among the first monks, he included Jonadab's children (Jeremiah 35:6-19) and John the Baptist, all of whom lived austerely in the desert, but who were, above all, faithful to God. "Their style of life has no comparison with the monks of our day."[45] Then he summarized some of the monastic developments in the first three centuries of the Christian era. These individuals he said lived differently from the people around them, in sobriety and purity. They loved God and praised him with psalms, prayers, and fasts. They held all things in common, wrote or copied books, and worked with their hands to earn their own necessities of life. They were free from special clothing, vows, and promises, but they praised God and helped one another voluntarily because of love.

Next, however, those who followed the Rule of St. Benedict began to give evidence of changes. Because of increasing gifts of money, clothing, jewels, and real estate, the orders became wealthy and indulged themselves in costly clothing, food and buildings. This diminished the Spirit of God and the love for one's fellow compatriots. Loyalty to the rule reigned supreme. There were certain times to sing, pray, fast, and do outward works. In the meantime, they forgot sobriety, mercy, and simple human kindness. Thereafter, the various groups vied among themselves as to who was greatest among them. Bernard of Clairvaux's reforms brought the orders back nearer to their own original profession, but these reforms were not permanent.

The Dominicans and Franciscans then arose. Rivalries continued, but there were even more negative results. From these orders came popes and cardinals who dispensed various privileges among their brother monks. Outer works became most important. In former times monastic groups were separated from the world; now they became a part of the world, indulging in carousing, brawls, and drinking. Outer ceremonies of singing, bowing, fasting and celebrating masses became all-important, and they lost the true spirit of their original founders. As the author concluded: "Because the monastic life is so much modified now, I do not see why anyone would go into a cloister."[46]

Chapter 17 began:[47] "Since the life of a monk is now completely absorbed in the world. . .I do not see how it can be thought to be more holy than the life of a burgher."[48] In fact, the devout burgher may exemplify a holier life than the monks, for at least he does not take alms, but works with his hands to gain the necessities for his life. In addition, he provides the very alms on which the monks are dependent. It is also possible that the burgher's life can be a better example because he can hold the rule of God before himself as his highest example, whereas the monk holds before himself, instead, the rule of the order and the human works. In contrast to the devout burgher, the monks and nuns are more like contemporary Pharisees than Christians.

Other aspects of the monastic life are condemned as well. Monastic groups too often further the Rule through coercion. God wants faith and love, neither of which can be developed through coercion. In fact, in some cases, vows should be broken. "No one is required to hold a vow or a promise which works against his own salvation." More important than vows is the inner freedom to act in these situations through faith and love. Thus it is better to live a holy life outside the monastery than to live unworthily within the cloister.[49]

Why is it then that monks do not live up to their own highest objectives? It is because they overemphasize the flesh, the letter of the Rule, and human commands. They do not act alone from love and concerns of the heart. To be sure, there are some monks and nuns who find a way of spiritual salvation and service in the cloister, but these are indeed few.

One group, however, which was a sharp contrast to the monks and nuns, was the sisterhood based on the model of the Brethren and Sisters of the Common Life.[50] They were closer to the ideal of the gospels, for they work with their hands and serve one another with true Christian love. They spend their time in weaving, washing, spinning, and other works for the common good. Surely the author had in mind the houses where he was a leader (if indeed our identification of the possible author is accurate)!

His view of Womanhood

Following his analysis and sharp criticism of the monastic orders, the author then applied his spiritual and ethical principles to other groups of the sixteenth-century. For example, Chapter 22 is entitled "How men and women should live together, a lesson from the gospels." A rather higher concept of womanhood is found here when he writes about how husbands and wives must work and live in cooperation. A man must love his wife for more than fleshly reasons. Many others—prostitutes, knaves and beasts—indulge in this type of love. Rather, the faithful man should serve his wife with love, seeing in her a sister in the faith and a fellow heir of the kingdom of God. She has participated in the same baptism and shares the same faith with her husband. The husband should protect his wife so that she will not be tempted with costly clothes or other outer symbols of worldliness. Interestingly, the author specifically counteracted the admonition attributed to Paul, that men should be the overlords of their wives. As scriptural evidence for the equality between men and women the author reminded us that "Eve was not taken from Adam's foot, but from his side."[51]

The Role of Parents

Parents have a particularly responsible role with respect to their children.[52] Too often parents have sent their children to cloisters to bring credit and merit to the parents. This is not condoned; instead, parents must be good examples of the Christian life, so that they may lead children into the true Christian faith. This is more important than for parents to travel to far-off places and leave their children under care of persons hired for the occasion. Rather than allow children to read unworthy material—such as strange history concerning love affairs or wars—parents should "buy them a Dutch Bible . . . and let them from an early age study and read the teachings of God and drink from the sweet fountain that has come down from heaven."[53] "There is no other food for souls than the Holy Spirit."[54] "A mother can serve God in no better way than in teaching her children well."[55] Parents should discipline their children out of love rather than out of anger. Children who obey only because of fear forget as soon as the punishment is over; but children who obey because of love remain always obedient in love.

God is Sovereign over All

One must not work only for one's own profit but always work for the glory of God. One must neither glory in one's wealth nor regret his/her poverty. All things come from God. Even a wealthy man must remember that all his wealth came from God and that he is only a warden or steward, and must use his gifts for the glory of God.[56]

Servants and hirelings are to live as devoted helpers, serving as though serving God, doing all tasks willingly and thoroughly, and learning to be content with their status in life. One receives his true reward not from the one she/he serves, but from God. God is not concerned with status—either servants or lords—but with the state of our hearts.[57]

Relation to Political Powers

Chapter 14 (in Latin, of the Second Part; parallel with Chapter 29 of the *Summa*) begins a summary of the relationship between political authorities and the Church. Then follows another chapter in the *Summa* for which there is no Latin parallel. This extra chapter (Chapter 26 of the *Summa*) was written two or more years after the original, and presents what is actually an alternative understanding of the political situation. We will analyze these two understandings of political life to understand their differences.

Chapter 14 (of the Second Part) of the *Oeconomica* is entitled "Evangelical doctrine concerning soldiers" (*Oeconomica*, pp. 101-108), or the relation of the Christian to war and the political order. The parallel section in the Dutch version, "Of Knights and war and whether one may wage war without sin" (*Summa*, Chapter 29, pp. 189-191) is a much-condensed version of some of the same ideas. Both versions begin with the question put to John the Baptist by the soldiers: "What should we do" (Luke 3:14). John answered, "Do not extort money from anyone by threats or false accusation, and be satisfied with your wages." The author emphasized that John was not laying down rules but acknowledging his role as a forerunner, preparing the way for Jesus.

The message of Jesus was that all should live in peace and exemplify love for all classes of people. How could one speak meaningfully to those outside the faith—even the Turks—if there was dissention or war within the Christian fold? Therefore, fighting is not allowed for any Christian. Using the reference in Matthew, "You have heard it said: 'an eye for an eye and a tooth for a tooth'; but I say to you do not resist any evil-doer" (Matthew 5:38-40). The author concluded that retaliation is not allowed: "It is better to suffer for doing good if suffering should be God's will than to suffer for doing evil" (I Peter 3:17).

The *Summa* asserted that the gospel knows nothing of warriors, or war, but refers only to peace (p. 189). Those *doctoren end theologi* who try to justify war do not understand John the Baptist's meaning (in Luke 3:17). The Dutch version elaborated further, using I John 3 as an example of how one must get along with one's associates, for "all who hate brother or sister are murderers" (I John 3:14). We must "hate no one, must have love for our enemies, and pray for them" (*Summa*, p. 190). If we do this how can we wage war and remain sinless? All persons must realize that "above them there is a King to whom all must give a reckoning of one's actions, whether the individual be king, emperor, pope or cardinal, noble or low born, young or old" (*Summa*, p. 191).

The Latin *Oeconomica* (p. 105) asserted that the various wars of the Israelites are to be taken figuratively [*figurae*, in the Latin version] and typologically [*per typos/typias*]. The Dutch translation elaborated on these supposed figures or typologies [*figuren* in the Dutch version, p. 191]. We are not to fight each other [*tegen malkander*], but to struggle "against ourselves, that is against our sins, against our presumptions, anger, avarice, hatred and envy" (*Summa*, p. 191).

The Dutch *Summa* has an additional chapter (26) which presents a different understanding of political power. This Chapter has no parallel in the Latin text. It is entitled "Concerning the two-fold authority [*regement*], the spiritual and the worldly." In the nineteenth century it was discovered that this added section parallels Luther's tract "Temporal Authority: to what extent it should be obeyed." [58] (In fact, in some places it is a shortened translation of Luther's text). Since Luther's work was completed in March, 1523, the Dutch translation which contains this material must be dated no earlier than 1523. Since the Latin original, *Oeconomica*, was written two or more years earlier, it could not have included the material related to Luther's tract.

The added chapter in the *Summa* began with the assertion that both the worldly and the spiritual authorities have been ordained by God. The supposed proof is from Romans 13:1-2: "There is no power but of God the powers that be are ordained of God; and the one who resists this power resists God." Luther quoted the same scripture with the same interpretation. Then both Luther and the *Summa* quote I Peter 1:13-14: "Submit yourselves to every human ordinance for the Lord's sake, whether it be of the King as supreme, or the governors as unto them that are sent for the punishment of evildoers, and for the praise of them that do well." For "governors" the Dutch uses "*Stadthouders*."

Again, paralleling Luther's argument, the temporal sword is meant to punish the wicked, and protect the good and upright Christians. Certainly, Christians are not burdened by such laws since they are already upright. Those who are not righteous, however, must be restrained by the world powers. Both the *Summa* and Luther use the example of a wild beast which must be restrained with chains for the protection of the sheep within the fold. Hence, worldly law and political authorities were established by God to maintain order and control those who would otherwise be unruly or even vicious.

The suggestion from the Sermon on the Mount, "do not resist evil," would seem to preclude Christians from participating in earthly governments or employing force. Is it then allowable for Christians to use the sword, to be involved in affairs of the earthly estate? Again, this chapter of the *Summa* and Luther argue in opposition to the Sermon on the Mount. The power of the sword can be and should be used by Christians for "maintaining peace, punishing sin, and hindering wickedness" (*Summa*, p. 184). The sword should be borne in "a Christian manner" (Luther, p. 95), never for oneself, but only in service of society.

In this way, both Luther and this chapter of the *Summa* support the theory of two kingdoms. Consequently they both denied the Roman Catholic theory of the Two Swords, that the spiritual kingdom has authority over the earthly (*i.e.* the papal bull, *Unam Sanctam*, of Pope Boniface VIII, 1302). Rather, both governments are equally under the power of God. This assertion would sharply contrast to the later Anabaptist views. Except for this "Lutheran" insertion in one chapter, however, the author otherwise anticipated later Anabaptist and/or Mennonite developments in The Netherlands. War and turbulence are completely forbidden in Christian society, asserted the author.[59] This is justified by I John 3: 15: "he who hates his brother has already killed." All persons must conduct themselves with the realization that they have a king—Christ—over them whether they are "king, emperor, pope or cardinal, noble or commoner, young or old." Israel's wars are to be taken as figurative illustrations that we must fight against ourselves and our own sins of presumption, wrath, hate and envy, not against each other.[60]

Conclusion

The *Oeconomica Christiana* (or its translation, *Summa der Godliker Scrifturen*), was based on several propositions not strictly Lutheran, but stemming from the Biblical Humanism and Erasmian thought in The Netherlands. While in many places the work is a paraphrase of Scripture it, nevertheless, contains certain distinctive emphases.

1. It exemplifies the use of Scripture to establish Christian truth rather than relying on the authority of the Roman Catholic Church.

2. Faith is central and must be present before good works are of any value.

3. Faith *must* result in works, hence there is a close relationship between faith and ethics.

4. The Spirit of Christ (or Grace) can be shared through faithful witness rather than through the channels of the church. It promoted a priesthood of all believers.

5. God, through faith in Christ, actually removes one's sins; they are not merely covered over.

6. External rites or sacraments are only signs of an inner faith. There is no automatic power or grace within the elements themselves. We must bring our faith and our interpretation to these symbols. The sacraments of baptism and the Eucharist depend on our internalizing their significance with a very spiritual meaning.

7. Some external signs are false and do not exemplify true inner faith; hence

vows and other church requirements are not necessary.

8. A pious life lived in faith could be exemplified in all vocations: among parents rearing their children; among husbands and wives; among burghers in "secular" life; among teachers and students; among servants, widows, rich and poor, noble and commoner.

These elements of an "evangelical " theology show clearly why the printing was thought to contain false doctrine. While it was not Lutheran in very many respects, it certainly represented an approach to Christianity different from the predominant Roman Catholic establishment in The Netherlands. The Inquisition, which the Emperor had already organized in The Netherlands, could do nothing less than condemn the work and burn all copies too protect the Church's faithful.

Notes for Chapter 9

1. Paul Fredericq, *Corpus Documentorum Inquisitionis* (5 vols., Gent: Université, 1889-1902), IV, 265f. The Emperor noted that some printers thought the publishing of these documents would be permissible because they did not have the name of Martin Luther on the cover. They contain false doctrines, nevertheless, and after eight days from the issuing of this decree, prosecution and punishment would begin, so he declared.

2. J. J. van Toorenenbergen, *Het oudste Nederlandsche Verboeden Boek*, (1523). Leiden: E. J. Brill, 1882. The original work, *Oeconomica Christiana*, was written in Latin probably in 1520 or 1521, although it was published only in 1527. The Dutch translation, *Summa der Godliker Scrifturen*, was published earlier than the Latin, and is listed as *NK* 3910, Leiden, 1523. Van Toorenenbergen had both these versions printed in the same volume. The Latin *Oeconomica* is on pp. 3-112; while the Dutch *Summa* is on pp. 115-193. There is also included "The Other Portion of the Summa der Godliker Scrifturen," on pp. 203-249, although there is no Latin version of the last-named work. The Toorenenbergen edition was used in this study.

3. *Mennonite Quarterly Review*, LVI (July 1982), number three, 242-255.

4. J. Trapman, *Summa der Godliker Scrifturen* (1523) (Leiden: New Rhine Publishers, 1978). He kindly provided me with a copy of his extensive analysis of this 16th century document.

5. Although available in edited form since 1880 in German and 1882 in both Latin and Dutch, this document has been little analyzed in Reformation scholarship since the end of the 19th century. Eduard Boehmer published an Italian version in 1877 as an example of Reformation thought in Italy. Karl Benrath published it in German in 1880, using an edition from 1526, *Die Summa der heiligen Schrift: Ein Zeugnis aus dem Zeitalter der Reformation für die Rechtfertigung aus dem Glauben* (Leipzig: Fernau, 1880). Benrath not only wrote a critical introduction to this volume, but expanded this into three articles in the next few years under the general title "Die Summa der heiligen Schrift: eine literarhistorische Untersuchung" *Jahrbuch für protestantische Theologie* Erster Artikel, VII (1881), 127-59; Zweiter Artikel, VIII (1882), 681-705; Dritter Artikel, IX (1883), 328-45. Johann Justus Toorenenbergen published the Latin and Dutch *Het oudste Nederlandsche verboden Boek* (Leiden: E.J. Brill, 1882), and two years later, an article concerning the supposed author in "Het oudste Nederlandsche verboden Boek," *Theologische Studien Tijdschrift*, II (1884), 145-62. H.G. Kleyn wrote two articles challenging the supposed authorship asserted by both Benrath and Toorenenbergen: "De auteur der 'Summa der godliker Schrifturen,'" *ibid.*, I (1883), 313-323; and "Nog eens der auteur der 'Summa,'" *ibid.*, II (1884), 447-451. Finally, N. Weiss wrote about the French edition: "Le premier traite protestante en langue francaise 'La summe de l'escripture saincte, 1523,'" *Societe de l'Histoire du Protestantisme Francaise Bulletin*, LXVII (5th Series; XVI, 1919), 63-79. It is interesting that a work as early in the Reformation period as 1523, and translated into Dutch, French, English and Italian, should have been little known except in scholarly circles during the past century. The Toorenenbergen volume, containing both the Latin original and the Dutch translation of 1523, was used in this present study. The other studies noted above have been consulted as well.

6. *CDI*, IV, 244.

7. *CDI*, IV, 255.

8. *CDI*, IV, 271.

9. *CDI*, IV, 282-283, 289-291.

10. *NK* 3451. There is a facsimile of the title page of this work on page 113 in M. E. Kronenberg, "Verboden Boeken en Opstandige Drukkers in de Hervormingstijd," in *Patria: Vaderlandse Cultuurgeschiedenis in Monografieën*, vol. 44, Leiden, 1947.

11. *CDI*, IV, 345, May 16, 17, 1525.

12. M. E. Kronenberg, *Lotgevallen van Jan Seversz, Boekdrukker te Leiden [ca. 1502-1524 and 1527-1530]* (The Hague: Martinus Nijhoff, 1924), pp. 22-23.

13. At the close of the document the name of the city and the date appear as follows: *Argentinae* [at Strasbourg] *excusae. Sesquimillessimo vicesimo septimo. Septimo August* [7 August, 1527], in the Toorenenbergen edition (1882) p. 112. J. Trapman has evidence that suggests the correct country of this printing was The Netherlands, although precise details are not available. Cf. Trapman, p. 15 and footnote 10 in his Chapter II.

14. The French edition is entitled: *La somme de le scripture saincte.*

15. The English edition was entitled: *The Summe of the holye scripture and ordinarye of the Christen teachying the true Christen faithe by the which we be all justified.* This English version was discussed briefly by William Clebsch, *England's Earliest Protestants: 1520-1535* (New Haven: Yale University Press, 1964), 245-51. A British bibliographer stated that Simon Fish translated it "from the Dutch."

16. The Italian work carried the title: *El summario de le scrittura et lordinario de Christiani il qual demonstra la vera fede christiana mediante la qua scamo giustificate.*

17. The prologue is found only in the Dutch translation, edited by Toorenenbergen, pp. 115-117. This quotation concludes the prologue.

18. This assertion is made in the articles by Benrath and by Toorenenbergen, as indicated in note 5, above. H.G. Kleyn wrote his objections to the identification, also indicated in note 5.

19. A Study of Henry of Bomelius was written by G. Kraft, "Der Niederlander Heinrich Bomelius zu Moers und Wesel als Historiker," *Monatsschrift für rheinischwestfälische Geschichsforschung und Alterthumskunde*, II (1876), 224-231.

20. This is the opening idea in the beginning sentence in both the Dutch and the Latin versions. Because the last half of the chapters in the Latin *Oeconomica* and the Dutch *Suumma* are numbered differently, for clarification where necessary each chapter number will be followed by the designation *Oeconomica* (Latin) or *Summa* (Dutch); the page numbers refer to Toorenenbergen's edition. Numbers in the Latin original following Chapter 15 continue as Chapter 1 (of the Second Part).

21. The "First Adam" and the "Second Adam" are noted in Chapter 1 in both editions.

22. Chapter 1

23. Faith is defined in Chapter 13 in both editions; translation from the *Summa*.

24. Baptism is thus described in Chapter 1 in both editions; translation from the *Summa*.

25. Chapters 1 through 16 in both the Latin and the Dutch editions parallel each other. Thereafter, there are major differences in numbering. Baptism is related typologically to the journey through the Red Sea in Chapter 2.

26. Baptism is related typologically to circumcision in Chapter 2.

27. The Augustinian concept of baptism, and the godparents are referred to in Chapter 3.

28. The Lord's Supper is thus described in Chapter 7. Translated from *Summa*.

29. Chapter 1.

30. Chapter 2.

31. Chapter 4.

32. Chapter 1.

33. Chapter 12.

34. *Ibid.*

35. Chapter 10.

36. Chapter 12.

37. Chapter 1.

38. Chapter 11 is entitled "There are Two Kinds of People in the World." The two thieves on the cross (he calls them murderers) exemplify the two types.

39. Chapter 11.

40. *Ibid.*

41. Chapter 3.

42. *Ibid.*

43. *Ibid.*

44. *Ibid.*

45. The four stages of monastic development are analyzed in Chapter 16 (*Summa*).

46. The ending of Chapter 16.

47. Chapter 17 (*Summa*) is entitled, "Which Life is Superior, That of a Monk or of a Burgher?" This is parallel with Chapter 1 (Second Part in *Oeconomica*).

48. Chapter 17 (*Summa*).

49. *Ibid.*

50. Chapter 21 (*Summa*) is entitled, "Concerning Cloisters of Sisters, and their Lives." The parallel Latin section is numbered Chapter 8 (in the Second Part) .The numbering for much of the remainder of the work differs between the Latin and the Dutch.

51. Chapter 26 (*Summa*) is entitled, "How Men and Women should live together: A Good Teaching from the Gospels." The parallel Latin comprises Chapters 9 and 10 (of the Second Part).

52. Chapter 23 (*Summa*) is entitled, "How Parents should rear their Children in a Christian Manner." There is no parallel section in the Latin original.

53. Chapter 23 (*Summa*).

54. *Ibid.*

55. *Ibid.*

56. Chapter 25 (*Summa*) is entitled, "How Rich Persons should live: Information and Instructions from the Gospel." This is parallel with Chapter 9, *Oeconomica* (of the Second Part).

57. Chapter 30 (*Summa*) is entitled, "How Man-Servants, Maid-Servants and Hirelings should live; Instruction from the Gospel." There is no Latin parallel.

58. *LW*, vol. 45, 81-129. While Luther's work is in three parts, the *Summa* is parallel only with the first part (pp. 81-104), in which Luther gave his main scriptural proofs, and summarized the basic presuppositions of his idea of the two kingdoms.

59. Chapter 29 (*Summa*) is entitled, "Concerning Knights, and making Wars, whether Men may engage in Wars without Sin: information from the Gospel." The Latin parallel is Chapter 14 (Second Part). This section and its strong aversion to war of all types parallels the later Anabaptist and pacifist developments.

60. This is the statement which concludes Chapter 29 (*Summa*), and is parallel with Chapter 14 (of the Second Part) of *Oeconomica*.

Chapter 10

Jan de Bakker (Johannes Pistorius)
A Priest martyred in 1525

The earliest scholar-priest in the northern Netherlands to undergo a trial by fire was Jan de Bakker (also known in Latin as Pistorius), a priest at Woerden, near Utrecht. In 1525 he was burned in the square outside the present Parliamentary buildings in The Hague. An analysis of his life, and especially his theological thought as gleaned from the extensive report of his trial, is instructive for us in at least two ways. *First*, it shows a theology not strictly Lutheran, but with tendencies related to the Biblical Humanism of Erasmus and others. *Second*, while we are not able to determine the permanent influence of the young priest among his followers, we see that his confidence in his faith was strong enough that he evidently did not waver even when confronted with the fiery alternative.

Life of Pistorius

Johannis Pistorius (Jan Janszoon de Bakker van Woerden) was born probably in 1499,[1] at Woerden, near Utrecht. His name of "Baker"—Bakker in Dutch and Pistorius in Latin—may indicate an early occupation, although it is assumed this means not baker of bread, but of stone, a brick-maker.[2] It is possible that the father of Pistorius, Jan Diercksz., studied for a time in a school of the Brethren of the Common Life and lived in the same house with Erasmus.[3] How much influence the great scholar had upon his fellow Dutch student is unknown. Later when the father went with his grown son to Louvain/Leuven to visit Erasmus, this earlier association was recalled.[4] Little is known of the youth of Pistorius.

At approximately age twelve young Jan was sent to the School of St. Martin, at the Cathedral in Utrecht. He probably studied the usual Latin *Trivium* and *Quadrivium*.[5] In approximately 1514 he entered the Hieronymus School in Utrecht where Hinne Rode was a leader.[6] There reforming tendencies, such as teaching the Bible in the mother tongue, were being introduced by Rode.[7] Evidently Rode's influence was widespread and his personality persuasive, for to guard Pistorius from heresy the father withdrew his son and kept him at home for a time,[8] making bricks we assume. Still the new evangelical teachings continued to spread, in part probably through Pistorius' efforts.[9] Therefore, the father, to make sure Pistorius had the right doctrines, went with him to Louvain/Leuven where they were with Erasmus for a time.[10] Yet Pistorius could have studied with Erasmus at the De Lelie house for only a short time, for in October 1521 Erasmus himself left Louvain/Leuven permanently for Basel.[11]

In around 1522 Pistorius became pastor, or chaplain, in the small town of Jacobswoude (sometimes called Woubrugge), near his home,[12] and in 1523 he was ordained as priest to serve at Woerden, his home town.[13] In this year, or perhaps in 1524, he went to Wittenberg where he may have heard the preaching of Luther,[14] an activity now banned by the Empire. About this time he married a widow, but we know almost nothing of his wife Jacoba Jansdochter[15] except the references in the trial proceedings. His inquisitors accused him of being "Lutheran." Later writers have suggested that he was "Calvinist," or a prototype of Calvinist. This was an anachronism because at the time John Calvin had not yet completed his University education, and there was no such thing as "Calvinism." It is probably more correct to think of him as a proto-Protestant, or early dissenter, before various distinctions became meaningful.

In 1524 the lenient Bishop of Utrecht, Philip of Burgundy died, and a more rigid and orthodox successor strengthened the administration against heretics. Pistorius was arrested in his home town in May, 1525, amid protests of the towns-folk that the authorities had no right to invade the privileges of this old town. He was taken to the Voorport prison in The Hague.[16] While there he had a chance to relate details of his trial to his friend Willem Gnapheus (See Chapter 11), who recorded it for posterity. Some of Pistorius' theological ideas can be gleaned from his sharp replies to the inquisitors. On 15 September, 1525, he was burned in The Hague, the first martyr for Protestantism (or at least early dissent) in the northern Netherlands. In 1925, four hundred years later, a special service of thanksgiving and remembrance was held in the Great St. Jacobs Church in The Hague. A part of this commemoration included dedicating a special window in the church known as the "Jan de Bakker, or Pistorius" window.[17]

The trial and execution of Pistorius

The record of the trial of Pistorius, as compiled by Gulielmus Gnapheus, must be used to analyze his theology and the reasons for his coming into conflict with the church and the civil authorities.[18] Gnapheus, a Humanist scholar and rector of the Latin School in The Hague, wrote this report of the trial between 1525 and 1529 when he himself was on the Inquisitors' list, and was himself in prison part of that time. Gnapheus ultimately fled to Germany in 1530 where he lived and taught for more than thirty more years.

Pistorius's life was short, and he left no theological writings of his own. Two theological concerns, however, stand out in his trial as most important. Subordinate to these, other ideas also emerge. His major concerns are, *first*, the centrality of the Scriptures; and *second*, the nature of the Church, and the ways in which an individual lives out his or her religious faith. We will analyze each of these in turn.

After preliminary discussion about how scripture is to be interpreted, who has the authority to interpret it and the extra-scriptural tradition in the Roman Catholic Church, Pistorius stated clearly:

> The meaning of the Holy Scriptures is not hidden under the commentaries of the doctors nor in the decrees of the councils. The conclusions are given to us by the clear and true Word of God, wherewith we determine what we should and should not do, if we would not be found in error. It is blasphemy against God that you understand the Word of God by means of your own opinions and fancies.[19]

He affirmed that he believed all scripture, all books of the Bible.[20] Then his inquisitors asked about the suggestion that many other things were done by Jesus not contained in the written scriptures (John 21:25).[21] They hoped to trick him into admitting the possibility of trust in tradition, ecclesiastical ceremonies or even the doctors of the church.

Pistorius, however, countered: "There is but one true holy doctor in the Holy Church, that is the Holy Ghost, who teaches all truth."[22] Furthermore, since Christ taught all that was necessary for eternal life, he added, "prove to me where Christ gave the right to any persons [*menschen*] or council or priest [*pater*] to teach to us what he had forgotten [*vergheten*]."[23] The prisoner was asked how he distinguished when the Holy Ghost spoke. He answered simply, "The one who has not the Spirit of Christ within himself does not belong to him."[24] "The scripture needs the help of no doctors to clarify what the scripture itself presents richly and fully."[25]

Pistorius then stated his concept of the Church. "I have said that the Holy Church is an invisible and a spiritual gathering of all who are loyal to Christ, and who rely on nothing more than the Word of God."[26] As such, it is constituted by spiritual authority and not by earthly power.

> Your church, however, which you serve on bended knee, is the *ecclesia malignantium* [the Church of the malicious], and the Pope sits there in the elevated chair called the *cathedra pestilentie*, [the chair of pestilence]. I will have nothing to do with this, your church, and will willingly be banned therefrom.[27]

> "You speak as a mad man, and blaspheme the Holy Roman Church."[28]

Pistorius insisted that the inquisitors state the accusations made against him, while quickly denying that they had any authority over him.

> The Church has no authority that it should be the instrument for damnation. She also does not have the power to make any new articles of faith, nor to pronounce any commands contrary to the Holy Scriptures. Therefore, this law against marriage is not valid. It behooves us all to disregard that command which is directly contrary to the clear Word of God.[29]

They accused him of denying the Church if he denied its authority. Pistorius, however, disagreed. He affirmed that he believed in the Holy Christian Church, and that he was a member thereof.

"How do you know?" they asked.

"The Spirit of God convinces me of that. . . . The Spirit of God convinces us that we are children of God."

The inquisitors replied, "How audaciously these Lutherans speak!"[30]

The accusers then reminded Pistorius that they had authority from the Church and power to condemn him if he did not listen to reason and admit his errors. Pistorius said that he could only listen to them as representing the Lord who sent them.

> You have indicated you are ambassadors and commissioners of the Emperor as indicated by your letter;" [therefore, you should not use Christ's words, 'whoever hears you hears me' (Luke 10:16)]. You inquisitors are actually new Scribes and Pharisees, whose works are wicked and malicious, and contrary to gospel truth and teaching. . . . You growl [brijst] as wolves in order to devour a sheep."[31]

The inquisitor continued: "Paul said, 'Servants, be submissive to your masters with all respect'" (I Pet. 2:18).

Pistorius reminded him that was not said by Paul but by Peter, "so well you know the scriptures!"[32]

The officials suggested that if it were not for the authority of the church the land would be over-run by murderers and robbers. Pistorius argued that this keeping of order was the function of the power of the prince. It should not be directed against heretics, but should be used to control unruly men such as these and Barabbas. That is the function of the state, but the sword of the Spirit is never for this type of punishment.[33] The inquisitors concluded that Pistorius was critical of Mother Church and denied the power of the Keys.

Pistorius agreed: "You understand me well,"[34]

The prisoner had an opportunity during the questioning to allude to several other aspects of the teaching of the Roman Catholic Church. One of the most serious charges the inquisitors brought against him was that as a priest he had dared to take a wife. They asked him about this rumor several times, and he turned the discussion to other issues; but they persisted. Pistorius then explained himself, referring to the admonition of the Scriptures, "Be fruitful and multiply " and Paul's admonition "It is better to marry than to burn" (Genesis 1:22, I Corinthians 7:9).

> The Scripture has not singled out any group as exceptions, and leaves all persons free. Those in priestly orders, therefore, are free according to God's command to marry rather than suffer serious danger of burning in the flesh.[35]

The inquisitors, however, continued the questioning. They insisted, "You have a wife and will not admit it openly. You are guilty of misdeed."[36]

Pistorius brought the discussion directly to the point with his question: "Which do you think would be better that a priest should sleep with one whore one night, and with another the next night, and then someone else's wife—or on the other hand, that he should be married to one wife?"[37] They answered: "Neither is commendable."[38] One of the accusers elaborated: "I would rather that you had slept with the devil, than with your wife; I would rather that you had associated with whores, than with your wife; for you have played such a game with us."[39] Pistorius finally admitted that he had a wife but even under threat of death he refused to renounce her.

In relation to Pistorius' criticism of the Roman Catholic hierarchy, the question of his own ordination arose. "How do you know you are really a priest. . .who has made you a priest, or has ordained you?"[40]

"The bishop ordained me."[41]

"Do you believe he had that power to ordain?. . . . Concerning this there is nothing in the Scriptures. . . . How do you come to believe he has this power?"[42]

Pistorius answered sharply,

> He received this power from the Pope, to create papal priests. . . . This kind of priest, however, I count as chaff, because it was done for money. . . . I hold this type of priesthood to be of no worth. Those who are made priests by the papal authority are not priests.[43]. . No one can make one a priest, but one should choose servants of the community following the apostolic examples, as the Apostle Paul wrote for us.[44]

In the Latin text there is a marginal note asserting that Pistorius said: "In Christ all of us are priests" [*sacerdotes*].[45]

The inquisitors then asked,

> Do you then believe that all Christian men are Priests?. . .All men can perform masses, baptism and administer the sacraments? . . . It is written that only those of the class of the Levites were of the priestly estate.[46]

Pistorius quoted scripture as he answered,

Thus speaks the Lord God. `All the Kingdoms of the world have become His Kingdom, and belong to Him (Rev. 11:15).' Here he speaks not only of the Levites, but of all the people of Israel. Peter also writes to us, `You shall be a chosen race, and a royal priesthood (I Pet. 2:9).' I do not say that all should preach or that all should perform the services for the community. . . . Furthermore, I say that we are all called to the priesthood of Christ; and the priesthood of the Law in Christ is as follows. We all must offer to God the killing [stervinge] of our bodies [the old Adam] as a worthy offering, so should we pray for each other through the law of brotherly love.[47]

The inquisitors understood the implication clearly and complained, "You have qualms about the sacrament of orders, which Martin Luther has completely cast out."[48]

When the sentence of death was about to be pronounced Pistorius was given the opportunity for a final confession. Rather than the usual confession of various types of sins, he gave a confession of faith.[49] This took the inquisitors off their guard, so they began to question him about the sacrament of penance. "Is that a confession?"[50] "You shall go to your death without absolution."[51]

Pistorius answered, "I know who shall give me absolution."[52]

"Again, you seem like a Lutheran, when you do not ask for absolution from a priest."[53]

Pistorius insisted: "Christ has promised me forgiveness of all my sins through the shedding of his blood, which promises he has confirmed with his death."[54]

The inquisitors agreed among themselves, "He speaks his confession secretly, as the heretics do."[55] Then they asked him, "Who shall forgive your sins?"[56]

Pistorius responded, "The Lamb of God, who takes away the sins of the world, who has borne our sickness [cranckheyden], and has offered an eternal sacrifice for our sins."[57]

The discussion moved to in the sacrament of the Eucharist. "The Church has said that if the consecration is to be valid, no one can perform a mass other than upon an altar with appropriate ornamentation [ornamenten]. Should you not be sinning then if you speak the verba consecrationis [words of consecration] using only a table without ornamentation?"[58]

The prisoner answered, summarizing his view in one statement.

The Lord's Supper receives its power [cracht] not from outer ornaments, or times, or from hours, but from the words of God alone. In that mysterium the apostles never became concerned with such things. So, in whatever place and time, whenever the words are narrated and proffered among believing Christians, there is the true celebration of the sacrament.[59]

"I think you are more harmful than Luther himself!"[60] exclaimed the inquisitor.

There is little mention of baptism. Pistorius, however, was accused of baptizing in the name of Jesus only, and not the three persons of the Trinity. He was reminded that this trinitarian formula was biblical![61] He said that baptism was really a baptism of the power of God. Baptism in the name of Jesus only was not meant to diminish the importance of baptism, but there was no value in merely speaking the precise words. It was the reference to the power of God alone that was the important element,[62] and not the exact formula. The inquisitor then turned to the question of fasting. "Didn't Moses fast for forty days—and isn't that sufficiently Biblical?"[63]

Pistorius said,

> I hear you well; but how is it that one, on pain of committing a deadly sin, must fast on certain days, with certain foods, and on another day he may eat that food? Does this agree with the scriptures? I think not. . . . We do read of fasting in the Scriptures. I do not, however, find mention of specific days or foods. I also do not find that any banning or excommunication, or any punishments which they who disobey must suffer.[64]

"Would you even eat meat on Friday?"[65] they asked.
The prisoner replied,

> I say to you that my conscience is free to do that, on all days and at all times. One day is no better than another. Paul criticized the Galatians because they distinguished between days and times. In that criticism the Roman Church and all her adherents are also criticized.[66]

Pistorius was convinced that this faith was not unique to him, for he commented that "there are many thousands in Holland who have the same faith and understanding that I do."[67] He was ready to face martyrdom and was not concerned for the life of the flesh, because "Christ taught me that I must lose the life here in order to find eternal life."[68]

"Don't you have concern for your parents, or for your wife?" he was asked. Yes, he loved them, but he loved the truth of God more.[69]

Toward the end of the trial Pistorius's father was brought in to plead with him to recant, believing that his son's sins were small and that he would be set free. As they discussed the situation, in which Pistorius explained that a recantation was much more serious than that, it became obvious that the faith of the father was very similar to that of the son. The inquisitors asked the father if he had read these theological errors for himself, or had he been taught by his son? He replied "I do not know what to say, except that I got this from the New Testament that I have read. I have never read your decrees."[70] He bade farewell to his son, never to see him in this life again. Gnapheus reported that the father's parting words were: "I pray, my beloved son, that you will never stray from the Word of God. I will gladly offer you as Abraham offered his son, a parting will not be sorrowful for us."[71] The father's possible earlier study with Erasmus may have emboldened his determined action to support his son.

Even at the end, Pistorius did not lose confidence. He continued his sharp replies to his accusers, never evading issues, and never wavering from what he believed God and the Biblical record should mean to the church of his day. Even his humor was evident. For example, in one interplay of accusation and reply his accusers wanted to trick him with a complicated question about the writings of the fathers of the church. They demanded a simple answer. He knew it was a trick, so he said to his accusers, "You smear your knife with honey!"[72]

Finally, for the last time they asked, "Will you not recant?"[73] He answered: "In no way." Furthermore, the prisoner concluded, "I shall advocate the Word of God to the end of my life, with the help of God."[74]

On 15 September, 1525, Pistorius was "burned to ashes."[75] The analysis of his death as written by his friend Gnapheus, gave the setting and listed all church and state dignitaries who were there. Gnapheus told how Pistorius's priestly robes were taken off and the yellow robe and yellow hat of a traitor put on him instead. Then, as he mounted the scaffold, he began to sing "*Te Deum Laudamus*." Gnapheus said that he seemed as happy as though it were his wedding day![76] The final sentence of the inquisitors included, according to Gnapheus (See Appendix VI), eight items of erroneous belief.[77]

Shortly after this, possibly before the end of 1525, an unknown follower wrote a hymn celebrating Pistorius's life and criticizing the inquisitors who had demanded the execution.[78] The reference began: "History of a Martyr who was burned." In nine verses the author really wrote more of a praise or eulogy than an actual history, beginning with the words: "Now we lift up a new song." This beginning is reminiscent of the "new song" which Luther wrote praising the first martyrs in Antwerp, 1 July, 1523 (See Chapter 7). This may not be a coincidence, but a deliberate comparison. The hymnist stated that there was a Christian, born in Woerden, and very devoted to the faith. Furiously Masters of Leuven/Louvain, monks and priests, came to threaten him. He met their challenges with devotion without fear, and constantly admonished his followers to remain faithful. The worldly inquisitors were characterized as wolves who acted as Pilate did. In the trial report Pistorius, himself, had already made this comparison with the inquisitors/wolves who came to devour the sheep, so the unknown hymn writer chose to use this same imagery as he included a scathing ridicule in his concluding verse:[79]

(Verse 9) Suck [*suypt*] up, you wolves, the blood of the martyrs.
Suck up, and satisfy [*versaden=verzagd/verzadigen*] your angry mood.
Grope toward it and carve from the one burned.
Is Cain never to be satisfied with the blood of his brother Abel?

It hardly seems that this hymn was meant to be sung in any group, but instead to incite further animosity toward the inquisitors. It was not published until a half-century later.[80]

Theological Conclusions of Pistorius

The theological implications in Pistorius's statements at his trial are many, although not thoroughly presented in this trial document. The document probably contains—in summary form—many of his main ideas. He insisted that the scriptures give straight-forward direction to life, and no human institution, whether Imperial or Ecclesiastical, has any authority to make changes to delete requirements or to establish new commands for the religious life. In this he reflected the Humanist emphasis on the centrality of the Bible as interpreted simply, without metaphor, allegory or other philosophical modifications or qualifications. He contrasted this view to of the medieval Roman Catholic developments, especially its sacramental system. This sacramentalism seemed to make God's action too rigid, or *ex opere operato*, and extra-scriptural. The Bible-centered approach criticized the use of Aristotle, Aquinas and Scotus in the medieval church's attempt to substantiate its sacramental doctrine.

Another implication arose from his contrast between what we call the "secular" authority and the "spiritual." The former is the power to control unruly individuals, such as Barabbas and to mete out physical punishment for crimes against the temporal order. Spiritual authority, however, is quite different. This comes from God and is manifest by an inner conviction that the Spirit of God or of Christ, has spoken directly to an individual. The "Kingdom of God is within you" Pistorius would say, and the authority of that Kingdom is an inward authority. As a corollary to this understanding denied that either papal or imperial authority—and he probably equated the two—could make any new requirement or legislate beliefs or actions contrary to the straight-forward scriptural admonition, or the Spirit of God speaking from within.

As he analyzed this spiritual authority within and the external or literal interpretation of the Scriptures, Pistorius held a concept of the Church which rejected the sacramental system of his day—hence in his non-sacramental interpretation he anticipated later Protestant developments. One of the main charges against Pistorius concerned his marriage. His reference to Paul's admonition to "marry rather than burn" can hardly be thought of as a positive interpretation of marriage. It was, however, an opposition based on scriptural grounds.

The record of his trial also revealed his criticisms of other sacraments. In baptism one called on the power of God neither through the elements nor a precise formula. The grace of God was received directly, on the basis of the true inner intention of the participants. Likewise, concerning priestly orders, priests are consecrated by God directly—not by means of an earthly ordination or by men, unworthy authority, or false motives.

He made modifications to the doctrine of the Eucharist. Neither the ornamentations, the place, the times, nor words spoken were basic. The crucial aspect was that it be done for pure motives in the presence of believing Christians. This leads us to assume that the doctrine of transubstantiation was totally rejected.

Repentance, Pistorius insisted, was not dispensed by the Roman Catholic hierarchy. Forgiveness for true penitence came from God directly, when one had faith in the already-accomplished sacrifice of the Lamb of God, "a full and sufficient sacrifice," for us all. Thus, at the time of his martyrdom, he could reject the offer of a priestly confessor with a clear conscience, and know that he was already forgiven. There is no mention of confirmation, nor anything which gives us any idea of his approach to this sacrament. Neither is last unction mentioned. One of his contemporaries, however, had already stated that since the power of life and death was in the hands of God, the oil itself was useful only for one's shoes [See Chapter 12].

The question of fasting was not officially a part of the sacramental system, but it was often treated as though it were. Pistorius rejected the idea that there was any benefit from following human laws about fasting.law as determined by human authority as to when to fast, or with reference to which foods to exclude. He would have argued that it is not what goes into the body in eating (Matthew 15:11) or what one does not eat that makes the difference. What is important is the inner disposition of faith, trust, confidence, discipline, and assurance of forgiveness and salvation. This came from God through the community of believers, the church, and through reading and meditating on the Biblical record. In the last analysis inner faith—inner Spirit—was neither affected by outer authority, threat of punishment, nor by fire itself.

Thus the first martyr of the Reformation in the northern Netherlands met the inquisitorial flames. His faith was inspired not only by the theology of Luther, but more directly by a love of learning and careful Scriptural (and Humanist) interpretation. His theological interpretations assumed a straightforward interpretation of the Scripture. His rejection of the church's hierarchy and earthly authority, and his criticisms of the abuses and moral lapses of his day, have some similarities with Erasmus' *Enchiridion,* and perhaps also with *Praise of Folly*. His steadfastness in face of martyrdom witnessed to a strong faith. Above all, his example shows us the difficulty of a Reformation, spiritual in character, which does not enjoy political or ecclesiastical support.

Notes for Chapter 10

1. Gulielmus Gnapheus wrote a Latin record of the trial of Pistorius in "*Johannis Pistorii a Worden, ob evangelicae doctrinae assertionem, apud Hollandos primo omnium exusti, vita,*" hereafter referred to as "*Joannis Pistorii martyrium*," published in Paul Fredericq, *Corpus Documentorum Inquisitionorum* (hereafter *CDI*) (5 vols., Ghent: University, 1889-1902), IV, 406-452. There is uncertainty about the publication date of this Latin version, although he concluded his writing in 1529—"*Ex exilio nostro, kalendas Decembris, anno* 1529—i.e., 1 December. There is also a Dutch translation, which is slightly condensed *Een Suuerlicke ende sehr schoone disputacie, welcke geschiet is in den Haghe in Hollant, tusschen de kettermeesters ende eenen christlijcken priester ghenaemt Jan van Woorden, aldaer ghevangen ende verbrant.* This was published between 1525 and 1529 by Nicolaas Oldenborch in Emden, or under a false name possibly in Antwerp between 1525 and 1529 [See *NK* # 1009]. The Dutch version is reprinted in *CDI*, IV, pp. 453-495. We note these words: When the young priest was martyred "*xxvii enim annum vix attingerat* [or touched, *vix attingerat*, from *attingere*, had barely touched or attained]." This is usually translated, "he had barely entered his 27th year," *i.e.* he had just passed his twenty-sixth birthday," *CDI*, IV, p. 410. Such is the interpretation used by his biographer, J.W. Gunst, *Joannes Pistorius Woerdensis* (Hilversum, The Netherlands: De Blauwvoet, 1925), p. 323. Others have written about him: Cf. Nico Plomp, *Woerden 600 Jaar Stad* (Woerden, The Netherlands: Stichts-Hollandse Bijdragen, 1972, pp. 88-94; for a chapter on Pistorius; the article "Pistorius" by J.N. Bakhuizen van den Brink in *Die Religion in Geschichte und Gegenwart* (7 vols., Tübingen: Mohr, 3rd ed., 1961), V, 388; and "Pistorius" by van der Zijp in *The Mennonite Encyclopedia* (4 vols., Scottdale, Pennsylvania: Mennonite Publishing House, 1959), IV, 182.

2. Plomp, *Woerden 600 Jaar Stad*, p. 88.

3. Whether this was during Erasmus's study at Deventer (1475-1483) or later at the Steyn monastery at Gouda (1486-1493) is not clear. J.G. de Hoop Scheffer, *Geschiedenis der Kerkbervorming in Nederland van haar outstaan tot* 1531 (Amsterdam: G.L. Funke, 1873), p. 362, seems to favor Gouda, while J.W. Gunst, *Johannes Pistorius*, pp. 27f., argues for Deventer. This early relationship with Erasmus was indicated in the Gnapheus biography of Pistorius in *CDI*, IV, 408.

4. The father feared his son's growing interest in Luther's ideas and took him instead, to study with Erasmus in Louvain. The father tells us he stayed eight days. Cf. Gnapheus's "Martyrdom," in Fredericq, *CDI*, IV, 483, "daer was ik acht daghen lanck."

5. J.W. Gunst, *Pistorius*, p. 42, Gnapheus' record in the "Martyrdom" states that he was "natus duodecim annus" when he went to this school.

6. J.W. Gunst, *Pistorius*, p. 42.

7. *Ibid*, p. 48.

8. The "Martyrdom" of Gnapheus states it: "Pater vero optimus filio timens exitium, gliscente...magis odiosa Lutheranismi suspicione, eum iam e ludo domum revocatum." *CDI*, IV 408.

9. "...inculcare et multos proselytos Christo adducere." *Ibid.*, 408.

10. *Ibid.*, p. 408.

11. Erasmus went to Basel in October, 1521. Pistorius left Louvain/Leuven probably by 1522. Gunst, *Pistorius*, p. 83.

12. J.N. Bakhuizen van den Brink, in his article "Pistorius" in *Die Religion in Geschichte und Gegenwart*, V, 388; cf J.W. Gunst, *Pistorius*, pp. 93ff.

13. J.W. Gunst, *Pistorius*, p. 103.

14. A statement to this effect appears in Gnapheus's "Martyrdom," *CDI*, IV, 409. This speculation is discussed in Gunst, *Pistorius*, pp. 125-128.

15. J.W. Gunst, *Pistorius*, pp. 153-156.

16. J.W. Gunst, *Pistorius*, p. 197.

17. Plomp, *Woerden 600 Jaar Stad*, p. 96.

18. The "Martyrdom," by Gnapheus, including a summary of the trial, is published in Fredericq, *CDI*, IV, 406-452 in Latin, and 453-495 in a slightly condensed Dutch translation.

19. *Ibid.*, IV, 473.

20. *Ibid.*, IV, 456.

21. *Ibid.*, IV, 457.

22. *Ibid.*, IV, 457.

23. *Ibid.*, IV, 457.

24. *Ibid.*, IV, 457.

25. *Ibid.*, IV, 467.

26. *Ibid.*, IV, 477.

27. *Ibid.*, IV, 477.

28. *Ibid.*, IV, 477.

29. *Ibid.*, IV, 474f.

30. *Ibid.*, IV, 482.

31. *Ibid.*, IV, 455.

32. *Ibid.*, IV, 468.

33. *Ibid.*, IV, 469.

34. *Ibid.*, IV, 491.

35. *Ibid.*, IV, 461.

36. *Ibid.*, IV, 469.

37. *Ibid.*, IV, 469.

38. *Ibid.*, IV, 469.

39. *Ibid.*, IV, 493.

40. *Ibid.*, IV, 457.

41. *Ibid.*, IV, 458.

42. *Ibid.*, IV, 458.

43. *Ibid.*, IV, 458.

44. *Ibid.*, IV, 458.

45. The Latin text, *Ibid.*, 418.

46. *Ibid.*, IV, 458.

47. *Ibid.*, IV, 458.

48. *Ibid.*, IV, 459.

49. *Ibid.*, IV, 489.

50. *Ibid.*, IV, 489.

51. *Ibid.*, IV, 490.

52. *Ibid.*, IV, 490.

53. *Ibid.*, IV, 490.

54. *Ibid.*, IV, 490.

55. *Ibid.*, IV, 491.

56. *Ibid.*, IV, 491.

57. *Ibid.*, IV, 491.

58. *Ibid.*, IV, 482.

59. *Ibid.*

60. *Ibid.*

61. *Ibid.*, IV, 455.

62. *Ibid.*, IV, 456.

63. *Ibid.*, IV, 460.

64. *Ibid.*, IV, 460.

65. *Ibid.*, IV, 480.

66. *Ibid.*, IV, 481.

67. *Ibid.*, IV, 488.

68. *Ibid.*, IV, 491.

69. *Ibid.*,IV, 492.

70. *Ibid.*, IV, 484.

71. *Ibid.*, IV, 487. The interview with the father appeared only in the Dutch version of the trial, pp. 483-487.

72. *Ibid.*, IV, 459.

73. *Ibid.*, IV, 488.

74. *Ibid.*, IV, 487.

75. *Ibid.*, IV, 495.

76. *Ibid.*

77. *Ibid.*, IV, 494.

78. *CDI*, V, 78-80. The editor of the *CDI* has included no details other than the date 1525.

79. *CDI*, V, 80.

80. Notes are included on *CDI*, V, 80, where three publications are listed.

Chapter 11

Gulielmus Gnapheus (1493-1568)
A Latin Scholar in Delft and The Hague

We now turn our attention to an interesting scholar who not only wrote a defense of Pistorius, but who also had a literary and personal influence on early Dutch opposition to the abuses of the Roman Catholic Church. Gulielmus Gnapheus was a member of the circle of Humanists in Delft,[1] but he ultimately chose to flee from his native land rather than to compromise his beliefs under Roman Catholic pressure.[2] It is not certain whether he was ordained, but he was sometimes referred to as a priest. He was married in the 1530s.

Life of Gnapheus (Willem de Volder)

Willem de Volder, [or Willem Voldersgraft] also known by the Greek name Gulielmus [also Guilhelmus] Gnapheus or in Latin as Fullonius, was born around 1493 in The Hague—hence still another appellation, Willem de Haghe, or "Hagiensis."[3] We know little of his early life. Johannes Bolte[4] suggested, and others have followed his lead, that Gnapheus may have attended a school administered by the Brethren of the Common Life and may have attended the University of Louvain/Leuven. Documents for both these assumptions are lacking. In any case, Gnapheus appeared in Cologne in 1511 and took his baccalaureate degree in 1512.[5] Shortly after 1520 he became rector of a Latin School in The Hague, and in 1523 he was charged with heresy. He said that Satan had sent some of his henchmen to apprehend him because he had been more critical of some church ceremonies and false religion than the devil wished.[6] Gnapheus was incarcerated in The Hague in 1523, where for three months he was a fellow-prisoner with Cornelis Hoen.[7] While in prison he was visited by Pistorius, whose place in our story has already been analyzed (Chapter 10). Although Gnapheus came before the harsh inquisitor, Frans van der Hulst, he was set free on bail because of the influence of Dutch officials, who were then testing their independence from the imperial and ecclesiastical authorities.[8]

In 1524 Cornelis Hoen died and in 1525 Gnapheus's friend, Pistorius (Jan de Bakker), was himself imprisoned, and ultimately executed. Gnapheus took pen in hand to write—although in vain—his defense of Pistorius. It was not only because of this, however, that he again came into conflict with the authorities. In the meantime, he had written a criticism of cloistered living. His criticisms were a pastoral response to a mother who grieved the flight of her son from holy orders. Gnapheus argued that the Kingdom of God was not served in food, drink, or set times for monastic prayers, clothing, or places—but by a firm faith in God and unending love for neighbor. The son could surely carry on this faith and love as well now as if he still wore his monastic habit.[9] Gnapheus, as a consequence, was sentenced in 1525 to live in a cloister for three months on "beer and bread" [*te bier ende te broode*]. He was cloistered from 31 May to 15 September, 1525. Later he analyzed his critical attitude toward the church.

> When I sojourned in this cloister I thought about what a sorrowful time we are experiencing because of the great persecutions in The Netherlands, and the gruesome bloodshed of the rebellious peasants in other lands. Because of this many sorrowing women in many lands became widows and many children are orphans. Then I originally began to compose this book from Holy Scripture to bring comfort to myself and to bring damage to the Kingdom of the devil—for he has so severely persecuted me already for a letter of comfort. That this book [*Een troost ende spiegel der siecken*] originally appeared in print was without my knowledge and against my wishes, for it was not so carefully written as to appear in print in that form. Nevertheless, it has produced much fruit and has brought many good persons to knowledge of the truth. . . . Indeed, one of the book printers has been beheaded because of this book.[10]

Evidently it was in 1525 or 1526 that he finished writing his critique published later in 1531 as "*Een Troost ende spiegel der siecken, end der ghenen die in lijden zijn*" [A Comfort and a mirror for the sick, and for those who suffer].[11] He had evidently worked on this document for quite some time. It was later revised (1557), and we assume corrected to his satisfaction, under the title "Tobias and Lazarus." It was published in Emden. We shall analyze this theological work shortly.

Gnapheus served his sentence in the cloister and was released. His problems, however, were not over. In 1528 he was again a hunted man. He was accused of breaking a fast because a piece of meat was found in his home during Lent. When the authorities came, Gnapheus was not at home, but a sentence was passed urging anyone who could find him to capture him and kill him if possible. The other members of his family, also, did not escape at this time. His mother was placed in chains, his only sister was sent to jail, and Gnapheus's personal property was seized.[12] His whereabouts for the next several months are unknown.

In Antwerp, in 1529, another work by Gnapheus appeared—a later work than *Troost ende Spiegel* but published first—the *Acolastus*. In an introductory letter he dedicated this to Johann Sartorius, a fellow colleague of Gnapheus and Hoen in The Hague-Delft circle of Humanists (See Chapter 3). *Acolastus* was a dramatic and poetic work, in Latin, based on the story of the Prodigal Son (Luke 15)— "Acolastus" was the name of the son. It was written to be performed by his students of the Latin School. The title page of the publication stated that Gnapheus was leader of the "*Gymnasium*" [*i.e.*, the Latin school] at The Hague.[13] Whether this is meant to indicate that Gnapheus actually was still in this position in 1529 is not known. *Acolastus* has been translated from the Latin into several languages (Dutch, German, French, English), and there were forty-eight editions in the 16th century alone, as listed by Bolte in 1891.[14] In the introductory dedication Gnapheus told Sartorius about the problems he had experienced and how he would have liked to write more Latin works, but he had been too severely persecuted.[15]

> My original intention had been to make this first attempt a prelude to the writing of a true comedy. The malice and envy of certain people made them begrudge me my efforts. Stirred up by jealousy, they have driven me from my pastime, deprived me of leisure for writing and forced me into exile, and goodness knows how many enemies they have brought me.[16]

In any case, it was in the year 1530 or 1531 that Gnapheus chose to flee from his homeland rather than compromise his religious beliefs.[17] In exile he said that he "had indeed found his cross" [*mijn cruys wel ghevonden*].[18] He traveled to Elbing, East Prussia [now Poland], where he connected with other Dutch refugees. Since the later life of Gnapheus is not closely related to our story of the religious movements in The Netherlands, it will be merely summarized here. In 1535 or 1536 he became rector of a Gymnasium or Latin School, newly-formed in Elbing. While there he wrote his "*Eloquentiae triumphus*" [The triumph of Eloquence], published in Antwerp in 1541. Also, while at Elbing, Gnapheus married, and subsequent Roman Catholic agitation led to his leaving this position.[19]

Seven years after having begun his work at Elbing, that is in 1542 or 1543, Gnapheus became leader of the Gymnasium at Königsberg [now Kaliningrad], East Prussia, where he also gave lectures on the Bible, mainly on the gospels.[20] Pijper's introduction suggests that he taught in the University.[21] The school was supported by Duke Albert of Brandenburg, who had recently led his territories into the Lutheran movement. Here, however, Gnapheus came into conflict with one of the professors, Frederic Staphylus, a former student at Wittenberg and a friend of both Luther and Melanchthon. Gnapheus was accused of being an Anabaptist and that he devalued the sacrament of the Eucharist. Furthermore, his antagonists argued that he placed too much emphasis on philosophy and human reasoning, in contrast to what the Lutherans signified of as "pure theology." He was accused of diminishing the power of the sacraments by placing too much emphasis on the power of the human mind rather than relying on the power of God in both sacraments.[22] Indeed, Gnapheus did deny that the power of God was present in the Eucharist more than as a "memorial" or "contemplation." Roodhuyzen concluded that a similar non-sacramental view of baptism also was part of Gnapheus's thought in that he denied any inherent power in the act of baptism itself. He thought it gained significance only as the participant contemplated what the act represented.[23] Melanchthon wrote to Staphylus suggesting that he was continuing the controversy more than evidence warranted.[24] Staphylus, however, continued until Gnapheus was excluded from his position.[25] He was accused of "heresy" and "Anabaptism," which indicated once again how close a "proto-Protestant" view of the Lord's Supper is related to a modified view of baptism as advocated in Anabaptism. Gnapheus wrote an apology, "*Antiloga contra Frederikum Staphylum*" (1548), addressed to Duke Albert of Brandenburg.

By the time it was received by the Duke (and before the final excommunication) Gnapheus and his family had moved to Emden, in East Friesland, where through the influence of John à Lasco, he became tutor to the children of a noble lady, Anna of East Friesland.[26] He remained there until approximately 1560. While in Emden he revised his "*Troost ende Spiegel*" and republished it as "*Tobias and Lazarus*" (1557).[27] (These are the names of the two main figures in the document). In the meantime, his old antagonist in Königsberg, Staphylus, had returned to the fold of the Roman Catholic Church and had moved to Ingolstadt. There were many who tried to convince Gnapheus to return to Königsberg, but nothing came of their pleas.[28]

Gnapheus spent his last years, after 1560, at Norden, also in East Friesland, where he was "steward of spiritual goods"—perhaps a type of chaplain or welfare worker. Here he translated Heinrich Bullinger's theological work, *Somma der christliken Religions* (1562), from German into Dutch.[29] Here he died 29 September, 1568,[30] at the age of 75.

Gnapheus's Theology: Centrality of the Scriptures

In all of Gnapheus's writings Scripture provided the model for the true Christian life. Scripture quotations and paraphrases abound. As the son, Acolastus, was prepared to leave home, his father gave him a Bible. The importance of Scripture was expressed in the father's ensuing advice.

> Finally, take this memorial [*monumentum*] as a model on which you may pattern your behavior, your life, your thought. Study it assiduously, reflect on it, make it your star by which you steer. Let it be for you a kind of touch-stone by which to test yourself, so that you may learn inwardly to know yourself.[31]

Shortly after this Acolastus talked with his friend, Philautus [the name, from the Greek, may be translated "blind self-love"].

Philautus: What is that book you're carrying?

Acolastus: A memento from my father.

Philautus: Bah! It's the book of the Law. Away with it. Concentrate now on arrangements for your journey abroad. That book is as much our foe as your father himself. Presently I'll teach you a different set of principles.

Acolastus: My father solemnly warned me not lose it.[32]

Troost ende Spiegel der siecken

Since the two writings of Gnapheus are quite different, we will analyze first the theological content of *Troost ende Spiegel* and then later return to *Acolastus*. We have noted Gnapheus's high regard for the Scriptures as the pattern for the Christian life and his assumption that knowledge of self and true humility prepares one for true worship and service of God. Let us follow some of his theological assumptions as they are found in his dialogue in *Troost ende Spiegel* between Timothy and two of his neighbors, Tobias and the sick Lazarus.[33] We assume that the comments of Timothy reflected Gnapheus's own criticisms.

Timothy, coming from his priest where he had asked the priest to make a pastoral call to visit his poor sick friend, Lazarus, was talking to himself.

> Dear Christ Jesus, true Shepherd and Bishop of our souls, how seldom do we find such shepherds who give their souls for their sheep—as you did with so much love and so diligently to the end of your life. Our shepherds don't watch over the sheep. . . but leave them and allow the wolves to come upon the sheep. Yes, and they even join the wolves.[34]

Just then a neighbor, Tobias, happened along and realized that Timothy was deeply concerned. He asked what was concerning him. Timothy continued, "I am grieved that we see so few examples of love, so few of our Shepherds who give themselves in cure of souls." Tobias still did not understand until Timothy told him that their neighbor, Lazarus, was very ill. Timothy had asked their chaplain if he would visit Lazarus to bring him comforts of the Christian faith. This entreaty, however, fell on deaf ears. The chaplain had told him: "I must read my devotions, and say masses. Indeed, I have no time. When I have some leisure, I will go to him."[35] The two neighbors agreed that the chaplain, in whom they had placed their confidence, was really a hypocrite. He was always ready to take the sacrament or the holy oil if it would net him a little profit. He wore his faith on his sleeve, and had good words in his mouth. Nor would he do Evangelical deeds with his hands.[36] They continue with the shepherd/sheep motif.

Timothy said about the chaplain:

> One does not want to ask him to go to the widow of the Burgermaster who is
> lying sick. There he came by each day, alas, uninvited, and watched after her soul
> like a vulture watching its carrion, in order to receive from her a last will and a
> compliment. Is that being a pastor? (Tobias joined in) Like a pastor, not at all.
> They are like wolves as Ezekiel stated: they eat the fat from their sheep and are
> clothed with wool. [They referred to Ezekiel 34:2-3 where we read 'Thus says the
> Lord God: Ho, shepherds of Israel who have been feeding yourselves! Should not
> shepherds feed the sheep? You eat the fat, you clothe yourselves with the wool,
> you slaughter the fatlings; but you do not feed the sheep.'] (Tobias continued)
> They visited the widow's house and offerred long prayers, or read the liturgy, for
> which they receives hefty rewards. This pained me. They are false prophets going
> around in sheep's clothing, but within they are grasping wolves.[37]

This set the situation for Timothy and Tobias to discuss the meaning of the
faith as they understood it. They bemoaned the fact that the Papists and members of
religious orders did not realize that real Christian work consisted in comforting the
oppressed, visiting the sick, helping the poor people, and serving in love. Papists
assumed that it was sufficient only to give the sacrament to the sick. One should,
instead, sing a song of praise to God the Father who won for believers a victory
over death. This was to proclaim the Lord's death (I Corinthians 11:26). We will be
judged as to whether or not we have shown works of love to our neighbor.[38]

Likewise, Timothy and Tobias agreed that works of the law were now useless.
Christ was the fulfillment of the law. Christ showed his love for us when he shed
his blood as a true priest and overcame the Jewish law. Legalistic, false ceremonies
have no value for those who are brought to Christ.[39] God said, "I desire mercy and
not sacrifice" (Matthew 9:13).

The neighbors finally concluded that they themselves must be better pastors
than their pastor. Tobias noted,

> Let us then, on behalf of our neighbor, help, comfort, assist, advise, and render
> service wherever there is most need. Don't you think that is the best way, brother
> Timothy?[40]

When they compared their idea with the parable of the Good Samaritan,
Timothy and Tobias decided the Roman Catholic priests were the Levites.[41] In
contrast they would let the light of their beliefs (faith) shine among all people that
when others saw their good works, God would be glorified. This is the Christian
life—not of ceremonies, church-going, and sacrifices, not of the flesh of the world.
It is, rather, a life of spirit, truth, love, and mercy. It is the death of sinfulness and a
life of peace and calm, possible only through God. This is the true Christian faith—
that which works through love.[42]

They decided to go themselves to Lazarus and help him bear the suffering of his sickness by explaining the truth of this faith. Timothy visited first. When he asked Lazarus how he was, Lazarus told him how ill he was and that he would surely die.[43] Timothy replied that if he did not wish to continue in his sickness and remain discouraged, he must understand the truth of the Christian faith. He reminded him that he was named for the biblical Lazarus who bore his sickness without complaint. Rather than feel sorry for himself in his sickness, he must realize that it is God's will that he suffer—God is testing his faith. He should realize that the true servant of Christ has confidence in God. "The more the inner person [mensche] grows in grace and goodness, the more the outer flesh is humbled and killed."[44]

Lazarus wanted to know more about this type of faith; but for this to happen he must first be convinced of the depth of his unbelief. Timothy said:

In order to instruct you gently so that you may understand my spoken words I shall first present the basis and the depth of your unbelief. I shall show you clearly how far a person [mensche] is separated from God because of unbelief. Out of this unbelief all other sins come forth, like bad branches and fruits come from bad roots. That unbelief alone is the sin for which the world will be punished by the Spirit of God—so Christ said.[45]

He continued: "Have you read of the *Vader onse* [in Dutch] or the *Pater Noster* [in Latin]?"

Lazarus responded sharply: "What kind of question is that? Do you think I am a Turk that I would not read my *Pater Noster?*"

Timothy: "How do you read it, in Dutch or in Latin?"

Lazarus: "I read it just as my father has taught me: '*Pater noster qui es in caelis. . .*' [*i.e.* in Latin]." Timothy responded with a plea for the vernacular language: "You ought to read it in Dutch, so you could understand it better, for you do not know any [*gheen*] Latin."

Because Lazarus has prayed the "Our Father" many times, Timothy used this as an example for his message of faith. Those who believe that God really is their Father truly believe that they are heirs of God's blessings. One must feel as much love for the Father God as an earthly son does for an earthly father—otherwise the prayer is uttered in unbelief.[46]

Lazarus was surprised that he was accused of unbelief. Timothy told him: "Faith is a gift of God, not given to all persons, but without which no one may be pleasing to God."[47] As there were two types of children of Israel—those of the flesh and those of the promise, there are two kinds of Christians—those of works and those of faith; but what is faith? Timothy told him:

Faith is a living and firm feeling in the heart that we are pleasing to God, and that God, through the loving son, is gracious to us in all that we do, or in all that may come upon us, as well in death as in life. The strength of this belief will grow and be more certainly felt and tasted by the believer than one can express.[48]

God had given humankind power to become God's children through the name of Him who because of the Father's command became human for humanity's sake, and who chose us to be heirs.[49] This faith manifests itself in rest and joy of heart which believers feel even in the midst of their sufferings. This is the fruit of the Holy Spirit.[50] This is the faith awakened, tested, and strengthened through pain and suffering. Lazarus admitted that his reading of "Our Father" never had this meaning for him.[51]

Furthermore, Timothy stated that the true believer must be convinced that God hates sin, proving this by bearing the cross unto death. As the Children of Israel had to go through the Red Sea to get to the promised land, so must we undergo suffering and tribulations like Christ in order to participate in the glory. In this way the old Adam is destroyed, along with all desires and lust of the flesh.[52] "Then we are crucified with Christ, as we kill our own lusts and sinful desires—which we should continue as a life-long task."[53] As we are one with Christ in suffering and in death, so shall we be like him in resurrection to newness of life.[54]

This process of purification through suffering is likened also to the medicine which one is given in sickness--it is bitter at the time, but in the end makes one whole again.[55] Thus we believe that the hand of God is within us and upholds and strengthens us so that we come to no desperation or murmuring against God. Without this help from God we could not stand for an instant.[56]

Using Malachi 1:11 the text then criticized the Roman Catholic Church.

From the rising of the sun to its setting my name is great among the nations, and in every place incense is offered to my name, and a pure offering, for my name is great among the nations, says the Lord of hosts.

What offering? Of candles, flax or silver of gold? No, a sacrifice of fleshly and sinful desires, as in Romans 12:1:

I appeal to you therefore, by the mercies of God, to present your bodies as a living sacrifice, holy and acceptable to God, which is your spiritual worship.

The Roman Catholic Church took this to mean a pilgrimage outside oneself or out of one's own territory. The Church refused to look within or to those directly around them. Rather than take pilgrimages to far-away places, we should comfort the sick. Pilgrimages have too often venerated false gods. It is, therefore, of no value to go to Rome, Jerusalem, or Campostello.[57]

By emphasizing the centrality of Christ and the work he had done for human salvation, Gnapheus had to deny any real spiritual power or authority to Roman

Catholic or earthly authorities. "I am the Way, and the Truth and the Life" (John 14:6). Hypocrites think, instead, that God's kingdom is a complex, not simple nature or composed of many parts. They think that God has parcelled his kingdom out piece by piece to counts, dukes, presidents, *stadthouders*, magistrates. . . and other worldly authorities.[58] God, however, said "I will give my power to no other." God is one God who is over all kings. Therefore, in order not to wander astray from the true faith the believer must act to glorify God through Christ. This cannot be done through some earthly means, for that is darkness instead of light. Christ's death frees the believer from imprisonment of flesh and slavery to sin. As it is said for you "Seek the Kingdom of God within you, seek in your heart the King of Glory." It is a kingdom adorned not with gold, silver, and other ornaments, but with "patience, peace, gladness, belief and love."[59]

Lazarus promised that he would never again place a candle before the picture of St. Anne. Rather than pay his money for this votive privilege, he would give his money to the poor in order to light within them the fire of the living temple wherein the mercy of God lives.[60] The true believer cannot seek God in pilgrimages, candles, vestments, or any other material object, for God is not material. God cannot be worshipped in material ways; God is a spirit. God desires only the elimination of all evil thoughts such as unbelief, mistrust, impurity, hate, envy, avarice, and presumption. Only then will one's heart be pure and one will truly be poor in spirit.[61] We are told in scripture to follow God, listen to his Word, and serve Him. "These words very clearly cast out all service to and worship of false gods, that is the saints and images."[62]

Lazarus then asked about miracles, which Timothy said are of no value-- except where Jonah was prefiguring the death and resurrection of Christ and Moses was confirming the law with miracles. Beyond this, however, the use of the miraculous is sacrilege. Especially criticized are the miracles of canonization through which the Pope and Cardinals designate certain people and acts holy. This is an idle and godless thing whereby the Pope builds up his own kingdom in opposition to that of Christ. Lazarus was admonished to place no belief in miters, staffs, capes, casuals, crosses, oil or singing. The process of sanctification is God's alone who does not use objects of sight or hearing, but brings truth in a spiritual unseen way[63] unlike the Romans who "seek their own profit, or their earthly glory, because from these canonizations they receive much money."[64]

They discussed the Mass. Timothy likened it to superstition because in all his Bible reading he had not found anything about Masses. He found the stories concerning the Lord's Supper, but when he compared this with the Mass, there was nothing which was comparable.[65]

So do this in a commemorating [*commemoratie*] or remembrance [*ghedachtenisse*] of me—that is: that we in the use of the Lord's supper proclaim the death of the Lord—as Paul teaches: we also proclaim the death of the Lord as we hold before our fellow believers and the community how Christ has given his body in death for us, so that we in eternity should not suffer death. . . . As you celebrate this evening meal [*avontmael*=communion] for this purpose, as Christ has established—so you are inwardly stimulated to despise the bodily death . . . and to desire the future life."[66]

Any other use of this sacrament is a ridicule of the suffering of Christ and seeks only bodily comfort.

God's saving power works inwardly, without our own works. God empowers us through faith alone to profit through suffering and sacrifice. The believer must trust in the example of Christ. Baptism begins the work of a new birth which gradually purifies the old self, bringing it to new birth—a new creature in God.[67] One must continually "seek Christ in the depth [*graf*, grave] of the Holy Scriptures, seek him in the bedroom [*slaepcamer*] of your heart; there shall you most certainly find him."[68] Tobias admonished Lazarus not to fear temptations of the world. "It is the proclamation of the Word of God that if you have peace and forgiveness in your heart, you have God; where rest is, there is God. There is an eternal inner freedom. . . .Love shuts out fear [of death]."[69]

God brought forth a new creature, Eve, from the side of Adam—while the latter was in a sleep resembling death. In like manner God brought forth a new truth from the sleep—the death—of Christ. Lazarus (Luke 11) rested in the faith of Abraham; Stephen (Acts 7) slept in the Lord. We, too, must die to earthly pleasure before our true life is revealed by God.[70]

Theses to be discussed

In addition to the biblical orientation in his thinking, we note in Gnapheus a close relation between philosophy and theology. Undoubtedly it was this which brought him into conflict with some Lutheran theologians. In Königsberg, when Gnapheus was accused of heresy in 1547, he composed thirteen theses to be debated. Although they never were discussed formally, they gave some indication of the general direction of his thought. Perhaps we may assume that this latter evidence is not substantially different from concepts Gnapheus had been expounding during the decade he was in The Netherlands. The basic criticism Staphylus made against Gnapheus was that he related too closely the truth which God gives to us with the information that human knowledge can gain on its own.

Gnapheus's first thesis was: "Indeed, heavenly and divine philosophy (*i.e.* theology?) consists in two parts: knowledge of God and of ourselves."[71] We have no evidence that Gnapheus had read the work of Calvin by this date [1547], where this formulation is basic to the first section of Calvin's *Institutes*. It reflected, however, a presupposition widely held in Humanistic circles.

Two other theses (XI and XIII) probably reflected Gnapheus's assumptions even more clearly. Gnapheus asserted:

(XI) Through knowledge of God we learn and truly believe not only the mode of God's being and that he ought to be worshipped, but also that he is truly the source of all goodness, all justice and all truth;[72] [and]
(XII) Our own self knowledge, to which we are led only by words of truth [Scripture?], not only thrusts us into true humility of spirit, but when we are freed from all self love [*philautia*=from Greek], which we may interpret along with the poets as blind self love, we are overcome with desire to seek God.[73]

The person who has self knowledge, and then humility of spirit, is prepared—in fact is driven—to seek God and all that implies. This is much more synergistic than Lutheran theologians would have accepted, perhaps the reason for Gnapheus's controversy. Even more important, however, this reflected again the theme of many Humanists that one's religious experience must result in ethical, moral activity—imitation of Christ—otherwise the faith is not genuine.

A Latin Play: Acolastus

In a quite different work Gnapheus treated the question of growing self-knowledge and humility in relation to seeking God. We now turn to the drama of *Acolastus*[74] to analyze the theological content embedded in Gnapheus's treatment of the story of the Prodigal Son.[75] This Biblical account, so Gnapheus assumed, is not simply a story, but a moral example of how one's own destiny is to be interpreted. In the Epilogue to *Acolastus*, the author gave his reasoning.

I will not have you think, most worthy spectators, that this is nothing more than a play. Beneath the surface of the plot there lies a mystery. Indeed, we have revealed to you by means of an image, brought as it were before your eyes, how salvation is procured for fallen man. From it you may readily learn the nature of man's rebellion against God, and of the arrogance for which he richly deserves to die. On the other hand, however, it teaches you how deep is the compassion of the Heavenly Father who gladly welcomes back his son when the latter is restored; never reproaching the boy for the sins he has committed against his father, but with his whole heart running to embrace his son, yes, to kiss him, without the least regard for his filthy condition. Love takes no heed of imperfection and quickly forgets past sins. . . . We summon all of you who are present here for this drama to this same joy, if only you will acknowledge your sins and come to your senses; and we promise that like the Prodigal Son you will receive your Father's forgiveness.[76]

This drama was one of the first such works in this period based on a Biblical theme. Indeed, it was written to be performed by students in the Latin schools. So widespread was its popularity that it enjoyed no less than forty-eight editions in Latin, German, French, and English before the end of the Sixteenth Century. An English edition of 1540 was dedicated to King Henry VIII.[77]

The play has four major actors as well as eight others who are involved in its intrigue and debauchery. The Prodigal Son is named Acolastus, which may be translated from the Greek [*akolasia*] as "prodigality, or profligacy." His companion is Philautus, whose name is translated from Greek classical drama as "blind self love." The father is Philargus, sometimes translated as "admonish or correct," but the term does not exactly fit the character of the father who is often hesitant and tends to be pessimistic, fearing the worst. The counselor for the father is Eubulus, translated "good companion," who optimistically assumed all will turn out well. The elder son in the biblical story is almost totally ignored in the drama. The eight other actors play supplemental roles as the drama moves toward the "fall," (*i.e.* the departure of the son), through debauchery and despair to the final return to the father through the "Grace" of God.

In his literary analysis of the play, Atkinson asserted that it is thoroughly "deterministic." He assumed that the satisfactory end of the play is suggested even as the play opens. The intervening actions and conversations are merely a literary device to get the reader from the beginning good relation between the father and the son, through the prodigal's succumbing to self-love, through debauchery, through total loss of property, to servanthood in feeding the hogs, and finally, to the son's return to the father, an outcome predicted from the beginning.

Although Atkinson found many literary parallels in classical literature which Grapheus could have used as models—Terrence, Horace, Plautus, for example—he argued that Gnapheus used a Lutheran model. Erasmus and Luther debated free will or bound will in 1524 and 1525, and Atkinson assumed that Grapheus would have known of this literature, subsequently borrowing Luther's idea of the bound will. Based on Atkinson's own thorough analysis, however, it seems more likely that Gnapheus used classical models more than he used Luther. In fact, in the document itself, Gnapheus referred to characters in the play of Terrence and never made reference to any Lutheran or Evangelical doctrines. There do not seem to be any obvious parallels with Luther. Yet Atkinson was convinced that the play's "determinism" came from Luther. While Luther was a thorough predestinarian, Atkinson is not technically correct to refer to it as "deterministic." Luther did, however, argue that all human acts are based on God's foreknowledge and that God is involved in every act. Predestination in the sense of Luther, of Zwingli, or even a generation later in Calvin, is based on the "Providence" of a very active God, and is not, strictly speaking, determinism such as that advocated by Thomas Hobbes.

Familiarity with its plot, however, did not detract from the play's popularity. The story had been dramatized in Europe as far back as 13th century France.[78] It was depicted in stained glass windows in the cathedrals at Chartres, Bourges, Sens, Poitiers, and Auxerre.[79] It appeared in tapestries in France and Germany. Clearly

Gnapheus must have been familiar with the widespread use of this parable in drama, literature and art before his time. Indeed, there were several such plays based on this theme in the early decades of the 16th century. Atkinson himself singled out two for special consideration. In 1527 (two years before Gnapheus published his *Acolastus*) a play was published in Germany with many strikingly similar details and development.[80] Atkinson found no documentation that Gnapheus might have known the German play, so there must have been a common source used by both playwrites. Likewise, an Italian version of the play appeared in the 15th century in Venice.[81] Again, there does not seem to be evidence that Gnapheus knew this Italian version, although again there are other obvious similarities.

Since there was a long tradition of the story of the Prodigal Son in the art of Europe, and because it was a Biblical parable, we must ask why the *Acolastus* version was suspect in the eyes of the inquisitors. This is especially interesting since the 1559 version was printed in Antwerp with approval of the imperial authorities. As we have noted above, as compared with *Acolastus*, the *Troost ende Spiegel* had many more theological references which could be taken as criticism of the Roman Catholic establishment, and perhaps since the author was the same person, it became a case of guilt by association. The first *Index of Prohibited Books* of 1559 included all books written by Gulielmus Gnapheus, although they are not listed by title.

Another reason for the Roman Catholic censorship of *Acolastus* might have been that the German play of 1527 did include a long exposition of the Lutheran doctrine of Justification by Faith and a long condemnation of the Roman Catholic Church. These Lutheran additions to the story may be explained in part by the fact that the author, Burkhard Waldis, was formerly a Franciscan who had previously served as a Roman Catholic official opposing Protestantism.[82] His conversion to Protestantism probably influenced his anti-Roman rhetoric.

Theological Assumptions which made Gnapheus suspect in the eyes of the Roman Catholic Church

In his *Troost ende Spiegel* especially, Gnapheus presented an alternative pastoral model with many theological implications differing from contemporary Roman Catholic practice. His exposition, written as an example of pastoral counseling for the sick, emphasized several concerns of the Humanists.

The drama *Acolastus* carries some of these concerns further in the strong emphasis on God's forgiveness for the imperfections of humans, and the need for the believer to respond. Consequently, self knowledge was necessary as was humility. In the end God's love for humans is shown to be eternal, despite human imperfections. In both these works Gnapheus asserted that theology should emphasize practical concerns rather than theoretical, it should be person-centered not institution-centered, and it must be closely related to the Scriptural model. Consequently, several of these practical directives were seen as a contrast, or even opposition to the Roman Catholic practices.

Notes for Chapter 11.

1. The two works of this humanist scholar which will be analyzed in this chapter are those which are most closely related to the decade of the 1520s in The Netherlands. **FIRST**, "*Een Troost ende Spiegel der Siecken end der ghenen die in Lijden zijn.*" Published in vol.I., Dr. F. Pijper, ed. *Bibliotheca Reformatoria Neerlandica (BRN):* (The Hague: Martinus Nijhoff, 1903), pp. 137-149, Introduction; 150-249. This was originally published in 1531, probably in Antwerp, by Niclaes Oldenborch (pseud.), according to *NK* 1010. Bart Spruyt, however, suggested, without documentation, that the *NK* 1010 should really be dated in 1552-1554—see his thesis on Hoen, p. 80. A second edition was published in Antwerp, 1532, *NK* 3108. A later, revised edition was published as *Tobias and Lazarus* in Emden, 1557. These are the names of the two main participants in this discussion in both these editions. These works were originally published in Dutch, whereas Gnapheus's other works were in Latin. There were at least forty-seven editions of this work published, including three in German, one in English and one in French, *BRN*, I, 140, Introduction to *Troost ende Spiegel*.
SECOND, *Acolastus*, a poetic drama based on the parable of the Prodigal Son, Luke 15:11-32. Seven editions of this work appeared within a decade, all printed in Antwerp: July 1529. *NK* 3102; August 1530, *NK* 3103; June 1532, *NK* 3104; July 1533, *NK* 1007; March 1535, *NK* 3105; August 1535, *NK* 1108; 1539, *NK* 3106.
Other recent studies will also be used as our sources. Johannes Bolt, ed., vol. I , *Acolastus, Lateinische Literaturdenkmäler des XV und XVI Jahrhunderts* (Berlin: Speyer and Peters, 1891); P. Minderaa, *Latijnse tekst met Nederlandsche Vertaling* (Zwolle: W. E. J. Tjeenk Willink, 1956). English translation by W. E. D. Atkinson (London, Ontario, Canada: Humanities Department, University of Western Ontario, 1964).
All his works [*Auctores quorum Libri & Scripta omnia prohibenter*] were placed on the *Index Librorum Prohibitorum* of 1559.
2. A thorough study of this scholar appears in H. Roodhuyzen, *Het leven van Guilhelmus Gnapheus.* (Amsterdam: J. C. Loman, 1858), a doctoral thesis of the mid 19th century written at the University of Leiden. A recent biographical reference was prepared originally by G. J. Graafland, and after his death in 1992, was completed by J. Trapman "Gnapheus, Gulielmus,." in *Biografisch Lexicon voor de Geschiedenis van het Nederlandse Protestantisme* (Kampen, The Netherlands: Uitgeverij Kok, 1998), IV, 142-144.
3. The Dutch word "volder" is translated "fuller," a worker in cloth. The Latin "fullonius," and the Greek "gnapheus," imply the same. See P. Minderaa, ed., *Acolastus*, p. 14. We note here a common tendency among sixteenth century Humanists to change their names to the Latin or Greek equivalent.
4. Johannes Bolte, edition of *Acolastus*, p. xi; and Minderaa, *Acolastus*, pp. 14ff. In both of these editions we have not only an analysis of the work under discussion, but also a sketch

of the author, his life and his 16th century career.

5. Minderaa, *Acolastus*, p. 15. Bolte, Introduction to his edition of *Acolastus*, p. xii.

6. In the 1557 edition of *Tobias and Lazarus*, a revision of his 1531 publication, *Een Troost ende Spiegel*, Gnapheus included a letter to the leaders in Holland, Zeeland and West Friesland. This biographical letter does not carry page numbers, but this quotation is taken from the eighth page of the text, opposite his marginal note, "*Ann.* 1523." The title page of the copy of this 1557 edition at the University of Amsterdam gives us the following details: "*Ghedruckte te Embden* by Gellium Crematium, an. 1557."

7. The biographical letter, dated 20 September, 1557, in the 1557 edition of *Tobias and Lazarus*, p. 8 (although unnumbered in this edition).

8. Introduction by F. Pijper to his edition of "*Een Troost ende Spiegel der Siecken,*" vol. I of *Bibliotheca Reformatoria Neerlandica*. For information on various editions, see endnote 1, above, and also Minderaa, *Acolastus*, p. 15.

9. The biographical letter is included in the 1557 edition of *Tobias and Lazarus*, p. 9 of the text.

10. This statement is included on the ninth and tenth pages of the letter, *ibid.*

11. "A Comfort and a mirror for the sick, and for those who suffer" was published (1531) by Niclaes van Oldenborch [pseud.], [in Antwerp, *NK* 1010]. The edition used here is that by S. Cramer and F. Pijper, eds. *Bibliotheca Reformatoria Neerlandica*, volume I of this ten-volume collection.

12. The biographical letter included in the 1557 edition of *Tobias and Lazarus*, the tenth and eleventh pages of the text.

13. Minderaa, *Acolastus,* included a photograph of this title page, facing p. 47.

14. Johannes Bolte's edition of *Acolastus.* He listed the forty-eight editions in his bibliography, pp. xxiv-xxvii. One edition, in English (1540) was dedicated to King Henry VIII.

15. The biographical letter included in the 1557 edition of *Tobias and Lazarus*, the eleventh page of the text.

16. This letter to Sartorius was included at the beginning of the *Acolastus*. This translation is from Atkinson, p. 87.

17. Hendrik Roodhuyzen, *Het Leven van Guilhelmus Gnapheus*, 1858. Gnapheus gave us this information in his biographical letter from the 1557 edition of Tobias and Lazarus, opposite the marginal note, "*Anno.* 1530." Graafland/Trapman's article also summarizes the work and the publications of Gnapheus from the 1530s to the 1560s.

18. The biographical letter, *Ibid.*

19. J. P. de Bie and J. Loosjes, eds., *Biographisch Woordenboek van Protestantische Godgeleerden in Nederland* (5 vols., The Hague: Nijhoff, 1913-1943), II, 270.

20. Roodhuyzen, *Het Leven van Guilhelmus Gnapheus*, p. 35, gave the date as 1542. The editors of *Bibliotheca Reformatoria Neerlandica*, I, 141, gave it as 1543.

21. Pijper, edition of *Troost ende Spiegel*, p. 140.

22. Minderaa, *Acolastus*, pp. 16ff. This theological controversy is thoroughly analyzed in Roodhuyzen, *Het Leven van Guilhelmus Gnapheus*, pp. 38-54.

23. Roodhuyzen, *Leven van Gnapheus*, p. 63.

24. Melanchthon's letter is printed in Roodhuyzen, *Leven van Gnapheus*, p. 46.

25. The text of the excommunication of Gnapheus is printed in Roodhuyzen's study, pp. 57-60, dated 9 June, 1547.

26. Roodhuyzen, *Leven van Gnapheus*, p. 66; Bie and Loosjes, *Biographisch Woordenboek*, II, 270.

27. A copy of this 1557 edition is in the library of the University of Amsterdam.

28. Minderaa, *Acolastus*, p. 17.

29. According to Pijper, the first edition of this work, with the place of publication unknown, was 1562. The 1567 edition was published in Leiden.

30. Roodhuyzen, *Leven van Gnapheus*, p. 78.

31. *Acolastus*, Act I, Scene III, from the translation by Atkinson, p. 113.

32. *Acolastus*, Act I, Scene IV, from the translation by Atkinson, p. 115.

33. Gnapheus, *Een Troost ende Spiegel van de siecken end der Ghenen die in Lijden zijn*, from the *BRN* edition of Pijper and Cramer, I, 150-249. The 1557 edition of the work is entitled *"Tobias and Lazarus,"* after the two main spokesmen.

34. *"Troost ende Spiegel," BRN* edition, p. 153.

35. *Ibid.*, p. 154.

36. *Ibid.*, p. 155.

37. *Ibid.*, p. 155.

38. *Ibid.*, p. 156.

39. *Ibid.*, p. 157.

40. *Ibid.*, p. 160.

41. *Ibid.*, p. 161.

42. *Ibid.*, p. 161.

43. *Ibid.*, p. 168.

44. *"Troost ende Spiegel,"* p. 168. Bastian (Bart) Spruyt is convinced that this discussion reflects a knowledge of Luther's thought concerning bearing one's suffering as one proof of one's faith: faith grows through suffering. Bastian Spruyt, *Cornelius Henrici Hoen (Honius) and his epistle on the Eucharist (1525)*, p. 86.

45. "Troost ende Spiegel," p. 168-169.

46. *Ibid.*, p. 169.

47. *Ibid.*, p. 170.

48. *Ibid.*, p. 170.

49. *Ibid.*, p. 171.

50. *Ibid.*, p. 171.

51. *Ibid.*, p. 172.

52. *Ibid.*, p. 175.

53. *Ibid.*, p. 176.

54. *Ibid.*, p. 176.

55. *Ibid.*, p. 178.

56. *Ibid.*, p. 178.

57. *"Troost ende Spiegel,"* p. 191. St. James in Campostello, a famous shrine in northwestern Spain, was well-known to Netherlanders of his day.

58. *Ibid.*, p. 191.

59. *Ibid.*, p. 190.

60. *Ibid.*, p. 192.

61. *Ibid.*, p. 193.

62. *Ibid.*, p. 195.

63. *Ibid.*, p. 199.

64. *Ibid.*, p. 199.

65. *Ibid.*, p. 202.

66. *Ibid.*, p. 203.

67. *Ibid.*, p. 207.

68. *Ibid.*, p. 192-193.

69. *Ibid.*, p. 232.

70. *Ibid.*, p. 241.

71. Roodhuyzen, *Leven van Gnapheus*, p. 39. This first thesis reads: "*Philosophiae vera coelestis atque divinae summam duabus partibus contineri, cognitione videlicet Dei atque nostri, certum est.*"

72. Roodhuyzen, *Leven van Gnapheus*, p. 41. The thesis reads: "*Sic futurum est ut cognitione Dei discamus, vereque credamus, non modo Deum esse et adorari oportere verum etiam omnis bonitatis justitiae ac veritatis fontem esse.*"

73. Roodhuyzen, *Leven van Gnapheus*, p. 41. The thesis reads: "*Cognitione nostri ad quam solo veritatis sermone adducimur, non modo in veram animi humilitatem dejiciamur, sed remota etiam omni philautia, quam caecum nostri amorem cum poeta interpretamur, requirendi Deum desiderio accendamur.*"

74. Gnapheus, *Acolastus*, (Antwerp, 1529). *NK* 3102.

75. W. E. D. Atkinson, trans and ed., *Acolastus* (London, Ontario, Canada: University of Western Ontario, 1964).

76. *Acolastus*, Epilogue, from the translation by Atkinson, p. 203.

77. These editions are listed in a bibliography compiled by Johannes Bolte in 1890: Johannes Bolte, *Gulielmus Gnapheus: Acolastus* (Berlin: Speyer and Peters, 1891), pp. xxiv-xxvii.

78. Atkinson edition, p. 207.

79. *Ibid.*, p. 210, where Atkinson gave many references to art histories of this period.

80. Burkhard Waldis, *Der Parabell vom verlorene Sohn* (Riga: 1527). See Atkinson, pp. 207-211.

81. Castellano Castellani, *Rappresentazione del Figliuol Prodigo*, (Venice: 15th Century). See Atkinson, pp. 217

82. These suggestions are from the Minderaa introduction and his Latin/Dutch edition and analysis of *Acolastus*, pp. 22-23.

Chapter 12

Religious Dissent among the Common People

Continuing Agitation for Reforms in Religion

From afar in Basel, Erasmus continued to be informed about the problems concerning religion in his native land. For example, in 1524 he wrote to Willibald Pirckheimer, the Humanist scholar in Nürnberg:

> The thing [religious turmoil] spreads more widely every day. Neither side takes any steps toward reconciliation; most of them in fact have no other purpose than to pour oil on the flames. In my native Holland nuns everywhere are leaving the cloister and getting married in the Lord. The Camel (Nicholas Baechem of Egmont, the Carmelite), has been disowned by both emperor and pope. His colleague Hulst has barely escaped a death sentence [because of aggressive opposition to Cornelis Hoen while he was in prison]. Literary studies flourish and go forward to the impotent fury of the theologians. They proclaim that I am a heretic, but no one believes them (lines 11-18).[1]

We have already analyzed many examples of these religious difficulties in the monasteries, and among priests and Humanist scholars. Indeed, many of the teachers were known to Erasmus at least by name if not personally. Now let us turn to the more popular reactions among the less educated, common people. Our major source are various legal documents from all parts of The Netherlands. In 1889-1902 Paul Fredericq, Professor at the University of Gent, along with several students compiled five volumes of trial records and correspondence in The Netherlands.[2] The last two volumes cover the period from 1515 to 1528. He originally had hoped to extend his work a few more years, but the volumes as now published extend only to 1528. Volume IV includes documents numbered from #1 (beginning in 1515) thorough #391, while Volume V continues to number #786 (13 July, 1528). We will include a sampling of these records from all parts of The Netherlands. They involve individuals in all walks of life. Unfortunately, many of these trial records do not give enough detail to determine the precise theological ideas behind the actions of those who were tried as suspects or punished as heretics.

Imperial Edicts meant to Control Religious Dissent

That the agitation for religious reform continued is seen in the number of anti-heresy Edicts or Placards [*Plakkaaten*] which the Emperor issued in The Netherlands. Although there were already three edicts which would seem to cover almost all possible dissenting opinions or actions with respect to new religious ideas—*Exsurge Domine* (15 June, 1520), *Decet Romanum Pontificem* (3 January, 1521) and the Edict of Worms (8 May, 1521)—there were several additional edicts promulgated covering much of the same material. The **First Edict** of the Emperor against Luther was actually issued on 29 March, 1521, during the meetings at the Diet of Worms, but before Luther's appearance. It was issued in French and directed to the Council of Flanders. A further Edict was issued against two specific books, neither of which had the name of Luther, nor were written by him. (These two publications were analyzed in Chapters 8 and 9.) A **Second Edict** specifically against Luther, 1 April, 1524, was directed to the Councils of Holland, Zeeland and Friesland.[3] Although edicts had been published against heretical writings, so the edict read, still many erroneous books were being published without permission. The edict specifically forbade the printing of books unless they had been approved by authorized censors. The penalty would be loss of life, confiscation of possessions, or probably both.

The **Third Edict** against Lutherans, 24 September, 1525, was much more extensive[4] and was directed to the Council of Holland. The emperor reminded them that in 1521 he prohibited buying, selling or reading Lutheran books. Later he repeated the prohibition, but the Lutheran "errors" continued to spread. Heretical ideas were even known by laity and unlearned [*ongeleerde*] persons. Consequently, he forbade any meetings, public or private, where anyone discussed the gospels, the epistles of Paul or other spiritual writings in Latin, Dutch/Flemish [*Duytsche*] or Walloon/French [*Walsh*]. Furthermore, no one was to discuss articles of the holy faith, sacraments of the church, the power of the pope, councils, bishops, and other authorities. The fines for anyone who disobeyed these were listed—for the first offense, the second, the third, and so on. Any income derived through prosecution was to be divided three ways, one-third each to the accuser, the judge and the Emperor.

This edict expanded the prohibited writers from Luther to other reformers. This is interesting with respect to those other individuals who were identified as reformers as early as 1525:

Pomerani (Bugenhagen), Carlstadt, Melanchthon, Oecolampadius (of Basel), Francis Lambert [formerly a Franciscan of Avignon, translator of German reformation materials into French and Italian, and Professor at Wittenberg and at Marburg, all in this decade], and Justus Jonas [of Erfurt and later professor of theology at Wittenberg], and any others whose understanding of the Holy Scripture was sympathetic with that of Luther.

Authorities were to collect all their books, even those printed without titles, and take them to a public place. There they were to be burned to ashes [*tot pulver verbrant*]. Further restrictions were directed toward schoolmasters. They were to teach and expound only on books dealing with grammar, logic and rhetoric. Hereafter, anyone found with other forbidden books would be banned from this region, upon pain of forfeiture of life and all possessions. The edict reiterated that no books should be printed, bought, or sold in the Netherlands—even those printed elsewhere and brought into the country—if related to Lutheran or other heresies. The next day the Regent, Margaret, added her authority by repeating the necessity of enforcing this edict[5]

A **Fourth Edict**, 17 July, 1526, was issued from Mechelen/Malines. and directed to the President and members of the Court of Flanders.[6] This Edict was similar to the Third Edict of the previous year. Despite earlier edicts, the heretical teachings were continuing because some unlearned persons were reading religious writings in Flemish/Dutch or Walloon/French and interpreting them according to their own opinions without the help of their superiors. Even regular priests were preaching Lutheran doctrines and reminding the people of erroneous ideas from ancient times. The edict re-affirmed that unlawful gatherings to read, speak, discuss, or preach from the Gospels, the Epistles of Paul or other sections of the Holy Scriptures in any of the above-mentioned languages were strictly forbidden. Hereafter, no one may teach or promote any doctrines of Martin Luther, especially as related to the Eucharist, the Confession, and other Sacraments of the church or anything which was related to the honor of Holy Mother Mary, or the saints [*santen*] or "saintesses" [*santinnen*] and their images. The people were also forbidden to discuss the powers of the councils, the pope, bishops, prelates, prayers for the dead, observation of lent, or other fasts. In short, they were forbidden to discuss any ideas different from the strict and narrowly-defined faith of the Roman Catholic Church. Punishments were similar to those stipulated in previous edicts. In the case of fines, again one third would go to the accuser, one third for judges, and one third for the Emperor. An interesting modification, however, appeared in this Edict. It was left to the discretion of judges to raise or lower the fines. The works of the same six reformers, mentioned in the third edict, in addition to Luther, were forbidden. All such books were to be burned, and anyone not complying must forfeit life and property.

A **Fifth Edict**, 14 March, 1527, was a reissue of the Third Edict of 24 September, 1525.[7] A **Sixth Edict**, 18 January, 1528, was issued from Brussels and directed to the *Stadthouder* and Council of Holland.[8] It stated that earlier prohibitions against printing had not been effective, so the later prohibitions must be more diligently enforced. Furthermore all printers were required to put their names and their city on all publications. A further concern was raised about the number of people leaving their cloisters to live on the outside as laypersons. Henceforth, no one was to take off his/her religious garb without dispensation from church authorities. No one in the community was allowed to give comfort or lodging to any of these who had left their cloister without permission.

A **Seventh Edict**, even more strict, was issued 14 October, 1529.[9] Concerning the possession of prohibited books the edict noted that those who possessed them, or did not surrender them as requested, would be condemned to death. Those who relapsed after confessing were "sentenced to die by fire." Others were subjected to even stricter punishments "the men were to die by the sword, and the women by the pit [that is, to be buried alive]." Several more names were added to the previous list of those whose works were forbidden: the total list now included Luther, Wyclif, Huss, Marsilius of Padua, Oecolampadius, Zwingli, Melanchthon, Francis Lambert, Bugenhagen, Otto Brunfels, Justus Jonas and John Pupper of Goch. Brunfels left the Carthusian monastery to follow Luther and he was also interested in Zwingli's movement. He wrote in support of many Reformation ideas, was influenced by Anabaptism in Strasbourg and eventually became a physician. Justus Jonas was a theologian in Wittenberg already mentioned in the Third Edict. As we have already seen, John Pupper was considered an early anticipator of reformation ideas.

Attempts to limit printing and printers, especially works of Luther

Following the condemnation of Luther's work at both Cologne and Louvain/Leuven in 1519, the authorities emphasized controlling the printing presses, and identifying anyone who might have copies of any of his works. In Gent/Gans a pastry-baker, Lieven de Zomere, was interrogated because he possessed many writings of Luther. The books were burned on 24 June, 1521,[10] and he was commanded not to speak of Luther's ideas again. Within a year, however, he was again arrested for the same charge because the authorities thought that he had secured and read other volumes.[11] Some authorities claimed that he had even proclaimed Lutheran ideas in sermons. He was reported to have said that "he would rather go into a fire than to depart from Luther or to be separated from his books."[12] Nevertheless, by April 24 the books were burned. The case was reopened three years later when more books were found. We assume it was the same Lieven de Zomere and his wife, Lijsbeth, who were required to recant on the scaffold and were banished from the vicinity of Flanders for fifty years.[13]

More accusatioins, more book burnings, and more punishments ensued in The Netherlands. In Amsterdam in early December a shoeworker [*schoenlapper*] named Jan Ysbrantz was discovered with Lutheran materials. Usually in the judicial proceedings the books were not identified, but in this case Ysbrantz had some annotations by Phillip Melanchthon concerning the Gospel of John, comments on the Gospel of Matthew, a commentary on Paul's letter to the Galatians, and one more book discussing the "abomination [*gruwel*] of the Mass."[14] It was assumed that these were related to the "sect of Luther." His punishment was banishment from the city of Amsterdam for six years. In Antwerp Hendrik Henricxsens from Bergen op Zoom and Tanneken Zwolfs from Brussels were accused of circulating Lutheran books. Within three days they were ordered out of the city of Antwerp. Hendrik was required to make a pilgrimage to Boulogne, from which he returned on 12 November, 1526. Tanneken was to make a pilgrimage to O. L. V. [*Onze lieve Vrouw* =Our Beloved lady=Notre Dame] church in Paris.[15]   At Duinkerke Jan Corbel had sold Lutheran books. He was condemned to pay a fine for penance and on Sunday to make a public proclamation of penance. He had to walk barefooted in a procession at the church to renounce his errors. Following this he was banished from the bishopric of Thorenburg (Tournai/Dornik) for three months.[16] In Brugge/Bruges Hector van Dommenne, a hatmaker, was apprehended with 36 suspicious books. The authorities declared he was a heretic because he had separated himself from the French Roman Catholic faith. He was condemned to death by fire.[17] In Antwerp Cornelis van der Plassen was convicted of having sold heretical books, even though they did not carry the name of the author or the place of publication. He was required to pay a fine, and was banished from Antwerp for one year. Local authorities discovered that Lutheran books translated into Spanish were being printed in Antwerp.[18]

In addition to books and pamphlets other questionable printings appeared. In Hoorn, Claes Hendricxz received a sentence of six years in exile because he gave heretical lectures and possessed books of heretical songs from which he had actually sung on the street as well as in his home.[19] In Leiden Gijsbrecht Aelbrechtsz, clothing maker or tailor from Delft, was accused of spreading heretical writings. He had distributed heretical writings on the door of the church of St. Peter in Delft, and even placed a copy on the pulpit. He was apprehended and was required to promise he would not do this again. He was scourged with a sharp sword, and was commanded to return to the church bare-headed, and walk in procession with a burning candle which he had to offer before the Holy Sacrament. He was then imprisoned for two weeks, supplied only with bread and water. Finally, he was banished from Leiden for ten years.[20]

Evidence of suspected Lutheran influence

An early historian summarized some of the developments he observed before and during the year 1524, in Amsterdam and in Friesland.[21] He reported that there were great disturbances because of the writings of Luther. He also explained how dangerous Luther was. Luther, so he wrote, had written against the

Pope and the cardinals, bishops, and others in the hierarchy. He opposed indulgences and the money spent on them. He opposed the mendicant orders, although he himself was a member of the Augustinian order. He opposed cloisters and said that it would be better if men and women left the monasteries and cloisters and got married. Indeed, the historian remarked we find that is exactly what many individuals did, not only in Amsterdam but in all other parts of The Netherlands. Interested people discussed these ideas every chance they got. For example, in Amsterdam before 15 February, 1524, the authorities discovered several offenses, including gatherings [*conventiculen*] of Lutherans in Amsterdam.[22] The disposition of these cases is unknown. A few months later there was another report of some "Lutherans" who were questioned in Amsterdam but transferred to The Hague for investigation.[23] Indeed, a few years later in 1528, it was reported that there still were many citizens of Amsterdam who were infected with heresy, and furthermore, there was no city in Holland more susceptible to corruption.[24]

North and east of Amsterdam, across the *IJsselmeer* in the region known as Friesland, there were similar disturbances. Concerning that area in particular, this same historian continued:

> In our Friesland there is also discord, because now many priests or educated lay people, both in orders [*gheestelick*] and secular [*wereltlick*], feel a close affinity with Luther. They know what he advocates because he proves his message clearly with the Holy Gospel and with Paul's Epistles; he proceeds with the principal scriptures so that many learned people become sympathetic with his message.[25]

Three examples of this unrest may suffice. George Schenck, Governor of Friesland wrote to the Magistrates of Leeuwarden in 1526 that all books of Luther, Carlstadt, Melanchthon, Oecolampadius, Lambert, Jonas, and others who were thought to be sympathetic with Luther were to be forbidden. This was true whether they were in Latin or German, even if printed without title. No one was to share these ideas or opinions in private or public. Any one possessing any of these works was to bring them to be burned to ashes. Otherwise, these persons would be subjected to the strongest punishment.[26] Two days before this, Willem Tanckles was accused: "this one has blasphemed the Holy Mary."[27] His tongue was bored with a sharp instrument, and his hands were bound as he stood on a scaffold for one hour. The next Sunday he came to the church wearing the sign of the cross on his chest, and carrying a candle in procession. He proceeded to the statue of the Virgin Mary and said an "Ave Maria" while asking for forgiveness. In Leeuwarden on 16 July, 1527, Marten Mathysz van Bergen in Henegouwe/Hainaut spoke heresy. His tongue was bored, and he was condemned to eternal banishment from Friesland. This punishment was especially severe because he had earlier been banned from the County of Holland.[28]

Unrest within the monasteries

Some of the monasteries were the locus of questionable religious developments. We wonder exactly what may have been the content of the message of an
Augustinian in Antwerp who was preaching against indulgences as early as
1520.[29] Frustration was exemplified in the monastery at Doesburg (a short distance east of Arnhem) where the authorities reported that "*Hoc tempore* (1525)
nondum cessavit doctrina Lutherana" [At this time—1525—the doctrines of
Luther have not yet ceased]. One of the brothers was suspected of heresy and
denounced or reprimanded [*denunciatur est*]. Details of any punishment were
not given.[30] The next year in the same monastery a similar problem was reported.[31] The spread of Lutheran thought was discovered among the younger
monks. Some were expelled from the monastery, some fled. The remaining
monks were ordered to Arnhem where punishment or imprisonment would be
determined. In 1525 in Mechelen/Malines Jacob Neut from the nearby town of
Geervliet, was reported to be a heretic priest.[32] He had earlier been forbidden to
preach, although he ignored this prohibition and continued preaching. The inquisitors were asked to suggest appropriate punishment for him. In 1527, in Ri-
jsel (l'Ille=now Lille, France) the prior of the Domincans, Jan Frelin, read the
Bible in a vulgar language, preached erroneous ideas in sermons, and associated
with those who were heretical.[33]

On 14 August, 1527, at Maastricht, there was a general investigation against
some citizens who were "infected" with the suspected evil, and un-Christian sect
of Luther.[34] In Tournai/Dornik in 1527, Jaspar Bernard was suspected of heresy
and imprisoned 183 days because he held the false opinions of Luther.[35] Sometime before 30 September, 1528, also at Dornik/Tournai Damiaan de la Motte, a
merchant, and Jan de la Frelie, a carpet-maker, were investigated.[36] They were
accused of holding the heretical teachings of Martin Luther, which the accusers
stated were against the Christian faith. The accused were required to pay the fine
determined by the imperial Edict. In May, 1528, an Augustinian suspected of
heresy was spreading his views in Dordrecht.[37]

Unrest outside the monasteries

Outside the monasteries there was considerable interest in Lutheran ideas as
well. Those suspected of Lutheran sympathies among the common folks (un-
ordained and usually uneducated lay persons) appeared from almost all walks of
life. One summary report in The Hague and Leiden during the summer of 1527[38]
listed many names and noted various occupations which were represented:
bookbinder, glass-maker, lantern-maker, brewer, bookbinder, a Beguine, an Augustinian of Dordrecht, a priest, carpenter, vice curate at a Delft church, harness-
maker, and barrel-maker. All paid their required fines. In Arnhem in 1526 a
young woman from Welz and two from Nijmegen were charged as Lutherans.[39]
The last two were burned. A few months later, also in Arnhem (or nearby Tiel), a

woman was suspected of being Lutheran because she despised and scorned the sacrament of the Eucharist.[40] She became sick and died. Evidently the authorities felt cheated, because they had planned to accuse her of heresy. As an example to others they promptly disinterred the body and burned it.

In Amsterdam in 1526 Peter Govertsz's house was suspected as a center of heretical Lutheran opinions.[41] He was commanded to make a pilgrimage to *O. L. V.* Church at l'Insul (Rijsel=Lille, France). Also in Amsterdam on the same day, Jan Ysbrantsz, shoeworker, was convicted of blasphemies. During the services he had called loudly that he was leaving the church because he had listened to seducers or tempters [*verleyders*] of God long enough.[42] He also was accused of a similar blasphemy against the minister. He was not to return for six years; otherwise he would lose his right hand.

In 1526 at Ypres/Ieperen, a barber, Jan Paeuwaert, had to pay a penalty because he associated with persons suspect of reading Luther's books, clearly against the imperial Edicts.[43] Two years later, also at Ypres/Ieperen another barber, Joachim Uutendale, was suspected of heresy because he associated with persons thought to have Lutheran sympathies and had read heretical books.[44] He was required to do penance and pay the required fine. In Antwerp, in February 1528, a judgment was recorded against Christiaan Boeye, a dealer in clothing.[45] The court decided that he was infected [*besmet*] with certain heresies. He had to remain within the walls of the city, and until the coming Easter season he had to attend O. L. V. [*Onse Lieve Vrouw*=Our Beloved Lady=St. Mary] Church every Sunday, hearing the mass and the sermon "from beginning to the end" while kneeling. Furthermore, he had to carry a burning candle in the procession to show penance. In 1528 in Luik/Liege it was reported that many in city were of Lutheran sympathies disregarding the Edict of Worms.[46] In connection with this investigation, one heretical priest was burned on the banks of the Maas River.

In Antwerp a widow, Duyf Dirck Pauwelsz, and another person, Lysbet in den Spiegel, were charged by the bishop of Utrecht with being Lutheran sympathizers.[47] They were commanded to wear a cross on their clothing, pay fines, and do penance in the church. Alas, five years later, Lijsbet was brought in for questioning again, this time in Amsterdam.[48] She was charged with disobeying the earlier sentence—she had not worn the cross conspicuously on her clothing. The penalties were similar to those in the previous court session. It was reiterated that she was to wear the red cross conspicuously on her clothing, to pay penalties, and to act so others could see she was modest and repentant.

During the court proceedings there sometimes appeared a twist in the circumstances, like false accusation. Whether for profit or spite one of these was reported in Utrecht, when in 1525 Cornelis Wyman was falsely charged with being of the sect of Luther.[49] This time, however, the accuser, instead of the accused, was reprimanded. Reyer Slory, the accuser, was confined to his house for fourteen days. After this he was required to pay a fine and beg forgiveness from the courts.

Unspecified heresies and suspicions

There were also many instances of unspecified heresy charges because of the ambiguity or unclarity of the accusations. In Leiden, someone affixed libelous or slanderous posters on the doors of St. Peters Church and on the confessional of the traveling monks.[50] They read:

> [First] "This confessional is to be sold and not rented out, because those louts" (perhaps a more derogatory meaning is implied—*beichtheyncxten* or [*beicht*]=confession, and [*heyncxten=hengst*]=stallion. Probably the meaning was not only derogatory, but sexual as well—*i.e.* a confession stallion)— "because those louts who hear confessions will not remain here long; for soon you will hear: 'it is God's will that it shall no longer be tolerated'."
> [Second] "These four chairs are for sale and not for rent, for what people buy here is awful and much too expensive."
> [Third] "Watch out, Watch out, o sir bailiff, woe! to you, for protecting those monks."
> [Fourth] "You pious men, keep your wives away from all monks, for if you don't you will be sorry."

If it were children who did this, the parents would be required to do penance. Those who knew the instigators of these crimes and did not come forth would be punished. We do not know if any one was apprehended. In Ertvelde (north of Gent/Gans) some persons placed a scandalous painting in the church in derision of God, the Apostles and the Christian faith.[51] In Amsterdam Hans Schroeder of Bremen was sentenced to be exhibited on a pillory and required to pay penance because he had abused two observant Franciscan monks by calling them names.[52] The monks, who were on their way to bury the dead, were dubbed "you gray wolves." After his hour on the pillory he was required to beg forgiveness of the monks. In Antwerp Jacob Roder, saddle-maker, was suspected of heresy.[53] He was to remain in the city, and not leave without consent, until such time when his guilt had been confirmed, or he was absolved from suspicion.

Secret meetings—Conventicles

In Amsterdam, in 1523, a law was passed concerning secret meetings. No gatherings were to be held for religious instructions; no preaching was to be conducted in private or in public. Any one who had information of such gatherings was required to notify authorities. Punishments meant confiscation of goods, a possible fine, pilgrimage, or death.[54] Despite this law, within a very few months, an investigation was conducted to investigate secret meetings in Amsterdam itself.[55] Likewise, in May in Amsterdam, a sentence was pronounced against eight persons (who were named) and Weijn Zybrantsedochter, in whose home a meeting was held. They were ordered to go to St. Nicholas Church in Amsterdam and walk in the procession between the cross and the school children, while carrying burning candles for penance. Then they were separated, with the men going to one place and the women to another— in each case to be held in prison eight days on bread and water. Should any one not repent and pay the required penalty, he or she would be banned from the city for seven years. Zybrantsedochter had to make a pilgrimage to Brabant.[56] Two months later Aechgen Aerntsdochter was charged with using her house for a conventicle—a gathering of miscellaneous persons, married men and women, priests, and girls. She was condemned to leave the city of Amsterdam permanently.[57] In March 1528 a judgment was pronounced against Brecht, wife of Baernt de Guldenberch, because she had held a conventicle meeting in her house where forbidden books were read. She was required to pay a penitential fine within eight days.[58]

In other areas outside Amsterdam there were many breaches of the law prohibiting secret meetings. In Antwerp in 1524 a secret gathering was discovered in which 37 names were listed, giving the occupation of each person—working class lay persons from the nearby region. They had read and interpreted the Gospels and other holy Scripture. All had to promise never to conduct or attend such a meeting again. In addition, they had to remain in prison until they paid the required fine.[59] Also in Antwerp in 1524, there were secret meetings led by Adriaan, a house painter. They read and discussed the Gospels. The sentence was that within three days he had to leave Antwerp, make a holy pilgrimage to The Holy Blood of Wilseneken (now Bad Wilsnack, about 60 miles west of Berlin near the Havel River where it joins the Elbe. [This was a popular destination for pilgrims in the 14th-16th centuries]) and not return to Antwerp for six years.[60] In Gent/Gans Jan de Pruet, a utensil maker [kettelboeter], was banned for fifty years because he held secret meetings for discussing heretical ideas.[61] In May 1527 at Den Briel/Brielle, a lock-maker, Lambrecht Lambrechtsz, circulated heretical publications and held forbidden gatherings where they discussed the Gospels, the Epistles and other questionable literature. He was required to attend church that Sunday bareheaded, carry a candle in procession for penance, stand before everyone in the choir, and confess to authorities that he was rejected all his errors (while begging forgiveness). Thereafter he had to place the candle before the Holy Sacrament at the church in Den Briel/Brielle.[62]

Marriage of Priests and general unrest in the Waterland area

While many infractions of the laws were related to the larger cities or to monasteries, the area immediately north of Amsterdam was also the location of several incidents of "heresy." The section of the country approximately ten miles north of Amsterdam was known as the Waterland area because it is below sea level and protected by dikes and polders. While this area was not known as a center of Humanistic scholarship, it was, nevertheless, involved in religious controversies in early days of the Reformation. This was true, especially in the towns of Monnikendam and Hoorn. The town of Monnikendam got its name from a dam built by a monastic group three centuries earlier. Since this area was subject to flooding, the ending "dam" appears in the names of several towns in this region. The authorities investigated many churches in the area. For example, in March 1524 officials from The Hague made a trip to Monnikendam to investigate "certain abuses and unauthorized conventicles held there among the villagers, including both religious [*i.e.* those in orders] and secular people."[63] While we do not know the outcome, the fact that their investigation lasted seven days indicated that they must have interviewed many people and made a thorough investigation. Another trip was made the next year to investigate "certain abuses which have taken place there, related to the Lutheran sect."[64] The investigation lasted nine days. Many names of suspected Lutheran followers were listed in 1526 in a long summary in the legal records, including names of several priests and several lay persons. We know nothing about most of them, but their numbers indicate a very strong movement toward dissent in this region.[65]

In 1525 there was a report concerning the well-publicized imprisonment of Willem Ottenzoen [Ottenis, Ottens], a priest in Hoorn because of his outspoken support of Luther's ideas.[66] He was evidently also known as William of Utrecht, from the place of his birth, although details of his connection to Utrecht and the Waterland area are not known. The authorities in Hoorn did not want him to remain in the local prison so they transferred him to The Hague, where he was imprisoned 2-27 September.[67] He was then confined briefly in the castle of Medemblik on 28 September,[68] but was immediately returned to The Hague where he remained from 28 September to 26 December, 1525. On the latter date he agreed to recant his "false" ideas and did the required penance.[69]

Very soon, however, on 19 February, 1526 authorities returned to Monnikendam to arrest Ottens again, who, although he had recanted his Lutheran "heresy" and had been released, was now accused of contracting a marriage in Monnikendam. He was also accused of teaching heresy concerning the sacrament of the Eucharist and the Mass. Before the authorities got there, however, he had taken his wife and fled to Emden, outside the authority of the Emperor and the inquisition.[70] To guarantee that he would remain outside the empire, he was threatened with immediate imprisonment and deportation to prison in The Hague if he returned.[71] We know nothing further concerning Ottens. In an act of retaliation, the inquisitors turned their attention instead to the sheriff who had performed the wedding and to Yde Pouwels, the mother of the bride, because she had been a party to the illegal marriage of her daughter to a priest. She was sentenced to stand on a scaffold for one hour holding a placard indicating that she had allowed a priest to marry her daughter and sleep in her house. Furthermore, she had to walk in the procession on the next two Sundays with her head uncovered, carrying a burning candle in penance.[72]

At about the same time at Hoorn, four persons were sentenced because of heretical opinions. It was said that an evil spirit compelled them to blasphemy and ostentatiously speaking out against Almighty God and the Sacrament of the Eucharist. As punishment they were to walk in the morning procession bareheaded and barefooted, following the Holy Sacrament. They were to carry burning candles or a torch. Their clothing had to exhibit a symbol of the chalice and the host. Furthermore, they were to make an offering before the Holy Sacrament in the parish church.[73]

A court report in The Hague, listing expenses for various investigations of unrest or heresy, included the names of 22 persons from Monnikendam.[74] In October 1526 three suspected priests from Monnikendam, Gerbrant Paul, Jan Jacobs and a third, unnamed, were arrested and taken to The Hague because of suspicious teachings concerning the sacrament of the Eucharist.[75] Other heretical problems were also discovered at Monnikendam: some refrained from going to Mass and did not go to confession.[76] In 1527 Dieuwer, wife of Jan van Matten of Monnikendam, was charged with speaking erroneously and scandalizing the Eucharist and the Confession. She was required to recant and pay a fine.[77]

One of the best-known woman heretics was from the Waterland area, Wendelmoet Claesdochter (i.e. daughter of Claes). On 18 May, 1527 a financial account was submitted to the Court of Holland for expenses incurred while the officials made yet another trip to Monnikendam the previous month. The investigators were charged with bringing a certain widow, "Wendelmoet" or Weynken, from the jail in her home town to The Hague. How long she was in jail in Monnikendam and the details of her arrest there are not known. The total trip to investigate and return took sixteen days.[78] In May she arrived with her captors in The Hague, to remain until June 10.[79] Further details in the case were contained in a report by Arnold Sandelin, the government Secretary in The Hague, who had summarized all these events of the past few years. On 12 May, 1527, Sandelin stated that when Wendelmoet was examined in prison she was found to be in error concerning the sacraments. She was opposed, furthermore, to "all rites instituted by humans, and generally all outward forms that the holy church has practiced and has required." She assumed "much authority from the holy scripture," and she seemed prepared to die for her faith.[80]

Although the officials had little hope that they could change her mind, they made one last try. They sent Roelof of Monnikendam, vice-curate of Gouda, and a blood relative [maech] of the prisoner, to see if he could convince her of her errors.[81] Evidently, he was no more successful, despite his learning and family ties, for the court decided to move her after being imprisoned at The Hague from 2 May to 10 June, 1527.[82]

Having been thus far unsuccessful in changing her opinions, they took her to a castle at Woerden, near Utrecht, and kept her there with the false hope that she might change her mind and confess her errors. Her diet at Woerden was be bread and water for two months. If she still persisted, the Dean of Naaldewijk was to assume authority to proceed with further punishment as he saw fit. The authorization letter was signed by the Emperor's aunt, Margaret, who along with the Emperor, as she said, had complete confidence in the decision the inquisitor would make.[83] A few weeks later, an inquiry about her was addressed to the Lord of the castle at Woerden, asking if there had been any change. The reply confirmed that she persisted in her heresy. She had been in this castle "157 days" from 10 June to early November.[84]

Finally, the inquisitors decided that they must take more drastic steps. They returned her from Woerden to the prison in The Hague arriving 15 November, 1527.[85] On 18 November they began to question her only to find she still clung to "all errors." A summary of many of her ideas is printed in both German and Dutch.[86] Even when the sentence was about to be pronounced monks, priests and nuns could not dissuade her from her faith. She was sentenced by the Dean of Naaldewijk to be burned in The Hague "such that no memory of her will remain."[87] Her case was turned over to the executioners and all of her property was declared confiscated. A simple note summarized the final details: "On the 20th of November, 1527, Wendelmoet, daughter of Jacob of Monnikendam, was burned to ashes because she said that Christ did not descend into the Host; and it was Wednesday."[88]

Memory of her, however, was not erased. Within a few months the inquisitors had another problem to investigate. They sent inspectors to the "printers and librarians of the land" to inquire how there could have been printed a "certain scandalous document pertaining to the woman recently burned in The Hague because of her evil and erroneous beliefs." They were asked to check all witnesses as well as all sources of rumors.[89] All inquiries were sent especially to The Hague, Leiden and Delft. Perhaps the publication referred to was the summary of the trial of the heretic as printed the previous year. There is no original Dutch version of this work extant, but three German copies, dating from shortly after the recorded happenings, are available.[90] It was a copy of this document from the Royal Library at Munich which was used for the edition in *CDI*.[91] [A translation of the German record of this trial is in Appendix VII].

One further mention of continuing heresy in Monnikendam was recorded in September 1528 when a man from the same town was apprehended in Delfshaven (Rotterdam). He had said openly that he would have been willing to die with the widow Wendelmoet. They took this to mean that he was a guilty of "other Lutheran errors" as well. The final disposition of this case is unknown.[92]

Dissent concerning the Sacraments, especially The Sacrament of the Eucharist

The Roman Catholic teaching that the Sacraments are special means of Grace and have special benefit for the believer often became the center of controversies. When compared with the number of criticisms against the Sacraments of penance, the oil of unction and the Sacrament of the Eucharist, it is surprising that the documents collected by Fredericq do not reflect a comparable number of criticisms of baptism. The Roman Catholic teaching about this sacrament was that baptized individuals, especially infants and young children, were free of original sin and need not fear eternal damnation. As such, baptism was an institutional requirement, administered and controlled by the Church hierarchy, often tainted by the payment of money. It is surprising that the strong emphasis on baptism emphasizing human responsibility which we noted in the *Summa* (Chapter 9) seems not to have been known in the early popular reactions in The Netherlands. This is especially noteworthy because within the next decade the Anabaptist movement made their interpretation of baptism of believers much more central in their faith. They insisted on adult baptism and on human responsibility for one's faith and actions; this, in turn, led them to modify all other sacraments and their whole church order, including their emphasis on a disciplined life.

In the decade of the 1520s, however, criticism of the doctrine of the Eucharist seemed to attract considerable attention. The Roman Catholic teaching that the elements of the Sacrament of the Eucharist had been transubstantiated into the actual body and blood of Jesus was challenged. Some stated that there was nothing special about the bread or wine. The critics seemed to suggest that it was not valuable, maybe even misleading, to emphasize a physical element so strongly instead of its spiritual meaning. The processions of the Host were common in all towns and cities, so the purported nature of the elements was obvious to believer and skeptic alike. Heretics who denied the power of this sacrament of the Eucharist were often required to march in those regular processions to express their penance toward the Sacrament as well as the Virgin Mary.

From Worms the papal legate, Girolamo (Jerome) Aleander, wrote a letter to the Pope on 28 February, 1521, in which he reported that many heretics had been discovered and apprehended in many parts of The Netherlands. Some of those mentioned, specifically in Artois and l'Isola [Rijsel, now Lille, France], supposedly were influenced by the thought of Wyclif and Berengar of Tours. They said that the true body of Christ was not in the sacrament of the altar, but was only present as a sign [*sed tantum in signum fieri*].[93] It was in this same year that Cornelis Hoen was writing about the Eucharist. It is difficult, however, to imagine that this specific incident was directly connected with the writing of Hoen, since these locations are quite some distance away in the extreme south part of Netherlands near the French border [indeed, they are now located in northern France]. Also there is no indication that Hoen's work was known in The

Netherlands at this time. The similarity probably stems from a widespread and common understanding of Wyclif's teachings.

Many ecclesial investigations concerned individuals who had expressed disrespect, even disbelief, in the Sacrament of the Eucharist. Probably some of them were not sufficiently informed about the subtleties of this doctrine, and reacted mainly against the external appearances. For example, in January 1526 in Leiden six men and two women were charged with blasphemy.[94] They stated that they did not believe that the sacraments had any power to work on behalf of individual persons.

On 23 June, 1526, another interesting exchange concerning the Eucharist took place between the authorities in Leiden and a certain slate roofer [*leydekker*] named Jan Cornelisz.[95] The questioners thought he held horrible [*afgryselicke=afgrijselijk*] opinions concerning the Sacrament, contrary to the church and apostolic beliefs. It was reported that on the day after Easter he and some others were working in a monastery at Warmonde [just north of Leiden]. One of his companions mentioned a conversation he had recently heard in Germany. Someone there had taken the chalice and the ciborium, thrown the wine and the bread on the floor, and walked on them. Jan Cornelisz said that this was no concern, for the bread was only bread, nothing more. One companion argued, however, that the bread was both God and Man together. Cornelisz said that it was no more than bread, and he took a piece and said that whether he ate this piece or that, it did not matter. His companions wondered, "How can that idea be true?" Cornelisz said

> St. Matthew says it in Chapter 24: (23-26), Watch out for false prophets who shall say to you 'behold Christ is there' but in fact it is not so. If you should be told that Christ is in the wilderness, or in an inner room, do not believe it.

Furthermore, it is reported in Acts 17: (22-25) where Paul spoke to the Athenians and proclaimed that your "unknown God" is really the Lord of heavens and earth. "God lives not in temples which are made with hands, nor is God served by human hands," concluded Cornelisz.

After spending fourteen days investigating the charges, the authorities saw that Cornelisz had a courageous spirit [*oetmoedicheyt*]. In the meantime he stated that he was ready for repentance, and would remain penitent. The sentence for his blasphemy was that he should stand on a scaffold barefoot and bareheaded. Then carrying a burning candle he must go to St. Peter Church, presumably in Leiden, pray before the holy sacrament and offer his candle. He should do the same at O.L.V. [*Onze Lieve Vrouw*=our beloved lady=St Mary's] Church in Antwerp. Thereafter he had to wear a cross on his clothing for a year as an example for others, warning them not to be blasphemous. Finally, he received absolution, and nothing more is known about him.

The Carthusian cloister at s'Hertogenbosh in 1527 had some of the works of Oecolampadius of Basel.[96] Summarizing his views, the monks reflected ideas of this Swiss leader when they concluded: *"in Eucharistia non est Christum nisi in signa"* [In the Eucharist Christ is present only as a sign]. This is interesting to note since Oecolampadius did not reform Basel until 1529. How widespread his views were known before that date is unclear.

In Delft, in 1528, a woman was accused of erroneous belief concerning the Eucharist.[97] The woman, Dieuwer Reyersdochter, was asked: "Do you believe that under the host in the Mass or in the church there is the body of God?" She answered: "No, it is not there." She continued to "speak erroneously and to blaspheme the Holy Sacrament and other sacraments of the Holy Church, of Mary the Mother of God and of the Saints." Furthermore, she had not observed holy days and fasting days. She even received into her house renegade monks and dissolute persons. She was sentenced to stand on a scaffold in Delft as an example to all, have her tongue bored, pay a fine, and be banned for three years. Should she return in less time, part of her tongue would be cut off. Hildebrand of Zwolle was condemned for blasphemy in 1528.[98] She said that in the Holy Sacrament there was only common bread. She was sentenced to stand on the scaffold a half hour, her tongue bored, and be banned from the city the remainder of her life. Should she return, the sentence would be death. Also in Delft, Woolfert the locksmith [*slootemaker*] was accused of having spoken heretical words against the sacrament.[99] He said that "it must be a foolish God [*het mach wel een sot=zot God wesen*] which could be held between the hands of your priest." After he had been in prison for 66 days (12 July-25 September, 1528) he was sentenced to have his tongue bored, and he had to pay the required fine.

Infractions of other aspects of the Roman Catholic faith

Required respect for the Virgin Mary as a mediator in the faith brought reactions. For example, in September 1526, in Namen/Namur, Jehan Adam was arrested because he spoke humiliating and scornful words against the Virgin Mary and the Saints.[100] He was branded [*fer chaud*] on the right side of his face, required to stand on a scaffold, and then imprisoned in the city for one year. The next year in Den Briel/Brielle a knife-maker, Cornelis Maertsze, had accused a woman of blasphemy when she said "Mary the Mother of God was no better than any other woman."[101] This was blasphemy, although may have been a commonly held opinion. In the trial Cornelis could produce no proof of his accusation, however, so instead, the accuser was charged and had to carry a torch in the procession and ask forgiveness from the city officials. He may have made his false accusation because he hoped to profit from a share of the fine.

Food laws were another source of contention. In Amsterdam in April 1528 Albert Dircx of Gelderland openly ate flesh during a time of fasting—against the ordinances of the church.[102] He was condemned to scourging and had to make a pilgrimage to Naples. He could not return without a certificate stating he had completed this trip. What the significance of Naples was in this situation is not known. The same year in The Hague a roasted chicken was found at the home of Klaas Coebel. Obviously he was not observing the fast.[103] We have no record of his punishment. We remember that Cornelis Grapheus was also charged with breaking the laws of fasting (See Chapter 6).

Criticisms of the monastic life evoked various reactions. The criticisms or the problems with the monasteries were among the growing concerns in the society which Erasmus had earlier reported. In 1526 the court in Mechelen/Malines issued warnings against those who left their cloisters to live secular lives.[104] The government thought this posed a great danger for the faith, so the Emperor directed that no one should give accommodation to these renegade persons. Whoever knew of any of these hiding places must divulge their knowledge or face consequences. In s'Hertogenbosch in 1526 Otto Bollix Janssoen was charged with helping his daughter, Margrieten, escape from the convent.[105] He denied that he had anything to do with her escape, and nor had he provided her with any heretical books. Furthermore, he did not know where she was. In 1528, Brother Mathias Kempis fled from the Doesburg monastery.[106] Shortly thereafter, he asked forgiveness, but the authorities judged that he was still infected with new doctrines. They noted that he appeared stupid [insipientia] and even unstable [inconstantia]. He did not receive forgiveness and was not allowed to return to the monastery. In Waal and Burg op Tessel (two neighboring villages on the island of Texel) a brewmaster was asked to explain why he kept a renegade monk, Willem Bruynessesz, in his employ as a brewery assistant, since the Emperor's edicts had forbade anyone to befriend or give lodging to such a person.[107] The fugitive had lived at the brewery for two years and had recently married. Before that he had left his monastery in Amsterdam, but was actually originally from Alkmaar. The brewmaster used the defense that his son was really the manager of the brewery, and that since their questionable employee was not from the local area, neither of them knew he was a fugitive, especially since he had discarded his monastic garb.

Other heretical opinions

Two other heresetical groups were reported in this period, spiritualist in nature and certainly not strictly Lutheran, although perhaps encouraged by the religious unrest which was in the region. They were, **first**, the "Loists," and, **second**, the followers of David Joris, whose influence would soon spread to other parts of Europe. In Antwerp in 1526, there are reports of a group of ten "Loists" from the extreme Spiritualist branch of the Radical Reformation.[108] They were called the "Loists" from the name from their founder, Eligius (Loy) Pruystinck, a slate roofer [schaliedekker]. They spiritualized the sacraments so thoroughly that they considered the physical form of no value.[109] As a consequence, they denied any

physical use of baptism, denied the sacrament of the Eucharist, and said that
Christ is not God. They were found guilty of heresy, were required to stand in
public on a scaffold, and their books burned. Since in the minds of the government authorities there was no clear distinction between the "Loists" and the Lutherans some books from both groups were probably burned. Sensing the problems of being associated with these ideas, Luther wrote to Spalatin in 1525[110]
that they taught "*Spiritum Sanctum nihil aliud esse quam ingenium et rationem
naturalem*" [The Holy Spirit is nothing other than one's natural endowment and
human reason]. Luther then wrote a long letter to the Christians in Antwerp[111]
alerting the believers of this dangerous sect. He thought their appearance was the
work of the devil. The teachings of the Loists persisted for twenty years until
Loy Pruystinck was finally executed by burning in 1544. Three other leaders
were beheaded the next year. This effectively ended the movement.[112]

David Joris, a glassmaker [*glaesemaker*], or perhaps glass painter in Delft,
was convicted of heresy on 30 July, 1528.[113] He was critical of the use of pictures and statues in churches. Specifically during a procession for Ascension
Day, he demeaned the value of statues, especially that of *Onze Lieve Vrouw*
[*O.L.V.* = Our Beloved Lady]. He taught that they were misleading the people
and was quoted as saying

> these false hypocrites, monks and papists have deluded us when they said they
> [statues and pictures] were the books for the unlearned. The spirit of the Lord
> says, however, that they are snares that will cause the downfall of the illiterate
> and that they try to seduce people's souls.[114]

The more he talked the more he seemed to deny the basic teachings of the
church. He denied that the body and blood of Christ was under the form of the
consecrated elements. He referred to the Pope as Anti-Christ and added that the
prohibition against allowing simple people to read the scriptures, even though
enforced by imperial edicts, was opposed to the truth.

He was required to go before the procession in linen clothing with a burning
candle and his scandalous pamphlets tied to his body and bound to his neck. He
was required to remain six weeks in his home and then be confined to the city
until the end of the year. Some, however, thought this was too lenient so stronger
punishments were demanded. Subsequently, he was flogged, his tongue was
bored, his property was confiscated, and he was banned for three years. This
punishment evidently did not deter him for very long, because he would have a
radical influence continuing for more than twenty-five years both in The Netherlands and beyond.[115]

There were suspicions that some individuals were adherents of Waldensian
thought, although it is not clear what specific ideas they might have espoused. In
1526, for example, a financial report was submitted to authorities outlining an
inquisitors' trip to investigate Hanskin Luucx at Veurne/Furnes [in the far west-

ern section of Flanders] who was accused of being a follower of Waldensian ideas.[116] No further details were given. The charges are not clear in cases where two women prisoners in southern part of The Netherlands (Fleurus/Fleru, now southern Belgium) were accused of being Waldensian and engaging in withcraft. Marye de Beauvolz was held in prison for 25 days. Pierette Pourreau had been accused two years earlier, but because of lack of evidence she was released. She was arrested again and held in prison for 18 more days. Both of these women were charged with of "false" Waldensian ideas and were ultimately condemned to be burned.[117] In 1527 it was also reported that persons in many other places were accused of being Waldensian or Lutherans.[118] They were severely punished or burned. No details were given, but these persons were charged in Brabant, Henegouwen/Hainault, Namen/Namur, Dornik/Tournai, and Antwerp.

Common punishments: burning, boring the tongue, drowning

Undoubtedly the most well-known burning in the Northern Netherlands was that of Jan de Bakker (Pistorius). As a priest he had denied many aspects of the Roman Catholic faith, but more serious was the charge that he had taken a wife and would not denounce her, nor call her his "concubine." His execution may reflect the frustration of the authorities. The inquisitors gradually realized such punishments as forced confession, walking in a public procession with a burning candle for penance, paying a fine, and being banished from the area were not sufficient deterrents. Increasingly during the decade more severe measures were adopted. During the year 1522 Geertruyt Cuypers was tortured and burned in Utrecht because she was thought to be a heretic.[119] On 22 January, 1523, at Brugge/Bruges, Moddert de Brievere was accused of blaspshemy. He was flogged and a hole bored in his tongue.[120] In the town of Heusden (north of s'Hertogenbosch), on 25 July, 1524, Jacob Jansz de Coster was beheaded.[121] The cost was carefully documented, but the charges leading to the execution were not indicated. In a letter dated 22 February, 1525, Luther wrote to Johannes Lang that Bernhard, a Carmelite, was burned as a martyr for Christ in Mechelen/Malines.[122] On 29 July, 1525, in Antwerp, an Augustinian monk named Nicholaas was caught preaching while standing in a boat. He was clothed not in his monastic garb but in "working clothes" of a layman. He was bound, stuffed into a sack, and thrown into the river.[123] It was reported that this caused quite a stir among the people watching the proceedings! In Mechelen/Malines in 1526 Philip Goessens was charged with blasphemy of God's holy name, and accused of "detestable sermons." He was flogged, a hole bored in his tongue and part of the tongue cut off. [124]

In Delft on 1 July, 1528, Jan Dircsz of Amsterdam was charged with derogatory comments about the Holy Sacrament and possessing certain forbidden writings. He was subjected to exhibition on the scaffold, a hole was bored in his tongue, and he had to pay the required fine. Following this he was subjected to "strong flagellation" which led to bleeding. This punishment was said to be an example to others.[125] Two days later, in Gent/Gans on 15 July, 1528, Joost de Backere was subjected not only to boring his tongue, but having his hair burned off because he spoke erroneously of the Holy Sacrament and held other heretical Lutheran opinions. Another heretic at the same time only had his hair burned. They were required to wear a red cross on their clothing and march in the procession of St. Peters for three Sundays.[126] In Gent/Gans on 17 June, 1528, Jacob van Keymeulen was convicted of heresy.[127] He had often spoken against articles of church belief, despising the Holy Sacrament, the Saints, and Purgatory, and had disregard for the Holy Church in general. He said that in the sacrament of the altar there was no more power than in regular bread; it is not necessary to pray to Our Lady; and the Mass which the priests pronounced over the dead do not profit the deceased but bring profit only to the priest. He had also led others in the city to similar errors. His sentence was carried out on July 25 of the same year. He was ordered to ask forgiveness, walk barefoot and bareheaded in the procession and carrying a torch to the pillory. His hair was burned off. He was branded on his jaw with a cross, and banned from Flanders for 50 years.

On 11 July, 1528, a trial was begun concerning Hendrik, an Augustinian monk originally from Westphalia. He had been imprisoned for twenty-seven months in Kortrijk/Courtrai, where he had been accused of heresy and other complaints "concerning the Catholic and the Christian faith."[128] He was also married. Authorities wanted to spare his life, if he would only declare that his wife was his concubine [*bijzit*=Dutch; *concubine*=French]. This he refused and "insisted on continuing in the heresy of Luther." He was transferred to Dornik/Tournai where the trial was held. Stripped of his Augustinian orders, he was turned over to the secular authorities for punishment. After questioning him they declared that he must be burned and all his goods confiscated. As preparations were proceeding on 13 July, 1528, penance was offered to him, but he refused. The Sacrament of the Eucharist was offered, which he also refused. As the preparations for the execution continued, someone in the crowd ran forward, embraced the prisoner, called him "brother" and declared that he wanted to die with him. The intruder was pulled away and taken to prison until an honorable decision could be made in his case.[129] After Hendrik's execution his ashes were thrown into the Scheldt River.

Even some of the entourage of King Christian of Denmark who was living in exile in The Netherlands were in danger of execution. The Danish king had been deposed in 1523 because of political problems including his interest in reformed ideas. He lived in exile for several years in Flanders, although he was in a difficult position. He was a brother-in-law of Emperor Charles V, having married Charles's sister, Isabella. At the same time he was a nephew of Elector Frederick the Wise, Luther's protector. His reforming sympathies were perhaps nurtured by his relation with Frederick the Wise, but he hesitated to cause conflict with his Roman Catholic host in The Netherlands. Some of his associates, however, were arrested and taken to Vilvoord prison.[130] Four persons were named. The first two were: Hendrik van Zwolle burned as a heretic at Mechelen/Malines on 20 October, 1529; and Hans Michelsen of Malmo (Sweden), the king's banker. Michelsen had published an edition of the New Testament translated by Christiaan Pedersen into Danish. The two others were Hendrik Smit, assistant to Michelsen, and Pieter van Keulen, servant of the king. The decisions concerning the last three cases are not known.

Notes for Chapter 12

1. *CWE*, X, # 1466, from Basel, 21 July, 1524.

2. *Corpus Documentorum Inquisitionorum Pravitatis Neerlandicae*, (5 volumes, Gent: J. Vuylsteke; and The Hague, Martinus Nijhoff, 1889-1902).

3. *CDI*, IV, 268-269.

4. *CDI*, V, 2-5. Also, M. E. Kroonenberg, *Verboden Boeken en opstandige Drukkers in de Hervomingstijd* [hereafter, *Forbidden Books*] Amsterdam: P. N. Van Kampen en Zoon, N.V., 1948), p. 16.

5. *CDI*, V, 5-6. She issued this from The Hague.

6. *CDI*, V, 143-147.

7. *CDI*, V, 190.

8. *CDI*, V, 320-321. Also, Gerard Brandt, *The History of the Reformation and other Ecclesiastical Transactions in and about the Low Countries* (4 vols. London: T. Wood, 1720-1723), Reprint of English Translation, (2 volumes, New York: A. M. S. Press, 1979), p. 57.

9. Kronenberg, *Forbidden Books*, p. 19. Brandt, pp. 57-58.

10. *CDI*, IV, 77, in Gent, 24 June, 1521.

11. *CDI*, IV, 110-113, 10 April, 1522.

12. *CDI*, IV, 113.

13. *CDI*, V, 64, 9 July, 1525.

14. *CDI*, V, 162, a report covering proceedings in Amsterdam, 10-16 December, 1526.

15. *CDI*, V, 155, 30 October, 1526, in Antwerp.

16. *CDI*, V, 267, 13 October, 1527, at Duinkerke.

17. *CDI*, V, 355, 12 August, 1528 at Bruges/Brugge.

18. *CDI*, V, 394, 28 February, 1521.

19. *CDI*, V, 12 August, 1526 at Hoorn.

20. *CDI*, V, 353, 31 July, 1528, recorded at Leiden.

21. Petrus Taborita, *History of Friesland*, as printed in *CDI*, IV, 245-247.

22. *CDI*, IV, 255-256. This report in Amsterdam on 15 February, 1524, included many incidents before that date.

23. *CDI*, IV, 383-384, as reported in Amsterdam, 3 August, 1525.

24. *CDI*, V, 331, the report covered 20-27 March, 1528.

25. *CDI*, IV, 245; this paragraph concerning Friesland is also included in De Hoop Scheffer's *History*, p. 484.

26. *CDI*, V, 164, 22 December, 1526, reported in Leeuwarden.

27. *CDI*, V, 163, 20 December, 1526, also at Leeuwarden.

28. *CDI*, V, 252, 16 July, 1527.

29. *CDI*, IV, 36, October, 1520.

30. *CDI*, V, 89, at Doesburg, 1525.

31. *CDI*, V, 166-167, at Doesburg, 1526.

32. *CDI*, IV, 335, reported from Mechelen, 23 April, 1525.

33. *CDI*, V, 319.

34. *CDI*, V, 14 August, 1527, at Maastricht.

35. *CDI*, V, 304, in 1527.

36. *CDI*, V, 365, reported before 30 September at Dornik/Tournai.

37. *CDI*, V, 375, 28 May, 1528, reported in Dordrecht.

38. *CDI*, V, 9-11. The report includes details from 11 May through 27 September, 1525.

39. *CDI*, V, 153, 19 May, 1526.

40. *CDI*, V, 150, 17 September, 1526.

41. *CDI*, V, 159, Amsterdam, 14 November, 1526.

42. *CDI*, V, 159, 14 November, 1526.

43. *CDI*, V, 303.

44. *CDI*, V, 389. This was part of an extensive listing for the year 1528.

45. *CDI*, V, 328, 28 February, 1528.

46. *CDI*, V, 331, 15 April, 1528.

47. *CDI*, IV, 232, 7 September, 1523 in Antwerp.

48. *CDI*, V, 408-410, 28 July, 1528, in Amsterdam.

49. *CDI*, V, 89, Utrecht, 1525.

50. *CDI*, V, 105-106, 20 January, 1525. I thank Gerrit W. Sheeres of Grand Rapids, Michigan, for suggestion on to how to translate some of the archaic words in these quotations.

51. *CDI*, V, 108, 2 May, 1526.

52. *CDI*, V, 332 4 April, 1528.

53. *CDI*, V, 330, 23 March, 1528.

54. *CDI*, V, 239, 30 November, 1523, Amsterdam.

55. *CDI*, IV, 255-256, before 15 February, 1524.

56. *CDI*, IV, 21 May, 1524, in Amsterdam.

57. *CDI*, IV, 284, 21 July, 1524.

58. *CDI*, V, 329, 18 March, 1528 in Amsterdam.

59. *CDI*, IV, 266-267, 24 March, 1524.

60. *CDI*, IV, 266, 26 March, 1524.

61. *CDI*, V, 149, 13 August, 1526.

62. *CDI*, V, 221-223, 11-12 May, 1527, in Den Briel/Brielle.

63. *CDI*, IV, 264, before 20 March, 1524.

64. *CDI*, V, 84, dated 1525, without either day or month.

65. Approximately two dozen names appear in the records, although no information is available for most of them. *CDI*, V, 1526, 168-173.

66. *Chroniick van Hoorn*, as printed in *CDI*, V, 89.

67. *CDI*, V, 10, September, 1525.

68. *CDI*, V, 21, September, 1525.

69. *CDI*, V, 77, 109, September, 1525.

70. A long collection of letter giving many details concerning this suspected "heretic" is printed in *CDI*, V, 111-114. The reference to his flight to Emden is on p. 111.

71. *Ibid.*, p. 111.

72. *CDI*, V, 126, dated 18 April, 1525.

73. *CDI*, V, 176, 1526.

74. *CDI*, V, 168-171, at The Hague, during the year 1526.

75. *CDI*, V, 156-158, 30 October, 1526, at The Hague.

76. *CDI*, V, 160-161, 15 November, 1526.

77. *CDI*, V, 305, in 1527.

78. *CDI*, V, 229f., dated 18 May, 1527.

79. *CDI*, V, 236.

80. *CDI*, V. 225.

81. *Ibid.*, V, 225.

82. *CDI*, V, 236.

83. *CDI*, V, 232. *"Si qui l'Empereur et nos en avons en vous entiere confidence."*

84. *CDI*, V, 385.

85. *CDI*, V, 274.

86. This summary of many of her ideas is printed in *CDI*, V, 274-279 in German, and in *CDI*, V, 279-283 in Dutch. The German is probably the older, and contains several statements which the later Dutch version omits. All copies of the original Dutch, printed the year after the sentence, are evidently lost. A translation of this German report appears as Appendix VII.

87. *CDI*, V, 272f.

88. *CDI*, V, 273, 285.

89. *CDI*, V, 370f. This letter is not specifically dated but appeared in a collection covering the calendar year, 1528. This "scandalous" document may have been the summary of her trial and the "heretical" ideas expressed therein; *CDI*, V, 274-279.

90. *CDI*, V, 274-279. Dr. J. C. van Slee, in his "Wendelmoet Claesdochter van Monnikendam 20 November, 1527," *Nederlandsch Archief voor Kerkgeschiedenis*, XX (1927). On pages 140 and 141 of his article he has printed an extensive note concerning these sources. Here he indicated a third copy of the document not known to Paul Fredericq when he compiled the five volumes of *CDI* at the end of the century (1889-1902).

91. *CDI*, V, 279.

92. *CDI*, V, 385, dated 9 September, 1528.

93. *CDI*, V, 394. This letter of Aleander summarized heretical ideas in many other locations in The Netherlands: Antwerp, Gent/Gans, Flanders, Utrecht and Holland.

94. *CDI*, V, 98, 14 January, 1526, reported in Leiden.

95. *CDI*, V, 139-141.

96. *CDI*, V, 189-190, 27 March, 1527.

97. *CDI*, V, 347, 30 July, 1528.

98. *CDI*, V, 366, 28 November, 1528.

99. *CDI*, V, 364, 25 September, 1528.

100. *CDI*, V, 149, 15 September, 1526.

101. *CDI*, 227, 14 May, 1527.

102. *CDI*, V, 332, Amsterdam, 2 April, 1528.

103. *CDI*, V, 374, The Hague, 1528.

104. *CDI*, V, 124, Mechelen, 12 April, 1526.

105. *CDI*, V, 131-132, 26 May, 1526, s'Hertogenbosch.

106. *CDI*, V, 335, Doesburg, 6 July, 1528.

107. *CDI*, V, 356-357, 9 September, 1528. The case was discussed in The Hague.

108. *CDI*, V, 116, February, 1526.

109. George H. Williams, *The Radical Reformation* (Kirksville, Missouri: Sixteenth Century Essays and Studies, 1992), p. 535-537.

110. *CDI*, IV, 325, 25 March, 1525, where an excerpt from the letter of Luther is given.

111. *CDI*, IV, 326-330, April, 1525.

112. George H. Williams in his *Radical Reformation (1992)*, included in his footnotes some recent bibliography concerning this movement, pp. 535-537.

113. *CDI*, V, 349-351, 30 July, 1528.

114. *CDI*, V, 349.

115. Gary Waite analyzed Joris's career in the Netherlands to 1544 when he went into exile in Basel. He lived there in relative peace, under an assumed name, until his death in 1556. Three years later (1559) the truth was discovered and his body was exhumed and burned as a heretic. Gary K. Waite, *David Joris and Dutch Anabaptism, 1524-1543* (Waterloo, Ontario: Wilfrid Laurier University Press, 1990).

116. *CDI*, V, 177-178, Veurne/Furnes, 1526.

117. CDI, V, 213-216, records from 1524 to conclusion of punishment, March-April, 1527, Fleurus/Fleru. This location is in the province of Hainaut, north of Charleroi.

118. *CDI*, V, 217, April, 1527.

119. *CDI*, IV, 162, during the year 1522, at Utrecht.

120. *CDI*, IV, 177, 22 January, 1523, at Bruges/Brugge.

121. *CDI*, IV, 285, in The Hague.

122. *CDI*, IV, 312, the execution was at Mechelen/Malines.

123. *CDI*, V, 379, 29 July, 1525 at Antwerp.

124. *CDI*, V, 177, 1526, in Mechelen/Malines.

125. *CDI*, V, 334-335, 1 July, 1528, in Delft.

126. *CDI*, V, 343, 389, 15 July, 1528, in Gent/Gans.

127. *CDI*, V, 333-334, 344-345, 17 June, 1528, in Gent/Gans.

128. *CDI*, V, 337, 338, 340, 342, 11 July, 1528.

129. *CDI*, V, 340, 13 July, 1528.

130. *CDI*, V, 336, 7 July, 1528.

Afterword

As we have clearly noted many times, the earliest dissenting tendencies in The Netherlands did not form a unified approach. There was no recognized leader or school of thought, but out of these divergences we have noted many key ideas which would be developed in later decades. These were summarized in relation to the documents analyzed in each chapter. The religious and theological discussions and controversies of the 1520s, while not resulting in an organized movement, nevertheless provided some of the building blocks for further religious developments in later decades. Having noted this, still we may hazard a tentative summary or conclusion for this turbulent decade as we are reminded of the concept of Cornelis Grapheus [as quoted above in Chapter 6, p. 105]. He suggested that the freedoms brought by Christ have been subverted over the centuries, taking the church back to the slavery in Egypt. As he summarized the problems the solutions to these problems were implied.

> We have regressed from Christ to Moses and backslidden from Moses to Pharaoh. [From the promises of the Savior we have begun to trust in "human fables"—*fabulis hominum*]. For the Gospel we have substituted decrees [of the Pope]; for Christ, a certain Aristotle; for piety, ceremonies; for truth, deception and division; fearing all things we do nothing because of faith or love.[1]

The political situation in The Netherlands differed significantly from that in both Germany and Switzerland where reformers had political protection. For this reason especially, the contemporaneous Reformation movements in the 1520s in those two countries developed in quite different ways from the situation which existed in The Netherlands. The Burgundian territories were more directly controlled by imperial leaders, and the imperial and Papal inquisition—although local governments did exert influence at some points. Independent scholars usually affected their own close followers, and these tended to be the elite and the educated. Dissenting leaders did not have widespread influential in provinces as a whole. Each center was virtually independent of others except for a migrating scholar who carried religious ideas or documents from one place to another, such as the migration of Wouter or Gualterius from Utrecht to Delft/Hague in 1520, or traveling Augustinian monks to and from Germany.

Whether in The Netherlands or other parts of Europe, however, the weight of centuries-long theological and institutional dominance of the Roman Catholic establishment held a reverence for many people even though they might be critical of portions of this tradition. Even more important, this religious reality was coupled with a political system which usually supported the traditional faith and practice while conversely, the political order was often supported by the traditional church. Their mutual interrelationship usually proved formidable so that a forced change, or even a gradual modification proved to be very difficult. Early in the sixteenth century two parallel intellectual movements in Europe insisted on just such changes. To a large extent they supported each other, used some of the same methodologies, and interacted with each other in unique ways in The Netherlands. Although these two intellectual tendencies had different premises and objectives, both looking to new directions and new objectives as contrast to the centuries-long tradition of the Medieval Church.

One movement embodied the reforms advocated by Martin Luther and various Augustinian leaders in The Netherlands who emphasized theological reinterpretations and church reforms. This monastic and intellectual movement came to insist that the Biblical message, as they interpreted it, should be central, and that "man-made" or "worldly" rules should be replaced. They advocated "spiritual" objectives in contrast to very concrete forms and rituals which reflected the past establishment. When there was a conflict they assumed that God was on their side, and that God was a directive force in their efforts toward their objectives. They reverted back to the early Church Fathers, and especially to Augustine, as their authority. The changes these individuals and movements brought to their society often led to more serious rifts than they might have imagined at the outset.

The other movement was symbolized largely by Erasmus and the intellectual strands of the Renaissance and Biblical Humanism of Northern Europe where the emphasis was on philology, new translations, scholarly precision and education methodologies. They came to assume that a church tradition, which was based more on inherited tradition than on their modern scholarship, should be reevaluated if not quietly abandoned. Their concern, however, was gradual change without disrupting various aspects of the fabric of the society.

We lift up four major generalizations from all theological ideas in these documents. 1) Both the Lutheran and the Humanist emphasis on the centrality of Scripture was evident many times. For example, Cornelis Hoen sought correct scriptural interpretation in the discussion of "*est*" versus "*significat*" [Chapter 5]. Pelt's translation of the Gospel of Matthew was an attempt to provide yet another vernacular version, but, in addition, his own commentaries gave a particular dissenting flavor to the text. The concern for lack of use of Scripture is the whole point of the satire *The Lamentation of Peter* [Chapter 4]. The document analyzed in Chapter 9 purported to be a summary of the Scripture and of the faith. 2) The Humanist emphasis on the human person is dealt with in many ways. The strong emphasis on baptism in Chapter 9 implies a more positive view of human nature than the medieval concept, yes, even more positive than that of Luther himself. Here we note a strong emphasis on human responsibility, hence "free" will is presupposed, rather than a "bound" will. 3) Not only was the dissent intellectual or abstract, but there was also a use of the practical embodiment of the "philosophy of Christ." They sought to disseminate a practical and usable personal appropriation of the faith, beginning in schools and monasteries, but gradually spreading to the common people who were gradually taking their place in the growing middle class. This was a population, sosme of whom were privileged to own, read, and understand books and were thus encouraged to begin thinking for themselves. One example of this concern for persons in their existential situation is the pastoral counseling of Gnapheus in his *Troost ende Spiegel* [Chapter 11]. The main thrust in Chapter 5 concerning the Eucharist points to a more inner appropriation of the faith in contrast to an abstract or "official" understanding. 4) There was a yearning for "freedom" from what they considered Roman Catholic "tyranny," and the people as well as the scholars sought relief from compulsion concerning rituals and practices of the Church which they were beginning to question. They sought freedom especially from clerical controls and ecclesiastical demands which in turn might lead to a more meaningful and "spiritual" understanding of the faith. Some priests ignored the church's ban on clerical marriage and suffered the consequences. Perhaps this growing tendency toward independence and self-determination in the faith could also be seen as parallel with their aspirations for their own political developments.

The majority of the population, although they were not completely conversant with the concerns of either of the scholarly groups, nevertheless sensed a need for some re-working of the system. The sources for many of these grievances often extended prior to the beginning of the sixteenth century, and often the Lutheran and the Humanist influences served as a catalyst for these grievances as much as their source. Some people reacted to the need for changes in rather overt ways. The Roman Catholic establishment was symbolized in the minds of many people by the Pope and the hierarchy which placed demanding requirements on the believers. This included certain aspects of belief such as the presence of God in the Eucharist, abstinence of food at certain seasons, required confession, special reverence for saints and the Virgin Mary, requirements of monastic vows and a celibate clergy. The reaction to the Roman Catholic establishment took two forms. First, in so far as one recognized these aspects of the faith as valuable these requirements were accepted as helpful in directing the devotional life. On the contrary, a second group thought the church represented unwelcome social control or irrelevant strictures. This was the case in so far as they sensed that these rituals and beliefs were coercive, were meant to enrich the priests or the church through extra fees or taxes, or otherwise were intrusive in one's family life or community activities. They then saw the Church as more insistent on worldly motives than on spiritual purposes.

In the case of the common people it is easy to understand their rejection of the dogmas, their tendency toward non-conformity, their civil disobedience with respect to the Church's requirements, or even anti-clericalism and their anti-intellectual rejection of certain scholastic scholarship. What is more difficult for us to understand, however, is the willingness of those in all these categories who were ready to suffer many severe hardships, punishments, torture and even imminent execution for their faith. Undoubtedly while these attitudes and these actions had little immediate effect in weakening the Church's authority in this decade, it probably went a long way to strengthen the various communities for even stronger opposition they would meet in the two or three decades which lay immediately ahead.

The religious and theological discussions and controversies of the 1520s, while not resulting in any organized movement, nevertheless provided some of the building blocks for further religious developments in The Netherlands. Up until the 1530s the Dissenting movements can generally be considered to have had little success, if we notice they did not result in organized congregations, or associations of like-minded people across geographical areas. Few government officials embraced reforming ideas, and for the most part did not lend their support to reforming principles. Immediately in the coming decades, however, significant developments would take place. In the decade of the 1530s the Anabaptist/Melchiorite/Mennonite developments were forming their organizations, undoubtedly using ideas, and even leaders who were nurtured in the Dissent of the 1520s. During the 1550s, the Calvinist influence in The Netherlands would bring discipline and a differently-structured theological formulation involving in addition, certain new relations with political and governmental authorities. During the last few decades of the sixteenth century the discussions concerning the doctrines of Jacob Arminius proceeded simultaneously with, and then became intertwined in, the wars seeking independence from Spain. These developments later in the century were worthy outcomes not unrelated to the struggles of a decade of the 1520s, which at the time seemed to meet with more defeat than success for the believers.

Note for the Afterword

1. *BRN*, VI, 35-36, in his preface to his edition of Goch's *Libertate*

Appendices

I. Pope Leo X, *Decet Romanum Pontificem* [3 January, 1521]

This papal document is translated from Francisco Gaude, *Bullarum diplomatum et Privilegiorum Sanctorum Romanorum Pontificum* (Augustae Taurinorum: by Seb. Franco et Henrico Dalmazzo, editors, 1860), V, 761-764. Translated by Dr. Michael Woodward, July, 1999.

Condemnation and excommunication of the heretic Martin Luther and his followers.

Leo, bishop, servant of the servants of God, unto everlasting memory.

It is right for the Roman pontiff, from the power given him from heaven, made a dispenser of spiritual and temporal penalties for the diversity of merits, to suppress the heinous efforts of the perverse, whom a depraved intention of harmful will has taken captive to such an extent that they, having laid aside the fear of God, and having neglected and despised canonical sanctions and apostolic commands, are not afraid to devise new and false dogmas and to introduce nefarious schism into the Church of God, or to offer support, assist, and adhere to these schismatics who are trying to rend the seamless tunic of our Redeemer and the unity of the orthodox faith. Lest the bark of Peter seem to navigate without a pilot and oarsman, it is right for the pontiff to rise up more severely against these men and their followers and so to provide for an intensification of penalties and at the same time an opportune remedy. In order that these despisers, who are given over to a depraved understanding, as well as those who cling to them, may not deceive the simple crowd by their false inventions and cunning tricks, to drag them along with themselves into their error and ruin, and to contaminate them as though with a contagious disease, and for the greater shame of those condemned, it is right for the pontiff to show publicly to all the Christian faithful and declare openly how these fearful censures and penalties exist for this end, that those who have been so declared and published, finally shamed and prodded to return to their own heart, might in obedience completely withdraw themselves from the excommunicated and anathematized, that they might avoid divine punishment and not be made partakers of their damnation.

1. Rightly at other times, when certain worshipers of a false faith, seeking the glory of the world, etc. [The remainder of this section is omitted because the entire bull *Exsurge Domine* is repeated here. It is found under *Ibid.*, number 44, pp. 748ff].

2. As we have learned, after the affixing and publication of our letter, after the elapse of such time or times set by us in the letter (which time has and is elapsed, as we declare and solemnly affirm here to the Christian faithful), some of those who had followed the errors of this Martin, being aware of our letter, warning, and commands, hav-

ing returned to their heart in a spirit of wiser counsel, confessing their errors and abjuring
the heresy in our presence, and turning back to the true catholic faith, obtained the grace
of absolution according to the faculty conferred from above on our nuncios; and the writings and words of Martin in some cities and locations of Germany, according to our
commands, were publicly burned. Yet Martin himself (which we relate not without grave
trouble of spirit and disturbance of our mind), given over to a reprobate understanding,
not only neglected to revoke his errors within the allotted time and to make us the more
sure of his revocation, or to come to us, but, as a rock of scandal, was not afraid to write
and preach worse things than before against us and this holy see and the catholic faith,
and to induce others to do the same. For this reason, just as he has already been declared
a heretic, so too others, also not of slight authority and dignity, not mindful of their own
salvation, publicly and notoriously following the pernicious and heretical sect of Martin,
openly and publicly furnishing aid, counsel and support, encouraging Martin in their own
disobedience and defiance, and others impeding the publication of our mentioned letter,
have damnably incurred the contents of our letter and should rightly be considered heretics to be avoided by all the Christian faithful, according to the Apostle's words: Avoid a
heretical man after a first and a second correction, knowing that such a one is corrupted
and is doing wrong, since he is condemned by his own judgment.

  3. Therefore they should be joined with Martin and the other excommunicated,
anathematized, and accursed heretics; and just as they continue stubbornly in the wrong-
doing of Martin and so share in his penalties and name, they should bear in themselves
the name of Luther and the due penalties, when such clear and public admonitions have
been made and continue in effect, so that they need no proof or warning or summons, as
we decree and declare will be so. We thus decree that excommunication and anathema,
eternal malediction and interdict, have damnably come upon Martin and the others who
continue obstinately in his perverse and condemned effort. This also applies to those
who, with military assistance, defend, guard, and do not fear to sustain them with their
own resources or in some other way, and have presumed and presume to offer and supply
aid, counsel, or support in any way. All of their names and surnames and titles, even if
they shine with lofty and grand dignity, we here determine to be held as expressed, even
if they are expressed by name; and in the publication of them, to be carried out with the
force of this document, they can be expressed by name. They and their descendants also
incur the loss of dignities, honors, goods and the disqualification to the same, as well as
the confiscation of goods and the other judgments, censures, and penalties for the crime
of wounded majesty that are contained in the said letter and inflicted on heretics in the
canons.

  4. We also declare by apostolic authority in the course of this letter that all cities,
lands, castles, towns and villages in which they lived at the time, and which turned aside
to them, and the places therein, including the cathedrals, metropolitan churches, monasteries, and other religious and holy sites, both exempt and non-exempt, have been placed
under ecclesiastical interdict. Thus, while it lasts, no masses or other divine services may
be celebrated there, under any pretext of apostolic permission, except in cases permitted
by law, and then not other than with their doors closed to the excommunicated and interdicted. We order that these places be proclaimed and publicized everywhere as excommunicated, anathematized, cursed, interdicted, deprived and disqualified, and we command that they be very strictly avoided by all the Christian faithful.

5. In order that all might come to know of the great contempt for God and their
Church shown in the recklessness of obstinate temerity of Martin, his followers, and of
other disobedient ones, lest the sick sheep infect the flock and the healthy part be drawn
into infection, we entrust to all prelates to denounce publicly this Martin and the other
excommunicated, anathematized, cursed and declared heretics, hardened, interdicted, deprived and disqualified and named in the execution of the present letter. They should
cause and order them to be denounced by others and to be strictly avoided by all the
Christian faithful. This is entrusted to each and every patriarch, archbishop, bishop, to the
prelates of patriarchal, metropolitan, cathedral, and collegiate churches, to the chapters
and ecclesiastical leaders of all orders, both mendicant and religious, exempt and non-
exempt, wherever they are established, in virtue of holy obedience and under penalty of
the broad sentence of excommunication as far as we ourselves command. This goes into
effect if and after they have been required by the force of the present letter, within three
days, one of which is the first, another the second, and the next the third and final term,
and with canonical warning sent out beforehand. The declaration should be made in their
churches on a Sunday or other feast day (when a greater multitude of people meet in them
for divine services), with the standard of the cross and ringing of bells, with lit candles
that are extinguished and thrown on the ground and trampled, with a triple tossing of
stones, and other ceremonies and similar rites accustomed to be observed. To the greater
consternation of this Martin and the other heretics, adherents, followers, and supporters,
in virtue of holy obedience we command each and every patriarch, archbishop, bishop
and prelate of other churches, since they have been established, as Jerome says, to
squelch schisms, so now, by urgent necessity, in as much as it is part of their duty, to establish themselves as a wall for the Christian people, not being silent like mute dogs unable to bark, but crying out and lifting their voice incessantly, and preaching and causing
to be preached the word of God and the truth of the catholic faith against these heretics
and their condemned articles.

6. We also command that each and every rector of parochial churches and the rec-
tors of all orders, including the mendicant orders, exempt and non-exempt, in the same
way as stated above, in virtue of holy obedience, like those clouds established by the
Lord to sow spiritual rain on the people of God, should not fear to preach publicly, as is
also part of their duty, against these condemned articles. It is written that perfect love
casts out all fear; therefore, may you show yourselves zealous and diligent in word and
deed, taking up with a devoted mind the burden of such a meritorious work for each
member of your flock, so concerned in its execution, that from your labors, supported by
divine grace within us, the hoped for fruits may come. Through our solicitude, which is
owed for payment to those carrying out holy causes, may you not only merit to attain the
palm of glory, but may you also be able rightfully to be commended more richly for your
proven diligence by us and the holy see.

7. Because it would be difficult personally to conduct this letter of declaration and
publication into the presence and unto the very person of Martin and the others that are
declared excommunicate, because of the power of those protecting them, we determine
that the affixing and publication of this letter on the main doors of two cathedrals or metropolitan churches standing in Germany, or of one cathedral and one metropolitan
church, accomplished by one of our nuncios staying there, might thus bind and restrain
them and might demonstrate in all and in every respect that Martin and the others are de-

clared condemned, as if this letter had been presented and made known to them and to each one of them personally.

8. Because it would also be difficult for this letter to be delivered to every location where its publication is necessary, we determine and decree by our authority that it is established everywhere after it has been adopted and secured with the seal of any ecclesiastical prelate or one of our nuncios and signed by the hand of any public notary, as much as it would be established by the original letter, if it were exhibited and shown.

9. With nothing contrary to apostolic constitutions and ordinations, and nothing contrary to all the things that we determined in our previous letter, and in all other letters.

10. It is not lawful, therefore, for any person [hominum] to tear up this page of our constitution, declaration, precept, mandate, assignation, will, and decree, or to oppose it by a rash deed. If, however, anyone presumes to attempt this, he/she should know that he will incur the indignation of almighty God and of his apostles, blessed Peter and Paul.

Given at Rome at Saint Peter's, in the 1,521st year of the Lord's incarnation, on the third day of January, in the eighth year of our pontificate.

II.   Nine articles revoked by Herman Gerrits [or Gherardi], after 15 January, 1522.

This was in St. Caecilia Church, Utrecht. These nine Propositions are translated from the Latin, printed in *CDI*, IV, 86-87.

1. It is possible for a person [homo] by faith without works to be saved.
2. Merits of the saints are of no value [nulla].
3. Whoever prays or indeed works toward acquiring indulgences, blasphemes God.
4. Fasting is not to be observed for merit or satisfaction of sins, but only for restraining sensualities; and at any time that is subject to reason, then all the more we are not obligated to fast.
5. To wear a coarse garment is not good or to be praised, but to be censured; it is not commanded by God, but invented by hypocrites and is without reason or utility for human purposes.
6. All expenditures which do not go to the advantage of the poor are useless; and on that account ruin the comeliness and the respected image of the churches.
7. Whoever serves God by exertion, and in hope of retribution wastes the effort [perdit operam].
8. No Christian person [homo] has power to obligate himself/herself [seipsum] to a certain form of living outside the mandates of God, but he/she ought to remain free.
9. No one has power to impart his/her [sua] good merits or spiritual blessings [bona] to another.

III.   Articles which Jacob Proost (Propst, or Praepositus) recanted [on 9 February, 1522].

Translated from the articles, printed in *CDI*, IV, 90-92.

1. The threes sacraments of the church, namely, baptism, penitence and Eucharist, are divinely instituted expressly in the Holy Scripture. The remaining four, however, [are instituted] by humans [*humanus*] through the church.
2. One should not put trust [*confidendum*] in indulgences.
3. The pope is not able to give indulgences.
4. Indulgences are not efficacious.
5. It is not possible to apply merits of the saints to others.
6. All works of the saints are sins and lead one to overlook and draw back from mercy [of God].
7. There is no treasury of the church except for the merits of Christ, which are applied only by Christ himself to each according to his or her own [*suam*] faith.
8. Luther, along with his doctrines, is not legitimately condemned by the apostolic see.
9. An act of free will of one's own interior good is not an effective cause, but only a receptive cause, so that one might hold himself/herself [*se*] passive toward them.
10. Every work of free will, however much it is good, is sin, leading one to overlook and draw back from the mercy of God
11. Whatever motivates a person [*homo*], before justifying grace, is sin.
12. Eating certain foods and abstinence from certain foods leads to irrational fasting time and [is] contrary to sacred scriptures.
13. Christians are free from this type of observance of fasting.
14. Neither does this prepare one for observance of the laws of God.
15. It is doubtful whether a human [*homo*], himself/herself [*se*] is able to undertake a vow with respect to the above-mentioned fasting.
16. The pope or the church does want nor is it able to obligate their [*suos*] subjects with a penalty of mortal sin, in the sense that a person [*homo*] transgressing a precept of a superior person [*hominis*] does not sin mortally.
17. It is understood that superiors do not wish to obligate their subjects under penalty of mortal sin.
18. The subject himself/herself [*sui*] transgressing a precept of a superior because of supreme ignorance, or of passion, apart from scandal, does not sin.
19. The little document *Omnis utriusque sextus* irrationally prescribes that one should confess once in a year. [This was the directive of the IV Lateran Council (1215) where the requirement for yearly confession was established].
20. The pope is not head of the church by divine law.
21. Peter, by human law alone, was made first or supreme among the apostles, and the same is to be agreed to [*censendum*] concerning each successor of Peter.
22. In every gathering [*foro*] whether inwardly or outwardly, all bishops are equal.
23. A council properly constituted is rightly able to decide what is expressly contained in the Sacred Scriptures.
24. Concupiscence [or lust], which is relinquished in baptism, is [still] properly called sin against this law of God: 'do not covet' [*non concupisces*].
25. Flesh, tainted with concupiscence, accompanies every work of free will so that whatever human work is done, is sinful.
26. The same is the opinion concerning the martyrdom of Peter and of works of the other saints.
27. All lay people are priests [*sacerdotes*].

28. The one who remains in mortal sin does not remain [*non manet, i.e.*, is not worthy of] baptism, the priesthood, the episcopate or the papacy.
29. Displeasure concerning admission of sin is not the way to justifying grace, but on the contrary, grace is the way to that displeasure.
30. Sorrow for one sin, without sorrow for all sins, is [still] sin.

Therefore, I revoke, I disapprove, I condemn all and every single article stated above.

IV.   The 18 propositions which Grapheus was asked to renounce and condemn [on 23 April, 1522].

They were printed in the Latin by Gerdes in *Scrinium Antiquarium* (Groningen, 1756), Section VI, Part I. Translated here in their entirety from the Latin original, printed in *CDI*, IV, 105f.

1. Christians have been reduced to slavery through [practices such as] fasting as presently observed in the Church, and through other rites of ecclesiastics such as the teaching concerning confession once per year, and the vows of the religious. No observances such as fasting, distinctions among foods, confession once per year, nor other institutions of the church which are not explicitly contained in the scriptures, nor vows of the religious, are obligatory for Christian men upon pain of mortal sin.
2. We have been reduced from liberty to miserable slavery, for the last 800 years and more, namely from the time of Boniface III [607] who first assumed for himself the name 'supreme pontiff' from Phokas [602-610] the Emperor. Because of the usurpation of this name his followers and successors have assumed for themselves the authority to make laws.
3. No Pope has power to impose any law on persons [*hominibus*], especially not Christian individuals, which obligates them under some penalty of mortal sin. It is doubtful whether Peter, the apostle, possessed any authority superior to any of the other apostles, at least this [proof] does not exist in scripture.
4. The supreme pontiff is set up as an idol for us.
5. All the laity are priests, just as those who are called consecrated priests; also all laity (excepting of course women and children) have the right to consecrate the venerable sacrament, although they would sin if they have not been given permission to consecrate.
6. The mode of prayer, which ecclesiastics observe in reading the canonical hours, in singing and other rites as rosaries, frequent prayers, and similar things, is superstitious and Jewish ceremonialism.
7. It is slavery that we are commanded to convene in church for prayer on certain days and hours, for of old worship in all places was within the teachings [of the early church].
8. It is not legal to accept money for administration of the sacraments, conducting burials and preaching the word of God.
9. Preachers of the divine word are to be censured who so often in their speaking introduce the opinions of the scholastic doctors.

10. Just as of old all, with the same discrimination excepting women and children, were allowed to teach and to interpret the sacred literature in public legally; so now it is legal [for all] and not only our own masters, bachelors or licentiates or those appointed by the church for this purpose.
11. The gospel is born anew, and Paul raised to life, because of the writings of Luther and others who adhere to his doctrines and whoever in their own works make known evangelical freedom.
12. None of our own works are meritorious, and we should in no way place confidence in them.
13. When Paul wrote to the Galatians: "If you be circumcised, Christ will be nothing to you," he meant that if you put confidence in your own works, Christ will be nothing to you.
14. The books of Martin Luther and his followers ought to be read because they teach Christ to us, [and] they exclude and reject all subtleties of the scholastic doctors.
15. The book of John of Goch, entitled *de libertate Christiana*, should be read before all the rest of the scholastic doctors, sacred as they may be.
16. The condemnation by the supreme pontiff of Luther, his person and his doctrines was unjust and iniquitous. The same may be said for the edict of the Emperor because the doctrines of Luther ought to be regarded as sound especially those herein mentioned, and ought not be condemned except by means of thorough and reasonable analysis.
17. Sacramental confession is not according to divine law, but is a human institution.
18. Indulgences are not efficacious.

V.   Articles asserted by brother Henry and others, prior to their being burned in Brussels on 1 July, 1523.

Translated from *Bibliotheca Reformatoria Neerlandica*, VIII, 39-43.

1. No one is obligated, because of a mandate of the pope or the emperor, to abstain from reading books of Luther.
2. Those who require one to abstain from reading books of Luther, act more according to the wishes of the one who commands rather than from the Spirit of God

3. Those who decide beforehand to abstain from reading the works of Luther operate against Scriptures which says: "Test all things" (I Thess. 5:21); and "Test the Spirits to see whether they are of God" (I John 4:1).

4. After the authorities spoke sharply [to brother Henry], he said to them that they wished to deceive him by means of enticing words [flattery?].

5. The books of Luther themselves shed more light on the Holy Scriptures than all other doctors he had read.

6. Luther leads one closer to the gospel of Christ than does Augustine or Jerome.

7. It is not possible to prove from Sacred Scripture that the Pope or any other prelate should have more [authority] than the simple ministry of the Word of Christ.

8. Neither the pope nor any other prelate has power to command or prohibit anything which the Holy Scripture does not contain, or what God does not command or prohibit, lest the conscience be injured.

9. The secular authority has power to anticipate and prohibit whatever concerns the bodily aspects, but not in so far as it concerns the conscience.

10. The church has not yet prohibited the books of Luther: and after the explanation of the text: "test everything that is said to be sure it is true, and if it is, then accept it" [I John 4:1]; and "don't believe everything you hear just because someone says it is a message from God: test it first to see if it really is" [I John 4:1]; then he introduced the article saying "The Church should not prohibit books of Luther."

11. Some articles condemned in the bull of Pope Leo X are nevertheless found to be true and by this bull were wrongly condemned. We wait until such time as it [the decree of the pope] is better instructed and an example made concerning it.

12. All persons [homines] are priests [sacerdotes] before God.

13. All persons [homines] have power to remit sins of Christians, whom they know are members of the congregation. [This is related to Matthew 18:15f].

14. Women have power to absolve persons [homines] from sins, which is recognized concerning evangelical absolution. This is contained in that scripture [Matt 18:15-17]: If your brother sins against you. . . .

15. The power of the gospel asserts: "Who are able to remit sin?" It is a power common to the whole community. [see John 20:23].

16. In the mass the body of Christ is not offered by a human person [ab homine] because what is given in remedy or cure [remedium] and commemoration is not offered.

17. He was asked whether the words of the canon of the mass were false: Whatever might be said concerning the canonical words: he said: "The body of Christ is not offered in the mass, but they [words] are taken up [sumitur] only in his [Christ's] memory."

18. He did not know whether the bread remains in the Eucharist after the consecration.[He was shown a text and responded] "If it is contained in the scripture, then I believe it, otherwise I do not believe it."

19. Nothing ought to be believed, under danger of conscience, except what is stated in the Divine Word, or can be derived [illici potest] from the divine word.

20. If a council should define something which is not contained in the Sacred Scripture, one ought to be have suspicion [suspectum haberi] concerning this.

21. He did not want to respond further whether one ought to believe or not believe. He was nevertheless questioned about what he knew concerning M. Luther. He said that through these writings he had come to knowledge of the gospel. He was asked if Martin Luther had the Spirit of God. He did not answer.

22. He said he did not understand, as asked, if he thought there was a difference between priest and lay in consecration of Eucharist and if consecration pertained to the priesthood of Christ and to the priesthood of the New Testament.

23. Unjustly he said, Christ will regard well the least among you.

24. If up to this point they should consider well, all laity had been counted priest just as if they themselves were ordained by them.

25. He did not know if a bishop's consecrating one in priesthood confers a new power of consecrating [the sacramental elements].

26. It is better to gather together the body of Christ which brings together all faithful, than to consecrate in so far as this applies in ministry of this sacrament. He did not know, however, if a bishop should say to a lay person "you are consecrated," whether that lay person without other ordination might consecrate the body of Christ.

27. It is not divine law, neither a precept from God, that all mortal sins should be confessed to a human person [*homini*], because no person [*hominum*] is able to recognize one's own sins, much less to confess [them].

28. Baptism, Eucharist and penance rest on the promises of Christ which arouse faith; for that reason he believes that they confer faith and grace.

29. He rejects four sacraments, that is Confirmation, ordination, matrimony and extreme unction, which do not include word of promise, but which are, rather, observed as ancient rites, and for that reason they do not confer grace, and are able to be abandoned because they are not sacraments.

30. Sacraments confer no more grace than other rites of the church, which the church does not count sacraments because only by the word of God is grace conferred.

31. Priesthood [*sacerdotium*] is not a sacrament, nevertheless the office of ministry is necessary.

32. Extreme unction does not contain the promise.

33. Neither the pope nor bishop nor any other spiritual prelate has power to obligate a person [*hominem*] to those things which are not of divine law such that by transgressing them one should sin mortally-for example: the assumption that one is purified by fasting during lent, by confessing once a year, by celebration of feasts, etc. Except when such omission might cause a brother to stumble, then one [the accused] should refrain from these until he/she may be better instructed.

34. Christ works in persons [*hominibus*] and through persons [*homines*] every good work, such that persons [*homines*] do nothing actively, but passively in so far as Christ works in him/her [*se*] just as with a tool.

35. The Roman Pontiff, successor of Peter, is not the vicar [*i.e.*, substitute for] of Christ over all churches of the world as instituted by Christ in St. Peter, because Christ instituted not a vicar [*vicarium, i.e.* taking the place of] but Christ instituted ministry of the supreme pontiff.

36. All perpetual vows, issued outside the precepts of Christ, so as to be a vow of the religious, are imprudently issued through ignorance of the Christian liberty, and thus are not obligatory.

37. After one puts Christian liberty to the test, his conscience is not to be bound by means of vows.

38. He is not able to separate true, Christian, catholic faith from charity [*charitate*] because charity [*charitas*] is a fruit of faith, and Christian faith without love [*dilectione*] is dead.
39. The sacrament in the mass is advantageous for those who partake.
40. Wherever God dismisses sins of the sinner, then through the death of Christ God even dismisses every penalty [*poenam*]; he believes this piously.
41. He does not know whether there is a purgatory or not.
42. He said: "My lords, you deal unfairly with us, and not according to the gospel."
43. The sacrament of the Eucharist does not contain an oblation on the altar, but on the cross a great oblation was made.
44. After a sinner has confessed and been absolved, he/she is not obligated by divine law to perform any other penalty [satisfaction]; he/she merely does not offend by scandalizing a brother or the churches by any accusation public or private. Therefore there are only two parts of penance [*i.e.* contrition and confession].
45. He did not know whether any help of the living benefits the dead.
46. It was better to observe the mode of celebration of mass as was served by the primitive church, than these involved things you set up and put forth beyond the precepts of God.
47. These statutes established through the church about the mass are instituted against the precepts of God and of Christ.
48. If the aforementioned statutes or ceremonies are because of human arrangement rather than by divine precepts, then they are against the divine law.
49. We are not obliged to read canonical hours under penalty of mortal sin.
50. This reading of the canonical hours is always done against divine law because one never prays to the father in spirit and in truth.
51. Rather, he wishes that his neck should be amputated, even though he might have ten necks, than that he should respond to the questions you pose.
52. If a sinner believes himself/herself [*se*] truly absolved, the sins are forgiven.
53. He would prefer not to deny to the laity what Christ left behind for all; that is, communion in both species.
54. By prohibiting lay people from communing in both species they act against divine intention.
55. Words of consecration ought to be spoken loudly. [The Roman Catholic usage of the day was to speak the words of consecration "this is my body" softly].
56. He was asked whether it was lawful to adore saints. He said he would not respond further.
57. He was asked whether he was led astray [*seductus*] by Luther (and because he feared being led astray by Luther, therefore they put forth other questions): He said: "I am seduced [or led astray, *seductus*] as Christ led astray [*seduxit*] his apostles."
58. It is against divine law that clergy are exempt from the jurisdiction of the emperor.
59. The pope has no other power than preaching the word of God, and feeding his sheep by preaching the word of God.
60. He saw well that the word of God is not in the possession of the authorities [*dominis Commissariis*].
61. He took too little care concerning his life; he commended his soul to God.
62. He did not think that he could deny all and every error through this confession. Although they required and commanded him, he refused to deny [his understanding.]

VI.   "Erroneous" beliefs of Jan de Bakker (Pistorius) as determined by the inquisitors, 15 September, 1525.

Translated from *CDI*, IV, 494,

1. The Pope was not the Vicar of Christ, and he was not greater than any other apostle;
2. The Pope could bind no one to sin, nor release one therefrom;
3. One could eat meat on Friday without sin;
4. A priest could marry one wife and sleep with her without sin;
5. He had gone to Wittenberg and had there read and listened to Luther's sermons, after the Imperial ban against Luther and his works had been pronounced;
6. He had been accused earlier in Utrecht of certain heresy; he had promised to assert the articles no more, but he reverted to the former heresy;
7. No one was guilty if he or she confessed sins secretly, *i.e.* not to a priest;
8. A worthy person, possessing the Holy Ghost, could consecrate the sacraments at the altar.

VII   The German account of the imprisonment, trial and burning of Wendelmoet Claesdochter, a widow of Monnikendam [15-20 November, 1527].

Translated from *CDI*, V, 275-279. The original Dutch version is not extant. The Dutch
version in this *CDI* volume was probably a translation from the German, made at a
later date. [*CDI*, V, 279-283].

[Page 275]. On the 18th day of November, Wendelmoet Claesdochter was brought
before the full council [in The Hague]. She was asked if she had slept well and had collected her thoughts to be prepared for the beginning of the trial.

She answered "Yes, and what I have said, I will stand by staunchly."

The questioner said: "It will be then, if you deny and recant your errors, otherwise
you will meet a severe death."

Wendelmoet: "If there is given to you a power from the Lord on high, then I am
ready to suffer."

Questioner: "Do you not fear death, which you have not sought [*versucht*; Dutch,
tasted, *gesmaect*]?"

Wendelmoet: "That is true. I will not taste death because Christ has said: 'Who
hears my word, to him will be no taste of death in eternity; but the rich man tastes death
and will taste it in eternity'."

Questioner: "What do you understand about the Sacrament?"

Wendelmoet: "I hold it to be bread and meal, and any one who holds it for a real
God, I say, it is really your devil."

Questioner: "What do you believe concerning Saints?"

Wendelmoet: "I recognize no other advocate and mediator than Christ."

[Page 276] Questioner: "You will be required to die, will you not recant and thereby
remain [*bleiben*]?"

Wendelmoet: "I am already dead."

Questioner: "Are you dead and can yet speak?"

Wendelmoet: "The Spirit lives in me and the Lord is in me and I in him."

Questioner: "Do you wish to have a father confessor or not?"

Wendelmoet: "I have Christ: I confess to him; if there is anyone whom I have
wronged, I will gladly pray that he/she will forgive me."

Questioner: "From whom have you learned these opinions, and how came you
thereto?"

Wendelmoet: "The Lord who calls all persons to himself and has said: 'My sheep
hear my voice;' I am of his flock, so I hear his voice."

Questioner: "Are you alone called?"

Wendelmoet: "No. The Lord calls all who belong to him."

After more questions she was returned to prison and during the two days following
she was visited and challenged by others such as monks, priests, women, a blood relative
[*vetter*=cousin?]; among others came a simple woman to visit and to speak plaintively:

Woman: "Therefore, beloved woman, can you not carry what you will in your heart and
yet remain outwardly silent and so not be required to die such a death?"

Wendelmoet: "Ah! beloved sister, the Lord my God has called me not to be silent but that I should speak the truth; therefore I cannot remain silent."

Woman: "I am concerned that they will put you to death."

Wendelmoet: "God grant that they will drown me [Dutch, *in eenen sack staecken*] or burn me; it means the same. As the Lord has foreseen, so it must happen and not be altered; therefore I will remain with the Lord."

Woman: "So I hope if you had not done anything other than this that they would not kill you."

Wendelmoet: "For me it matters not; but when I came from the hall above I cried bitterly in my heart and was deeply grieved, and I lamented that I so much want these good persons for my cause but they are so blinded; but I will pray to the Lord for them."

Then black monks also came to her [Dominicans] to be her father confessors and to give her counsel. One showed her a crucifix and said, "Look, here is your Lord and God."

Wendelmoet: "That is not my God. It is quite a different cross through which I am redeemed. That is a wooden god. Throw it into the fire and warm yourself with it."

Another asked, since she would die in the morning, whether she wanted to have the Sacrament. He wanted to administer it to her himself.

Wendelmoet: "What, do you want to give me the god, which you offered that I might buy for a penny at Easter [Dutch has: perishable, which sold for very little]?" She said to a priest, who was proud of his good works because he had held Mass that same day, that he had crucified the Christ yet once again. Then the priest took her to be a fool [*naarinen*; Dutch, *verdolt*=misguided].

[P. 277]. "I can do nothing. God has made me so; if, however, I had made myself, I should like to have made myself much wiser [*weyser*]."

She was also asked if she desired the holy oil.

Wendelmoet: " Oil is good to spread on salad, or to smear on shoes."

On Wednesday morning she was brought to the court. As she came into the hall [*saal*] another monk ran forward with a crucifix and shouted: "Look, repent before the sentence is given."

She turned away from the crucifix and said, "I remain with my Lord and God. Neither death nor life will separate me from him."

As she was led to the judge, a monk whispered to her saying that she should fall to her knees before the judge and plead for grace.

Wendelmoet: "Be still! Have I not told you that you shall not lead me from God my Lord?"

The Dean of Naaldwijk, sub-commissioner and inquisitor, read the sentence in Latin from a letter, repeated it in Dutch, and said briefly: that she was found to be in error with regard to the sacraments, and that she persistently adhered to it; hence he decided that she was a heretic, and delivered Wendelmoet to the secular arm with the protest that he did not want to consent to her death. He then retired from the council, together with his two associate ecclesiastics.

Her sentence was read by her captors, after which she was found to be a stubborn heretic [*Ketzerin*; Dutch, *kettersse*], and she ought not go unpunished. Her sentence was that she be burned to ashes [*zu pulver verbrennen*] as a heretic and her goods should be confiscated.

Wendelmoet: "It is now accomplished; so I beg for forgiveness if there is anyone I have wronged, that he/she may forgive me."

A monk ran to her: "Kiss once again the cross of your eternal Lord God."

Wendelmoet: "That is not my Lord God."

On the way out of the room a monk said: "Call to Our Lady that she may intercede for you."

Wendelmoet: "Mary is fully satisfied in God."

Monk: "Call on her!"

Wendelmoet: "We have the Lord, who sits at the right of his Father, he intercedes for us."

Along the way out a monk said, "Call on your eternal God who died for you."

Wendelmoet: "That is not my Lord God, My Lord God is in me and I in him."

Monk: "Look around you, do you judge all these sheep, and shall they all be damned?"

Wendelmoet: "Not all: the decision belongs to God."

Monk: "Do you not fear the strong judgment of God?"

Wendelmoet: "God is not coming to judge but to give us freedom."

Monk: "Is it not an article of the Christian belief that he will come to judge the living and the dead?"

[Page 278]. Wendelmoet: "That, however, is not now."

Monk: "Do you not see the judgment which in one hour will come over you?"

Wendelmoet: "No, because I know well that I shall remain with the Lord."

She was put on a scaffold and a monk spoke: "Look around yourself, and ask the people to forgive you for the bad example which you have exhibited for them." She made no response.

Another said: "Turn to the crowd and if you have misled any, seek his/her pardon; it will bring much fruit."

This she did; then she helped the executioner [*Hencker*] place the powder in her bosom. A monk, fearful for her, pressed a crucifix close to her.

She pushed it away with her hand and turned and said: "Why do you torment [*plagen*] me thus. My Lord and God is in heaven."

With a joyful mind, and without any fright, she went to the fire. [the Dutch adds "as to a wedding"].

Monk: "Will you remain strongly in God."

Wendelmoet: "Yes."

Monk: "Do you believe in the Gospel?" [the Dutch omits this question].

Wendelmoet: "Yes."

Monk: "Look, you must go into the fire. Repent now!"

Wendelmoet: "I am certain that the Lord's will is to be done."

Monk: "This is not God's will. God's will is to save souls-to bring sanctification [*Seeligmachung*]."

The executioner said: "Woman, remain in God and do not be led away from that."

Then she stepped undaunted to the chair and asked: "Is this chair standing firm so I will not fall?" She placed herself firmly at the stake. Then the executioner prepared the rope and tied it over and under her clothing. She removed her scarf and adjusted the rope with which she was to be strangled. Another monk came to her to ask:

Monk: "Wendelmoet, will you yet die as a Christian person?"

Wendelmoet: "Yes."

Monk. "Do you deny all heresy?"

Wendelmoet: "Yes."

Monk: "Do you hold to the Christian Church and deny all errors?"

Wendelmoet: "Yes."

Monk: "That is good. Is it not painful [*leid*] that you have erred?"

Wendelmoet: "In previous times I have erred, and I am sorry; but this is not error and is the right way and I remain in God."

Then the executioner began to tighten the rope. As this was done she closed her eyes and mouth, as if she were asleep, and moved not even a finger of her hand, and gave up her spirit.

Thus, the above-mentioned Wendelmoet died, XX November, 1527.

Bibliography

Abbreviations

BRN   Pijper, F. *Bibliotheca Reformatoria Neerlandica.* 10 vols.. The Hague: Nijhoff, 1903-1904.

CDI   *Corpus documentorum inquisitionorum haereticae Pravitatis Neerlandicae, Verzameling von stukken betreffende de pauslijke en bishoppelijke inquisitie in de Nederlanden.* Ed. Paul Fredericq, five volumes: Gent and The Hague, 1889-1902.

CR   *Corpus Reformatorum.* Edited by C. G. Breitschneider and H. E. Binsdeil. Halle, 1834-1860.

CWE   *Collected Works of Erasmus.* Toronto: University of Toronto Press, 1974-   .

Contemporaries of Erasmus: a biographical register of the Renaissance and Reformation, edited by Peter G. Bietenholz., 3 vols., Toronto: University of Toronto Press, 1985-1987.

LW   American Edition of *Luther's Works*, 55 vols., Philadelphia: Fortress Press, Saint Louis: Concordia Publishing House, 1955-

NK   Nijhoff-Kronenberg, *Nederlandsche bibliographie van 1500 tot 1540.* 3 vols:, s'Gravenhage, Martinus Nijhoff, 1940.

RE   *Realencyklopädie für protestantische Theologie und Kirche*, Third ed. Leipzig: 1896-1913.

RGG   *Die Religion in Geschichte und Gegenwart*, Third ed. Tübingen: 1957-

WA   *D. Martin Luthers Werke. Kritische Gesamtausgabe.* Weimar, 1883-

WA Br. *D. Martin Luthers Werke, Briefwechsel.* Weimar, 1930-

ZW   *Zwinglis Werke.* Leipzig, 1927

Primary Sources

Castellio, Sebastian. *An sint persequendi* [1554], as translated by Roland Bainton in *Concerning Heretics, whether they are to be persecuted.* New York: Columbia University Press, 1935

Decet Romanum Pontificem, Bull issued by Pope Leo X, January 3, 1521, (excommunication of Luther). Translated from Francisco Gaude, *Bullarum diplomatum et Privilegiorum Sanctorum Romanorum Pontificum.* Augustae Taurinorum: by Seb. Franco et Henrick Dalmazzo, editors, 1860, V, 761-764. Because no English translation of this bull is available, an English translation is included in Appendix # I.

Erasmus, D. *Paraphrase of Matthew*, published in England, 1548.

Exsurge Domine, Bull issued by Pope Leo X, June 15, 1520.

Gansfort, M. Wesselli, Groningensis, *Opera* (Groningen: Johannes Sassius Typographus, 1614); reprint, Gansfort, Wessel, *Opera*. (Facsimile of Edition of Groningen, 1614); Groningen, Nieuwkoop: B. De Graaf, 1966.

Gnapheus, Gulielmus. *Acolastus*. English Trans. W. E. D. Atkinson. London, Ontario, Canada: Humanities Department, University of Western Ontario, 1964.

Gnapheus, Gulielmus. *Een Troost ende Spiegel der siecken ende der ghenen die in Lijden zijn* [*NK* 1010, Antwerp,1531; *NK* 3108, Antwerp, 1532]. Vol. 1, Pijper, F. ed. *Bibliotheca Reformatoria Neerlandica*: The Hague: Martinus Nijhoff, 1903.

Hillerbrand, Hans. *The Reformation in its own words*. London: S. C. M. Press, 1964; also New York: Harper and Row, 1964.

Hoen, Cornelius. *"Christiana Admodum. . . ."* Trans., Paul Nyhus, "A Most Christian Letter. . . ," in Oberman, Heiko A. *Forerunners of the Reformation: The Shape of Late Medieval Thought*. New York: Holt, Rinehart and Winston, 1966, pp. 268-278.

[Index of Prohibited Books] *Index librorum prohibitorum. Romae: Ex officina salviana*, February, 1559 (reprint 1980).

Lamentationes Petri, [*NK* 2985], microfilm copy from The Bibliothéque Nationale, Paris.

Lamentationes Petri, microfilm copy from the library, Wolfenbüttel, Germany.

Miller, Edward and Scudder, Jared Waterbury, trans. and ed. *Wessel Gansfort: life and works*. 2 vols., New York: G. P. Putnam Sons, 1917.

Pelt, John, [*NK* 369]. *Evangelie van Matthaeus*. (Dutch trans.), Amsterdam: 1522.

Smith, Preserved and Jacobs, Charles, trans. and eds. *Luther's Correspondence and Other Contemporary Letters*. Philadelphia: The Luther Publication Society, 1918.

Toorenenbergen, J. J. van. *Het oudste Nederlandsche Verboeden Boek, (1523)*. Leiden: E. J. Brill, 1882. This volume contains both the Latin *Oeconomica Christiana* (written perhaps in 1520, but published only in 1527); and the Dutch translation, *Summa der Godliker Scrifturen* (Leiden, 1523).

Zwingli, Huldrych, "Friendly Exegesis, that is, Exposition of the Matter of the Eucharist to Martin Luther, February 1527," *ZW*, V [=*CR* 92]; trans in Edward Furcha and Wayne Pipkin, *Huldrych Zwingli Writings*. 2 vols. Allison Park, Pennsylvania: Pickwick Publications, 1984. Vol. II trans. H. Wayne Pipkin, 238-369.

Secondary Sources: Published Books

Akkerman, Fokke, Huisman, Gerda .C., and Vanderjagt, Arie Johan, eds. *Wessel Gansfort and Northern Humanism*. Leiden: Brill, 1993.

Akkerman, Fokke, Vanderjagt, Arie Johan, and, Van der Laan, A.H. *Northern Humanism in European Context, 1469-1625*. Leiden: Brill, 1999.

Atkinson, W.E.D. *Acolastus*, English trans. London, Ontario, Canada: Humanities Department, University of Western Ontario, 1964.

Augustijn, Cornelis, *Erasmus der Humarist als Theologe und Kirchenreformer*. Leiden, New York: Brill, 1996.

Bender, Harold, and Smith, C. Henry. *The Mennonite Encyclopedia*. 4 vols., Scottdale, Pennsylvania: Mennonite Publishing House, 1955.

Benrath, Karl. *Die Summa der heiligen Schrift: Ein Zeugnis aus dem Zeitalter der Reformation für die Rechtfertigung aus dem Glauben*. Leipzig: Vernau, 1880.

Bietenholz, Peter G., ed. *Contemporaries of Erasmus: a Biographical Register of the Renaissance and Reformation.* 3 vols., Toronto: University of Toronto Press, 1985-1987.

Bolt, Johannes, ed., *Lateinische Literaturdenkmäler des XV und XVI Jahrhunderts* Vol. I, Berlin: Speyer and Peters, 1891.

Boyle, Marjorie O'Rourke. *Erasmus on Language and Method in Theology.* Toronto: University of Toronto Press, 1977.

Brandt, Gerard. *The History of the Reformation and other ecclesiastical transactions in and about the Low Countries.* 2 vols., London: T. Wood, 1720-1732; reprint, London: A. M. S. Press, 1979.

Clebsch, William. *England's Earliest Protestants: 1520-1535.* New Haven: Yale University Press, 1964.

Clemen, Otto. *Johann Pupper von Goch.* Leipzig: Duncker and Humboldt, 1896.

d'Aubigne, J. A. Merle. *History of the Reformation in the Sixteenth Century.* 2 Vols., Lancaster, Pennsylvania: W. W. Freeman. [18??].

De Bie, J. P. and Loosjes, J., eds., *Biographisch Woordenboek van Protestantische Godgeleerden in Nederland.* 5 vols., The Hague: Martinus Nijhoff, 1913-1943.

De Bruin, C. C. *De Statenbijbel en Zijne Voorgangers.* Leiden: A. W. Sijthoff's Uitgevermaatshcappij, 1937.

De Greef, W., De Jong, O. J., Van Oort, J., Spruyt, B. J., editors. *Reformatie Studies, Reformatie in Meervoud.* Kampen, The Netherlands: Uitgeverij de Groot Goudriaan, 1991.

De Vocht, Henry. *History of the Foundation and the Rise of the Collegium Trilinguae Lovaniense, 1517-1550.* 3 vols., Louvain/Leuven: Publications Universitaires, 1953; reprinted Nedeln, Liechtenstein: Kraus reprint, 1976.

Duke, Alastair. *Reformation and Revolt in The Low Countries.* London: Hambledon Press, 1990.

Ekker, A. *De Hieronymusschool te Utrecht.* Utrecht: Bosch and Son, 1863.

Erasmus, Desiderius. *Opus Epistolarum D. Erasmi Rotterdami.* 12 vols. ed. P. S. Allen. Oxford: Clarendon, 1906-1963.

Erasmus, Desiderius. *The First Tome or Volume of the Paraphrases of Erasmus on the Newe Testamente.* London: Fleet Street, the last daie of Januarie, 1548.

Eubel, Conradus, ed., *Hierarchie Catholica.* Münster: 1923.

Gavin, J. Austin. *The Commentary of Gerardus Listrius on Erasmuis;'s "Praise of Folly." A Critical Edition and Translation with Introduction and Commentary.* Ph. D. Thesis, St. Louis University, 1973.

Gunst, J. A. *Johannes Pistorius Woerdensis.* Hilversum, The Netherlands: De Blauwvoet, 1925.

Herzog, J. J., *et al. Realencyklopädie für protestantische Theologie und Kirche* Leipzig: J. C. Hinrichs, 1896-1913.

Hillerbrand, Hans J. *The Oxford Encyclopedia of the Reformation.* 4 vols., New York: Oxford University Press, 1996.

Israel, Jonathan I. *The Dutch Republic: Its Rise, Greatness, and fall, 1477-1806.* Oxford: The Clarendon Press, 1988.

Jackson, Samuel Macauley. *Huldrych Zwingli: Selected Works.* Philadelphia: University of Pennsylvania Press, 1901, 1972.

Janssen, H. Q. *Jacob Praepositus: Luther's Leerling en Friend*. Amsterdam: G. L. Funke, 1866.

Knappert, L. *Geschiedenis der Nederlandsh Hervormde Kerk de 16e en 17e eeuw*. Amsterdam: 1911.

Knappert, L. *Het ontstaan en de vestiging van het Protestantisme in de Nederlande*. Utrecht, 1924.

Knappert, Laurentius, P. J. Blok, and Molhuyzen, P. C., eds. *Nieuw Nederlandsch Biographisch Woordenboek*. 10 vols., Leiden: A. W. Sijthoff's Uitgevers, 1911-1937.

Krahn, Cornelius. *Dutch Anabaptism, Origin, Spread, Life and Thought (1450-1600)*. The Hague: Martinus Nijhoff, 1968. Reprinted: Scottdale, Pennsylvania: Herald Press, 1981.

Kristeller, Paul Oscar. *Renaissance Thought and its Sources*. New York: Columbia University Press, 1979.

Kronenberg, M. E. *Lotgevallen van Jan Seversz, Boekdrukker te Leiden [ca. 1502-1524 and 1527-1530]*. The Hague: Martinus Nijhoff, 1924.

Kronenberg, M. E. *Verboden Boeken en opstandige Drukkers in de Hervormingstijd*. Amsterdam: P. N. Van Kampen & Zoon, 1948.

Lindeboom, J. *De Confessioneele outwikkeling der Reformatie in de Nederlanden van haar onstaan tot 1531*. Amsterdam: G. L. Funke, 1873.

Lindeboom, J. *Het Biblisch Humanisme in Nederland*. Leiden: A. H. Adriani, 1913.

Miller, Edward Waite, and Scudder, Jared Waterbury, *Wessel Gansfort: Life and Writings*. 2 vols., New York: G. P. Putnam's Sons, 1917.

Minderaa, P. *Acolastus: Latijnse tekst met Nederlandsche Vertaling*, Zwolle: W. E. J. Tjeenk Willink, 1956.

Oberman, Heiko A., *Forerunners of the Reformation: The Shape of Late Medieval Thought*. New York: Holt, Rinehart and Winston, 1966.

Ozment, Steven. *The Age of Reform, 1250-1550: An Intellectual and Religious History of Late Medieval and Reformation Europe*. New Haven: Yale University Press, 1980.

Pipkin, Wayne. *Huldrych Zwingli Writings. II*. Allison Park, Pennsylvania: Pickwick Publications, 1984.

Plomp, Nico. *Woerden 600 Jaar Stad*. Woerden, The Netherlands: Stichts-Hollandse Bijdragen, 1972.

Post, Regnerus Richardus. *The Modern Devotion*. Leiden: E. J. Brill, 1968.

Post, Regnerus Richardus. *Kerkelijke verhouding in Nederland voor de Reformatie: van 1500 tot 1580*. Utrecht, Antwerp: Het Spectrum, 1954.

Prinsen, Jacob. *Gerardus Geldenhauer Noviomagus: Bijdrage tot de kennis van zijn Leven en Werken*. The Hague; Martin Nijhoff, 1898.

Reitsma, J. *Geschiedenis van de Hervorming en de Hervormde Kerk des Nederlanden*. The Hague: Martinus Nijhoff, 1949.

Roodhuyzen, Hendrik. *Het leven van Gulielmus Gnapheus*. Amsterdam: J. C. Loman, 1858.

Rummel, Erika. *The Confessionalization of Humanism in Reformation Germany*. Oxford: Oxford University Press, 2000.

Rummel, Erika. *The Humanist-Scholastic Debate in the Renaissance and Reformation*. Cambridge, Massachusetts, London, England: Harvard University Press, 1995.

Scheffer, J. G. De Hoop, *Geschiedenis der Kerkhervorming in Nederland van haar ontstaan tot 1531*. Amsterdam: G. L. Funke, 1873.

Schmitz, Wolfgang, O.F.M. *Het Aandeel der Minderbroeters in onze Middeleeuwse Literatuur: Inleiding tot een Bibliografie der Nederlandse Franciscanen*. Nijmegen, Utrecht: Dekker & van de Vegt en J. A. van Leeuwen, 1936.

Smith, Preserved. *Erasmus*. New York: Harper, 1923; reprint 1962.

Snyder, C. Arnold. *Anabaptist History and Theology: An Introduction*. Kitchener, Ontario: Pandora Press, 1995.

Spruyt, Bastian (Bart) Jan. *Cornelius Henrici Hoen (Honius) and his Epistle on the Eucharist*. Houten, The Netherlands: 1996; a doctoral thesis completed at the University of Leiden.

Spruyt, Bart Jan. *Ketter aan het Binnenhof: Cornelius Hoen en zijn tracktaat tegen de transubstantieleer*. Heerenbeen, The Netherlands: J. J. Groen en Zoon, 1997.

Steinmetz, David. *Misericordia Dei: The Theology of Johannes von Staupitz in its Late Medieval Setting*. Leiden: E. J. Brill, 1968.

Tracy, James D. *Holland under Hapsburg Rule, 1506-1566: The formation of a Body Politic*. Berkeley, Los Angeles: University of California Press, 1990.

Trapman, J. *De Summa der Godliker Scrifturen (1523)*. Leiden: New Rhine Publishers, 1978.

Ullmann, Karl C., *Reformers Before the Reformation: principally in Germany and The Netherlands*. Trans. Robert Menzies, 2 vols., Edinburgh: T. and T. Clark, 1855.

Valvekens, P. E. *De Inquisitie in de Nederlanden der zestiende eeuw*. Brussels, Amsterdam: De Klinkhoren, 1949.

Van Rhijn, Maartin. *Studien over Wessel Gansfort en zijn Tijd*. Utrecht: Kemink en Zoon, 1933.

Van Rhijn, Maartin. *Wessel Gansfort*. The Hague: 1917.

Visser, C. Ch. G. *Luther's Geschriften in de Nederlanden tot 1546*. Assen, The Netherlands: Van Gorcum & Comp. N. V., 1969.

Waite, Gary K. *David Joris and Dutch Anabaptism, 1524-1543*. Waterloo, Ontario: Wilfrid Laurier Press, 1990.

Weiland, J. Sperna, Frijhoff, W.Th.M. *Erasmus of Rotterdam:The Man and The Scholar*. Leiden: Brill, 1988.

Williams, George H. *The Radical Reformation*. Philadelphia: Westminster Press, 1962. A much-expanded version was published thirty years later: Kirksville, Missouri: Sixteenth Century Journal Publishers, 1992.

Wolfs, Petrus Franciscus. *Das Groninger "Religionsgespräch" (1523) und seiner Hintergründe*. Doctoral thesis at the University of Nijmegen, The Netherlands, printed at the Centrale Drukkerij, Nijmegen, 1959.

Zuidema, Willem, *Wilhelm Frederici, persona van Sint-Martin te Groningen (1489-1525), en de Groninger staatkunde van zijn tijd*. Doctoral thesis, University of Groningen, 1888.

Secondary Sources: Book Chapters and Periodical Articles

Akkerman, Fokke. "The Early Reformation in Groningen. On Two Latin Disputations" in Ackerman, F., Vanderjagt, A.J., and van der Laan, A.H., eds. *Northern Humanism in European Context, 1465-1625.* Leiden: Brill, 1999, pp. 1-42.

Arblaster, Paul. "Totius Mundi Emporium: Antwerp as a Center for the Vernacular Bible translations: 1523-1545." In Arie-Jan Gelderblom, Jan L. De Jong, Marc van Vaeck, eds., *The Low Countries as a Crossroads of Religious Belief.* Leiden, Boston: Brill Publishers, 2004.

Augustijn, Cornelis. "Gerard Geldenhauwer und die religiöse Toleranz, *Archiv fur Reformationsgeschichte,* 69 (1978), 132-156.

Benrath, Karl. "Der Summa er heilgen Schrift: Eine literarhistorische Untersuchung." *Jahrbuch für protestantische Theologia.* Three articles, 1881, 1882, 1883.

Bouwsma, William. "The Spirit of Renaissance Humanism," in Jill Raitt, ed., *Christian Spirituality: High Middle Ages and Reformation.* New York: Crossroads, 1987, pp. 236-237.

Clemen, Otto. "Das Antwerper Augustiner-kloster bei Beginn der Reformation (1513-1523)," *Monatshefte der Comenius-Gesellschaft,* X (1901), 306-313.

Clemen, Otto, "Die Lamentationes Petri," *Zeitschrift für Kirchengeschichte,* XIX (1899), pp. 431-448

Clemen, Otto, "Hinne Rode in Wittenberg, Basel, Zürich und die frühesten Ausgaben Wesselscher Schriften," *Zeitschrift für Kirchengeschichte, Vol. XVIII (1898),* 346-373.

Gavin, J. Austin and Walsh, Thomas M. "The Praise of Folly in Context: The Commentary of Gerardus Listrius." *The Renaissance Quarterly,* 24 (1971), pp. 193-209.

Graafland, G.J. and Trapman, J. "Gnapheus, Gulielmus" in *Biografisch Lexicon voor de Geschiedenis van het Nederlandse Protestantisme.* Kampen, The Netherlands; Uitgeverij Kok, 1998, IV, 142-144.

Hendriks, Olof. "Gerardus Geldenhauwer Noviomagus (1484-1542)." *Studia Catholica.* 31 (1956), 129-139 and 176-196.

Ijsewijn, Joseph. "Humanism in the Low Countries," in Albert Rabil, ed., *Renaissance Humanism: Foundations, Forms, and Legacy,* vol. 2, *Humanism beyond Italy.* Philadelphia: University of Pennsylvania Press, 1988, pp. 156-215

Iken, Friedrich. "Heinrich von Zütphen," *Schriften des Vereins für Reformationsgeschichte,* No. 12, Halle, 1886.

Kleyn, H. G. "De auteur der 'Summa der godliker Scrifturen'," *Theologische Studie Tijdschrift,* I,(1883), 313-323, and "Nog eens der auteur der 'Summa'," *ibid.,* II (1884), 447-451.

Kraft, G. "Der Niederlander Heinrich Bomelius zu Moers und Wesel als Historiker," *Monatschrift für rheinischwestfälische Geschichtsforschung und Altertumskunde, II (1976), 224-231.*

Kronenberg, M. E. "Uitgaven van Luther in de Nederlanden verschenen tot 1541," *Archief voor Kerkgeschiedenis,* XL, (1954), 1-25.

Kronenberg, M. E. "Verboeden Boeken en Opstandige Drukkers in de Hervorminngstijd" in *Patria: Vaderlandse Cultuurgeschiedenis in Monografieën,* Vol. 44, Leiden: 1947

Lindberg, Carter. "Prierias and his Significance for Luther's development." *Sixteenth Century Journal*, III 2 (October 1972), pp. 45-64.

Peteghem, P.P.J.L. van. "Erasmus's Last Will," in Weiland, J. Sperna, and Frijhoff, W.Th.M.Frijhoff, *Erasmus of Rotterdam: The Man and The Scholar.* Leiden: Brill, 1988, pp. 88-98.

Post, R. R. "Het Groningsche Godsdienstgesprek van 1523." *Studia Catholica*, XX (1944), 113-124.

Royards, H. J. "Proeve eener Geschidenis der Hervorming in de Stad en province Utrecht," *Archief voor Kerkgeschiedenis*, XVI, (1845), 360-363.

Scheffer, J. G. De Hoop. "Cornelius Woutersz, van Dordrecht, een Martelaar der Hervorming (1525-1529)." *Kerkhistorisch Archief*, IV (1866), 1-22.

Spruyt, Bastian (Bart) J. "Hinne Rode (*c.* 1480-*c* 1539: Het Leven en de Ontwikkeling van de Dissidente Rector van het Utrechtse Fraterhuis, pp. 21-42, in ten Boom, H, Geudeke, E. Leeuwenberg, H.L.Ph.Leeuwenberg, and Abels, P.H.A.M., eds. *Utrechters Entre-Deux: Stad en Sticht in de Eeuwe van de Reformatie, 1520-1620.* Delft, The Netherlands: Eburon, 1992.

Spruyt, Bart Jan. "Humanisme, evangelisme en reformatie in de Nederlanden, 1520-1530," pp. 26-54, in W. De Greef *et al.*, eds, *Reformatie in meervoud: Congressbundel, 1990.* Kampen, The Netherlands: 1991.

Spruyt, Bart Jan. "Laat middeleeuwse Ketterijen en de vroege hervorming in de Nederlanden: Cornelius Hendrickxz Hoen en zijn Epistola Christiana (1525)," *Doopsgezinde Bijdragen*, Vol 19 (1933), 115-128.

Spruyt, Bart Jan. "Listrius lutherizans: His Epistola theologica adversus Dominicanus Suollenses [written in 1520, first published in 1733], *Sixteenth Century Journal*, XXII, No. 4, (1991), 727-751.

Spruyt, Bart Jan. "Wessel Gansfort and Cornelius Hoen's *Epistola Christiana*: 'The Ring as a pledge of my love,'" in Ackerman, Fokke, Huisman, Gerda C., and Vanderjagt, A. J., eds, *Wessel Gansfort (1419-1489) and the Northern Humanism.* Leiden, New York, Köln: E. J. Brill, 1993.

Toorenenbergen, Johann Justus van. "Het oudste Nederlandsche verboden Boek," pp. 145-162. *Theologische Studien Tijdschrift*, II, 1884

Toorenenbergen, J. J. van. "Hinne Rode (John Rhodius), rector van de Hieronyusschool te Utrecht (-1522), predikant te Norden (-1530), in betrekking tot de Anabaptisten." *Archief van Nederlandsche Kerkgeschiedenis*, III (1889), 90-101.

Trapman, J. "Afscheid van de sacramentariërs?" *Doopsgezinde Bijdragen, Nieuw reeks* 15(1989), pp. 143-147.

Trapman, J. "Erasmianism in the Early Reformation in The Netherlands," pp. 169-176, in M.R.H.N. Mount, H. Smolinsky and J. Trapman, eds., *Idea and Reality*, Amsterdam, Oxford, New York, Tokyo: Koninklijke Nederlandse Akademie van Wetenschappen Verhandlingen, Nieuw Reeks, deel 174. Colloquium held in 1996, published 1997.

Trapman, J. "Johannes Sartorius (*ca.* 1500-1557) Gymnasiarch te Amsterdam en Noordwijk, als Erasmiaan en Spiritualist." *Nederlandsche Archief voor Kerkgeschiedenis*, 70 (1990), 30-51.

Trapman, J., "Le role des 'Sacramentaires' des Origens de la réforme jusqu'en 1530 aux Pays Bas." *Nederlands Archief voor Kerkgeschiedenis*, 63(1983), pp. 1-24.

Van Peteghem, P. P. J. L., "Erasmus's Last will," in Weiland, J. Sperna, and Frijhoff, W. Th. M. *Erasmus of Rotterdam: The Man and The Scholar*. Leiden and New York: Brill, 1988.

Van Slee, J.C. "Wendelmoet Claesdochter van Monnikendam, 20 November, 1527." *Nederlandsch Archief voor Kerkgeschiedenis*, XX (1927).

Volz, Hans. "Die Ersten Sammelausgaben von Lutherschriften und ihre Drucker (1518-1520)." *Gutenberg Jahrbuch*, 1960, pp. 185-200.

Waite, Gary K., "Popular Drama and Radical Religion: The Chambers of Rhetoric and Anabaptism in The Netherlands," *Mennonite Quarterly Review*. 65 (1991), pp. 227-255.

Waite, Gary K., "Reformers on Stage: Rhetorical drama and Reformation Propaganda in The Netherlands of Charles V, 15199-1556," *Archiv für Reformationsgeschichte*, 83 (1992), 209-239.

Waite, Gary K., "Vernacular Drama and the early urban Reformation: The Chambers of Rhetoric in Amsterdam, 1520-1555," *Journal of Medieval and Renaissance Studies*, 21 (1991), 187-206.

Weiss, N. "Le premier traite protestante en langue francaise 'la summe de l'escripture sante,' 1523," *Societe de l'Histoire du Protestantisme Francaise Bulletin*, LXVII (5th Series; XVI, 1919), pp. 63-79.

INDEX

Saganus, George, 45
Sartorius, Johannes, 45-6, 56-7, 191
scripture, centrality of, 177, 179, 181,
    192-3,
Seversz. Jan, 156, 170n12
sola fide [by faith alone], 161, 192-3
sovereignty of God, 166
Spruyt, Bart J., xvii, xxixn2, xxixn4,
    52, 85,
    Ketter an het Binnenhof, xix, 100n27
    *Cornelius Henrici Hoen and his
    Epistle,* 56n39, 57n54, 94-6
    Summa der Godliker Scrifturen
    [*Oeconomica Christiana*], 139,
    (Chapter 9)

The Hague, city of, 44, 176, 191, 217,
    218
Theologia Deutsch, 130, 135n52
Thomas à Kempis, 78
Tracy, James D., xix
transubstantiation, doctrine of, iii, 45,
    46, 77, 87, 94, 220
Trapman, Johannes, xxviii, 61, 75n1,
    155, 202n2
    Sartorius, 45-6, 57n3
    De Summa der Godliker Scrifturen,
    155-6, 170n4

ubiquity, doctrine of, 91
Utrecht, city of, 24, 175

Van Bommel, Henry, 157
Van der Hulst, Frans, (inquisitor), 29,
    30, 31, 106, 121, 189, 207
Van Pelt, John, translation of the Gos-
    pel of Matthew (Chapter 8).

Van Rhijn, Maartin, 93, 99n25
Van Ruysbroeck, Jan, 138
Van Toorenenbergen, J. J., xxi,
    56n18, 158, 169n2
Visser, C. Ch., xviii, 9-10
Vives, Juan Luis, Humanist scholar,
    119
Voes, Hendrik, Augustinian brother ,
    123-28
    the articles which led to his mar-
    tyrdom, translated in Appendix
    V
Von Staupitz, Johannes, 16, 117

Waite, Gary, xix, 230n115
Wartburg Castle, 80
Weimar Ausgabe (Luther's Works),
    16
wheat and weeds, parable of, 51,
    143,152
Williams, George H., xxviii, xxix,
    232n112
Wittenberg, city of, 122
Wolfs, Petrus Franciscus, 75
Wolsey, Thomas, Cardinal, 12
womanhood, evaluation of, 165
Worms, Diet of (1521), 25-7, 41, 74,
    118
Wouter, (or Gualterius), 40, 44, 47
Wouterszoon, Cornelis, 130-2
Wyclif, John, 93-5, 97, 210

Zwingli, Huldrych, 10, 83-4, 97
Zwolle, city of, 9, 52, 61, 82, 121
Zutphen, city of, 121-3

About the Author

J. Alton Templin has spent most of his career teaching Historical Theology and Church History of the Reformation period. He is a graduate of The University of Denver (B.A.), The Iliff School of Theology (Th.M. and Th. D.) and Harvard University (Ph. D.).

He is an ordained minister of the United Methodist Church whose main emphasis has been in educational ministry. He has taught at Southwestern College (Kansas), the University of South Dakota, and for the last thirty years to his retirement (1997) as Professor at The Iliff School of Theology in Denver. Regular seminars were offered concerning each of the following: Luther, Calvin, Erasmus, Zwingli, Radical Reformation and English Reformation. Beyond published research related to the Continental Reformation, two of his publications concern the misuse of Calvinist Ideology in the development of South African *Apartheid.*

In addition to this teaching he has also taught one term at Kenya Methodist University in Meru, Kenya, and one term at the Russian United Methodist Theological Seminary in Moscow.